TRAVEL WISE

ITALIAN

Barbara Huter

and

Serena Kästel

This material was purchased as part of an
Indian Prairie Public Library District grant
**"Our Multicultural Neighborhood:
Promoting Awareness."**
Funding for this grant was provided by the
Illinois State Library, a division of the Office of the
Secretary of State using federal LSTA funding.
Indian Prairie Public Library District
Darien, Illinois 60561
630/887-8760

BARRON'S

Text Copyright © Ernst Klett Verlag GmbH,
Stuttgart, Federal Republic of Germany, 1992
The title of the German book is *Reisewörterbuch Italienisch*

English version translated
and edited by Mary Root Taucher.
Phonetics by Gabriella Romani.

All inquiries should be addressed to:
Barron's Educational Series, Inc.
250 Wireless Boulevard
Hauppauge, NY 11788
http://www.barronseduc.com

Library of Congress Catalog Card No. 97-49402

International Standard Book No. 0-7641-0378-4 (book)
0-7641-7104-6 (complete package)

Library of Congress Cataloging-in-Publication Data

Huter, Barbara
    [Reisewörterbuch Italienisch. English]
    Travelwise Italian/Barbara Hunter, Serena Kästel ; translated by
Mary Root Taucher.
        p. cm.
    Text in English and Italian.
    ISBN 0-7641-0378-4 (pbk).—ISBN 0-7641-7104-6 (bk./cassette)
    1. Italian language—Conversation and phrasebooks—English.
I. Kästel, Serena. II. Root Taucher, Mary. III. Title.
PC1121.H8413   1998
    458.3'421—dc21   97–49402
                                                                   CIP

Printed in Hong Kong
9 8 7 6 5 4 3 2 1

Contents

Preface

TravelWise Italian is a guide to both comprehension and conversation in Italian. By using it you will not only acquire a series of useful words and phrases, but, more importantly, you will learn how to understand and be understood.

The most commonly heard expressions are provided for everyday situations you will encounter during your travels. These are structured as dialogues, so that you not only learn what to say, but will also understand the corresponding responses.

TravelWise Italian is divided into eleven topical units, which accompany you through every phase of your travel: your arrival, checking into a hotel, at the beach, and even a meeting with business associates.

With the help of phrases and word lists, as well as the additional glossary provided at the end of the book, you can readily adapt the sample sentences to your own individual, real-life situations.

The following Pronunciation Guide and the Short Grammar toward the back of the book will help familiarize you with the sounds and constructions of the Italian language, while pictures and useful tips provided throughout the book will help you better appreciate the special cultural features and natural scenic attractions of Italy.

Pronunciation

Vowels

In Italian, as in English, the letters that represent vowel sounds are **a, e, i, o, u.** Italian vowels are clear, pronounced with no nasal or other kinds of features. If the vowels are stressed (i.e., if they bear the main emphasis) they are slightly longer than when they are not stressed.

To show primary stress, the vowel of the stressed syllable is underlined in this book.

LETTERS	PRONUNCIATION SYMBOLS USED	PRONUNCIATION	EXAMPLES
a	[ah]	as in exclamation *Ah!*	**cane** *dog* [k<u>ah</u>-neh]
e	[eh]	as in exclamation *Eh!*	**bene** *well* [b<u>eh</u>-neh]
i	[ee]	as in exclamation *Eeh!*	**vino** *wine* [v<u>ee</u>-noh]
o	[oh]	as in exclamation *Oh!*	**oro** *gold* [<u>oh</u>-roh]
u	[oo]	as in exclamation *Ooh!*	**uso** *use* [<u>oo</u>-soh]

The **i** in Italian can also stand for a **y-sound** as the *y* in *yes,* and the **u** for a **w-sound** as the *w* in *way.* Notice that this applies when **i** or **u** occur before (or after) a stressed vowel:

i = *y*		u = *w*	
chiuso *closed*	[kyoo-zoh]	**buono** *good*	[bw<u>oh</u>-noh]
ieri *yesterday*	[yeh-ree]	**quanto** *how much*	[kw<u>ah</u>n-toh]
piano *soft*	[pyah-noh]	**uomo** *man*	[w<u>oh</u>-moh]
fiore *flower*	[fyoh rch]	**qui** *here*	[kw<u>ee</u>]

Consonants

Most of the Italian consonants are similar to corresponding English consonants. Differences are shown in the chart below.

In general, most of the Italian single consonants have "double" counterparts. Double consonants do not exist in English, even though double letters are often used (to represent single consonants). When pronounced, Italian double consonants last approximately twice as long as corresponding single ones. In this book they are shown with double letters. Note that the *h* is always silent.

LETTERS	SYMBOLS USED	PRONUN.	EXAMPLES
b	[b]	as in *bat*	**bene** *well* [beh-neh] **babbo** *dad* [bah-bboh]
c (hard) /**ch**	[k]	as in *cat*	**cane** *dog* [kah-neh] **chi** *who* [kee] **pacco** *package* [pah-kkoh]
c (soft) / **ci**	[ch]	as in *chin*	**cena** *dinner* [cheh-nah] **ciao** *hi/bye* [chah-oh] **accento** *accent* [ah-cchehn-toh]
d	[d]	as in *day*	**dopo** *after* [doh-poh]
f	[f]	as in *fair*	**fare** *to do* [fah-reh]
g (hard) / **gh**	[gh]	as in *gas*	**gatto** *cat* [ghah-ttoh] **ghetto** *ghetto* [gheh-ttoh]
g (soft) / **gi**	[j]/[dj] when doubled	as in *gym*	**gente** *people* [jehn-teh] **giacca** *jacket* [jah-kkah] **spiaggia** *beach* [spyah-djah]
gli	[ly]	as in *million*	**figlio** *son* [fee-lyoh]
gn	[ny]	as in *canyon*	**bagno** *bathroom* [bah-nyoh]
l	[l]	as in *love*	**latte** *milk* [lah-tteh]
m	[m]	as in *man*	**mano** *hand* [mah-noh]
n	[p]	as in *name*	**nome** *name* [noh-meh]

p	[p]	as in *pet*	**pane** *bread* [p<u>ah</u>-neh]
q	[k]	as in *quick*	**que** *here* [kw<u>ee</u>]
r	[r]	as in *brrr....!*	**rosso** *red* [r<u>oh</u>-ssoh]
s (voiceless)	[s]	as in *sip*	**sale** *salt* [sah-leh] **specchio** *mirror* [sp<u>eh</u>-kkyoh]
s (voiced)	[z]	as in *zip*	**casa** *house* [k<u>ah</u>-zah]
sc (hard) / sch	[sk]	as in *skill*	**scuola** *school* [sw<u>oh</u>-lah] **scusi** *excuse me* [sk<u>oo</u>-zee]
sc (soft) / sci	[sh]	as in *shave*	**scena** *scene* [sh<u>eh</u>-nah] **sciarpa** *scarf* [sh<u>ah</u>r-pah]
t	[t]	as in *rent*	**tanto** *a lot* [t<u>ah</u>n-toh]
v	[v]	as in *vine*	**vino** *wine* [v<u>ee</u>-noh]
z	[tz]	as in *cats*	**zio** *uncle* [tz<u>ee</u>-oh]

Most nouns ending in *o* are masculine; most nouns ending in *a* are feminine. Nouns ending in e can be either masculine or feminine; for example, canzone *song,* is feminine. Double consonants must be pronounced with a strong emphasis. Notice the difference between casa [<u>kah</u>-sah][house] and cassa [<u>kah</u>-ssah][box].

The Italian Alphabet

A a [ah]	J j [ee loon-ghah]	S s [eh-sseh]
B b [bee]	K k [kah-ppah]	T t [tee]
C c [chee]	L l [eh-lleh]	U u [oo]
D d [dee]	M m [eh-mmeh]	V v [voo]
E e [eh]	N n [eh-nneh]	W w [doh-ppyah voo]
F f [eh-ffeh]	O o [oh]	X x [eeks]
G g [jee]	P p [pee]	Y y [eep-see-lohnn]
H h [ah-kkah]	Q q [koo]	Z z [zeh-tah]
I i [ee]	R r [eh-rreh]	

Abbreviations

adj	adjective
adv	adverb
conj	conjunction
dir obj	direct object
el	electricity
qlco	something
f	feminine
ind obj	indirect object
a qlcu	to someone
qlcu	someone
m	masculine
mech	mechanical
med	medicine
pers pro	personal pronoun
pl	plural
poss pro	possessive pronoun
pron	pronoun
prep	preposition
rel	religion
tel	telephone, telegraph

Some Common Italian Abbreviations

a	arrivo	arrival
a. C.	avanti Cristo	B.C.
ACI	Automobile Club Italiano	Automobile Club of Italy
CEE	Comunità Economica Europea	European Economic Community
CIT	Compagnia Italiana Turismo	Italian Travel Agency
D	diretto	direct train making major stops

d. C.	dopo Cristo	A.D.
DD	direttissimo	fast train stopping at main stations in large cities
dott.	dottore	doctor
ecc.	eccetera	etc.
ENIT	Ente Nazionale Italiano per il Turismo	Italian National Tourism Agency
F. S.	Ferrovie dello Stato	Italian national railroad
IVA	imposta sul valore aggiunto	value-added tax
m.	monte/metro	meter
MEC	Mercato Comune Europeo	European Common Market
mq.	metro quadrato	square meter
p.	pagina	page
part.	partenza	departure
p. es.	per esempio	e.g., for example
P. S.	Pubblica Sicurezza	police
rag.	ragioniere	certified accountant
RAI	Radio Audizioni Italiane	Italian Broadcasting Corporation
S. A.	società anonima	Inc. (i.e., publicly owned company)
S. r. l.	società a responsabilità limitata	Ltd. (limited partnership)
Sig.	signor	Mr.
Sig.ra	signora	Mrs.
Sig.na	signorina	Miss
SME	sistema monetario europeo	European Monetary System

1 **The Essentials**
A colpo d'occhio

Frequently Used Expressions
Espressioni di uso comune

Yes	Sì. [see]
No.	No. [noh]
Please.	Per favore. [pehr fah-voh-reh]
Thank you.	Grazie. [grah-tsyeh]
You're welcome/It's nothing.	Non c'è di che. [nohn cheh dee keh]
What did you say?	Come dice? [koh-meh dee-cheh]
Certainly.	Certo. [chehr-toh]
Of course! Agreed!	D'accordo! [dah-kkohr-doh]
Okay!	Va bene! [vah beh-neh]
Excuse me!	Scusi! [skoo-zee]
It's nothing.	Non fa nulla. [nohn fah noo-llah]
One moment, please.	Un momento, prego! [oon moh-mehn-toh preh-ghoh]
Enough!	Basta! [bah-stah]
Help!	Aiuto! [ah-yoo-toh]
Who?	Chi? [kee]
What?	Che cosa? [keh koh-sah]
Which?	Quale? [kwah-leh]
To whom?	A chi? [ah kee]
Where is/Where are…?	Dov'è/Dove sono…? [doh-veh/doh-veh soh-noh]
From where?	Da dove? [dah doh-veh]
Where?	Dove? [doh-veh]
Why?	Perchè? [pehr-keh]
Why not?	Come mai? [koh-meh mah-ee]
What … for?	Per che cosa?/A che cosa? [pehr keh koh-sah/ah keh koh-sah]

How?	Come? [koh-meh]
How much/many?	Quanto/Quanti/Quanta/Quante? [kwahn-toh/kwahn-tee/kwahn-tah/kwahn-tweh]
For how long?	Per quanto tempo? [pehr kwahn-toh tehm-poh]
When?	Quando? [kwahn-doh]
I would like...	Vorrei... [voh-rreh-ee]
There is/There are...	C'è/Ci sono... [cheh/chee soh-noh]

Numbers/Measures/Weights
I numeri/Le misure/I pesi

0	zero [zeh-roh]
1	uno [oo-noh]
2	due [doo-eh]
3	tre [treh]
4	quattro [kwah-ttroh]
5	cinque [cheen-kweh]
6	sei [seh-ee]
7	sette [seh-tteh]
8	otto [oh-ttoh]
9	nove [noh-veh]
10	dieci [dyeh-chee]
11	undici [oon-dee-chee]
12	dodici [doh-dee-chee]
13	tredici [treh-dee-chee]
14	quattordici [kwah-ttohr-dee-chee]
15	quindici [kween-dee-chee]
16	sedici [seh-dee-chee]
17	diciassette [dee-chah-sseh-tteh]

18	diciotto [dee-<u>choh</u>-ttoh]
19	diciannove [dee-chah-<u>nnoh</u>-veh]
20	venti [<u>vehn</u>-tee]
21	ventuno [vehn-<u>too</u>-noh]
22	ventidue [vehn-tee-<u>doo</u>-eh]
23	ventitré [vehn-tee-<u>treh</u>]
24	ventiquattro [vehn-tee-<u>kwah</u>-ttroh]
25	venticinque [vehn-tee-<u>cheen</u>-kweh]
26	ventisei [vehn-tee-<u>seh</u>-ee]
27	ventisette [vehn-tee-<u>seh</u>-tteh]
28	ventotto [vehn-<u>toh</u>-ttoh]
29	ventinove [vehntee-<u>noh</u>-veh]
30	trenta [<u>trehn</u>-tah]
31	trentuno [trehn-<u>too</u>-noh]
32	trentadue [trhn-tah-<u>doo</u>-eh]
40	quaranta [kwah-<u>rahn</u>-tah]
50	cinquanta [cheen-<u>kwahn</u>-tah]
60	sessanta [seh-<u>ssahn</u>-tah]
70	settanta [seh-<u>ttahn</u>-tah]
80	ottanta [oh-<u>ttahn</u>-tah]
90	novanta [noh-<u>vahn</u>-tah]
100	cento [<u>chehn</u>-toh]
101	centouno [chehn-toh-<u>oo</u>-noh]
200	duecento [doo-eh-<u>chehn</u>-toh]
300	trecento [treh-<u>chehn</u>-toh]
1,000	mille [<u>mee</u>-lleh]
2,000	duemila [doo-eh-<u>mee</u>-lah]
3,000	tremila [treh-<u>mee</u>-lah]
10,000	diecimila [dyeh-chee-<u>mee</u>-lah]
100,000	centomila [chehn-toh-mee-lah]

1,000,000	un milione [oon mee-_lyoh_-neh]
1st	primo [_pree_-moh]
2nd	secondo [seh-_kohn_-doh]
3rd	terzo [_tehr_-tsoh]
4th	quarto [_kwahr_-toh]
5th	quinto [_kween_-toh]
6th	sesto [_seh_-stoh]
7th	settimo [_seh_-ttee-moh]
8th	ottavo [oh-_ttah_-voh]
9th	nono [_noh_-noh]
10th	decimo [_deh_-chee-moh]
1/2	un mezzo [oon _meh_-zoh]
1/3	un terzo [oon _tehr_-tsoh]
1/4	un quarto [oon _kwahr_-toh]
3/4	tre quarti [treh kwahr-tee]
3,5%	tre virgola cinque per cento [treh _veer_-ghoh-lah cheen-kweh pehr chehn-toh]
27°C	ventisette gradi [vehn-tee-_seh_-tteh _ghrah_-dee]
-5°C	cinque gradi sotto zero [_cheen_-kweh _ghrah_-dee _soh_-ttoh _zeh_-roh]
1992	millenovecentonovantadue [mee-lleh-noh-veh-_chehn_-toh-noh-vahn-tah-_doo_-eh]
1997	millenovecentonovantasette [mee-lleh-noh-veh-chehn-toh-noh-vahn-tah-seh-tteh]
millimeter	millimetro [mee-_llee_-moh troh]
centimeter	centimetro [chen-_tee_-meh-troh]
meter	metro [_moh_ troh]
kilometer	chilometro [kee-_loh_-meh-troh]

mile	miglio [mee-lyoh]
square meter	metro quadrato [meh-troh kwah-drah-toh]
square kilometer	chilometro quadrato [kee-loh-meh-troh kwah-drah-toh]
hectar	ettaro [eh-ttah-roh]
liter	litro [lee-troh]
gram	grammo [ghrah-mmoh]
half kilo	mezzo chilo [meh-zoh kee-loh]
100 grams	un etto oon eh-ttoh]
kilogram	chilogrammo [kee-loh-ghrah-mmoh]
dozen	dozzina [doh-zee-nah]

Expressions of Time
L'ora

Telling Time	**L'ora**
What time is it?	Che ore sono? [keh oh-reh soh-noh]
Can you tell me the time, please?	Mi può dire che ore sono, per favore? [mee poo-oh dee-reh keh oh-reh soh-noh]
It's exactly ...	Sono… in punto. [soh-noh.. een poon-toh]
It's about …	Sono circa… [soh-noh cheer-kah]
3 o'clock.	le tre. [leh treh]
3:05.	le tre e cinque. [leh treh eh cheen-kweh]
3:10.	le tre e dieci. [leh treh eh dych-chee]
3:15/quarter past three.	le tre e un quarto. [leh treh eh oon kwahr-toh]

3:30.	le tre e mezza. [leh treh eh meh-zah]
3:45/quarter to four.	le quattro meno un quarto. [leh kwah-ttroh meh-noh oon kwahr-toh]
3:55/five to four.	le quattro meno cinque. [le kwah-ttroh meh-noh cheen-kweh]
It's one o'clock.	È l'una. [eh loo-nah]
It's noon/midnight.	È mezzogiorno/mezzanotte. [eh moh-zoh-john-noh/meh-zah-noh-tteh]
Is this clock right?	Questo orologio va bene? [kweh-stoh oh-roh-loh-joh vah ben-neh]
It's fast/slow.	Va avanti/indietro. [vah ah-vahn-tee/een-dyeh-troh]
It's late/too early.	È tardi/troppo presto. [eh tahr-dee/troh-ppoh preh-stoh]
At what time?/When?	A che ora?/Quando? [ah keh oh-rah/kwahn-doh]
At 1:00.	All'una. [ah-lloo-nah]
At 2:00.	Alle due. [ah-lleh doo-eh]
Around 4:00.	Verso le quattro. [vehr-soh leh kwah-ttroh]
In an hour.	Fra un'ora. [trah oo-noh-rah]
In two hours.	Fra due ore. [frah doo-eh oh-reh]
Not before 9 A.M.	Non prima delle nove del mattino. [nohn pree-mah deh-lle noh-veh dehl mah-ttee-noh]
After 8 P.M.	Dopo le otto di sera. [doh-poh leh oh-ttoh dee seh-rah]
Between 3 and 4.	Tra le tre e le quattro. [trah leh treh eh leh kwah-ttroh]
For how long?	Per quanto tempo? [pehr kwahn-toh tehm-poh]
For two hours.	Per due ore. [pehr doo-eh oh-reh]

From 10 to 11.	Dalle dieci alle undici. [<u>dah</u>-lleh <u>dyeh</u>-chee <u>ah</u>-lle <u>oon</u>-dee-chee]
Until 5.	Fino alle cinque. [<u>fee</u>-noh <u>ah</u>-lleh <u>cheen</u>-kweh]
Since when?	Da quando? [dah <u>kwahn</u>-doh]
Since 8 A.M.	Fin dalle otto del mattino. [feen <u>dah</u>-lle <u>oh</u>-ttoh dehl mah-<u>ttee</u>-noh]
For half an hour.	Da mezz'ora. [dah meh-<u>zoh</u>-rah]
For a week.	Da una settimana. [dah <u>oo</u>-nah seh-ttee-<u>mah</u>-nah]

Other Expressions of Time / Altre espressioni per indicare l'ora

(in the) morning	la mattina [lah mah-<u>ttee</u>-nah]
at noon/midday	a mezzogiorno [ah <u>meh</u>-zoh-<u>johr</u>-noh]
about this time	verso quest'ora [<u>vehr</u>-soh kweh-<u>stoh</u>-rah]
afternoon	il pomeriggio [eel poh-meh-<u>ree</u>-djoh]
at night	di sera, di notte [dee <u>seh</u>-rah]
day after tomorrow	dopo domani [<u>doh</u>-poh doh-<u>mah</u>-nee]
day before yesterday	l'altro ieri [<u>lahl</u>-troh <u>yeh</u>-ree]
during the day	di giorno [dee <u>johr</u>-noh]
every day	ogni giorno [<u>oh</u>-nyee <u>johr</u>-noh]
every day/daily	tutti i giorni, giornaliero [<u>too</u>-ttee ee <u>johr</u>-nee, johr-nah-<u>lyeh</u>-roh]
every half hour	ogni mezz'ora [<u>oh</u>-nyee meh-<u>zoh</u>-rah]
every hour	ogni ora [<u>oh</u>-nyee oh-rah]
every two days	ogni due giorni [<u>oh</u>-nyee doo-eh <u>johr</u>-nee]

from time to time	di tanto in tanto [dee <u>tahn</u>-toh een <u>tahn</u>-toh]
in the morning	la mattina (presto) [lah mah-<u>ttee</u>-nah-<u>preh</u>-stoh]
in two weeks	fra quindici giorni [frah <u>kween</u>-dee-chee <u>johr</u>-nee]
last Monday	lunedì scorso [loo-neh-<u>dee</u> <u>skohr</u>-soh]
next year	l'anno prossimo [<u>lah</u>-nnoh <u>proh</u>-ssee-moh]
now	ora [oh-rah]
recently	recentemente [reh-chehn-teh-<u>mehn</u>-teh]
sometimes	a volte [ah <u>vohl</u>-teh]
soon	presto [<u>preh</u>-stoh]
on Sunday	domenica [doh-<u>meh</u>-nee-kah]
ten minutes ago	dieci minuti fa [<u>dyeh</u>-chee mee-<u>noo</u>-tee fah]
this morning/evening	stamattina/stasera [stah-mah-<u>ttee</u>-nah/ stah-seh-rah]
this week	questa settimana [<u>kweh</u>-stah seh-ttee-<u>mah</u>-nah]
today	oggi [<u>oh</u>-djee]
tomorrow	domani [doh-<u>mah</u>-nee]
tomorrow morning/evening	domattina/domani sera [doh-mah-<u>ttee</u>-nah/doh mah-nee <u>seh</u>-ra]
toward afternoon	verso mezzogiorno [vehr-soh <u>meh</u>-zoh-<u>johr</u>-noh]
weekend	il fine settimana [eel <u>fee</u>-neh seh-ttee-<u>mah</u>-nah]
within a week	entro una settimana [<u>ehn</u>-troh <u>oo</u>-nah seh-ttee-mah-nah]
yesterday	ieri [<u>ych</u> ree]

Days of the Week	**I giorni della settimana**
Monday	lunedì [loo-neh-<u>dee</u>]
Tuesday	martedì [mahr-teh-<u>dee</u>]
Wednesday	mercoledì [mehr-koh-leh-<u>dee</u>]
Thursday	giovedì [joh-veh-<u>dee</u>]
Friday	venerdì [veh-nehr-<u>dee</u>]
Saturday	sabato [<u>sah</u>-bah-toh]
Sunday	domenica [doh-<u>meh</u>-nee-kah]

Months of the Year	**I mesi**
January	gennaio [jeh-<u>nnah</u>-yoh]
February	febbraio [feh-<u>brah</u>-yoh]
March	marzo [<u>mahr</u>-tsoh]
April	aprile [ah-<u>pree</u>-leh]
May	maggio [<u>mah</u>-djoh]
June	giugno [<u>joo</u>-nyoh]
July	luglio [<u>loo</u>-lyoh]
August	agosto [ah-<u>ghoh</u>-stoh]
September	settembre [seh-<u>ttehm</u>-breh]
October	ottobre [oh-<u>ttoh</u>-breh]
November	novembre [noh-<u>vehm</u>-breh]
December	dicembre [dee-<u>chehm</u>-breh]

Seasons	**Le stagioni**
spring	primavera [pree-mah-<u>veh</u>-rah]
summer	l'estate f [eh-<u>stah</u>-teh]
autumn/fall	autunno [ah-oo-<u>too</u>-nnoh]
winter	inverno [een-<u>vehr</u>-noh]

Holidays	**Giorni festivi**
New Year's Day	Capodanno [kah-poh-<u>dah</u>-nnoh]
Epiphany	Epifania [leh-pee-fah-<u>nee</u>-ah]
carnival	Carnevale [kuhr-neh-<u>vah</u>-leh]
Mardi Gras (Fat Tuesday)	Martedì grasso [mahr-teh-<u>dee</u> <u>grah</u>-ssoh]
Ash Wednesday	Mercoledì delle ceneri [mehr-koh-leh-<u>dee</u> deh-lle <u>cheh</u>-<u>neh</u>-ree]
Maundy Thursday (Thursday before Easter)	Giovedì Santo [joh-veh-<u>dee</u> <u>sahn</u>-toh]
Good Friday	Venerdì Santo [veh-nehr-<u>dee</u> <u>sahn</u>-toh]
Easter	Pasqua [<u>pah</u>-skwah]
Easter Monday	Lunedì dell'Angelo [loo-neh-<u>dee</u> deh-<u>llahn</u>-jeh-loh]
Italian Liberation Day	Liberazione [loo beh-rah-<u>tsyoh</u>-neh]

Labor Day	Festa del lavoro [feh-stah dehl lah-voh-roh]
Day of Assumption (August 15)	Assunzione, Ferragosto [ah-ssoon-tsyoh-neh]
All Saints' Day (November 1)	Ognissanti [oh-nyee-sahn-tee]
Immaculate Conception (December 8)	Immacolata Concezione [ee-mmah-koh-lah-tah kohn-chen-tsyoh-neh]
Christmas Eve	Vigilia di Natale [vee-jee-lyah dee nah-tah-leh]
Christmas	Natale [nah-tah-leh]
Christmas Day	il giorno di Natale [eel johr-noh dee nah-tah-leh]
New Year's Eve	S. Silvestro [sahn seel-veh-stroh]

The Date

Data e età

What's the date today?	Quanti ne abbiamo oggi? [kwahn-tee neh ah-byah-moh oh-djee]
Today is May first.	Oggi è il primo maggio. [oh-djee eh eel pree-moh mah-djoh]
Today is May 2, 3,...	Oggi è il due/il tre/il... maggio. [oh-djee eh eel doo-eh/eel treh/eel...mah-djoh]

*The first day of the month in Italian is expressed with the ordinal number **primo**. All other dates are expressed with cardinal numbers (**due, tre, quattro, etc.**)*

Weather
Il tempo

What's the weather going to be like today?	Che tempo farà oggi? [keh tehm-poh fah-rah oh-djee]
It's going to be...	Farà... [fah-rah]
nice.	bel tempo. [behl tehm-poh]
awful/bad.	brutto tempo. [broo-ttoh tehm-poh]
variable.	un tempo variable. [oon tehm-poh vah·ryah-bee-leh]
It's going to stay nice/awful.	Rimane bello/brutto. [ree-mah-neh beh-lloh/broo-ttoh]
It's getting hotter/colder.	Sta diventando più caldo/freddo. [stah dee-vehn-tahn-doh pee-oo kahl-doh/freh-ddoh]
It's going to rain/snow.	Pioverà/Nevicherà. [pyoh-veh-rah/neh-vee-keh-rah]
It's hot/cold.	Fa caldo/freddo. [fah kahl-doh/freh-ddoh]
It's muggy.	C'è afa. [cheh ah-fah]
A storm is brewing.	S'avvicina un temporale. [sah-vvee-chee-nah eel tehm-poh-rah-leh]
We're going to have a storm.	Avremo un temporale/una tempesta. [ah-vreh-moh oon tehm-poh-rah-leh/oo-nah tehm-peh-stah]
It's foggy/windy.	C'è nebbia/vento. [cheh neh-byah vehn-toh]
It's sunny.	C'è il sole. [cheh eel soh-leh]

The sky is clear/cloudy.	Il cielo è sereno/coperto. [eel <u>cheh</u>-loh eh seh-<u>reh</u>-noh/koh-<u>pehr</u>-toh]
What's the temperature today?	Quanti gradi abbiamo oggi? [<u>kwahn</u>-tee <u>ghrah</u>-dee ah-<u>byah</u>-moh <u>oh</u>-djee]
It's 20 degrees (Centigrade).	Abbiamo una temperatura di 20 gradi. [ah-<u>byah</u>-moh <u>oo</u>-nah tehm-peh-rah-<u>too</u>-rah dee <u>vehn</u>-tee <u>ghrah</u>-dee]
What is the condition of the roads in the Dolomites?	In che stato si trovano le strade nelle Dolomiti? [een keh <u>stah</u>-toh see <u>troh</u>-vah-noh leh <u>strah</u>-deh <u>neh</u>-lle doh-loh-<u>mee</u>-tee]
The roads are icy.	Le strade sono ghiacciate. [leh <u>strah</u>-deh <u>soh</u>-noh ghyah-<u>chah</u>-teh]
Visibility is only 20 meters/ less than 50 meters.	C'è una visibilità di soli 20 m/inferiore ai 50 m. [cheh oo-na vee-see-bee-lee-<u>tah</u> dee <u>soh</u>-lee <u>vehn</u>-tee <u>meh</u>-tree/een-feh-<u>ryoh</u>-reh <u>ah</u>-ee cheen-<u>kwahn</u>-tah <u>meh</u>-tree]
We need tire chains.	Ci vogliono le catene. [chee <u>voh</u>-lyoh-noh leh kah-<u>teh</u>-neh]

Word List: Weather

air	<u>a</u>ria [<u>ah</u>-ryah]
air pressure	la pressione atmosferica [preh-<u>ssyoh</u>-neh aht-moh-<u>sfeh</u>-ree-kah]
barometer	barometro [bah-<u>roh</u>-meh-troh]
calm	sereno [seh-<u>reh</u>-noh]
climate	il clima [eel <u>klee</u>-mah]
cloud	nuvola [<u>noo</u>-voh-lah]
cloudy	nuvoloso [noo-voh-<u>loh</u>-soh]
cold	freddo [<u>freh</u>-ddoh]
dawn	alba [<u>ahl</u>-bah]

dead calm	bonaccia [boh-<u>nah</u>-chah]
downpour	lo scroscio di pioggia [loh <u>skroh</u>-shoh dee <u>pyoh</u>-djah]
drenched/soaked	bagnato [bah-<u>nyah</u>-toh]
drizzly	piovigginoso [pyoh-vee-djee-<u>noh</u>-soh]
drought	siccità [see-chee-<u>tah</u>]
dusk	crepuscolo [kreh-<u>poo</u>-skoh-loh]
flood	l'alluvione (f) [lah-lloo-<u>vyoh</u>-neh]
fog haze/mist	nebbia [<u>neh</u>-byah]
frost	gelo [<u>jeh</u>-loh]
gust of wind	la raffica di vento [lah <u>rah</u>-ffee-kah dee <u>vehn</u>-toh]
hail	la grandine [lah <u>ghrahn</u>-dee-neh]
hailstone	gragnola [ghrah-<u>nyoh</u>-lah]
haze/mist	foschia [foh-<u>skee</u>-ah]
heat wave	ondata di caldo [ohn-<u>dah</u>-tah dee <u>kahl</u>-doh]
high pressure	l'anticiclone (m), l'alta pressione (f) [lahn-tee-chee-<u>kloh</u>-neh, lahl-tah preh-<u>ssyoh</u>-neh]
high tide	alta marea [<u>ahl</u>-tah mah-<u>reh</u>-ah]
hot	caldo, bollente [<u>kahl</u>-doh, boh-<u>llehn</u>-teh]
humid/hot and muggy	afoso, caldo [ah-<u>foh</u>-soh, <u>kahl</u>-doh]
ice	ghiaccio [<u>ghyah</u>-choh]
icy roads	strade ghiacciate [<u>strah</u>-deh ghyah-<u>chah</u>-teh]
lightning	il fulmine [eel <u>fool</u>-mee-neh]
low tide	bassa marea [<u>bah</u>-ssah mah-<u>reh</u>-ah]
muggy	caldo umido [<u>kahl</u>-doh oo-mee-doh]
powder (snow)	la neve farinosa [lah <u>neh</u>-veh fah-ree-<u>noh</u>-sah]

precipitation	le precipitazioni [leh preh-chee-pee-tah-tsyoh-nee]
rain	pioggia [pyoh-djah]
rainy	piovoso [pyoh-voh-soh]
snow	la neve [lah neh-veh]
snowstorm	bufera di neve [boo-feh-rah dee neh-veh]
starry (sky)	stellato [steh-llah-toh]
storm/cloudburst	nubifragio [noo-bee-frah-joh]
sultry/muggy	afoso [ah-foh-soh]
sun	il sole [eel soh-leh]
sunny	soleggiato [soh-leh-djah-toh]
sunrise	levata del sole/il sorgere del sole [leh-vah-tah dehl soh-leh/eel sohr-jeh-reh dehl soh-leh]
sunset	tramonto [trah-mohn-toh]
temperature	temperatura [tehm-peh-rah-too-rah]
thaw	disgelo [dee-sjeh-loh]
thunder	tuono [twoh-noh]
tornado, low pressure	il ciclone, la bassa pressione [eel chee-kloh-neh/lah bah-ssah preh-ssyoh-neh]
variable	variabile [vah-ryah-bee-leh]
warm	caldo [kahl-doh]
weather forecast	bollettino meteorologico/le previsioni meteorologiche [boh-lleh-ttee-noh meh-teh-oh-roh- loh-jee-koh, preh-vee-syoh-nee meh-teh-oh-roh-loh-jee-keh]
wind	vento [vehn-toh]
wind force	intensità del vento [een-tehn-see-tah dehl vehn-toh]

Word List: Colors

black	nero [neh-roh]
blue	blu [bloo]
brown	marrone [mah-rroh-neh]
chestnut	castano [cah-stah-noh]
colored	a colori [ah koh-loh-ree]
dark	scuro [skoo-roh]
golden	color oro [koh-lohr oh-roh]
gray	grigio [ghree-joh]
green	verde [vehr-deh]
light	chiaro [kyah-roh]
lilac	lilla [lee-llah]
multicolored	a più colori [ah pee-oo koh-loh-ree]
orange	arancione [ahran-choh-neh]
pink	rosa [roh-sah]
red	rosso [roh-ssoh]
silver	argento [ahr-jehn-toh]
solid-colored	a tinta unita [ah tee-tah oo-nce-tah]
turquoise	turchese [toor-keh-seh]
violet	viola [vyoh-lah]
white	bianco [byahn-koh]
yellow	giallo [jah-lloh]

2 **Making Contact**
Contatti

Saying Hello/Introductions/Getting Acquainted
Saluti/Presentazione/Relazioni

Good morning!/ Hi!/Hello!	Bom dia!
Good morning/afternoon. (until about 6 P.M.)	Buon giorno. [bwohn johr-noh]
Good evening/night.	Buona sera. [bwoh-nah seh-rah]

> Is used during the afternoon hours, especially in central and southern Italy!

Hello!/ Hi!	Ciao! [chah-oh]
What is your name? (formal)	Come si chiama? [koh-meh see kyah-mah]
What is your name? (informal)	Come ti chiami? [koh-meh tee kyah-mee]
My name is…	Mi chiamo… [mee kyah-moh]
May I introduce you to ...	Le posso presentare… [leh poh-ssoh preh-sehn-tah-reh]
Mrs. X.	la signora X. [lah see-nyoh-rah]
Miss X	la signorina X. [lah see-nyoh-ree-nah]
Mr. X.	il signor X. [eel see-nyohr]
my husband.	mio marito. [mee-oh mah-ree-toh]
my wife.	mia moglie. [mee-ah moh-lyeh]
my son.	mio figlio. [mee-oh fee-lyoh]
my daughter.	mia figlia. [mee-ah fee-lyah]
my brother/my sister.	mio fratello/mia sorella. [mee-oh frah-teh-lloh/mee-ah soh-reh-llah]
my friend.	il mio amico/la mia amica. [eel mee-oh ah-mee-koh/ lah mee-ah ah-mee-kah]
my colleague.	il mio collega/la mia collega. [eel mee-oh koh-lleh-ghah/lah mee-ah koh-lleh—ghah]

How are you?	Come sta? [<u>koh</u>-meh stah]
How are things?	Come va? [<u>koh</u>-meh vah]
Fine, thanks, and you?	Bene, gr<u>a</u>zie. E Lei/tu? [<u>beh</u>-neh, <u>ghrah</u>-tsyeh eh <u>leh</u>-ee/too]
Where are you from?	Di dov'è Lei?/Di dove sei tu? [dee doh-<u>veh</u> <u>leh</u>-ee/dee <u>doh</u>-veh <u>seh</u>-ee]
I am from...	Sono di... [<u>soh</u>-noh dee]
Have you been here a long time?	È/Sei qui da molto? [eh/<u>soh</u> ee kwee dah <u>mohl</u>-toh]
I've been here since...	Sono qui da... [<u>soh</u>-noh kwee dah]
How long are you staying?	Quanto si ferma/ti fermi [<u>kwahn</u>-toh see <u>fehr</u>-mah/tee <u>fehr</u>-mee]

Is this your first time here?	È/Sei qui per la prima volta? [eh/<u>seh</u>-ee kwee pehr lah <u>pree</u>-mah <u>vohl</u>-tah]
Are you alone?	È/Sei solo/a? [eh/<u>seh</u>-ee <u>soh</u>-loh/ah]
No, I'm here with my family./ I'm traveling with some friends.	No, sono qui con la mia fam<u>i</u>glia. /Sono in vi<u>a</u>ggio con degli amici. [noh, <u>soh</u>-noh kwee kohn lah <u>mee</u>-ah fah-<u>mee</u>-lyah/<u>soh</u>-noh een <u>vyah</u>-djoh kohn <u>deh</u>-lyee ah-<u>mee</u>-chee]

Are you also at the Astoria Hotel/at the campsite…?	È anche Lei/Sei anche tu all'hotel Astoria/al campeggio…? [eh ahn-keh leh-ee/<u>seh</u>-ee <u>ahn</u>-keh too ahl-loh-<u>tehl</u> ah-stoh-ryah/ahl-kahm-`pay-djoh]

Traveling Alone / Making a Date
In viaggio da solo / Appuntamento

Are you waiting for someone?	Aspetta/Aspetti qualcuno? [ah-<u>speh</u>-tta/ah-<u>speh</u>-ttee kwahl-<u>koo</u>-noh]
Do you already have plans for tomorrow?	Ha/Hai già un programma per domani? [ah/<u>ah</u>-ee jah oon proh-<u>ghrah</u>-mmah pehr doh-<u>mah</u>-nee]
Shall we go there together?	Ci andiamo insieme? [chee ahn-<u>dyah</u>-moh een-<u>syeh</u>-meh]
Shall we go out together tonight?	Vogliamo uscire insieme stasera? [voh-<u>lyah</u>-moh oo-<u>shee</u>-reh een-<u>syeh</u>-meh stah-<u>seh</u>-rah]
May I ask you to lunch/dinner?	La/Ti posso invitare a pranzo/cena? [lah/tee <u>poh</u>-ssoh een-vee-<u>tah</u>-reh ah <u>prahn</u>-tsoh/<u>cheh</u>-nah]
What time shall we meet?	A che ora ci incontriamo? [ah keh <u>oh</u>-rah chee een-kohn-<u>tryah</u>-moh]
May I come by to get you?	Posso venire a prenderLa/prenderti? [<u>poh</u>-ssoh veh-<u>nee</u>-reh ah <u>prehn</u>-dehr-lah/<u>prehn</u>-dehr-tee]
When should I come?	A che ora devo venire? [ah keh <u>oh</u>-rah <u>deh</u>-voh ve-<u>nee</u>-reh]
Let's meet at nine...	Ci incontriamo alle nove... [chee een-kohn-<u>tryah</u>-moh <u>ah</u>-lleh <u>noh</u>-veh]
in front of the movie theater.	davanti al cinema. [dah-<u>vahn</u>-tee ahl <u>chee</u>-neh-mah]
in the square.	in piazza. [een <u>pyah</u>-tsah]
at the café.	al bar. [ahl bahr]

Are you married?	È sposato/sposata? [eh spoh-<u>sah</u>-toh/spoh-<u>sah</u>-tah]
Do you have a boyfriend/girlfriend?	Hai un ragazzo/ragazza? [<u>ah</u>-ee oon rah-<u>gah</u>-tso/<u>oo</u>-nah rah-<u>gah</u>-tsah]
May I take you home?	La/Ti posso accompagnare a casa? [lah/tee poh-ssoh ah-kkohm-pah-<u>nyah</u>-reh ah <u>kah</u>-sah]
I will take you…	La/Ti porto… [lah/tee <u>pohr</u>-toh]
May I see you again?	La/Ti posso rivedere? La/Ti porto… [lah/tee poh-ssoh ree-veh-<u>deh</u>-reh? lah/tee <u>pohr</u>-toh]
I hope to see you again.	Spero di rivederLa/rivederti presto. [<u>speh</u>-roh dee ree-veh-<u>dehr</u>-lah/tee <u>preh</u>-stoh]
Thank you for the lovely evening.	Grazie della bella serata. [<u>grah</u>-tsyeh <u>deh</u>-llah <u>beh</u>-llah seh-<u>rah</u>-tah]
Leave me alone in peace, please!	Mi lasci in pace, per favore! [mee <u>lah</u>shee een <u>pah</u>cheh, pehr tah-<u>voh</u>-reh]
Out of here! Beat it!	Sparisci! [spah-<u>ree</u>-shee]
Enough!	Adesso basta! [ah-<u>deh</u>-ssoh <u>bah</u>-stah]

A Visit

Una visita

Excuse me, does Mr./Mrs./Miss X live here?	Scusi, abita qui il signor/la signora/la signorina X? [<u>skoo</u>-zee, <u>ah</u>-bee-tah kwee eel see-<u>nyohr</u>/lah see-<u>nyoh</u>-rah/lah see-nyoh-<u>ree</u>-nah?]
No, he/she has moved.	No, ha cambiato casa. [noh ha kahm-<u>byah</u>-toh <u>kah</u>-sah]
Do you know where he/she lives now?	Sa dove abita adesso? [sah <u>doh</u>-veh <u>ah</u>-bee-tah ah-<u>deh</u>-ssoh]

May I speak with Mr./Mrs./Miss X?	Posso parlare col signor/con la signora/con la signorina X? [poh-ssoh pahr-lah-reh kohl see-nyohr/kohn lah see-nyoh-rah/kohn lah see-nyoh-ree-nah]
When will he/she be at the house?	Quando sarà in casa? [kwahn-doh sah-rah een kah-sah]
May I leave a message?	Posso lasciare un messaggio? [poh-ssoh lah-shah-reh oon meh-ssah-djoh]
I'll come by again later.	Ripasso più tardi. [ree-pah-ssoh pee-oo tahr-dee]
Sit down./Make yourself comfortable.	Si accomodi/accomodati. [see ah-kkoh-moh-dee/ah-kkoh-moh-dah-tee]

*In Italy a visitor entering a house or the living room will often say **permesso** before entering.*

Greetings from Paul.	Tanti saluti da parte di Paul. [tahn-tee sah-loo-tee dah pahr-teh dee pohl]
May I offer you something to drink?	Che cosa Le/ti posso offrire da bere? [keh koh-sah leh/tee poh-ssoh oh-ffree-reh dah beh-reh]
To your health!/Cheers!	Alla Sua salute!/Alla tua! [ah-lla soo-ah sah-loo-teh/ah-llah too-ah]
Can't you stay for lunch/dinner?	Non può/puoi rimanere a pranzo/cena? [nohn poo-oh/pwo-ee ree-mah-neh-reh ah prahn-tsoh/cheh-nah]
Thank you. If it's no trouble, I'd like to stay.	Grazie. Se non disturbo, rimango volentieri. [ghra-tsyeh seh nohn dee-stoor-boh ree-mahn-goh voh-lehn-tyeh-ree]
I'm sorry, but I have to go now.	Mi dispiace, ma ora devo andare. [mee dee-spyah-cheh mah oh-rah deh-voh ahn-dah-reh]

Saying Good-bye
Congedo

Good-bye!	Arrivederci! [ah rree-veh-dohr-chee]
See you soon!	A presto! [ah preh-stoh]
See you later!	A più tardi! [ah pee-oo tahr-dee]
Till tomorrow!	A domani! [ah doh-mah-nee]
Good night! (used at the end of the evening)	Buona notte! [bwoh-nah noh-tteh]
Bye! (used with friends and family)	Ciao! [chah-oh]
Best regards!	Tante belle cose! [tahn-teh beh-lleh koh-seh]
Have a good time!	Buon divertimento! [bwohn dee-vehr-tee-mehn-toh]
Have a good trip!	Buon viaggio! [bwohn vyah-djoh]
Keep in touch!	Fatti sentire/fatti vivo/a! [fah-ttee sehn-tee-reh/fah-ttee vee-voh/ah]
Come see us!/Keep in touch!	Mi farò vivo/viva. [mee fah-roh vee-voh/ah
Give my regards to ...	Mi saluti.../Salutami... [mee sah-loo-tee /sah-loo-tah-mee]

Asking a Favor/Expressing Thanks
Chiedere e ringraziare

Yes, thank you.	Sì, grazie. [see ghrah-tsyeh]
No, thank you.	No, grazie. [noh ghrah-tsyeh]
May I ask you a favor?	Le posso chiedere un favore? [leh poh ssoh kyeh-deh-reh oon fah-voh-reh]
Excuse me?	Permette? [pehr-meh-tteh]
Can you please help me?	Mi può aiutare, per favore? [mee poo-oh ah-yoo-tah-reh pehr fah-voh-reh]

Thank you.	Grazie. [ghrah-tsyeh]
Thank you very much.	Tante grazie. [tahn-teh ghrah-tsyeh]
With pleasure!	Molto volentieri! [mohl-toh voh-lehn-tyeh-ree]
Thank you, the same to you.	Grazie, altrettanto. [grah-tsyeh ahl-treh-ttahn-toh]
That's very kind, thank you.	Molto gentile, grazie. [mohl-toh jehn-tee-leh]
Thank you for your help/kindness.	Grazie del Suo aiuto/della Sua premura. [ghrah-tsyeh dehl soo-oh ah-yoo-toh/deh-llah soo-ah preh-moo-rah]
You're welcome!/Don't mention it./It's nothing!	Prego!/Non c'è di che! [preh-ghoh nohn cheh dee keh]

Apologies/Regrets
Scusarsi e rammaricarsi

Excuse me!/I'm sorry!	Scusi! [skoo-zee]
I must apologize.	Devo scusarmi. [deh-voh skoo-zahr-mee]
I'm very sorry.	Mi dispiace tanto. [mee dee-spyah-cheh tahn-toh]
I didn't mean it.	Non intendevo questo. [nohn een-tehn-deh-voh kweh-stoh]
What a shame!	Peccato! [peh-kkah-toh]
Unfortunately, that's not possible.	Purtroppo non è possibile. [poor-troh-ppoh nohn eh poh-ssee-bee-leh]
Perhaps another time.	Forse un'altra volta. [fohr-seh oo-nahl-trah vohl-tah]

Congratulations/Best Wishes
Auguri

Best wishes!	Auguri! [ah-oo-ghoo-ree]
All the best!/Best regards!	Tante belle cose! [tahn-teh beh-lleh koh-seh]
Happy birthday!	Tanti auguri per il compleanno/per l'onomastico. [tahn tee ah-oo-ghoo-ree pehr eel kohm-pleh-ah-nnoh
Have a good day at work!	Buon lavoro! [bwohn lah-voh-roh]
Good luck!	Buona fortuna!/In bocca al lupo! [bwoh-nah fohr-too-nah/een boh-kkah ahl loo-poh]
Get well soon!	Buona guarigione! [bwoh-nah gwah-ree-joh-neh]
Happy holidays!	Buone feste! [bwoh-neh feh-ste]

Language Difficulties
Difficoltà di comprensione

Excuse me?/I beg your pardon?	Come dice? (Lei)/Come dici? (tu) [koh-meh dee-cheh? (lch-ee)/koh-meh dee-chee? (too)]
I don't understand. Please repeat that.	Non capisco. [nohn kah-pee-skoh] Ripeta/Ripeti, per favore. [ree-peh-tah/ree-peh-tee pehr fah-voh-reh]
Please speak more slowly/softly/louder.	Per favore, parli/parla più piano/forte. [pehr fah-voh-reh pahr lee/pahr-lah pee-oo pyah-noh/fohr-teh]
I understand.	Capisco/Ho capito. [kah-pee-skoh/oh kah-pee-toh]
Do you speak...	Parla/Parli... [pahr-lah/pahr-lee]
English?	inglese? [een-ghleh-seh]
French?	francese? [frahn-cheh-seh]
German?	tedesco? [teh-deh-skoh]

I speak only a little …	Parlo solo un po' di… [pahr-loh soh-loh oon poh dee]
How do you say…in Italian?	Come si dice…in italiano? [koh-meh see dee-che…een ee-tah-lyah-noh]
What does...mean?	Che cosa significa...? [keh koh-sah see-nyee-fee-kah]
How do you pronounce this word?	Come si pronuncia questa parola? [koh-meh see proh-noon-chah kweh-stah pah-roh-lah]
Please write it for me.	Me lo scriva/Scrivimelo, per favore! [meh loh skree-vah/skree-vee-meh-loh pehr fah-voh-reh]
Please spell it. Please write it for me.	Lo sillabi/Sillabalo, per favore! [lo see-llah-bee/see-llah-bah-loh pehr fah-voh-reh]

Expressing Opinions
Esprimere la propria opinione

I (don't) like it.	(Non) mi piace. [(nohn) mee pyah-cheh]
I prefer...	Preferisco…(Non) mi piace. [preh-feh-ree-skoh...(nohn) mee pyah-cheh]
More than anything, I really would like...	Più di tutto mi piacerebbe…[pee-oo dee too-ttoh mee pyah-cheh-reh-beh]
That would be nice.	Sarebbe bello. [sah-reh-beh beh-lloh]
With pleasure.	Con piacere. [kohn pyah-cheh-reh]
Great!	Magnifico! [mah-nyee-fee-koh]
I don't feel like it.	Non ne ho voglia. [nohn neh oh voh-lyah]
I don't want to.	Non voglio. [nohn voh-lyoh]
That's out of the question.	Non se ne parla neanche. [nohn seh neh pahr-lah neh-ahn-keh]

In no way./Certainly not.	In nessun caso. [een neh-ssoon kah-soh]
I don't know yet.	Non lo so ancora. [nohn loh soh ahn koh-rah]
Maybe.	Forse. [fohr-seh]
Probably.	Probabilmente. [proh-bah-beel-mehn-teh]

Personal Information
Dati personali

Age	**Età**
How old are you?	Quanti anni ha/hai? [kwahn-tee ah-nnee ah-ee]
I'm thirty-nine (39).	Ho trentanove anni. [oh trehn-tah-noh-veh ah-nnee]
When is your birthday?	Quando compie/compi gli anni? [kwahn-doh kohm-pyeh/kohm-pee lyee ah-nnee]
I was born on April 12, 1954.	Sono nato/nata il dodici aprile millenovecentocinquantaquattro. [soh-noh nah-toh/nah-tah eel doh-dee-chee ah-pree-leh mee-lleh-noh-veh-chehn-toh-cheen-kwahn-tah-kwah-ttroh]

Professions/Education/Training	**Professione e studio**
What is your profession?	Qual è la Sua/tua professione? [kwah-leh lah soo-ah/too-ah proh-feh-ssyoh-neh]
I work in a factory. (I'm a laborer.)	Sono operaio/a. [soh-noh oh peh-rah-yoh/yah]
I work in an office. (I'm a clerk.)	Sono impiegata/o. [soh-noh eem-pyeh-ghah-tah/oh]

I'm a civil servant.	Sono impiegato/a statale. [soh-noh eem-pyeh-ghah-toh/ah stah-tah-leh]
I'm a freelancer.	Sono libero/a professionista. [soh-noh lee-beh-roh proh-feh-ssyoh-nee-stah]
I'm retired.	Sono pensionato/a. [soh-noh pehn-syoh-nah-toh/ah]
I'm unemployed.	Sono disoccupato/a. [soh-noh dee-soh-kkoo-pah-toh/ah]
I work for ...	Lavoro presso… [lah-voh-roh preh-ssoh]
I'm still going to school.	Vado ancora a scuola. [vah-doh ah skwoh-lah]
I'm going to high school.	Frequento il liceo. [freh-kwehn-toh eel lee-cheh-oh]
I'm a student at the university.	Sono studente/essa universitario/a. [soh-noh stoo-dehn-teh/ssah oo-nee-vehr-see-tah-ryoh/yah]
Where/What are you studying?	Dove/Che cosa studia/i? [doh-veh/keh koh-sah stoo-dyah/dee]
I'm studying ... in Monaco.	Studio … a Monaco. [stoo-dyo ah moh-nah-koh]
What are your hobbies?	Quali hobby ha/hai? [kwah-lee oh-bee ah/ah-ee]

Word List: Professions/Education/Training

academy of fine arts	accademia delle belle arti [ah-kkah-deh-myah deh-lle beh-lle ahr-tee]
accountant	il/la contabile, il ragioniere/ragioniera [eel/lah kohn-tah-bee-leh eel rah-joh-nyeh-reh/rah-joh-nyeh-rah]
actor/actress	l'attore (m)/l'attrice (f) [lah-ttoh-reh lah-ttree-cheh]
agent	il/la rappresentante, l'agente (m) [eel/lah rah-ppreh-sehn-tahn-teh lah-jehn-teh]

apprentice	l'apprendista *(m/f)* [lah-ppreh-<u>dee</u>-stah]
archeology	archeologia [ah-keh-oh-loh-<u>jee</u>-ah]
architect	architetto/architetta [ahr-kee-<u>teh</u>-ttoh/ahr-kee-<u>teh</u>-ttah]
architecture	architettura [ahr-kee-teh-<u>ttoo</u>-rah]
art history	storia dell'arte [<u>stoh</u>-ryah deh-<u>llahr</u>-teh]
artisan/craftsman/-woman	artigiano/artigiana [ahr-tee-jah-noh/ahr-tee-<u>jah</u>-nah]
artist	l'artista *(m/f)* [ahr-<u>tee</u>-stah]
auditor	il revisore dei conti [reh-vee-<u>soh</u>-reh_<u>deh</u>-ee <u>kohn</u>-tee]
auto mechanic	meccanico per auto [meh-<u>kkah</u>-nee-koh pehr <u>ah</u>-oo-toh]
baker	fornaio/fornaia [fohr-<u>nah</u>-yoh/fohr-<u>nah</u>-yah]
biologist	biologo/biologa [bee-<u>oh</u>-loh-ghoh/bee-<u>oh</u>-loh ghah]
biology	biologia [bee-oh-loh-<u>jee</u>-ah]
blue-collar worker	operaio/operaia [oh-peh-<u>rah</u>-yoh/oh-peh-<u>rah</u>-yah]
bookseller	libraio/libraia [lee-<u>brah</u>-yoh/lee-<u>brah</u>-yah]
bricklayer	il muratore [eel moo-rah-<u>toh</u>-reh]
broker/agent	sensale *(m/f)*, il mediatore [sehn-<u>sah</u>-leh meh-dyah-<u>toh</u>-reh]
business management	l'economia *(f)* aziendale [leh-koh-noh-<u>mee</u>-ah ah-zyehn-<u>dah</u>-leh]
business school	scuola commerciale [<u>skwoh</u>-lah koh-mmehr-<u>chah</u>-leh]
butcher	macellaio/macellaia [mah-cheh-<u>llah</u>-yoh/mah-cheh-<u>llah</u>-yah]

caretaker	il portiere/la portiera, [eel pohr-<u>tyeh</u>-reh/lah pohr-<u>tyeh</u>-rah] il portin<u>a</u>io/la portin<u>a</u>ia [eel pohr-tee-<u>nah</u>- yoh/lah pohr-tee-<u>nah</u>-yah]
caretaker/doorman/janitor/custodian	il/la custode [eel/lah koo-<u>stoh</u>-deh]
carpenter	il falegname/donna falegname, carpentiere [eel fah-leh-<u>nyah</u>-meh/<u>doh</u>-nnah fa-leh-<u>nyah</u>-meh, cahr-pehn-<u>tyeh</u>-reh]
cashier	il cassiere/la cassiera [eel kah-<u>ssyeh</u>-reh/lah kah-<u>ssyeh</u>-rah]
chemist	ch<u>i</u>mico/ch<u>i</u>mica [<u>kee</u>-mee-koh/<u>kee</u>-mee-kah]
chemistry	ch<u>i</u>mica [<u>kee</u>-mee-kah]
civil servant (permanent)	impiegato/impiegata statale di ruolo [eem-pyeh-<u>ghah</u>-toh/eem-pyeh-<u>ghah</u>-tah stah-<u>tah</u>-leh dee <u>rwoh</u>-loh]
clerk	impiegata/impiegato [eem-pyeh-<u>ghah</u>-tah/eem-pyeh-<u>ghah</u>-toh]
computer processing specialist	t<u>e</u>cnico specializzato/tecnica specializzata nell'elaborazione elettr<u>o</u>nica dati [<u>tehk</u>-nee-koh speh-chah-lee-<u>zah</u>-toh neh-lleh-lah-boh-rah-<u>tsyoh</u>-neh eh-leh-<u>ttroh</u>-nee-kah <u>dah</u>-tee]
computer science	informatica [een-fohr-<u>mah</u>-tee-kah]
cook	cu<u>o</u>co/cu<u>o</u>ca [<u>kwoh</u>-koh/<u>kwoh</u>-kah]
course	mat<u>e</u>ria di st<u>u</u>dio [mah-<u>teh</u>-ryah dee <u>stoo</u>-dyoh]
decorator/window decorator	il decoratore/la decoratrice, il/la vetrinista [eel deh-koh-rah-<u>toh</u>-reh/lah deh-koh-rah-<u>tree</u>-cheh, eel/lah veh-tree-<u>nee</u>-stah]
dentist	il/la dentista [eel/lah dehn-<u>tee</u>-stah]
designer	il/la designer [eel/lah deh-<u>sah</u>-ee-nehr]

doctor	medico, il dottore/la dottoressa [<u>meh</u>-dee-koh, eel doh-<u>ttoh</u>-reh/lah doh-ttoh-<u>reh</u>-ssah]
draftsman(-woman)	il disegnatore *(m)* tecnico/la disegnatrice *(f)* tecnica [eel dee-seh-nyah-<u>toh</u>-reh tehk-nee-koh/lah dee-seh-nyah-<u>tree</u>-cheh tehk-nee-kah]
driver	l'autista *(m)* [lah-oo-<u>tee</u>-stah]
driving instructor	l'istruttore *(m)*/ l'istruttrice *(f)* di guida [lee-stroo-<u>ttoh</u>-reh, lee-stroo-<u>ttree</u>-cheh dee <u>gwee</u>-dah]
economist	l'economista *(m/f)* [leh-koh-noh-<u>mee</u>-stah]
editor	il redattore/la redattrice [eel reh-dah-<u>ttoh</u>-reh/lah reh-dah-<u>ttree</u>-cheh]
electrician	l'elettricista *(m)* [leh-leh-ttree-<u>chee</u>-stah]
elementary school	scuola elementare [<u>skwoh</u>-lah eh-leh-mehn-<u>tah</u>-reh]
engineer	l'ingegnere *(m)* [leen-jeh-<u>nyeh</u>-reh]
English studies	anglistica [ahn-<u>ghlee</u>-stee-kah]
environmental officer	addetto/addetta alle questioni ambientali [ah-<u>ddeh</u>-ttoh/ah-<u>ddeh</u>-ttah <u>ah</u>-lleh kweh-<u>styoh</u>-nee ahm-byehn-<u>tah</u>-lee]
farmer	l'agricoltore *(m)* [lah-ghree-kohl-<u>toh</u>-reh]
fashion model	l'indossatrice *(f)* [leen-doh-ssah-<u>tree</u>-cheh]
financial adviser	il/la consulente fiscale [eel/lah kohn-soo-<u>lehn</u>-teh fee-<u>skah</u>-leh]
fisherman	il pescatore/la pescatrice [eel peh-skah-<u>toh</u>-reh/lah peh-skah-<u>tree</u>-cheh]
flight attendant	assistente di vuolo [ah-ssee-<u>stehn</u>-teh dee <u>voh</u>-loh]

florist	il fioraio/la fioraia [eel fyoh-<u>rah</u>-yoh/lah fyoh-<u>rah</u>-yah]
gardener	il giardiniere/la giardiniera [eel jahr-dee-<u>nyeh</u>-reh/lah jahr-dee-<u>nyeh</u>-rah]
geography	la geografia [lah jeh-oh-ghrah-<u>fee</u>-ah]
geology	la geologia [lah jeh-oh-loh-<u>jee</u>-ah]
geriatric aide	assistente geriatrico [ah-ssee-<u>stehn</u>-teh jeh-<u>ryah</u>-tree-koh]
glazier	vetraio [veh-<u>trah</u>-yoh]
hairdresser	il parrucchiere/la parrucchiera [eel pah-rroo-<u>kkyeh</u>-reh/lah pah-rroo-<u>kkyeh</u>-rah]
healer	il guaritore/la guaritrice [eel gwah-ree-<u>toh</u>-reh/lah gwah-ree-<u>tree</u>-cheh]
high school	liceo [lee-<u>cheh</u>-oh]
history	storia [<u>stoh</u>-ryah]
house painter	il pittore, imbianchino [eel pee-<u>ttoh</u>-reh, eem-byahn-<u>kee</u>-noh]
househusband	casalingo [kah-sah-<u>leen</u>-ghoh]
housewife	casalinga [kah-sa-<u>leen</u>-ghah]
installer	l'installatore [leen-stah-llah-<u>toh</u>-reh]
institute	istituto [ee-stee-<u>too</u>-toh]
interpreter	l'interprete *(m)* [een-<u>tehr</u>-preh-teh]
jeweler	gioielliere [joh-yeh-<u>llyeh</u>-reh]
journalist	il/la giornalista [eel/lah johr-nah-<u>lee</u>-stah]
judge	giudice *(m/f)* [<u>joo</u>-dee-cheh]
junior high school	scuola media [<u>skwoh</u>-lah <u>meh</u>-dyah]
keyboarder	il perforatore/la perforatrice [eel pehr-foh-rah-<u>toh</u>-reh/ lah pehr-foh-rah-<u>tree</u>-cheh]

laboratory assistant	l'assistente *(m/f)* di laboratorio [ah-ssee-<u>stehn</u>-teh dee lah-boh-rah-<u>toh</u>-ryo]
law	legge *(f)*, diritto [<u>leh</u>-djeh, dee-<u>ree</u>-ttoh]
lawyer	avvocato/avvocatessa [ah-vvoh-<u>kah</u>-toh/ah-vvoh-kah-<u>teh</u>-ssah]
lessons	le lezioni [leh leh-<u>tsyoh</u>-nee]
letter carrier	il/la portalettere [eel/lah pohr-tah-<u>leh</u>-tteh-reh]
librarian	bibliotecario/bibliotecaria [bee-blyoh-teh-<u>kah</u>-ryoh/bee-blyoh-teh-<u>kah</u>-ryah]
locksmith	fabbro/donna fabbro [<u>fah</u>-broh/<u>doh</u>-nnah <u>fah</u>-broh]
machinist	l'utensilista *(m/f)* [loo-tehn-see-<u>lee</u>-stah]
management expert	diplomato/diplomata in economia aziendale [dee-ploh-<u>mah</u>-toh/dee-ploh-<u>mah</u>-tah een eh-koh-noh-<u>mee</u>-ah ah-zyehn-<u>dah</u>-leh]
manager	il gestore/la gestrice, il direttore/la direttrice [eel jeh-<u>stoh</u>-reh/lah jeh-<u>stree</u>-cheh, eel dee-reh-<u>ttoh</u>-reh/lah dee-reh-<u>ttree</u>-cheh]
masseur/masseuse	il massaggiatore/la massaggiatrice [eel mah-ssah-djah-<u>toh</u>-reh/lah mah-ssah-djah-<u>tree</u>-cheh]
mathematics	matematica [mah-teh-<u>mah</u>-tee-kah]
mechanic	meccanico [meh-<u>kkah</u>-nee-koh]
mechanical engineering	ingegneria meccanica [een-jeh-nyeh-<u>ree</u>-ah meh-<u>kkah</u>-nee-kah]
medical resident	assistente di studio medico [ah-ssee-<u>stehn</u>-teh dee <u>stoo</u>-dyoh <u>meh</u>-dee-koh]
medicine	medicina [meh-dee-chee-nah]

merchant	il/la commerciante [eel/lah koh-mmehr-<u>chahn</u>-teh]
meteorologist	meteorologo/meteorologa [meh-teh-oh-<u>roh</u>-loh-ghoh/meh-teh-oh-<u>roh</u>-loh-ghah]
music	m<u>u</u>sica [<u>moo</u>-see-kah]
musician	il/la musicista [eel/lah moo-see-<u>chee</u>-stah]
notary	not<u>ai</u>o [noh-<u>tah</u>-yoh]
novelist	romanziere [roh-mahn-<u>zyeh</u>-rehh]
nurse	l'infermi<u>e</u>re *(m)* / l'infermiera *(f)* [leen-fehr-<u>myeh</u>-reh/ leen-fehr-<u>myeh</u>-rah]
obstetrician	ost<u>e</u>trica [oh-<u>steh</u>-tree-kah]
official in charge	addetto/addetta [ah-<u>ddeh</u>-ttoh/ah-<u>ddeh</u>-ttah]
optician	<u>o</u>ttico [oh-ttee-koh]
orthodontist	odontot<u>e</u>cnico/odontot<u>e</u>cnica [oh-dohn-toh-<u>tehk</u>-nee-koh/oh-dohn-toh-<u>tehk</u>-nee-kah]
park ranger	gu<u>a</u>rdia forestale [<u>gwahr</u>-dya foh-reh-<u>stah</u>-leh]
pastry chef	il pasticc<u>e</u>re/la pasticc<u>e</u>ra [eel pah-stee-<u>cheh</u>-reh/ lah pah-stee-<u>cheh</u>-rah]
perfumer	il profumiere/la profumiera [eel proh-foo-<u>myeh</u>-reh/ lah proh-foo-<u>myeh</u>-rah]
pharmacist	il/la farmacista [eel/lah fahr-mah-<u>chee</u>-stah]
pharmacy	farmac<u>i</u>a [fahr-mah-<u>chee</u>-ah]
philosophy	filosof<u>i</u>a [fee-loh-soh-<u>fee</u>-ah]
photographer	fot<u>o</u>grafo [foh-<u>toh</u>-ghrah-foh]
physicist	f<u>i</u>sico [<u>fee</u>-see-koh]
physics	f<u>i</u>sica [<u>fee</u>-see-kah]

physiotherapist	il/la fisioterapista [eel-lah fee-syoh-teh-rah-<u>pee</u>-stah]
pilot	il/la pilota [eel/lah pee-<u>loh</u>-tah]
plumber	idraulico [ee-<u>drah</u>-oo-lee-koh]
police officer	l'agente *(m/f)*, il vigile/la vigilessa [lah-<u>jehn</u>-teh, eel <u>vee</u>-jee-leh/lah vee-jee-<u>leh</u>-ssah]
political science	le scienze politiche [leh <u>shehn</u>-tseh poh-<u>lee</u>-tee-keh]
postal worker	impiegato postale/impiegata postale [eem-pyeh-<u>ghah</u>-toh poh-<u>stah</u>-leh/eem-pyeh-<u>ghah</u>-tah poh-<u>stah</u>-leh]
priest	parroco [<u>pah</u>-rroh-koh]
primary school	scuola elementare [<u>skwoh</u>-lah eh-leh-mehn-<u>tah</u>-reh]

professor	il professore/la professoressa [ee proh-feh-<u>ssoh</u>-reh/lah proh-feh-ssoh-<u>roh</u> ssah]

psychologist	psicologo/psicologa [psee-koh-loh-ghoh/psee-koh-loh-ghah]
psychology	psicologia [psee-koh-loh-jee-ah]
pupil	allievo/a [ah-llyeh-voh/ah]
railroad employee	il ferroviere [eel feh-rroh-vyeh-reh]
restaurant owner	il restauratore/la restauratrice [eel reh-stah-oo-rah-toh-reh/lah reh-stah-oo-rah-tree-cheh]
restaurant/hotel manager	il gestore di ristorante [eel jeh-stoh-reh/lah jeh-stree-cheh dee ree-stoh-rahn-teh]; l'albergatore/l'albergatrice [lahl-behr-ghah-toh-reh/lahl-behr-ghah-tree-cheh]
retiree	pensionato/pensionata [pehn-syoh-nah-toh/pehn-syoh-nah-tah]
sailor	marinaio [mah-ree-nah-yoh]
school	scuola [skwoh-lah]
scientist	scienziato/scienziata [shehn-tsyah-toh/shehn-tsyah-tah]
secretary	segretario/segretaria [seh-ghreh-tah-ryoh/seh-ghreh-tah-ryah]
shoemaker	calzolaio/calzolaia [kahl-tsoh-lah-yoh/kahl-tsoh-lah-yah]
social worker	l'assistente (m/f) sociale [lah-ssee-stehn-teh soh-chah-leh]
sociology	sociologia [soh-choh-loh-jee-ah]
specialized worker	operaio specializzato/operaia specializzata [oh-peh-rah-yoh peh-chah-lee-zah-toh/oh-peh-rah-yah speh-chah-lee-zah-tah]
student	lo studente/la studentessa [loh stoo-dehn-teh/lah stoo-dehn-teh-ssah]
study	studio [stoo-dyoh]
tailor	sarto/sarta [sahr-toh/sahr-tah]
taxi driver	il/la tassista [eel/lah tah-ssee-stah]

teacher	il/la docente, l'insegnante *(m/f)* [eel-lah doh-<u>chehn</u>-teh, leen-seh-<u>nyahn</u>-teh]
teacher/kindergarten teacher	pedagogo/pedagoga [peh-dah-<u>ghoh</u>-ghoh/peh-dah-<u>ghoh</u>-ghah]; maestro/maestra d'asilo [mah-<u>eh</u>-stroh/mah-<u>eh</u>-strah dah-<u>see</u>-loh]
technical school (professional)	scuola d'avviamento (professionale) [<u>skwoh</u>-lah dah-vvyah-<u>mehn</u>-toh-proh-feh-ssyoh-nah-leh]
technician	tecnico/tecnica [<u>tehk</u>-nee-koh/<u>tehk</u>-nee-kah]
theater arts	le scienze teatrali [leh <u>shehn</u>-zeh nah-too-<u>rah</u>-lce]
theology	teologia [teh-oh-loh-<u>jee</u>-ah]
therapist	il/la terapeuta [eel/lah teh-rah-<u>peh</u>-oo-tah]
tiler/stonemason	il/la conciatetti [eel/lah kohn-chah-<u>teh</u>-ttee]
tourist guide	l'accompagnatore *(m)* turistico/l'accompagnatrice *(f)* turistica [lah-kkohm-pah-nyah-<u>toh</u>-reh too-<u>ree</u>-stee-koh/lah-kkohm-pah-nyah-<u>tree</u>-cheh too-<u>ree</u>-stee-kah]
translator	il traduttore/la traduttrice [eel trah-doo-<u>ttoh</u>-reh/lah trah-doo-<u>ttree</u>-cheh]
university	l'università [loo-ne-vehr-see-<u>tah</u>]
vendor/seller, salesclerk	il venditore/la venditrice, commesso/commessa [eel vehn-dee-<u>toh</u>-reh/lah vehn-dee-<u>tree</u>-cheh]
veterinarian	veterinario/veterinaria [veh-teh-ree-<u>nah</u>-ryoh/veh-teh-ree-<u>nah</u>-ryah]
waiter/waitress	il cameriere/la cameriera [eel kah-meh-<u>ryeh</u>-reh/lah kah-meh-<u>ryeh</u>-rah]
watchmaker	orologiaio/orologiaia [oh-roh-loh-<u>jah</u> yoh/oh-roh-loh-<u>jah</u>-yah]
writer	lo scrittore/la scrittrice [skree-<u>ttoh</u>-reh/skree-<u>ttree</u>-cheh]

3 **On the Go**
Per la strada

Giving Directions
Indicazione del luogo

after	dopo [doh-poh]
before	prima di [pree-mah dee]
behind	dietro [dyeh-troh]
crossing	incrocio [een-kroh-choh]
curve	curva [koor-vah]
far	lontano [lohn-tahn-noh]
here	qui [kwee]
in front of	di fronte [dee fronh-teh]
near	vicino [vee-chee-noh]
near to	vicino a [vee-chee-noh ah]
straight ahead	diritto [dee-ree-ttoh]
street	strada, via [strah-dah, vee-ah]
there	là [lah]
to the left	a sinistra [ah see-nee-strah]
to the right	a destra [ah deh-strah]

Signs and Notices

Attenzione Bambini	Watch Out: Children
Cambio corsia	Changing Lane
Circonvallazione	Bypass
Confluenza	Merge
Curva pericolosa	Dangerous Curve
Dare la precedenza	Yield
Deviazione	Detour
Discesa pericolosa	Dangerous Descent
Disco orario	Parking Meter Disk
Divieto di inversione	No U-Turn
Divieto di sorpasso	No Passing

Divieto di sosta	No Stopping
Divieto di svolta a destra	No Right Turn
Dogana	Toll
Doppio senso di circolazione	Two-Way Traffic
Galleria	Tunnel
Incrocio	Railroad Crossing
Ingorgo	Traffic Jam
Lavori in corso	Roadwork in Progress
Limitazione al peso	Weight Limit
Limite di velocità	Speed Limit
Mettersi in fila	Stay in Lane
Ospedale	Hospital
Parcheggio	Parking
Passaggio a livello incustodito	Unattended Railroad Crossing
Passaggio pedonale	Pedestrian Walkway
Pericolo	Danger
Pista ciclabile	Bicycle Path
Ponte	Bridge
Principiante	Student Driver
Rallentare	Slow Down
Rotatoria	Rotary (Traffic Circle)
Scontro, collisione	Crash
Scuola	School
Semaforo	Traffic Light
Senso unico	One Way
Sottopassaggio pedonale	Pedestrian Underpass
Strada sdrucciolevole	Slippery Road
Strettoia	Bottleneck
Tamponamento	Collision
Tenere la destra	Keep to the Right
Tenere libero l'accesso	Keep Access Free
Uscita	Exit
Vicolo cieco	Blind Alley
Vietato al traffico	No Through Traffic
Vietato l'accesso	No Trespassing
Zona a disco orario	Parking Disk Zone
Zona pedonale	Pedestrian Zone

Car/Motorcycle/Bicycle

Information

Information	Informazioni
Excuse me, how do I get to...?	Scusi, per andare a...? [skoo-zee, pehr ahn-dah-reh ah]
Can you show me the way on the map?/Can you show it to me on the map?	Mi può mostrare il percorso sulla cartina?/Me lo può mostrare sulla cartina? [mee poo-oh moh-strah-rrh eel pehr-kohr-soh soo-llah kahr-tee-nah/meh loh poo-oh moh-strah-reh soo-llah kahr-tee-nah]
How many kilometers is it?	Quanti chilometri sono? [kwahn-tee kee-loh-meh-tree soh-noh]
Excuse me, is this the street to...?	Scusi, è questa la strada per...? [skoo-zee eh kweh-stah lah strah-dah pehr]
Excuse me, (how do I get to) the highway...?	Scusi, l'autostrada per...? [skoo-zee lah-oo-toh-strah-dah pehr]
Straight ahead to... Then...	Sempre diritto fino a... Poi... [sehm-preh dee-ree-ttoh fee-noh ah... poh-ee]
at the light	al semaforo [ahl seh-mah-foh-roh]
at the next corner	al prossimo angolo [ahl proh-ssee-moh ahn-ghoh-loh]
turn left/right	svolti a sinistra/destra [zvohl-tee ah see-nee-strah/deh-strah]
Follow the signs.	Segua le indicazioni. [seh-gwah leh een-dee-kah-tsyoh-nee]
Is there also a street with less traffic to...?	C'è anche una strada con meno traffico per...? [cheh oo-nah strah-dah kohn meh-noh trah-ffee-koh pehr]

You have the wrong street. You must go back to…

Ha sbagliato strada. Deve tornare indietro fino a…[ah sbah-lyah-toh strah-da deh-veh torh-nah-reh een-dyeh-troh fee-noh ah]

Where is the next service station, please?

Dov'è la prossima stazione di servizio, per favore? [doh-veh lah proh-ssee-mah stah-tsyoh-neh dee sehr-vee-tsyoh pehr fah-voh-reh]

At the Service Station

Alla stazione di servizio

I'd like… liters of …

Vorrei… litri di… [voh-rreh-ee… lee-tree dee]

   regular.

   benzina normale. [behn-zee-nah nohr-mah-leh]

   super.

   super. [soo-pehr]

   diesel.

   gasolio. [gah-soh-lyoh]

   without lead.

   senza piombo (verde). [sehn-tsa pyohm-boh (vehr-deh)]

Fill it up, please.

Il pieno, per favore. [eel pyeh-noh pehr fah-voh-reh]

Please check …

Per favore, controlli… [pehr fah-voh-reh kohn-troh-llee]

   the oil.

   il livello dell'olio. [eel lee-veh-lloh deh-lloh-lyoh]

   the tire pressure.

   la pressione delle gomme. [lah preh-ssyoh-neh deh-lle ghoh-mmeh]

Also check the water in the radiator, please.

Controlli anche l'acqua del radiatore, per favore. [kohn-troh-llee ahn-keh lah-kwah dehl rah-dyah-toh-reh pehr fah-voh-reh]

Change the oil, please.

Cambi l'olio, per favore. [kahm-bee loh-lyoh pehr fah-voh-reh]

I'd like to have the car washed.

Vorrei far lavare la macchina. [voh-rreh-ee fahr lah-vah-reh lah mah-kkee-nah]

I'd like a street map of this area.

Desidero una carta stradale di questa zona. [deh-see-deh-roh oo-nah kahr-tah strah-dah-leh dee kweh-stah zoh-nah]

Excuse me, where is the restroom?

Scusi, dov'è la toilette? [skoo-zee doh-veh lah toh-ee-leht]

Parking

Il parcheggio

Excuse me, is there parking nearby?

Scusi, c'è un parcheggio qui vicino? [skoo-zee cheh oon pahr-keh-djoh kwee vee-chee-noh]

May I leave the car here?

Posso lasciare la macchina qui? [poh-ssoh lah-shah-reh lah mah-kkee-nah kwee]

Can you please change... lire for the parking meter?

Mi può cambiare... lire per il parchimetro, per favore? [mee poo-oh kahm-byah-reh... lee-re pehr eel pahr-kee-meh-troh pehr fah-voh-reh]

Is the parking lot attended?

Il parcheggio è custodito? [eel pahr-keh-djoh eh koo-stoh-dee-toh]

Unfortuately we're full.

Purtroppo siamo al completo. [poor-troh-ppoh syah-moh ahl kohm-pleh-toh]

How long can I park here?

Per quanto tempo posso parcheggiare qui? [pehr kwahn-toh tehm-poh poh-ssoh pahr-keh-djah-reh kwee]

What is the charge for ...

Qual è la tariffa per... [kwah-leh lah tah-ree-ffah pehr]

an hour?

un'ora? [oo-noh-rah]

a day?

un giorno? [oon johr-noh]

a night?

una notte? [oo-nah noh-tte]

Is this parking lot open all night?	Il parcheggio è aperto tutta la notte? [eel pahr-<u>keh</u>-djoh eh ah-<u>pehr</u>-toh <u>too</u>-ttah lah <u>noh</u>-tteh]

Car Trouble

Un guasto

I have a problem/a flat tire.	Ho un guasto/una gomma a terra. [oh oon <u>gwah</u>-stoh/<u>oo</u>-nah <u>ghoh</u>-mmah ah <u>teh</u>-rrah]
Could you call road assistance?	Potrebbe telefonare al soccorso stradale? [poh-<u>treh</u>-bbeh teh-leh-foh-<u>nah</u>-reh ahl soh-<u>kkohr</u>-soh strah-<u>dah</u>-leh]
My car's license plate number is...	La mia macchina è targata... /il mio motore è targato... [lah <u>mme</u>-ah <u>mah</u>-kkee-nah eh tahr-<u>ghah</u>-tah /eel <u>mee</u>-oh moh-<u>toh</u>-reh eh tahr-<u>ghah</u>-toh]
Could you send a mechanic/ a tow truck?	Mi potrebbe mandare un meccanico/un carro-attrezzi? [mee poh-<u>treh</u>-bbeh mahn-<u>dah</u>-reh oon meh-<u>kkah</u>-nee-koh/oon <u>kah</u>-rroh ah-<u>ttre</u>-tsee]
Could you please give me some gas?	Mi potrebbe dare un po' di benzina, per favore? [mee poh-<u>treh</u>-bbe <u>dah</u>-reh oon poh dee behn-<u>zee</u>-nah pehr fah-<u>voh</u>-reh]
Could you help me change the tire?	Mi potrebbe aiutare a cambiare la ruota? [mee poh-<u>treh</u>-bbeh ah-yoo-<u>tah</u>-reh ah kahm-<u>byah</u>-reh lah <u>rwoh</u>-tah]
Could you tow me/give me a lift to the next service station?	Mi potrebbe rimorchiare/dare un passaggio fino alla prossima officina/stazione di servizio? [mee poh-<u>treh</u>-bbeh ree-mohr-<u>kyah</u>-reh/<u>dah</u>-reh oon pah-<u>ssah</u>-djoh <u>fee</u>-noh ah-llah <u>proh</u>-ssee-mah oh-<u>ffee</u>-chee-nah/stah-<u>tsyoh</u>-neh dee sehr-<u>vee</u>-tsyoh]

At the Auto Repair Shop	All'officina

Excuse me sir/ma'am/miss, is there an auto repair shop nearby?

Scusi signore/signora/signorina, c'è un'officina qui vicino? [skoo-zee see-<u>nyoh</u>-re/see-<u>nyoh</u>-rah/see-nyoh-<u>ree</u>-nah cheh oo-noh-ffee-<u>chee</u>-nah kwee vee-<u>chee</u>-noh]

My car won't start.

La macchina non parte. [lah <u>mah</u>-kkee-nah nohn <u>pahr</u>-teh]

I don't know what the problem is.

Non so da che cosa dipenda. [nohn soh dah <u>koh</u>-sah dee-<u>pehn</u>-dah]

Could you please take me/ tow me?

Mi potrebbe accompagnare/rimorchiare, per favore? [mee poh-<u>treh</u>-bbe ah-kkohm-pahn-<u>nyah</u>-reh/ree-mohr-<u>kyah</u>-reh pehr fah-<u>voh</u>-reh]

There's something wrong with the engine.

Il motore non va bene. [eel moh-<u>toh</u>-reh nohn vah <u>beh</u>-neh]

The brakes don't work.

I freni non sono a posto. [ee <u>freh</u>-nee nohn <u>soh</u>-noh ah <u>poh</u>-stoh]

...are faulty.

...è/sono difettoso/difettosi. [eh/<u>soh</u>-noh dee-feh-<u>ttoh</u>-soh/dee-feh-<u>ttoh</u>-see]

My car is losing oil.

La macchina perde olio. [lah <u>mah</u>-kkee-nah <u>pehr</u>-deh <u>oh</u>-lyoh]

Could you please take a look?

Ci potrebbe dare un'occhiata, per favore? [chee poh-<u>treh</u>-bbeh <u>dah</u>-reh oo-noh-<u>kkyah</u>-tah pehr fah-<u>voh</u>-reh]

Change the spark plugs, please.

Cambi le candele, per favore. [<u>kahm</u>-bee leh kanh-<u>deh</u>-leh pehr fah-<u>voh</u>-reh]

Do you have replacement parts for this car?

Ha pezzi di ricambio (originali) per questa macchina? [ah <u>peh</u>-tsee dee ree-<u>kahm</u>-byoh (oh-ree-jee-<u>nah</u>-lee) pehr <u>kweh</u>-stah <u>mah</u>-kkee-nah]

Make only the necessary repairs, please.

Faccia soltanto le riparazioni indispensabili, per favore. [fah-chah sohl-tahn-toh leh ree-pah-rah-tsyoh-nee een-dee-speh-sah-bee-lee pehr fah-voh-reh]

When will the car/the motorcycle be ready?

Quando sarà pronta la macchina?/ la motocicletta? [kwahn-doh sah-rah prohn-tah lah mah-kkee-nah/lah moh-toh-chee-kleh-ttah]

How much will it cost?

Quanto costerà? [kwahn-toh koh-steh-rah]

A Traffic Accident

Un incidente stradale

There has been an accident.

C'è stato un incidente. [cheh stah-toh oon een-chee-dehn-teh]

Call... right away

Chiami subito... [kyah-mee soo-bee-toh]

an ambulance

un'autoambulanza [oo-nah-oo-toh-ahm-boo-lahn-tsah]

the police

la polizia [lah poh-lee-tsee-ah]

the fire department

i vigili del fuoco [ee vee-jee-lee dehl fwoh-koh]

Can you take care of the injured?

Può occuparsi dei feriti? [poo-oh oh-kkoo-pahr-see deh-ee feh-ree-tee]

Do you have first aid equipment?

Ha materiale di pronto soccorso? [ah mah-teh-ryah-leh dee prohn-toh soh-kkohr-soh]

It was my fault.

È stata colpa mia/Sua. [eh stah-tah kohl-pah mee-ah/soo-ah]

You...

Lei... [leh-ee]

did not yield.

non ha rispettato la precedenza. [nohn ah ree-speh-ttah-toh lah preh-cheh-dehn-tsah]

cut the curve.

ha tagliato la curva. [ah tah-lyah-toh lah koor-vah]

changed lanes without signaling.	ha cambiato corsia senza mettere la freccia. [ah kahm-<u>byah</u>-toh kohr-<u>see</u>-ah <u>sehn</u>-tsah <u>meh</u>-tteh-re lah <u>freh</u>-chah]
were going too fast.	andava troppo forte. [ahn-<u>dah</u>-vah <u>troh</u>-ppoh <u>fohr</u>-teh]
did not keep at a safe distance (were driving too close).	non ha mantenuto la distanza di sicurezza. [nohn ah mahn-teh-<u>noo</u>-toh lah dee-<u>stahn</u>-tsah dee see-koo-<u>reh</u>-tsah]
went through the red light.	è passato col rosso. [eh pah-<u>ssah</u>-toh kohl <u>roh</u>-ssoh]
I was going... kilometers an hour.	Sono andato a... km/h. [<u>soh</u>-noh ahn-<u>dah</u>-toh ah...kee-loh-<u>meh</u>-tree ah-<u>lloh</u>-rah]
Should we call the police, or do you want to settle this between ourselves?	Dobbiamo chiamare la polizia, o ci vogliamo mettere d'accordo fra noi? [doh-<u>byah</u>-moh kyah-<u>mah</u>-reh lah poh-lee-<u>tsee</u>-ah, oh chee voh-<u>lyah</u>-moh <u>meh</u>-tteh-reh dah-<u>kkohr</u>-doh frah <u>noh</u>-ee?]
I'd like to settle the damages with my insurance (company).	Vorrei far regolare il danno dalla mia assicurazione. [voh-<u>rreh</u>-ee fahr reh-ghoh-<u>lah</u>-reh eel <u>dah</u>-nnoh <u>dah</u>-llah <u>mee</u>-ah ah-ssee-koo-rah-<u>tsyoh</u>-neh]
I'll give you my address and my insurance number.	Le do il mio indirizzo e il numero della mia assicurazione. [leh doh eel <u>mee</u>-oh een-dee-<u>ree</u>-tsoh eh eel <u>noo</u>-meh-roh <u>deh</u>-llah <u>mee</u>-ah ah-ssee-koo-rah-<u>tsyoh</u>-neh]
Give me your name and address/name and the address of your insurance company.	Mi dia il Suo nome e indirizzo/ nome e l'indirizzo della Sua Assicurazione. [mee <u>dee</u>-ah eel <u>soo</u>-oh <u>noh</u>-meh eh leen-dee-<u>ree</u>-tsoh/<u>noh</u>-meh eh leen-dee-<u>ree</u>-tsoh <u>deh</u>-llah <u>soo</u>-ah ah-ssee-koo-rah-<u>tsyoh</u>-neh]
Can you be a witness?	Mi potrebbe fare da testimone? [mee poh-<u>treh</u>-beh <u>fah</u>-re dah teh-stee-<u>moh</u>-neh]

Traffic Signs

No Parking on the right side of the street on odd-numbered days, on the left side of the street on even-numbered days

No Parking on the right side of the street on even-numbered days, on the left side of the street on odd-numbered days

Road Used by Mountain Post Bus

Road Junction

No Right Turn

No U-turn

Traffic Circle

These signs indicate the nearest police station and give its location and phone number.

TRANSITO con CATENE o PNEUMATICI da NEVE
dal Km **174**

From km 174 on, snow chains or snow tires are required.

Thank you for your help.

Grazie dell'aiuto. [grah-tsyeh deh-llah-yoo-toh]

Car/Motorcycle/Bicycle Rental

Autonoleggio/Noleggio di motocicli

I'd like to rent for... days/a week...

Vorrei noleggiare per... giorni/una settimana... [voh-rreh-ee noh-leh-djah-reh pehr.. johr-nee/oo-nah seh-tte-mah-nah]

a four-wheel drive.

un fuoristrada. [fwoh-ree-strah-dah]

a car.

una macchina. [oo-nah mah-kkee-nah]

a moped/motorscooter.

ciclomotore/motorino/una motoretta. [oon moh-toh-reh/chee-kloh-moh-toh-reh/moh-toh-ree-noh/oo-nah moh-toh-reh-ttah]

a bicycle/a tandem bicycle

una bicicletta/un tandem. [oo-nah bee-chee-kleh-ttah/oon tahn-dehm]

What is the charge per day/ per week?

Qual è la tariffa al giorno/alla settimana? [kwah-leh lah tah-ree-ffah ahl johr-noh/ah-llah seh-ttee-mah-nah]

What is the charge per kilometer?

Quanto si paga per ogni chilometro percorso? [kwahn-toh see pah-ghah pehr oh-nyee kee-loh-meh-troh pehr-kohr-soh]

How much security deposit must I leave?

Quanto si deve lasciare di cauzione? [kwahn-toh see deh-veh lah-shah-reh dee kah-oo-tsyoh-neh]

I'll take the ...

Prendo la... [prehn-doh lah]

Do you want additional insurance?

Desidera un'assicurazione supplementare? [deh-see-deh-rah oo-nah-ssee-koo-rah-tsyoh-neh soo-ppleh-mehn-tah-reh]

Is the vehicle fully covered?	Il veicolo è assicurato contro tutti i rischi? [eel veh-<u>ee</u>-koh-loh eh ah-ssee-koo-<u>rah</u>-toh <u>kohn</u>-troh <u>too</u>-ttee ee <u>ree</u>-skee]
Show me your driver's license.	Favorisca la patente. [fah-voh-<u>ree</u>-skah lah pah-<u>tehn</u>-teh]
May I take the car right away?	Posso pr<u>e</u>ndere la m<u>a</u>cchina s<u>u</u>bito? [poh-ssoh pr<u>ehn</u>-deh-reh lah <u>mah</u>-kkee-nah <u>soo</u>-bee-toh]
Is it possible to return the car in... ?	È possibile riconsegnare la m<u>a</u>cchina a...? [eh poh-<u>ssee</u>-bee-leh ree-kohn-seh-<u>nyah</u>-reh lah <u>mah</u>-kkee-nah ah]

Word List: Car/Motorcycle/Bicycle

to accelerate	accelerare [ah-cheh-leh-<u>rah</u>-reh]
air filter	filtro dell'aria [<u>feel</u>-troh deh-<u>llah</u>-ryah]
air pump	pompa d'<u>a</u>ria [<u>pohm</u>-pah deh-<u>llah</u>-ryah]
alarm system	il sistema d'allarme [eel see-<u>steh</u>-mah dah-<u>llahr</u>-meh]
antifreeze	antigelo [ahn-tee-geh-loh]
automatic transmission	cambio autom<u>a</u>tico [<u>kahm</u>-byoh ah-oo-toh-<u>mah</u>-tee-koh]
axle	l'asse *(m)* carro [<u>lah</u>-sseh <u>kah</u>-rroh]
back pedal (coaster brake)	il contropedale [eel kohn-troh-peh-<u>dah</u>-leh]
battery	batteria [bah-tteh-<u>ree</u>-ah]
bearing	cuscinetto [koo-shee-<u>neh</u>-ttoh]
bell	campanello [kahm-pah-<u>neh</u>-lloh]
belt	cinghia [<u>cheen</u>-ghyah]
bicycle	bicicletta [bee-chee-kleh-ttah]
bicycle path	pista cicl<u>a</u>bile [<u>pee</u>-stah chee-<u>klah</u>-bee-leh]

bicyclist	pedaliera [peh-dah-<u>lyeh</u>-rah]
blinker, turning signal	freccia, l'indicatore *(m)* di direzione [<u>freh</u>-chah, leen-dee-kah-<u>toh</u>-reh dee dee-reh-<u>tsyoh</u>-neh]
body (work)	carrozzeria [kah-rroh-tseh-<u>ree</u>-ah]
brake	freno [<u>freh</u>-noh]
to brake	frenare [freh-<u>nah</u>-reh]
brake handle	leva del freno [<u>leh</u>-vah dehl <u>freh</u>-noh]
brake light	le luci di arresto [leh <u>loo</u>-cee dee ah-<u>rreh</u>-stoh]
brake lining/pad	la guarnizione dei freni [lah gwahr-nee-<u>tsyoh</u>-neh deh-ee <u>freh</u>-nee]
brake oil	olio per freni [<u>oh</u>-lyoh pehr ee <u>freh</u>-nee]
brake pedal	freno a pedale [<u>freh</u>-noh ah peh-<u>dah</u>-leh]
breakdown	guasto [<u>gwah</u>-stoh]
breakdown assistance	autosoccorso [ah-oo-toh-soh-<u>kkohr</u>-soh]
broken	rotto [<u>roh</u>-ttoh]
cable	cavo [<u>kah</u>-voh]
carburetor	il carburatore [eel kahr-boo-rah-<u>toh</u>-reh]
carwash	autolavaggio [ah-oo-toh-lah-<u>vah</u>-djoh]
chain	catena [kah-<u>teh</u>-nah]
change	cambio [<u>kahm</u>-byoh]
clutch	la frizione [lah free-<u>tsyoh</u>-neh]
clutch pedal	il pedale della frizione [peh-<u>dah</u>-leh <u>deh</u>-llah free-<u>tsyoh</u>-neh]
crash helmet	casco [<u>kah</u>-skoh]
cylinder	cilindro [chee-<u>leen</u>-droh]
cylinder head	testata del cilindro [teh-<u>stah</u>-tah dehl chee-<u>leen</u>-droh]
defect	difetto [dee-<u>feh</u>-ttoh]

detour	la deviazione [lah deh-vyah-<u>tsyoh</u>-neh]
distributor	spinter<u>o</u>geno [speen-teh-<u>roh</u>-jeh-noh]
emergency road assistance	soccorso stradale [soh-<u>kkohr</u>-soh strah-<u>dah</u>-leh]
emergency telephone	tel<u>e</u>fono d'emergenza [teh-<u>leh</u>-foh-noh deh-mehr-<u>jehn</u>-tsah]
exhaust/tailpipe	scappamento, tubo di sc<u>a</u>rico [skah-ppah-<u>mehn</u>-toh, <u>too</u>-boh dee <u>skah</u>-ree-koh]
fender	parafango [pah-rah-<u>fahn</u>-ghoh]
fender/bumper	il para<u>u</u>rti [eel pah-rah-<u>oor</u>-tee]
fine/ticket	ammenda [ah-<u>mmehn</u>-dah]
first gear	la prima m<u>a</u>rcia [lah <u>pree</u>-mah <u>mahr</u>-chah]
flat tire	gomma a terra [<u>ghoh</u>-mmah ah <u>teh</u>-rrah]
four speed	a quattro corsie [ah <u>kwah</u>-ttroh kohr-<u>see</u>-eh]
front axle	l'asse m anteriore [<u>lah</u>-sseh ahn-teh-<u>ryoh</u>-reh]
full liability insurance	l'assicurazione *(f)* di totale copertura [lah-ssee-koo-rah-<u>tsyoh</u>-neh dee toh-<u>tah</u>-leh koh-pehr-<u>too</u>-rah]
gas	benzina [behn-<u>zee</u>-nah]
gas can	lattina, t<u>a</u>nica [lah-<u>ttee</u>-nah, <u>tah</u>-nee-kah]
gas pedal	l'accelerat<u>o</u>re *(m)* [lah-cheh-lle-rah-<u>toh</u>-reh]
gas pump	pompa della benzina, pompa d'iniezione [<u>pohm</u>-pah <u>deh</u>-llah behn-<u>zee</u>-nah, <u>pohm</u>-pah dee-nyeh-<u>tsyoh</u>-neh]
gas/service station	la stazione di servizio, posto di ristoro [lah stah-<u>tsyoh</u>-neh dee sehr-<u>vee</u>-tsyoh, <u>poh</u>-stoh dee ree-<u>stoh</u>-roh]

gas tank	serbatoio [sehr-bah-toh-yoh]
gear brake	marcia freno [mahr-chah freh-noh]
gearshift	cambio [kahm-byoh]
gearshift lever	leva del cambio [leh-vah dehl kahm-hyoh]
generator	la dinamo [lah dee-nah-moh]
green card	carta verde [kahr-tah vehr-deh]
hand brake	freno a mano [treh-noh ah mah-noh]
handlebar	manubrio [mah-noo-bryoh]
headlight	faro [fah-roh]
headlights	lampeggio fari [lahm-peh-djoh fah-ree]
heating	riscaldamento [ree-skahl-dah-mehn-toh]
high beams	i fari abbaglianti [ee fah-ree ah-bah-lyahn-tee]
highway	autostrada [ah-oo-toh-strah-dah]
to hitchhike	viaggiare in autostop [vyah-djah-reh een ah-oo-toh-stohp]
hitchhiker	l'autostoppista (m/f) [lah-oo-toh-stoh-ppee-stah]
hood	cofano [koh-fah-noh]
horn	il clacson [eel klahk-sohn]
HP (horsepower) per mile	CV (cavalli vapore) [kah-vah-llee vah-poh-reh]
hub	mozzola [moh-zoh-lah]
idling	l'accensione (f) a vuoto [lah-chehn-syoh-neh ah vwoh-toh]
ignition	l'accensione (f) [lah-chehn-syoh-neh]
ignition key	chiavetta di accensione [kyah-veh-ttah dee ah-chehn-syoh-neh]
ignition switch	l'interrutore m dell'accensione [leen-teh-rroo-ttoh-reh deh-llah-chehn-syoh-neh]

inner tube	camera d'aria [kah-meh-rah dah-ryah]
jack	il cric [eel kreek]
jumper cable	cavo ausiliario di collegamento per la messa in moto [kah-voh ah-oo-see-lyah-ryoh pehr lah meh-ssah een moh-toh]
kickstand	cavalletto [kah-cvh-lleh-ttoh]
lane	corsia [kohr-see-ah]
lever	leva [leh-vah]
license	la patente [lah pah-tehn-teh]
license plate	targa [tahr-ghah]
light	semaforo [seh-mah-foh-roh]
low beams	le luci anabbaglianti [leh loo-chee ah-nah-bah-lyahn-tee]
to lower the lights	abbassare le luci [ah-bah-ssah-reh leh loo-chee]
lubricate	lubrificare [loo-bree-fee-kah-reh]
main street	strada maestra [strah-dah mah-eh-strah]
moped	il ciclomotore/motorino/ motocicletta [eel chee-kloh-moh-toh-reh/ moh-toh-ree-noh/moh-toh-chee-kleh-ttah]
motor	il motore [eel moh-toh-reh]
mountain bike	la mountain bike [lah mah-oon-tahn bah-eek]
neutral gear	in folle [een foh-lleh]
nozzle	ugello [oo-jeh-lloh]
nut (screw)	la madrevite [lah mah-dreh-vee-teh]
octane rating	numero di ottani [noo-meh-roh dee oh-ttah-nee]
oil	olio [oh-lyoh]
oil change	cambio dell'olio [kahm-byoh deh-lloh-lyoh]

oil stick	asta controllo [ah-stah kohn-<u>troh</u>-lloh]
papers	i documenti [ee doh-koo-<u>mehn</u>-tee]
parking (lot)	parcheggio [pahr-<u>keh</u>-djoh]
parking garage	parcheggio a più piani [pahr-keh-djoh ah pee-oo <u>pyah</u>-nee]
parking lights	le luci di posizione [leh <u>loo</u>-chee dee poh-see-<u>tsyoh</u>-neh]
parking meter	parchimetro [pahr-<u>kee</u>-meh-troh]
parking time indicator disk	disco orario [<u>dee</u>-skoh oh-<u>rah</u>-ryoh]
partial liability insurance	l'assicurazione *(f)* parziale per tutti i rischi [lah-ssee-koo-rah-<u>tsyoh</u>-neh pahr-<u>tsyah</u>-leh pehr <u>too</u>-ttee ee <u>ree</u>-skee]
pedal	il pedale [eel peh-<u>dah</u>-leh]
per mile	per mille [pehr <u>mee</u>-lleh]
piston	il pistone [eel pee-<u>stoh</u>-neh]
protective plates	lamiera di protezione [lah-<u>myeh</u>-rah dee proh-teh-<u>tsyoh</u>-neh]
to put on the high beams	abbagliare [ah-bah-<u>lyah</u>-reh]
racing bike	bicicletta da corsa [bee-chee-<u>kleh</u>-ttah dah <u>kohr</u>-sah]
radar control	controllo radar [kohn-<u>troh</u>-lloh <u>rah</u>-dahr]
radiator	il radiatore [eel rah-dyah-<u>toh</u>-reh]
rainwear	tuta impermeabile [<u>too</u>-tah eem-pehr-meh-<u>ah</u>-bee-leh]
rear axle	l'asse *(m)* posteriore [<u>lah</u>-sseh poh-steh-<u>ryoh</u>-reh]
rear light	il fanale anteriore [eel fah-<u>nah</u>-leh ahn-teh-<u>ryoh</u>-reh]
rear traction	la trazione posteriore [lah trah-<u>tsyoh</u>-neh poh-steh-<u>ryoh</u>-reh]
rear wheel	ruota posteriore [<u>rwoh</u>-tah poh-steh-<u>ryoh</u>-reh]

rearview mirror	specchietto retrovisore [speh-kkyeh-ttoh reh-troh-vee-soh-reh]
reflector	il riflettore [eel ree-fleh-ttoh-reh]
to release the clutch	disinnestare la frizione [dee-see-nneh-skah-reh lah free-tsyoh-neh]
reverse gear	marcia indietro [mahr-chah een-dyeh-troh]
rim	il cerchione [eel chehr-kyoh-ne]
roadworks	il cantiere edile [eel cahn-tyeh-reh eh-dee-leh]
saddlebag	borsa da sella [bohr-sah dah seh-llah]
safety	sicurezza [see-koo-reh-tsah]
sandpaper	carta vetrata [kahr-tah veh-trah-tah]
scooter	il motoscooter, motoretta [eel moh-toh-skoo-tehr, moh-toh-reh-ttah]
screw	la vite [lah vee-teh]
screwdriver	il cacciavite [eel kah-chah-vee-teh]
seat belt	cintura di sicurezza [cheen-too-rah dee see-koo-reh-tsah]
service station	officina [oh-ffee-chee-nah]
shock absorber	l'ammortizzatore (m) [lah-mmohr-tee-zah-toh-reh]
short circuit	corto circuito [kohr-toh cheer-koo-ee-toh]
signpost	il segnavia [eel seh-nyah-vee-ah]
sliding hood	tetto apribile [teh-ttoh ah-pree-bee-leh]
snow tires	gli pneumatici da neve parabrezza [lyee pneh-oo-mah-tee-chee dah neh-veh pah-rah-breh-tsah]
socket wrench	la chiave fissa a tubo [lah kyah-veh fee-ssah ah too-boh]
spare parts	i pezzi di ricambio [ee peh-tsee dee ree-kahm-byoh]
spare tire	ruota di scorta [rwoh-tah dee skohr-tah]

spark plug	candela [kahn-<u>deh</u>-lah]
spoke	raggio [<u>rah</u>-djoh]
starter	motorino d'avviamento [moh-toh-<u>ree</u>-noh dah-vvyah-<u>mehn</u>-toh]
steering wheel	il volante [eel voh-<u>lahn</u>-teh]
street map	carta stradale [<u>kahr</u>-tah strah-<u>dah</u>-leh]
super highway	superstrada [soo-pehr-<u>strah</u>-dah]
tachometer	tachimetro [tah-<u>kee</u>-meh-troh]
taillight	fanalino posteriore [fah-nah-<u>lee</u>-noh poh-steh-<u>ryoh</u>-reh]
tank	il distributore di benzina [eel dee-stree-boo-<u>toh</u>-reh dee ben-<u>zee</u>-nah]
tire	lo pneumatico, il copertone [loh pneh-oo-<u>mah</u>-tee-koh, eel koh-pehr-<u>toh</u>-neh]
tire iron	la chiave a crociera [lah <u>kyah</u>-veh ah kroh-<u>cheh</u>-rah]
tire repair kit	gli accessori per la riparazione di forature [lyee ah-cheh-<u>ssoh</u>-ree pehr lah ree-pah-rah-<u>tsyoh</u>-neh dee foh-rah-<u>too</u>-reh]
toll	pedaggio, pedaggio autostradale [peh-<u>dah</u>-djoh, peh-<u>dah</u>-djoh ah-oo-toh-strah-<u>dah</u>-leh]
tools	l'utensile *(m),* attrezzo [loo-<u>tehn</u>-see-leh, ah-ttreh-tsoh]
to tow	rimorchiare, trainare [ree-mohr-<u>kyah</u>-reh, trah-ee-<u>nah</u>-reh]
tow truck	carro attrezzi [<u>kah</u>-rroh ah-<u>ttreh</u>-tsee]
towing	rimorchio [ree-<u>mohr</u>-kyoh]
towing cable	cavo da rimorchio [<u>kah</u>-voh dah ree-<u>mohr</u>-kyoh]
traffic jam	ingorgo [een-<u>ghohr</u>-ghoh]
transmission	la trasmissione su tutte le ruote motrici [lah trah-smee-<u>ssyoh</u>-neh soo <u>too</u>-tteh leh roo-<u>oh</u>-teh moh-<u>tree</u>-chee]

truck	il camion [eel <u>kah</u>-myohn]
trunk	il portabagagli, bagagliaio [eel pohr-tah-bah-<u>ghah</u>-lyee, bah-ghah-<u>lyah</u>-lyoh]
to turn	svoltare [zvohl-<u>tah</u>-reh]
two-/three-speed bicycle	bicicletta a dieci/tre marce [bee-chee-<u>kleh</u>-ttah ah <u>dyeh</u>-chee/treh <u>mahr</u>-cheh]
valve	valvola [<u>vahl</u>-voh-lah]
vent	il ventilatore [vehn-tee-lah-<u>toh</u>-reh]
warning light	il lampeggiatore d'emergenza [eel lahm-peh-djah-<u>toh</u>-reh deh-mehr-<u>jehn</u>-tsah]
warning triangle	triangolo [tree-<u>ahn</u>-ghoh-loh]
wheel	ruota [<u>rwoh</u>-tah]
windshield	il parabrezza [eel pah-rah-<u>breh</u>-tsah]
windshield wiper	tergicristallo [tehr-jee-kree-<u>stah</u>-lloh]
wrench (impact)	la chiave per dadi [lah <u>kyah</u>-veh pehr <u>dah</u>-dee]

Airplane
L'aereo

At the Travel Agency/ At the Airport	**All'agenzia viaggi/All'aeroporto**
Where is the... counter?	Dov'è lo sportello della compagnia aerea...? [doh-<u>veh</u> loh spohr-<u>teh</u>-lloh <u>deh</u>-llah kohm-pah-<u>nyah</u> ah-<u>eh</u>-reh-ah]

When is there a flight to...?	Quando c'è un aereo per...? [kwahn-doh cheh oon ah-eh-reh-oh pehr]
I'd like to reserve a one-way/round-trip flight to ...	Vorrei prenotare un volo di sola andata/di andata e ritorno per... [voh-rreh-ee preh-noh-tah-reh oon voh-loh dee soh-lah anh-dah-tah eh ree-tohr-noh]
Are there still some available seats?	Ci sono ancora posti liberi? [chee soh-noh anh-koh-rah poh-stee lee-beh-ree]
Are there charter flights too?	Ci sono anche dei voli Charter? [chee soh-noh ahn-keh deh-ee voh-lee chahr-tehr]
How much is a tourist/first-class ticket?	Quanto costa un volo per la classe turistica/per la prima classe? [kwahn-toh koh-stah oon voh-loh pehr lah klah-sseh too-ree-stee-kah/pehr lah pree-mah klah-sseh]
How much luggage can I take with me?	Quanto bagaglio si può portare? [kwahn-toh bah-ghah-lyoh see poo-oh pohr-tah-reh]
What is the charge per kilo for excess luggage?	Quanto si paga per ogni chilo di sovrappeso? [kwahn-toh see pah-ghah pehr oh-nyee kee-loh dee soh-vrah-ppeh-soh]
I'd like to cancel this flight/take another flight.	Vorrei annullare questo volo/prendere un altro volo. [voh-rreh-ee ah-nnoo-llah-reh kweh-stoh voh-lo/prehn-deh-reh oon ahl-troh voh-loh]

At what time should I be at the airport?

A che ora devo essere all'aeroporto? [ah keh oh-rah deh-voh eh-sseh-reh ah-llah-eh-roh-pohr-toh]

Where is the information booth/the waiting room?

Dov'è lo sportello informazioni/la sala d'aspetto? [doh-veh loh spohr-teh-lloh een-fohr-mah-tsyoh-nee/lah sah-lah dah-speh-ttoh]

Can I have carry-on luggage?

Posso portare appresso il bagaglio a mano? [poh-ssoh pohr-tah-reh ah-ppreh-ssoh eel bah-ghah-lyoh ah mah-noh]

Is the plane to... late?

L'aereo per... è in ritardo? [lah-eh-reh-oh eh een ree-tahr-doh]

How late is it?

Quanto ritardo ha? [kwahn-toh ree-tahr-doh ah]

Has the plane from... already landed?

È già atterrato l'aereo da...? [eh jah ah-tteh-rrah-toh lah-eh-reh-oh dah]

Last call: Passengers going to..., flight..., please go to gate...

Ultimo avviso: I signori passeg geri per..., volo numero..., sono pregati di recarsi all'uscita... [ool-tee-moh ah-vvee-soh ee see-nyoh-ree pah-sseh-djeh-ree pehr ...voh-loh noo-meh-roh... soh-noh preh-ghah-tee dee reh-kahr-see ah-lloo-shee-tah]

On Board

A bordo

Please fasten your seat belts and do not smoke.

Si prega di allacciare le cinture di sicurezza e di non fumare. [see preh-ghah dee ah-llah-chah-reh leh cheen-too-reh dee see-koo-reh-tsah eh dee nohn foo-mah-reh]

What river/lake is that?

Che fiume/lago è? [keh fyoo-meh/lah-ghoh eh]

What mountains are they?

Che montagne sono? [keh mohn-tah-nyeh soh-noh]

Where are we now?

Dove siamo adesso? [doh-veh syah-moh ah-deh-ssoh]

When do we land in…?	Quando atterriamo a…? [kwahn-doh ah-tteh-rryah-moh ah]
We land in about… minutes.	Atterriamo fra circa… minuti. [ah-tteh-rryah-moh frah cheer-kah..mee-noo-tee]
What is the temperature in…?	Che tempo fa a…? [keh tehm-poh fah ah]

Arrival / Arrivo

I can't find my luggage/suitcase.	Non trovo il mio bagaglio/la mia valigia. [nohn troh-voh eel mee-oh bah-ghah-lyoh/lah mee-ah vah-lee-jah]
My luggage has been lost.	Il mio bagalio è stato smarrito. [eel mee-oh bah-ghah-lyoh eh stah-toh smah-rree-toh]
My luggage has been damaged.	La mia valigia è stata danneggiata. [lah mee-ah vah-lee-jah eh stah-tah dah-nneh-djah-tah]
Where can I report it?	A chi posso rivolgermi? [ah kee poh-ssoh ree-vohl-jehr-mee]
Where does the airport terminal bus leave from?	Da dove parte l'autobus per l'Air Terminal? [dah doh-veh pahr-teh lah-oo-toh-boos pehr lehr tehr-mee-nahl]

Word List: Airplane

air terminal	l'air terminal (m) [ehr tehr-mee-nahl]
airline	aereo di linea, compagnia aerea [kohm-pah-nyee-ah ah-eh-reh-ah, ah-eh-reh-oh dee lee-nah]
airplane ticket	biglietto aereo [bee-lyeh-ttoh ah-eh-reh-oh]
airport	aeroporto [ah-eh-roh-pohr-toh]
airport security tax	tassa per controlli di sicurezza [tah-ssah pehr kohn-troh-llee dee see-koo-reh-tsah]

airport shuttle bus	collegamento pullman con l'aeroporto [koh-lleh-ghah-<u>mehn</u>-toh <u>pool</u>-mahn kohn lah-eh-roh-<u>pohr</u>-toh]
airport tax	i diritti aeroportuali [ee dee-<u>ree</u>-ttee ah-eh-roh-pohr-<u>twah</u>-lee]
arrival	arrivo [ah-<u>rree</u>-voh]
arrival schedule	orario d'arrivo [oh-<u>rah</u>-ryoh dah-<u>rree</u>-voh]
arrival/landing	arrivo, atterraggio [ah-<u>rree</u>-voh ah-tteh-<u>rrah</u>-djoh]
baggage cart	carrello portabagagli [kah-<u>rreh</u>-lloh pohr-tah-bah-<u>ghah</u>-lyee]
baggage check	la spedizione bagagli [lah speh-dee-<u>tsyoh</u>-neh bah-<u>ghah</u>-lyee]
baggage claim	consegna del bagaglio [kohn-<u>seh</u>-nyah dehl bah-<u>ghah</u>-lyoh]
baggage/luggage	bagaglio [bah-<u>ghah</u>-lyoh]
boarding pass	carta d'imbarco [<u>kahr</u>-tah <u>deem</u>-bahr-koh]
to book	prenotare [preh-noh-<u>tah</u>-reh]
business class	la business class [lah <u>bees</u>-ness klahss]
to cancel	annullare [ah-nnoo-<u>llah</u>-reh]
captain	capitano [kah-pee-<u>tah</u>-noh]
to change the booking	cambiare il biglietto [kahm-<u>byah</u>-reh eel bee-<u>lyeh</u>-ttoh]
charter flight	volo charter [<u>voh</u>-loh <u>chahr</u>-tehr]
check-in	il check-in, la presentazione all'arrivo [eel chehk een, lah preh-sehn-tah-<u>tsyoh</u>-neh ah-llah-<u>rree</u>-voh]
connecting flight	coincidenza [koh-een-chee-dehn-tsah]
counter	sportello [spohr-<u>teh</u>-lloh]
crew	equipaggio [eh-kwee-<u>pah</u>-djoh]
delay	ritardo [ree-<u>tahr</u>-doh]

destination	meta del viaggio [meh-tah dehl vya-djoh]
direct flight	volo diretto [voh-loh dee-reh-ttoh]
domestic flight	volo nazionale [voh-loh na-tsyoh-nah-leh]
duty-free shop	spaccio porto-franco, duty free [spah-choh pohr-toh frahn-koh]
economy class	la classe economica, la classe turistica [lah klah-sseh eh-koh-noh-mee-kah, lah klah-sseh too-ree-stee-kah]
emergency chute	scivolo d'emergenza [shee-voh-loh deh-mehr-jehn-tsah]
emergency exit	uscita d'emergenza [oo-shee-tah deh-mehr-jehn-tsah]
emergency landing	atterraggio di fortuna [ah-tteh-rrah-djoh dee fohr-too-nah]
to fasten seatbelts	allaciare le cinture di sicurezza [ah-llah-chyah-reh leh cheen-too-reh dee see-koo-reh-tsah]
flight	volo [voh-loh]
flight attendant	lo steward, l'assistente *(m/f)* di bordo/l'hostess *(f)* [loh styoo-ahrd, lah-ssee-stehn-teh dee bohr-doh, loh-stehss]
gangway	marcia [mahr-chah]
hand luggage	bagaglio a mano [bah-ghah-lyoh ah mah-noh]
helicopter	elicottero [eh-lee-koh-tteh-roh]
identification tag	cartellino [kahr-teh-llee-noh]
international flight	volo internazionale [voh-loh een-tehr-nah-tsyoh-nah-leh]
jet	il jet [eel jeht]
to land	atterrare [ah-tteh-rrah-reh]
landing	atterraggio [ah-tteh-rrah-djoh]
layover	scalo [skah-loh]

life jacket	giubbetto di salvataggio [joo-<u>beh</u>-ttoh dee sahl-vah-<u>tah</u>-djoh]
nonsmoker	non fumatore [nohn foo-mah-<u>toh</u>-reh]
on board	a bordo [ah <u>bohr</u>-doh]
passenger	passeggero [pah-sseh-<u>djeh</u>-roh]
pilot	il pilota [eel pee-<u>loh</u>-tah]
plane	a<u>e</u>reo [ah-eh-reh-oh]
rear	coda [<u>koh</u>-dah]
reservation	la prenotazione [lah preh-noh-tah-<u>tsyoh</u>-neh]
route	tratto (di volo) [<u>trah</u>-ttoh (dee <u>voh</u>-loh)]
runway	pista [<u>pee</u>-stah]
scheduled departure time	volo regolare [<u>voh</u>-loh reh-ghoh-<u>lah</u>-reh]
seatbelt	cintura di sicurezza [cheen-<u>too</u>-rah dee see-koo-<u>reh</u>-tsah]
security control	controllo di sicurezza [kohn-<u>troh</u>-lloh dee see-koo-<u>reh</u>-tsah]
shuttle bus	il bus intercampo [eel boos een-tehr-<u>kahm</u>-byoh]
smoker	fumatore [foo-mah-<u>toh</u>-reh]
standby flight	volo stand by [<u>voh</u>-loh stehnd <u>bah</u>-ee]
timetable	or<u>a</u>rio (di volo) [oh-<u>rah</u>-ryoh (dee <u>voh</u>-loh)]
waiting room	sala d'attesa [<u>sah</u>-lah dah-<u>speh</u>-ttoh]
window seat	posto al finestrino [<u>poh</u>-sto ahl fee-neh-<u>stree</u>-noh]

Train

La ferrovia

At the Travel Agency/
At the Railroad Station

All'agenzia viaggi/
Alla stazione

A one-way second-/first-class ticket to ...

Un biglietto di andata, seconda/prima classe per... [oon bee-<u>lyeh</u>-ttoh dee ahn-dah-tah, seh-<u>kohn</u>-dah/<u>pree</u>-mah <u>klah</u>-sseh pehr]

Two round-trip tickets to ..., please.

Due biglietti per..., andata e ritorno, per favore. [<u>doo</u>-eh bee-<u>lyeh</u>-ttee pehr..., ahn-<u>dah</u>-tah eh ree-<u>tohr</u>-noh, pehr fah-<u>voh</u>-reh]

Is there a reduction for children/large families/students?

C'è una riduzione per bambini/per famiglie numerose/per studenti? [cheh <u>oo</u>-nah ree-doo-<u>tsyoh</u>-neh pehr bahm-<u>boo</u> nee/pehr fah-<u>mee</u>-lyeh noo-meh-<u>roh</u>-sch/pehr stoo-<u>dehn</u>-tee]

I'd like to reserve a seat on the... train from... to..., please.

Vorrei prenotare un posto per il treno delle... per..., per favore. [vo-<u>rreh</u>-ee preh-noh-<u>tah</u>-reh oon <u>poh</u>-stoh pehr eel <u>treh</u>-noh <u>deh</u>-lleh...pehr..., pehr fah-<u>voh</u>-reh]

A window seat?

Un posto vicino al finestrino? [oon <u>poh</u>-stoh vee-<u>chee</u>-noh ahl fee-neh-<u>stree</u>-noh]

I'd like to reserve a berth/sleeper on the eight o'clock train to...

Vorrei prenotare una cuccetta/un posto in vagone letto per il treno delle 20 per... [voh-<u>rreh</u>-ee preh-noh-<u>tah</u>-reh <u>oo</u>-na koo-<u>cheh</u>-ttah/oon <u>poh</u>-stoh een vah-<u>ghoh</u>-neh <u>leh</u>-ttoh pehr eel <u>treh</u>-noh <u>deh</u>-lle <u>vehn</u>-tee pehr]

Is there a ferry train service to...

C'è un treno-traghetto per...? [cheh oon <u>treh</u>-noh trah-<u>gheh</u>-ttoh pehr]

How much is it for a car and four people?	Quanto si paga per una macchina con quattro persone? [kwahn-toh see pah-ghah pehr oo-nah mah-kkee-nah kohn kwah-ttroh pehr-soh-neh]
I'd like to register this suitcase.	Vorrei spedire questa valigia come bagaglio espresso. [vo-rreh-ee speh-dee-re kweh-stah vah-lee-jah koh-meh bah-ghah-lyoh eh-spreh-ssoh]
Where can I register my bike?	Dove posso consegnare la mia bicicletta per la spedizione? [doh-veh poh-ssoh kohn-seh-nyah-reh lah mee-ah bee-chee-kleh-ttah pehr lah speh-dee-tsyoh-neh]
Do you want to insure your baggage?	Vuole far assicurare il Suo bagaglio? [vwoh-leh fahr ah-ssee-koo-rah-reh eel soo-oh bah-ghah-lyoh]
Will the baggage be on the... o'clock train?	Il bagaglio parte col treno delle...? [eel bah-ghah-lyoh pahr-teh kohl treh-noh deh-lleh]

Signs and Notices

Ai binari	To the Platforms
Arrivi	Arrivals
Capostazione	Main Station
Deposito a cassette	Lockers
Deposito bagagli	Baggage Check (room)
Gabinetti	Toilets/Restrooms
Informazioni	Information
Orario	Schedule
Partenze	Departure
Posto di pronto soccorso	First-Aid Office
Rinfreschi	Refreshments

Sala d'aspetto	Waiting Room
Signore	Women
Signori	Men
Sottopassaggio	Underpass
Sportello biglietti	Ticket Booth
Uscita	Exit

When does it arrive in…?

Quando arriva a…? [kwahn-doh ah-rree-vah ah]

Is the train from… running late?

È in ritardo il treno proveniente da…? [eh een ree-tahr-doh eel treh-noh proh-veh-nyehn-teh dah]

Is there a connection to…at…/with the ferry?

A…c'è la coincidenza per…/con il traghetto? [ah… cheh lah koh-een-chee-dehn-tsah pehr…/kohn eel trah-gheh-ttoh]

Where do I have to change?

Dove devo cambiare? [doh-veh deh-voh kahm-byah-reh]

Which platform does the train for… leave from?

Da quale binario parte il treno per…? [dah kwah-leh bee-nah-ryoh pahr-teh eel treh-noh]

Train… from… is arriving on platform one.

Il treno… proveniente da… è in arrivo sul primo binario. [eel treh-noh… proh-veh-nyeh teh dah… eh een ah-rree-voh sool bee-nah-ryoh]

Train… from… is running ten minutes late.

Il treno… proveniente da… arriverà con 10 minuti di ritardo. [eel treh-noh… proh-veh-nyehn-teh dah… ah-rree-veh-rah kohn dyeh-chee mee-noo-tee dee ree-tahr-doh]

Attention! Travelers please board and close doors.

Attenzione! I signori viaggiatori sono pregati di salire e di chiudere gli sportelli. [ah-ttehn-tsyoh-neh ee see-nyoh-ree vyah-djah-toh-ree soh-noh preh-ghah-tee dee dsh-lee-reh eh dee kyoo-deh-reh lyee spohr-teh-llee]

On the Train	**In treno**
Excuse me, is this seat free?	Scusi, è libero questo posto? [skoo-zee eh lee-beh-roh kweh-stoh poh-stoh]
Can you help me, please?	Mi può aiutare, per favore? [mee poo-oh ah-yoo-tah-reh pehr fah-voh-reh]
May I please open/close the window?	Posso aprire/chiudere il finestrino, per favore? [poh-sso ah-pree-re/kyoo-deh-reh eel fee-neh-stree-noh pehr fah-voh-reh]
Excuse me, but this is a nonsmoking compartment.	Scusi, ma questo è uno scomparti-mento non-fumatori. [skoo-zee mah kweh-stoh eh oo-noh skohm-pahr-tee-mehn-toh nohn foo-mah-toh-ree]
I'm sorry, but this is my seat.	Scusi, ma questo è il mio posto. [skoo-zee mah kweh-soh eh eel mee-oh poh-stoh]
It's reserved.	È prenotato. [eh preh-noh-tah-toh]
Tickets, please.	I biglietti, prego. [ee bee-lyeh-ttee]
Did someone else get on?	È salito qualcun altro? [eh sah-lee-toh kwahl-koon-ahl-troh]
Does this train stop in…?	Questo treno si ferma a…? [kweh-stoh treh-noh see fehr-mah ah]
Where are we now?	Dove siamo adesso? [doh-veh syah-moh ah-deh-ssoh]
How long does the train stop here?	Quanto tempo sta fermo qui il treno? [kwahn-toh tehm-poh stah fehr-moh kwee eel treh-noh]
Will we arrive on time?	Si arriva in orario? [see ah-rree-vah een oh-rah-ryoh]

Signs and Notices

Dining Car	Vagone-ristorante
Emergency Brake	Freno d'emergenza
Nonpotable Water	Acqua non potabile

Nonsmokers	Non Fumatori
Occupied	Occupato
Sleeping Car	Vagone-letto
Sleeping Compartment	Cuccetta
Sleeping Car	Fumatori
Toilet	Ritirata
Vacant	Libero

Word List: Train	➤ See also Word List: Airplane

to arrive	**arrivare** [ah-rree-vah-reh]
baggage cart	**carrello porta-bagagli** [kah-rreh-lloh pohr-tah bah-ghah-lyee]
baggage check counter	**sportello accettazione bagagli** [spohr-teh-lloh ah-cheh-ttah-tsyoh-neh bah-ghah-lyee]
baggage ticket	**lo scontrino bagagli** [loh skohn-tree-noh bah-ghah-lyee]
baggage/luggage	**bagaglio** [bah-ghah-lyoh]
baggage/luggage rack	**deposito bagagli** [deh-poh-see-toh bah-ghah-lyee]
berth reservation	**biglietto per la cuccetta** [bee-lyeh-ttoh pehr lah koo-cheh-ttah]
car number	**numero del vagone** [noo-meh-roh dehl vah-ghoh-neh]
child's ticket (half-fare)	**biglietto per ragazzi** [bee-lych-ttoh pehr rah-ghah-tsee]
closed	**fermata** [fehr-mah-tah]
compartment	**scompartimento** [skohm-pahr-tee-mehn-toh]
corridor	**corridoio** [koh-rree-doh-yoh]
departure	**partenza** [pahr-tehn-tsah]
departure schedule	**orario di partenza** [oh-rah-ryoh dee pahr-tehn-tsah]
dining car	**il vagone ristorante** [eel vah-ghoh-neh ree-stoh-rahn-teh]

direct	diretto [dee-<u>reh</u>-ttoh]
EC (Eurocity)	EC (Euro City) [eh-oo-roh <u>see</u>-tee]
emergency brake	freno d'emergenza [<u>freh</u>-noh deh-mehr-<u>jehn</u>-tsah]
fare	prezzo del biglietto [<u>preh</u>-tsoh dehl bee-<u>lyeh</u>-ttoh]
fast train	direttissimo [dee-reh-<u>ttee</u>-ssee-moh]
ferryboat	la nave traghetto [<u>nah</u>-veh trah-<u>gheh</u>-ttoh]
ferry train	treno traghetto [<u>treh</u>-noh trah-<u>gheh</u>-ttoh]
to get off	scendere
to get on	salire [sah-<u>lee</u>-reh]
group ticket	biglietto collettivo [bee-<u>lyeh</u>-ttoh koh-lleh-<u>ttee</u>-voh]
high-speed train	treno ad alta velocità [<u>treh</u>-noh ahd <u>ahl</u>-tah veh-loh-chee-<u>tah</u>]
intercity express train	ICE (Inter City Express) [een-ter <u>see</u>-tee eh-<u>sprehss</u>]
intercity train (connecting most large cities)	IC (Inter City) [een-<u>tehr</u> <u>see</u>-tee]
locker	deposito (bagagli) a cassette [deh-<u>poh</u>-see-toh (bah-<u>ghah</u>-lyee) ah kah-<u>sseh</u>-tteh]
locomotive	locomotiva [loh-koh-moh-<u>tee</u>-vah]
main station	la stazione centrale [lah stah-<u>tsyoh</u>-neh chehn-<u>trah</u>-leh]
nonsmoking compartment	scompartimento per non fumatori [skohm-pahr-tee-<u>mehn</u>-toh pehr nohn foo-mah-<u>toh</u>-ree]
occupied	occupato [oh-kkoo-<u>pah</u>-toh]
open car (without compartments)	il vagone senza suddivisione in scompartimenti [eel vah-<u>ghoh</u>-neh <u>sehn</u>-tsah soo-ddee-vee-<u>syoh</u>-neh een skohm-pahr-tee-<u>mehn</u>-tee]

to pay on the train (supplement)	pagare il supplemento [pah-<u>ghah</u>-reh eel soo-pleh-<u>mehn</u>-toh]
platform	binario [bee-<u>nah</u>-ryoh]
porter	il portabagagli, il facchino [eel pohr-tah-bah-<u>ghah</u>-lyee, eel fah-<u>kkee</u>-noh]
railroad	ferrovia [feh-rroh-<u>vee</u>-ah]
reduction	la riduzione [lah ree-doo-<u>tsyoh</u>-neh]
reservation	la prenotazione [lah preh-noh-tah-<u>tsyoh</u>-neh]
reservation ticket	biglietto di prenotazione posto [bee-<u>lyeh</u>-ttoh dee preh-noh-tah-<u>tsyoh</u>-neh]
round-trip ticket	biglietto di andata e ritorno [bee-<u>lyeh</u>-ttoh dee anh-<u>dah</u>-tah e ree-<u>tohr</u>-noh]
sleeping car ticket	biglietto per il vagone letto [bee-<u>lyeh</u>-ttoh pehr eel vah-<u>ghoh</u>-neh <u>leh</u>-ttoh]
smoking compartment	scompartimento per fumatori [skohm-par-tee-<u>mehn</u>-toh pehr foo-mah-<u>toh</u>-ree]
station	la stazione [lah stah-<u>tsyoh</u>-neh]
station restaurant	il ristorante della stazione [eel ree-stoh-<u>rahn</u>-teh <u>deh</u>-llah stah-<u>tsyoh</u>-neh]
subject to additional charge	con supplemento obbligatorio [kohn soo-ppleh-<u>mehn</u>-toh oh-blee-ghah-<u>toh</u>-tyoh]
supplement	supplemento [soo-ppleh-<u>mehn</u>-toh]
through coach	vettura diretta [veh-<u>ttoo</u>-rah dee-<u>reh</u>-ttah]

Camogli, Liguria

ticket	biglietto [bee-<u>lyeh</u>-ttoh]
ticket check	controllo dei biglietti [kohn-<u>troh</u>-lloh <u>deh</u>-ee bee-<u>lyeh</u>-ttee]
ticket office	biglietteria [bee-lyeh-tteh-<u>ree</u>-ah]
timetable	or<u>a</u>rio [oh-<u>rah</u>-ryoh]
toilet/restroom	gabinetto [gah-bee-<u>neh</u>-ttoh]
tourist guide	guida tur<u>i</u>stica [<u>gwee</u>-dah too-<u>ree</u>-stee-kah]
train	treno [<u>treh</u>-noh]
train personnel	il personale di scorta al treno [eel pehr-soh-<u>nah</u>-leh dee <u>skohr</u>-tah ahl <u>treh</u>-noh]
vacant	libero [<u>lee</u>-beh-roh]
waiting room	sala d'aspetto [<u>sah</u>-lah dah-<u>speh</u>-ttoh]
washroom	stanzino con lavabo [stahn-tsee-noh cohn lah-<u>vah</u>-boh]
window seat	posto vicino al finestrino [<u>poh</u>-stoh vee-<u>chee</u>-noh ahl fee-neh-<u>stree</u>-noh]

Ship
La nave

Information	Informazioni

Excuse me, which is the best way to get to... by ship?
Scusi, qual è il miglior collegamento via mare per...? [skoo-zee, kwah-<u>leh</u> eel mee-<u>lyohr</u> koh-lleh-ghah-<u>mehn</u>-toh <u>vee</u>-ah <u>mah</u>-reh pehr]

When does the next ship/ferry for... leave?
Da dove/Quando parte la prossima nave/il prossimo traghetto per...? [dah <u>doh</u>-veh/<u>kwahn</u>-do <u>pahr</u>-teh lah <u>proh</u>-ssee-mah <u>nah</u>-veh/eel <u>proh</u>-ssee-moh trah-<u>gheh</u>-ttoh pehr]

How long does the crossing take?
Quanto dura la traversata? [<u>kwahn</u>-toh <u>doo</u>-rah lah trah-vehr-<u>sah</u>-tah]

What are the ports of call?
Quali porti si toccano? [<u>kwah</u>-lee <u>pohr</u>-tee see <u>toh</u>-kkah-noh]

When do we land at... ?
Quando si fa scalo a...? [<u>kwahn</u>-doh see fah skah-loh ah]

How long do we stop at...?
Quanto ci fermiamo a...? [<u>kwahn</u>-doh chee fehr-<u>myah</u>-moh]

I'd like a... ticket...
Vorrei un biglietto... [voh <u>rreh</u>-ee oon bee-<u>lyeh</u>-ttoh]

    first-class
di prima classe. [dee <u>pree</u>-mah <u>klah</u>-sseh]

    tourist
di classe turistica. [dee <u>klah</u>-sseh too-<u>ree</u>-stee-kah]

    for a single-berth cabin.
per una cabina singola. [pehr <u>oo</u>-nah kah-<u>bee</u>-nah <u>seen</u>-ghoh-lah]

    for a double-berth cabin.
una cabina doppia. [<u>oo</u>-nah kah-<u>bee</u>-nah <u>doh</u>-ppyah]

I'd like a ticket for the... o'clock round trip at...
Vorrei un biglietto per il giro delle... [voh-<u>rreh</u>-ee oon bee-<u>lyeh</u>-ttoh pehr eel <u>jee</u>-roh <u>deh</u>-lleh]

On Board	A Bordo

Excuse me, I'm looking for cabin number…

Scusi, cerco la cabina numero… [skooh-zee chehr-koh lah kah-bee-nah noo-meh-oh]

Could I have another cabin?

Potrei avere un'altra cabina? [poh-treh-ee ah-veh-reh oo-nahl-trah kah-bee-nah]

Where is my suitcase/baggage?

Dov'è la mia valigia/il mio bagaglio? [doh-veh lah mee-ah vah-lee-jah/eel mee-oh bah-ghah-lyoh]

Where is the dining room/lounge?

Dov'è la sala da pranzo/il salone?

What time does one eat?

A che ora si mangia? [ah keh oh-rah see mahn-jah]

Waiter, please bring me…

Cameriere mi porti…per favore. [kah-meh-ryeh-reh mee pohr-tee pehr fah-voh-reh]

I don't feel well.

Non mi sento bene. [nohn mee sehn-toh beh-neh]

Call the (ship's) doctor, please.

Mi chiami il medico, per favore. [mee kyah-mee eel meh-dee-koh pehr fah-voh-reh]

Please give me something for seasickness.

Mi dia qualcosa contro il mal di mare, per favore. [mee dee-ah kwahl-koh-sah kohn-troh eel mahl dee mah-reh pehr fah-voh-reh]

Word List: Ship	➤ See also Word List: Airplane/Train

anchor	ancora [ahn-koh-rah]
to be seasick	avere il mal di mare [ah-veh-reh eel mahl dee mah-reh]
bow	prua [proo-ah]
to board/to embark	imbarcare [eem-bahr-kah-reh]
to call at	toccare, fare scalo [toh-kkah-reh, fah-reh skah-loh]

cabin	cabina [kah-<u>bee</u>-nah]
captain	capitano [kah-pee-<u>tah</u>-noh]
car ferry	autotraghetto [ah-oo-toh-trah-<u>gheh</u>-ttoh]
coast	costa [<u>koh</u>-stah]
course	rotta [<u>roh</u>-ttah]
crew	equipaggio [eh-kwee-<u>pah</u>-djoh]
crossing	crociera, traversata [kroh-<u>cheh</u>-rah, trah-vehr-<u>sah</u>-tah]
deck	coperta [koh-<u>pehr</u>-tah]
dock/pier	banchina [bahn-<u>kee</u>-nah]
dry land	terraferma [teh-rrah-<u>fehr</u>-mah]
excursion	l'escursione *(f)* a terra [leh-skoor-<u>syoh</u>-neh ah <u>teh</u>-rrah]
ferry	traghetto [trah-<u>gheh</u>-ttoh]
gondola	gondola [<u>ghohn</u>-doh-lah]
harbor dues	i diritti portuali [ee dee-<u>ree</u>-ttee pohr-<u>twah</u>-lee]
harbor/port	porto [<u>pohr</u>-toh]
hovercraft	l'hovercraft [oh-vehr-<u>krahft</u>]
hydrofoil	aliscafo [ah-lee-skah-foh]
interior cabin	cabina interna [kah-<u>bee</u>-nah een-<u>tehr</u>-nah]
knot	nodo [<u>noh</u>-doh]
to land	sbarcare [sbahr-<u>kah</u>-reh]
landing	approdo [ah-<u>pproh</u>-doh]
landing/docking wharf	il pontile d'approdo [eel pon-<u>tee</u>-leh dah-<u>pproh</u>-doh]
lifeboat	scialuppa di salvataggio [sha-<u>loo</u>-ppah dee sahl-vah-<u>tah</u>-djoh]
life jacket	giubbetto di salvataggio. [joo-beh-toh dee sahl-vah-<u>tah</u>-djoh]

life preserver	il salvagente [eel sahl-vah-jehn-teh]
lighthouse/beacon	faro [fah-roh]
lower deck	l'interponte *(m)* [leen-tehr-pohn-teh]
motorboat	motoscafo [moh-toh-skah-foh]
oar	remo [reh-moh]
outer cabin	cabina esterna [kah-bee-nah eh-stehr-nah]
passenger	passeggero [pah-sseh-djeh-roh]
port	approdo [ah-pproh-doh]
promenade deck	il ponte di passeggio [eel ponh-teh dee pah-sseh-djoh]
reservation	la prenotazione [lah preh-noh-tah-tsyoh-neh]
rough seas	moto ondoso [moh-toh ohn-doh-soh]
round trip	giro [jee-roh]
rowboat	barca a remi [bahr-kah ah reh-mee]
sailboat	barca a vela [bahr-kah ah veh-lah]
sailor	marinaio [mah-ree-nah-yoh]
starboard	tribordo [tree-bohr-doh]
steamship	prioscafo, nave a vapore [pee-roh-skah-foh, nah-veh ah vah-poh-reh]
stern	poppa [poh-ppah]
sundeck	il ponte del sole [eel pohn-teh dehl soh-leh]
ticket	biglietto [bee-lyeh-ttoh]
train ferry	la nave traghetto [lah nah-veh trah-gheh-ttoh]
waiter	il cameriere [eel kah-meh-ryeh-reh]
wave	il surf, onda [eel sehrf, ohn-dah]
to weigh anchor	uscire dal porto, salpare [oo-shee-reh dahl pohr-toh]
yacht	panfilo [pahn-fee-loh]
Your passport, please.	Il Suo passaporto, per favore. [eel

At the Border
Al confine

Passport Check	Controllo passaporti

soo-oh pah-ssah-pohr-toh pehr fah-voh-reh]

Your passport has expired.	Il Suo passaporto è scaduto. [eel soo-oh pah-ssah-pohr-toh eh skah-doo-toh]
I'm with the party from...	Appartengo alla comitiva proveniente da... [ah-ppahr-tehn-ghoh ah-llah koh-mee-tee-vah dah]
Could you please show me... for your dog/cat?	Mi può mostrare per favore... per il Suo cane/gatto? [mee poo-oh moh-strah-reh pehr fah-voh-reh... pehr eel soo-oh kah-neh/ghah-ttoh]
veterinary certificate	il certificato veterinario [eel chchr-tee-fee-kah-toh veh-teh-ree-nah-ryoh]
rabies vaccination certificate	il certificato di vaccinazione contro l'idrofobia [eel chehr-tee-fee-kah-toh dee vah-chee-nah-tsyoh-neh kohn-troh lee-droh-foh-bee-ah]
Do you have a visa?	Ha il visto? [ah eel vee-stoh]
Can I get a visa here?	Mi potete rilasciare qui il visto? [mee poh-teh-teh ree-lah-shah-reh kwee eel vee-stoh]

Customs	Dogana

Have you anything to declare?	Ha niente da dichiarare? [ah nyehn-teh dah dee-kyah-rah-reh]
No, I've only a few gifts.	No, ho soltanto alcuni regali. [noh oh sohl-tahn-toh ahl-koo-nee reh-ghah-lee]

Please move to the right/left.	Si metta lì a destra/a sinistra. [see meh-ttah lee ah deh-strah/ah see-nee-strah]
Please open your luggage/suitcase.	Apra, per favore, il bagaglio/questa valigia. [ah-prah pehr fah-voh-reh eel bah-ghah-lyoh/kweh-stah vah-lee-jah]
Do I have to pay duty on this?	Devo sdoganare questo? [deh-voh sdoh-ghah-nah-reh kweh-stoh]
How much duty do I have to pay?	Quanto devo pagare di dazio doganale? [kwahn-toh deh-voh pah-ghah-reh dee dah-tsyoh doh-ghah-nah-leh]

Word List: At the Border

birthplace	luogo di nascita [lwoh-ghoh dee nah-shee-tah]
border (crossing)	frontiera, il confine [frohn-tyeh-rah, kohn-fee-neh]
children's ID card	carta d'identità per bambini [kahr-tah dee-dehn-tee-tah pehr bahm-bee-nee]
customs	dogana [doh-ghah-nah]
customs check	ispezione (f) doganale [ee-speh-tsyoh-neh doh-ghah-nah-leh]
customs office	ufficio doganale [oo-ffee-choh doh-ghah-nah-leh]
customs officer	impiegato doganale [eem-pyeh-ghah-toh doh-ghah-nah-leh]
date of birth	data di nascita [dah-tah dee nah-shee-tah]
driver's license	la patente [lah pah-tehn-teh]
duty taxes	le tariffe doganali [leh tah-ree-ffeh doh-ghah-nah-lee]
duty-free	esente da dazio doganale [eh-sehn-teh dah dah-tsyoh doh-ghah-nah-leh]

entry (into a foreign country)	entrata (in territorio straniero) [ehn-trah-tah een teh-rree-toh-ryoh strah-nyeh-roh]
export	l'esportazione *(f)* [leh-spohr-tah-tsyoh-neh]
green card	carta verde [kahr-tah vehr-deh]
ID card	carta d'identità [kahr-tah dee-dehn-tee-tah]
import	l'importazione *(f)* [leem-pohr-tah-tsyoh-neh]
international license plate	targa di nazionalità [tahr-ghah dee nah-tsyoh-nah-lee-tah]
international vaccination certificate	certificato internazionale di vaccinazione [chehr-tee-fee-kah-toh een-tehr-nah-tsyoh-nah-leh dee vah-chee-nah-tsyoh-neh]
to leave (the country)	partire (per l'estero) [pahr-tee-reh pehr leh-steh-roh]
maiden name	il nome da ragazza [eel noh-meh dah rah-ghah tsah]
marital status	stato di famiglia [stah-toh dee fah-mee-lyah]
married	sposato [spoh-sah-toh]
name	il nome [eel noh-meh]
nationality	nazionalità [nah-tsyoh-nah-lee-tah]
passport	passaporto [pah-ssah-pohr-toh]
passport control	controllo dei passaporti [kohn-troh lloh pah-ssah-pohr-tee]
rabies	idrofobia [ee-droh-foh-hee-ah]
regulations	le disposizioni [leh dee-spoh-see-tsyoh-nee]
residence	domicilio [doh-mee-chee-lyoh]
single	celibe *(m)*, nubile *(f)* [cheh-lee-beh, noo-bee-leh]

subject to duty	soggetto a dazio doganale [soh-djeh-ttoh ah dah-tsyoh doh-ghah-nah-leh]
surname	il cognome [eel koh-nyoh-meh]
valid	valido [vah-lee-doh]
visa	visto [vee-stoh]
widow(er)	vedova, vedovo [veh-doh-vah, veh-doh-voh]

Local Transportation
Rete per traffico a breve distanza

Which bus/tram/subway goes to…?	Qual è l'autobus/il tram/la metropolitana che va a…? [kwah-leh lah-oo-toh-boos/eel trahm/lah meh-troh-poh-lee-tah-nah keh vah]
Where is the nearest…	Dov'è la prossima… [doh-veh lah proh-ssee-mah]
bus stop?	fermata dell'autobus? [fehr-mah-tah deh-llah-oo-toh-boos]
tram stop?	fermata del tram? [fehr-mah-tah dehl trahm]
subway stop?	stazione della metropolitana? [stah-tsyoh-neh deh-llah meh-troh-poh-lee-tah-nah]
Which line goes to...?	Qual è la linea che va a…? [kwah-leh lah lee-neh-ah keh vah ah]
Is this the right bus to…?	È l'autobus giusto per…? [eh lah-oo-toh-boos joo-stoh pehr]
When/From where does the bus leave?	Quando/Da dove parte l'autobus? [kwahn-do/dah doh-veh pahr-teh lah-oo-toh-boos]
When is the first/last subway to… ?	Quando parte la prima/l'ultima metropolitana per…? [kwahn-doh pahr-teh lah pree-mah/lool-tee-mah meh-tro-ph-lee-tah-nah pehr]

Which direction must I take?

In che direzione devo andare? [een keh dee-reh-<u>tsyoh</u>-neh <u>deh</u>-voh ah-<u>dah</u>-reh]

How many stops are there?

Quante fermate sono? [<u>kwahn</u>-teh fehr-mah-<u>teh</u> soh-noh]

Where do I get off/change?

Dove devo scendere/cambiare? [<u>doh</u>-veh <u>deh</u>-voh shehn-deh-reh/kahm-<u>byah</u>-reh]

EGEN-TASSA AHT 20 D.P.R. n 620 del 26-10-1972

Boarding is allowed only for ticket holders. Tickets are available in stores that have this or similar signs posted.

Excuse me, could you please tell me when to get off?

Mi dice, per favore quando devo scendere? [mee <u>dee</u>-cheh pehr fah-<u>voh</u>-reh <u>kwahn</u>-doh <u>deh</u>-voh shehn-deh-reh]

Where can I buy a ticket?

Dove si comprano i biglietti? [<u>doh</u>-veh see <u>kohm</u>-prah-noh ee bee-<u>lyeh</u>-ttee]

A ticket to... please

Un biglietto per..., per favore. [Oon bee-<u>lyeh</u>-ttoh pehr, pehr fah-<u>voh</u>-reh]

Do you also have one-day/weekly tickets?

Ci sono anche biglietti per più corse/abbonamenti settimanali? [chee <u>soh</u>-noh <u>ahn</u>-keh bee-<u>lyeh</u>-ttee pehr pee-<u>oo</u> <u>kohr</u>-seh/ah-boh-nah-<u>mehn</u>-tee seh-ttee-mah-<u>nah</u>-lee]

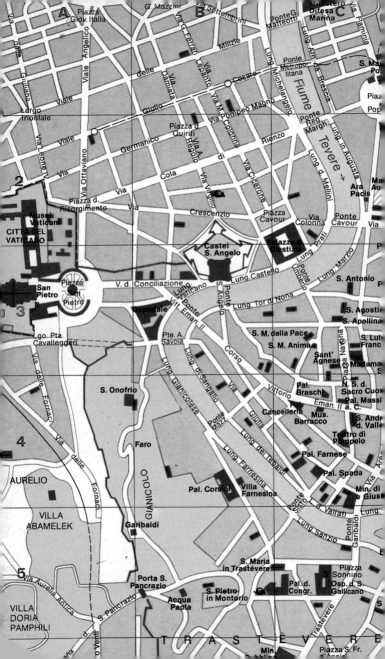

ROM

Taxi

Taxi

Where can I find a taxi?	Dove trovo un tassì? [doh-veh troh-voh oon tah-ssee]
At the station.	Alla stazione. [ah-llah stah-tsyoh-neh]
At the hotel.	All'albergo. [ah-llahl-behr-ghoh]
On… Street.	In via… [een vee-ah]
To…, please.	A…, per favore. [ah… pehr fah-voh-reh]
How much will it cost to go to… ?	Quanto costa andare a…? [kwahn-toh koh-stah ahn-dah-reh ah]
Please stop here.	Si fermi qui. [see fehr-mee kwee]
Wait, please. I'll be back in five minutes.	Aspetti, per favore. Fra 5 minuti sono di ritorno. [ah-speh-ttee pehr fah-voh-reh. frah cheen-kweh mee-noo-tee soh-noh dee ree-tohr-noh]
That's for you. (tip)	Questo è per Lei. [kweh-stoh eh pehr leh-ee]

On Foot

A piedi

Excuse me, where is… ?	Scusi signore/signora/signorina, dov'è…? [skoo-zee see-nyoh-re/see-nyoh-rah/see-nyoh-ree-nah. doh-veh]
Could you tell me how to get to…, please?	Mi potrebbe dire come si arriva a…, per favore? [mee poh-treh-beh dee-reh koh-meh see ah-rree-vah ah…pehr fah-voh-reh]
I'm sorry, I don't know.	Mi dispiace, non lo so. [mee dee-spyah-cheh, nohn loh soh]
Which is the quickest way to…?	Qual è la strada più breve per…? [kwah-leh lah strah-dah pee-oo breh-veh pehr..]

How far is it to… ?

Quanto ci vuole per andare a…? [kwahn-toh chee vwoh-leh pehr ahn-dah-reh ah]

It's (not) far.

(Non) è lontano. [(nohn) eh lohn-tah-noh]

It's very close.

È vicinissimo. [eh vee-chee-nee-ssee-moh]

Go straight/to the left/to the right.

Vada diritto/a sinistra/a destra. [vah-dah dee-ree-ttoh/ah see-nee-strah/ah deh-strah]

The first/second street on the left/right.

La prima/seconda strada a sinistra/a destra. [lah pree-mah/seh-kohn-dah strah-dah ah see-nee-strah/ah deh-strah]

Cross...

Attraversi… [ah-ttrah-vehr-see]

the bridge.

il ponte. [eel pohn-teh]

the square.

la piazza. [lah pyah-tsah]

the street.

la strada. [lah strah-dah]

Then ask again.

Poi chieda un'altra volta. [poh-ee kyeh-dah oo-nahl-trah vohl-tah]

St. Peter's Square, Rome

You can't miss it.   Non si può sbagliare. [nohn see poo-<u>oh</u> zbah-<u>lyah</u>-reh]

You can take…   Può pr<u>e</u>ndere… [poo-<u>oh</u> <u>prehn</u>-deh-reh]

  the bus.   l'<u>a</u>utobus. [<u>lah</u>-oo-toh-<u>boos</u>].

  the tram.   il tram. [eel trahm]

  the train.   il treno. [eel <u>treh</u>-noh]

  the subway.   la metropolitana. [lah meh-troh-poh-lee-<u>tah</u>-nah]

  the trolley.   il f<u>i</u>lobus. [eel <u>fee</u>-loh-boos]

Word List: On the Go in Town

alley	v<u>i</u>colo [<u>vee</u>-koh-loh]
announce	annunciare [ah-nnoon-<u>chah</u>-reh]
building	edif<u>i</u>cio [eh-dee-<u>fee</u>-choh]
bus	l'<u>a</u>utobus *(m)* [<u>lah</u>-oo-toh-<u>boos</u>]
bus station	la stazione degli autobus [lah stah-<u>tsyoh</u>-neh <u>deh</u>-lyee <u>ah</u>-oo-toh-<u>boos</u>]
to buy tickets	comprare i biglietti [kohm-<u>prah</u>-reh ee bee-<u>lyeh</u>-ttee]
to cancel	annullare [ah-nnoo-<u>llah</u>-reh]
church	chiesa [<u>kyeh</u>-sah]
city	l'<u>a</u>utobus *(m)* urbano [<u>lah</u>-oo-toh-<u>boos</u> oor-<u>bah</u>-noh]
daily travel ticket/pass	biglietto giornaliero [bee-<u>lyeh</u>-ttoh johr-nah-<u>lyeh</u>-roh]
departure	partenza [pahr-<u>tehn</u>-tsah]
direction	la direzione [lah dee-reh-<u>tsyoh</u>-neh]
district	il quarti<u>e</u>re [eel kwahr-<u>lyeh</u>-reh]
downtown/town center	centro [<u>chehn</u>-troh]
driver	il conducente [eel kohn-doo-<u>chehn</u>-teh]

fare	prezzo del biglietto [preh-tsoh dehl bee-lyeh-ttoh]
flat rate	prezzo forfettario [preh-tsoh fohr-feh-ttah-ryoh]
to get off/out	scendere [shehn-deh-reh]
to get on	salire [sah-lee-reh]
house	casa [kah-sah]
house number	numero civico [noo-meh-roh chee-vee-koh]
inspector	il controllore [eel kohn-troh-lloh-reh]
intercity bus	l'autobus (m) interurbano [lah-oo-toh-boos een-teh-roor-bah-noh]
to leave	partire [pahr-tee-reh]
local railroad	ferrovia urbana [feh-rroh-vee-ah oor-bah-nah]
local train	treno locale [treh-noh loh-kah-leh]
main street	strada principale [strah-dah preen-chee-pah-leh]
park	parco, giardino pubblico [pahr-koh, jahr-dee-noh poo-blee-koh]
pedestrian zone	zona pedonale [zoh-nah peh-doh-nah-leh]
to press the button	premere il pulsante [preh-meh-reh eel pool-sahn-teh]
price per kilometer	prezzo per chilometro [preh-tsoh pehr kee-loh-meh-troh]
receipt	ricevuta [ree-cheh-voo-tah]
schedule	orario [oh-rah-ryoh]
side street	strada secondaria [strah-dah seh-kohn-dah-rya]
sidewalk	il marciapiede [eel mahr-chah-pyeh-deh]
sightseeing tour	giro della città, escursioni [jee-roh deh-llah chee-ttah, eh-skoohr-syoh-nee]

stop	fermata [fehr-<u>mah</u>-tah]
to stop	fermarsi [fehr-<u>mahr</u>-see]
street	strada, via [<u>strah</u>-dah, <u>vee</u>-ah]
suburb	sobborgo [soh-<u>bohr</u>-ghoh]
subway	metropolitana [meh-troh-poh-lee-<u>tah</u>-nah]
taxi driver	il tassista [eel tah-<u>ssee</u>-stah]
taxi stand	posteggio di taxi [poh-<u>steh</u>-djoh dee tah-<u>ssee</u>]
terminus	il capolinea [eel kah-poh-<u>lee</u>-neh-ah]
ticket	biglietto [bee-<u>lyeh</u>-ttoh]
ticket machine	il distributore automatico di biglietti [eel dee-stree-boo-<u>toh</u>-reh ah-oo-toh-<u>mah</u>-tee-koh dee bee-<u>lyeh</u>-ttee]
ticket validator/puncher	l'obliteratore (m) [loh-blee-teh-rah-<u>toh</u>-reh]
tip	mancia [<u>mahn</u>-chah]
tram	il tram [eel trahm]
travel pass	abbonamento per tutta la rete [ah-boh-nah-<u>mehn</u>-toh pehr <u>too</u>-ttah lah <u>reh</u>-teh]
trolley	il filobus [eel <u>fee</u>-loh-boos]
weekly pass/ticket	abbonamento settimanale [ah-boh-nah-<u>mehn</u>-toh seh-ttee-mah-<u>nah</u>-leh]
weekly/monthly pass	tessera d'abbonamento [<u>teh</u>-sseh-rah dah-boh-nah-<u>mehn</u>-toh]

4 **Accommodations**
L'Alloggio

Information
Informazioni

Can you please recommend...	Scusi signora/signorina/signore, potrebbe consigliarmi... [skoo-zee see-nyoh-rah/see-nyoh-ree-nah/see-nyoh-reh, poh-treh-beh kohn-see-lyahr-mee]
a good hotel?	un buon albergo? [oon bwohn ahl-behr-ghoh]
a cheap hotel?	un albergo non troppo caro? [oon ahl-behr-ghoh nohn troh-ppo kah-roh]
a guest house?	una pensione? [oo-nah pehn-syoh-neh]
a bed and breakfast?	una camera privata? [oo-nah kah-meh-rah pree-vah-tah]
Is it in town/in a quiet spot/near the beach?	Si trova in centro/in una posizione tranquilla/vicino al mare? [see troh-vah een chehn-troh/een oo-nah poh-see-tsyoh-neh trahn-kwee-llah/vee-chee-noh ahl mah-reh]
How much will it cost a night?	Quanto costerà all'incirca il per nottamento? [kwahn-toh koh-steh-rah ah-lleen-cheer-kah eel pehr-noh-ttah-mehn-toh]
Is there a youth hostel/a campground here?	C'è un ostello della gioventù/un camping qui? [cheh oon oh-steh-lloh deh-llah joh-vehn-too/ oon kehm-peengh kwee]

Hotel/Guest House/Bed and Breakfast
Hotel/Pensione/Camera privata

At the Reception Desk

Alla sala di ricevimento

I've reserved a room. My name is…

Ho prenotato una camera. Il mio nome è… [oh preh-noh-<u>tah</u>-toh <u>oo</u>-nah <u>kah</u>-meh-rah. eel <u>mee</u>-oh <u>noh</u>-meh eh]

Have you any vacancies?

Ha camere libere? [ah <u>kah</u>-meh-reh <u>lee</u>-beh-reh]

… for one night.

… per una notte. [pehr <u>oo</u>-nah <u>noh</u>-tteh]

… for two days/a week.

… per due giorni/per una settimana. [pehr <u>doo</u>-eh <u>johr</u>-nee/pehr <u>oo</u>-nah seh-ttee-<u>mah</u>-nah]

No, unfortunately we're full.

No, purtroppo è tutto esaurito. [noh, poor-<u>troh</u>-ppoh eh <u>too</u>-ttoh ch sah oo-<u>ree</u>-toh]

Yes, what sort of room would you like?

Sì, che tipo di camera desidera? [see, keh <u>tee</u>-poh dee <u>kah</u>-meh-rah deh-<u>see</u>-deh-rah]

a single room

una singola [<u>oo</u>-nah <u>seen</u>-ghoh-lah]

a double room

una doppia [<u>oo</u>-nah <u>doh</u>-ppyah]

a double room, but with twin beds

una camera doppia, ma non con un letto francese [<u>oo</u>-nah <u>kah</u>-meh-rah <u>doh</u>-ppyah, mah kohn oon <u>leh</u>-ttoh frahn-<u>cheh</u>-seh]

a quiet room

una camera tranquilla [<u>oo</u>-nah <u>kah</u>-meh-rah trah-<u>kwee</u>-llah]

a sunny room

una camera soleggiata [<u>oo</u>-nah <u>kah</u>-meh-rah soh-leh-<u>djah</u>-tah]

with hot and cold water

con acqua corrente calda e fredda [kohn <u>ah</u>-kwah koh-<u>rrehn</u>-teh <u>kahl</u>-dah eh <u>freh</u>-ddah]

with a shower

con doccia [kohn <u>doh</u>-chah]

with a bath	con bagno [kohn <u>bah</u>-nyoh]
with a balcony/terrace	con balcone/con terrazza [kohn bahl-<u>koh</u>-neh/kohn teh-<u>rrah</u>-tsah]
with a view of the sea	con vista sul mare [kohn <u>vee</u>-stah sool <u>mah</u>-reh]
that faces the street	che dà sulla strada [keh dah <u>soo</u>-llah <u>strah</u>-dah]
that faces the courtyard	che dà sul cortile [keh dah sool kohr-<u>tee</u>-leh]
May I see the room?	Posso vedere la camera? [<u>poh</u>-ssoh veh-<u>deh</u>-reh lah <u>kah</u>-meh-rah]
I don't like this room. Please show me another one.	Questa camera non mi piace. Me ne mostri, un'altra, per favore. [<u>kweh</u>-sta <u>kah</u>-meh-rah nohn mee <u>pyah</u>-cheh meh neh <u>moh</u>-stree oo-<u>nahl</u>-trah pehr fah-<u>voh</u>-reh]
I like this room. I'll take it.	Questa camera mi piace molto. La prendo. [<u>kweh</u>-stah <u>kah</u>-meh-rah mee <u>pyah</u>-cheh <u>mohl</u>-toh lah <u>prehn</u>-doh]
Can you add another bed/cot (for children)?	Si può aggiungere un altro letto/un lettino (per bambini)? [see poo-<u>oh</u> ah-<u>djoon</u>-jeh-reh oon <u>ahl</u>-troh <u>leh</u>-ttoh/oon leh-<u>ttee</u>-noh (pehr bahm-<u>bee</u>-nee)]
How much is the room…	Quanto costa la camera… [<u>kwahn</u>-toh <u>koh</u>-stah lah <u>kah</u>-meh-rah]
with breakfast?	con la prima colazione? [kohn lah <u>pree</u>-mah koh-lah-<u>tsyoh</u>-neh]
with breakfast and dinner?	a mezza pensione? [ah <u>meh</u>-zah pehn-<u>syoh</u>-neh]
with all meals included (American plan)?	a pensione completa? [ah pehn-<u>syoh</u>-neh kohm-<u>pleh</u>-tah]
Would you please fill out the registration form?	Vuole riempire, per favore, il modulo d'accettazione? [<u>vwoh</u>-leh ryem-<u>pee</u>-reh pehr fah-<u>voh</u>-reh eel <u>moh</u>-doo-loh dah-cheh-ttah-<u>tsyoh</u>-neh]

Your passport/ID card, please.

Il Suo passaporto/La Sua carta d'identità, per favore. [eel soo-oh pah-ssah-pohr-toh/lah soo-ah kahr-tah dee-dehn-tee-tah]

Please have my luggage taken up to my room.

Faccia portare il mio bagaglio in camera, per piacere. [fah-chah pohr-tah-reh eel mee-oh bah-ghah-lyoh een kah-meh-rah pehr pyah-cheh-reh]

Where can I park the car?

Dove posso lasciare la macchina? [doh-veh poh-ssoh lah-shah-reh lah mah-kkee-nah]

In the garage/parking lot.

Nel nostro garage/parcheggio. [nehl noh-stroh ghah-rahj/pahr-keh-djoh]

Does the hotel have a pool/ a private beach?

L'albergo ha una piscina/una spiaggia riservata? [lahl-behr-ghoh ah oo-nah pee-shee-nah/oo-nah spyah-djah ree-sehr-vah-tah]

| Talking to the Hotel Staff | Col personale di servizio |

What time is breakfast?

Da che ora si può fare colazione? [dah keh oh-rah see poo-oh fah-reh koh-lah-tsyoh-neh]

When are meals served?

Quali sono gli orari per i pasti? [kwah-lee soh-noh lyee oh-rah-ree pehr ee pah-stee]

Where is the dining room?

Dov'è la sala da pranzo? [doh-veh lah sah-lah dah prah-tsoh]

Where is breakfast served?

Dove si fa colazione? [doh-veh see fah koh-lah-tsyoh-neh]

Downstairs.

Al piano inferiore. [ahl pyah-noh een-feh-ryoh-reh]

Would you like to have breakfast in your room?

Desidera far colazione in camera? [deh-see-deh-rah fahr koh-lah-tsyoh-neh een kah-meh-rah]

Please have breakfast brought to my room at…	Mi faccia portare, per favore, la colazione in camera alle… [mee fah-chah pohr-tah-reh pehr fah-voh-reh lah koh-lah-tsyoh-neh een kah-meh-rah ah-lleh]
For breakfast I'd like…	A colazione prendo… [ah koh-lah-tsyoh-neh prehn-doh]
black coffee.	caffè senza latte. [kah-ffeh sehn-tsah lah-tteh]
coffee with milk.	caffellatte. [kah-ffeh-llah-tteh]
decaffeinated coffee.	caffè decaffeinato. [kah-ffeh deh-kah-ffeh-ee-nah-toh]
tea with milk/lemon.	tè al latte/al limone. [teh ahl lah-tteh/ahl lee-moh-neh]
herbal tea.	una tisana. [oo-nah tee-sah-nah]
hot chocolate.	cioccolata. [choh-kkoh-lah-tah]
fruit juice.	una spremuta. [oo-nah spreh-moo-tah]
a soft-boiled egg.	un uovo à la coque. [oon woh-voh ah-llah kohk]
scrambled eggs.	uova strapazzate. [woh-vah strah-pah-tsah-teh]
eggs and bacon.	uova con lo speck. [woh-vah kohn loh spehk]
bread/rolls/toast.	pane/panini/pane tostato. [pah-neh/pah-nee-ne/pah-neh toh-stah-toh]
a croissant.	un cornetto. [oon kohr-neh-ttoh]
butter.	burro. [boo-rroh]
cheese.	formaggio. [fohr-mah-djoh]
cold cuts.	salume. [sah-loo-meh]
raw cured ham.	prosciutto. [proh-shoo-ttoh]
honey.	miele. [myeh-leh]
marmalade.	marmellata. [mahr-meh-llah-tah]

yogurt.	uno yogurt. [oo-noh yoh-ghoort]
some fruit.	della frutta. [deh-llah froo-ttah]
Could I have a lunch packed for tomorrow?	Per domani mi può preparare il cestino per il pranzo al sacco? [pehr doh-mah-nee mee poo-oh preh-pah-rah-reh eel cheh-stee-noh pehr eel prahn-tsoh ahl sah-kkoh]
Please wake me at…o'clock tomorrow morning.	Mi svegli domattina alle…, per favore. [mee zveh-lyee doh-mah-ttee-nah ah-lleh.. pehr fah-voh-reh]
Could you please bring me…	Potrebbe portarmi, per favore,… [poh-treh-beh pohr-tahr-mee pehr fah-voh-reh]
another towel?	un altro asciugamano? [oon ahl-troh ah shoo ghah-mah-noh]
some soap?	una saponetta? [oo-nah sah-poh-neh-ttah]
some coat hangers?	delle stampelli per i panni? [deh-lleh stahm-peh-lleh pehr ee pah-nnee]

How does... work?
Come funziona...? [koh-meh foon-tsyoh-nah]

My keys, please.
Per favore, la mia chiave. [pehr fah-voh-reh lah mee-ah kyah-veh]

Did anyone ask for me?
Mi ha cercato qualcuno? [mee ah chehr-kah-toh kwahl-koo-noh]

Is there any mail for me?
C'è posta per me? [cheh poh-stah pehr meh]

Do you have any postcards/ stamps?
Avete cartoline/francobolli? [ah-veh-teh kahr-toh-lee-neh/frahn-koh-boh-llee]

Where can I mail this letter?
Dove posso imbucare questa lettera? [doh-veh poh-ssoh eem-boo-kah-reh kweh-stah leh-tteh-rah]

Where can I rent... ?
Dove posso affittare/noleggiare...? [doh-veh poh-ssoh ah-ffee-ttah-re/noh-leh-djah-reh]

Where can I make a phone call?
Dove posso telefonare? [doh-veh poh-ssoh teh-leh-foh-nah-reh]

May I leave my valuables in your safe?
Posso lasciare i miei valori in deposito nella vostra cassaforte? [poh-ssoh lah-shah-reh ee myeh-ee vah-loh-ree een deh-poh-see-toh neh-llah voh-strah kah-ssah-fohr-teh]

May I leave my things here until I get back?
Posso lasciare qui le mie cose fino al mio ritorno? [poh-ssoh lah-shah-re kwee leh mee-eh koh-seh fee-noh ahl mee-oh ree-tohr-noh]

Complaints

Reclami

The room isn't clean.
La camera non è pulita. [lah kah-meh-rah nohn eh poo-lee-tah]

The shower...
La doccia... [lah doh-chah]

The toilet...
Lo sciacquone... [loh shah-kwoh-neh]

The heating… Il riscaldamento… [eel ree-skahl-dah-<u>mehn</u>-toh]

The light… La luce… [lah <u>loo</u>-cheh]

The radio… La radio… [lah <u>rah</u>-dyoh]

The television doesn't work. Il televisore non funziona. [eel teh-leh-vee-<u>soh</u>-reh nohn foon-<u>tsyoh</u>-nah]

The faucet drips. Il rubinetto gocciola. [eel roo-bee-<u>neh</u>-ttoh <u>ghoh</u>-choh-lah]

There's no (warm) water. Non c'è acqua (calda). [nohn cheh <u>ah</u>-kwah <u>kahl</u>-dah]

The toilet/sink is stopped up. Il gabinetto/Il lavandino è intasato. [eel ghah-bee-<u>neh</u>-ttoh/eel lah-vahn-<u>dee</u>-noh eh een-tah-<u>sah</u>-toh]

The window doesn't close/ open. La finestra non si chiude/non si apre. [lah fee-<u>neh</u>-strah nohn see <u>kyoo</u>-de/non see <u>ah</u>-preh]

The key doesn't fit. La chiave non va bene. [lah <u>kyah</u>-veh nohn vah <u>beh</u>-neh]

Checking Out

Partenza

I'll be leaving tonight/ tomorrow at… Parto stasera/domani alle…[<u>pahr</u>-toh stah-<u>seh</u>-rah/doh-<u>mah</u>-nee <u>ah</u>-lleh]

By what time must I be out of the room? Per quando devo liberare la stanza? [pehr kwahn-doh <u>deh</u>-voh lee-beh-<u>rah</u>-reh lah <u>stahn</u>-tsah]

I'd like my bill, please. Mi prepari il conto, per favore. [mee preh-<u>pah</u>-ree eel <u>kohn</u>-toh pehr fah-<u>voh</u>-reh]

Separate bills, please. Conti separati, per favore. [<u>kohn</u>-tee seh-pah-<u>rah</u>-tee pehr <u>fah</u>-voh-reh]

Do you accept traveler's checks? Accetta assegni turistici? [ah-<u>cheh</u>-ttah ah-<u>sseh</u>-nyee too-<u>ree</u>-stee-chee]

Please forward any mail for me to this address.	Per favore, rispedisca a questo indirizzo la posta che arriverà. [pehr fah-<u>voh</u>-reh ree-speh-<u>dee</u>-skah ah <u>kweh</u>-stoh een-dee-<u>ree</u>-tsoh lah <u>poh</u>-stah keh ah-rree-veh-<u>rah</u>]
Please have my luggage brought down.	Mi faccia portare giù il bagaglio, per favore. [mee <u>fah</u>-chah pohr-<u>tah</u>-reh joo eel bah-<u>ghah</u>-lyoh pehr fah-<u>voh</u>-reh]
Please have my luggage brought to the station/to the air terminal.	Mi faccia portare il bagaglio alla stazione/all'Air Terminal, per favore. [mee <u>fah</u>-chah pohr-<u>tah</u>-reh eel bah-<u>ghah</u>-lyoh <u>ah</u>-llah stah-<u>tsyoh</u>-neh/ah-<u>llehr</u> tehr-mee-<u>nahl</u> pehr fah-<u>voh</u>-reh]
Please call a taxi for me.	Mi chiami un tassì, per favore. [mee <u>kyah</u>-mee oon tah-<u>ssee</u> pehr fah-<u>voh</u>-reh]
Thank you for everything. Good-bye!	Grazie di tutto. Arrivederci! [<u>grah</u>-tsyeh dee <u>too</u>-ttoh. Ah-rree-veh-<u>dehr</u>-chee]

Word List: Hotel/Guest House/Bed and Breakfast

adapter	convertiture [kohn-vehr-tee-<u>toh</u>-reh]
air conditioning	aria condizionata [<u>ah</u>-ryah kohn-dee-tsyoh-<u>nah</u>-tah]
armchair	sedia [<u>seh</u>-dyah]
ashtray	il portacenere [eel pohr-tah-<u>cheh</u>-neh-reh]
baby-sitting service	assistenza ai bambini [ah-ssee-<u>stehn</u>-tsah <u>ah</u>-ee bahm-<u>bee</u>-nee]
balcony	il balcone [eel bahl-<u>koh</u>-neh]
bar	il bar [eel bahr]
bath	vasca da bagno [<u>vah</u>-skah dah <u>bah</u>-nyoh]
bathroom	bagno [<u>bah</u>-nyoh]

bed	letto [leh-ttoh]
bedside lamp	lampada del comodino [lahm-pah-dah dehl koh-moh-dee-noh]
bedside table	comodino [koh-moh-dee-noh]
bidet	il bidet, il bidè [eel bee deh]
blanket	coperta di lana [koh-pehr-tah dee lah-nah]
breakfast	la colazione [lah koh-lah-tsyoh-neh]
breakfast bar/buffet	il buffet della colazione [eel boo-ffeh deh-llah koh-lah-tsyoh-neh]
breakfast room	sala per la colazione [sah-lah pehr lah koh-lah-tsyoh-neh]
bus service	servizio pulman [sehr-vee-tsyoh pool-mahn]
category	categoria [kah-teh-ghoh-ree-ah]
change of sheets	cambio biancheria [kahm-byo byah-keh-ree-ah]
children's playground	parco giochi per bambini [pahr-koh joh-kee pehr bahm-bee-nee]
children's pool	piscina per bambini [pee-shee-nah pehr bahm-bee-nee]
to clean	pulire [poo-lee-reh]
closet	armadio [ahr-mah-dyoh]
coat hanger	stampella (per i panni) [stahm-peh-llah (pehr ee pah-nnee)]
cold water	acqua fredda [ah-kwah freh-ddah]
comforter	coperta [koh-pehr-tah]
cot	lettino (per bambini) [leh-ttee-noh (pehr bahm-bee-nee)]
dining room	sala da pranzo [sah-lah dah prahn-tsoh]
dinner	cena [cheh-nah]
electrical outlet	presa [preh-sah]

elevator	l'ascensore *(m)* [lah-shen-<u>soh</u>-reh]
extension cord	prolunga [proh-<u>loon</u>-ghah]
extra/additional week	settimana supplementare [seh-ttee-<u>mah</u>-nah soo-ppleh-mehn-<u>tah</u>-reh]
fan	il ventilatore [eel vehn-tee-lah-<u>toh</u>-reh]
faucet	rubinetto [roo-bee-<u>neh</u>-ttoh]
full board	la pensione completa [lah pehn-<u>syoh</u>-neh kohm-<u>pleh</u>-tah]
glass	il bicchiere da acqua [eel bee-<u>kyeh</u>-reh <u>dah</u>-kwah]
grilled meat dinner	cena a base di carne alla griglia [<u>cheh</u>-nah ah <u>bah</u>-seh dee <u>kahr</u>-neh <u>ah</u>-llah <u>gree</u>-lyah]
guest house	la pensione [lah pehn-<u>syoh</u>-neh]
half-board plan (breakfast and dinner)	la mezzapensione [lah <u>meh</u>-zah-pehn-<u>syoh</u>-neh]
heating	riscaldamento [ree-skahl-dah-<u>mehn</u>-toh]
hot water	acqua calda [<u>ah</u>-kwah <u>kahl</u>-dah]
key	la chiave [lah <u>kyah</u>-veh]
lamp	lampada [<u>lahm</u>-pah-dah]
lavatory/toilet	gabinetto [ghah-bee-<u>neh</u>-ttoh]
light switch	l'interruttore *(m)* [leen-teh-rroo-<u>ttoh</u>-reh]
linens	biancheria da letto [byah-keh-<u>ree</u>-ah dah <u>leh</u>-ttoh]
lounge	il soggiorno [eel soh-<u>djohr</u>-noh]
lunch	pranzo, il desinare [<u>prahn</u>-tsoh, eel deh-see-<u>nah</u>-reh]
maid/housekeeper	cameriera [kah-meh-<u>ryeh</u>-rah]
mattress	materasso [mah-teh-<u>rah</u>-ssoh]
minibar (in room)	il minibar [eel <u>mee</u>-nee-bahr]

mirror	specchio [speh-kkyoh]
motel	il motel [eel moh-tehl]
off-season/low season	bassa stagione *(f)* [bah-ssah stah-joh-neh]
overnight stay	pernottamento [pehr-noh-ttah-mehn-toh]
peak season	alta stagione *(f)* [ahl-tah stah-joh-neh]
pillow	cuscino [koo-shee-noh]
plug	spina [spee-nah]
pool bar	il bar della piscina [eel bahr deh-llah pee-shee-nah]
porter	il portiere [eel pohr-tyeh-reh]
program of activities	il programma d'animazione [proh-ghrah-mmah dah-nee-mah-tsyoh-neh]
radio	la radio [lah rah-dyoh]
reception	atrio [ah-tryoh]
registration	l'accettazione *(f)* [lah-cheh-ttah-tsyoh-neh]
reservation	la prenotazione [lah preh-noh-tah-tsyoh-neh]
reservation desk	l'accetazione *(f)*, la reception [lah-cheh-ttah-tsyoh-neh lah reh-sehp-shon]
room	camera [kah-meh-rah]
room and board	vitto e alloggio [vee-ttoh eh ah-lloh-djoh]
room telephone	telefono in camera [teh-leh-foh-noh een kah-meh-rah]
safe	la cassaforte [lah kah-ssah-fohr-teh]
sheet	lenzuolo [lehn-zwoh-loh]
shower	doccia [doh-chah]
sink	lavandino [lah-vahn-dee-noh]
story/floor	piano [pyah-noh]
television	il televisore [eel teh-leh-vee-soh-reh]

television room	camera della televisione [kah-meh-rah deh-llah teh-leh-vee-syoh-neh]
terrace/patio	terrazza [teh-rrah-tsah]
toilet paper	carta igienica [kahr-tah ee-jeh-nee-kah]
towel	asciugamano [ah-shoo-ghah-mah-noh]
wastepaper basket	cestino per la carta [cheh-stee-noh pehr lah kahr-tah]
water	acqua [ah-kwah]
window	finestra [fee-neh-strah]

Vacation Rentals: Houses/Apartments

Case/Appartamenti per le vacanze

Are water and electricity included in the price?	L'acqua e la luce sono comprese nel prezzo d'affitto? [lah-kwah eh lah loo-che soh-noh kohm-preh-seh nehl preh-tsoh]
Are pets allowed?	Si possono portare animali? [see poh-ssoh-noh pohr-tah-reh ah-nee-mah-lee]
Where can we pick up the keys to the house/apartment?	Dove possiamo ritirare le chiavi della casa/dell'appartamento? [doh-veh poh-ssyah-moh ree-tee-rah-reh leh kyah-vee deh-llah kah-sah/deh-llah-ppahr-tah-mehn-toh]
Do we have to return them there?	Le dobbiamo anche riconsegnare lì? [leh doh-byah-moh ahn-keh ree-kohn-seh-nyah-reh lee]
Where are the garbage cans?	Dov'è il bidone delle immondizie? [doh-veh eel bee-doh-neh deh-lle ee-mmohn-dee-tsye]
Are we expected to clean it before leaving?	Spetta a noi il lavoro di pulizia finale? [speh-ttah ah noh-ee eel lah-voh-roh dee poo-lee-tsee-ah fee-nah-leh]

Word List: Vacation Rentals: Houses/Apartments

additional costs	le spese (accessorie) [leh speh-seh (ah-cheh-ssoh-ryeh)]
apartment	appartamento [ah-ppahr-tah-mehn-toh]
bedroom	camera da letto [kah-meh-rah dah leh-ttoh]
brochure	opuscolo, il dépliant [oh-poo-skoh-loh, eel deh-plee-ahn]
bunk bed	letto a castello [leh-ttoh ah kah-steh-lloh]
central heating	riscaldamento centrale [ree-skahl-dah-mehn-toh chehn-trah-leh]
charge for electricity	prezzo forfettario per la corrente [preh-tsoh fohr-feh-ttah-ryoh pehr lah koh-rrehn-teh]
coffee machine	macchina del caffè [mah-kkee-nah dehl kah-ffeh]
cottage	il bungalow [eel boon-ghah-lohf]
day of arrival	giorno d'arrivo [johr-noh dah-rree-voh]
dining nook	zona pranzo [zoh-nah prahn-tsoh]
dishtowel	canovaccio per asciugare i piatti [kah-noh-vah-choh pehr ah-sho-ghah-reh ee pyah-ttee]
dishwasher	la lavastoviglie [lah lah-vah-stoh-vee-lych]
electric stove	cucina elettrica [koo-chee-nah eh-leh-ttree-kah]
electrical current	la corrente [lah koh-rrehn-teh]
final cleaning	pulizia finale [poo-lee-tsee-ah fee-nah-leh]
garbage	immondizia [ee-mmohn-dee-tsyah]
gas stove	cucina a gas [koo-chee-nah ah gahs]

homeowner	il padrone di casa [eel pah-<u>droh</u>-neh dee <u>kah</u>-sah]
key check	consegna delle chiavi [kohn-seh-<u>nyah</u> <u>deh</u>-lleh <u>kyah</u>-vee]
kitchenette	cucinino, cucinotto [koo-chee-<u>nee</u>-noh, koo-chee-<u>noh</u>-ttoh]
living room	soggiorno [soh-<u>djohr</u>-noh]
part of the day/night	la parte giorno/notte [lah <u>pahr</u>-teh <u>johr</u>-noh/<u>noh</u>-tteh]
pets	gli animali domestici [lyee ah-nee-<u>mah</u>-lee doh-<u>meh</u>-stee-chee]
refrigerator	frigorifero [free-ghoh-<u>ree</u>-feh-roh]
rent/lease	affitto, noleggio [ah-<u>ffee</u>-ttoh noh-<u>leh</u>-djoh]
to rent/lease	affittare, noleggiare [ah-ffee-<u>ttah</u>-reh noh-leh-<u>djah</u>-reh]
resort	centro vacanze [<u>chehn</u>-troh vah-<u>kahn</u>-tseh]
sofa bed	divano letto [dee-<u>vah</u>-noh <u>leh</u>-ttoh]
stove	cucina economica [koo-<u>chee</u>-nah eh-koh-<u>noh</u>-mee-kah]
studio	studio [<u>stoo</u>-dyoh]
toaster	il tostapane [eel <u>toh</u>-stah-<u>pah</u>-neh]
vacation apartment	appartamento per le vacanze [ah-ppahr-tah-<u>mehn</u>-toh pehr leh vah-<u>kahn</u>-tseh]
vacation home	casa per le vacanze [<u>kah</u>-sah pehr leh vah-<u>kahn</u>-tseh]
voltage	voltaggio [vohl-<u>tah</u>-djoh]
washing machine	la lavatrice [lah lah-vah-<u>tree</u>-cheh]
water use	consumo d'acqua [kohn-<u>soo</u>-moh <u>dah</u>-kwah]

Camping
Campeggio

Is there a campground/ campsite nearby?

C'è un camping nelle vicinanze? [cheh oon kahm-peen neh-lleh vee-chee-nahn-tseh]

Is there still room for another trailer/tent?

C'è ancora posto per una roulotte/una tenda? [cheh ahn-koh-rah poh-stoh pehr oo-nah roo-loht/oo-nah tehn-dah]

How much is it per person a day?

Quanto si paga al giorno a persona? [kwahn-toh see pah-ghah ahl johr-noh]

What's the charge for...

Quanto si paga per... [kwahn-toh see pah-ghah pehr]

a car?

l'auto? [lah-oo-toh]

a camper trailer?

la roulotte/il camper?

a tent?

la tenda? [lah tehn-dah]

Can you rent cabins/trailers?

Si possono affittare bungalows/roulottes? [see poh-ssoh-noh ah-ffee-ttah-reh boon-gah-lohf/roo-loht]

Where can I park my trailer/ pitch my tent?

Dove posso parcheggiare la mia roulotte/piantare la mia tenda? [doh-veh poh-ssoh pahr-keh-djah-reh lah mee-ah roo-loht/pyahn-tah-reh lah mee-ah tehn-dah]

We'll be staying for... days/ weeks.

Rimaniamo... giorni/settimane. [ree-mah-nyah-moh...johr nee/seh ttee-mah-neh]

Is there a grocery store here?

C'è un negozio di alimentari? [cheh oon neh-ghoh-tsyoh dee ah-lee-mehn-tah-ree]

Where are the...

Dove sono... [doh-veh soh-noh]

toilets?`

i servizi igienici? [ee sehr-vee-tsee ee-jeh-nee-chee]

washrooms?

i lavandini? [ee lah-vahn-dee-nee]

showers?

le docce? [leh doh-cheh]

Is there an outlet here?

C'è una presa di corrente? [cheh oo-nah preh-sah dee koh-rrehn-teh]

Is the current 220 or 110 volts?

Qui la corrente è da 220 o da 110 volt? [kwee lah koh-rrehn-teh eh dah dweh-chehn-toh-vehn-tee oh dah chehn-toh-dyeh-chee vohlt]

Where can I exchange/rent gas tanks?

Dove posso cambiare/affittare le bombole di gas? [doh-veh poh-ssoh kahm-byah-reh/ah-ffee-ttah-reh leh bohm-boh-leh ah gahs]

Is the campsite guarded at night?

Il campeggio è sorvegliato la notte? [eel kahm-peh-djoh eh sohr-veh-lyah-toh lah noh-tteh]

Is there a children's playground?

C'è un parco giochi per i bambini? [cheh oon pahr-koh joh-kee pehr ee bahm-bee-nee]

Could you please lend me…?

Per favore, potrebbe prestarmi…? [pehr fah-voh-reh poh-treh-beh preh-stahr-mee]

Youth Hostels
Ostelli per la gioventù

Can I borrow bed linens/a sleeping bag?

Posso affitare la biancheria da letto/un sacco a pelo? [poh-ssoh ah-ffee-ttah-reh lah byah-keh-ree-ah dah leh-ttoh/oon sah-kkoh ah peh-loh]

The front door is locked at midnight.

Il portone d'ingresso viene chiuso alle ore 24. [eel pohr-toh-neh deen-greh-ssoh vyeh-neh kyoo-soh ah-lleh oh-reh vehn-tee-kwah-ttroh]

Word List: Camping/Youth Hostels

to camp	campeggiare [kahm-peh-djah-reh]
camper	il camper [eel kahm-pehr]
camping card	tessera di campeggio [teh-sseh-rah dee kahm-peh-djoh]

camping guide	guida dei campeggi [gwee-dah deh-ee kahm-peh-djee]
camping/campground/ campsite	camping *(m)*, campeggio [kahm-peen, kahm-peh-djoh]
can/canister	tanica, latta [tah-nee-kah, lah-ttah]
children's playing area	parco giochi per bambini [pahr-koh joh-kee pehr bahm-bee-nee]
clothes dryer	l'asciugatrice *(f)* [lah-shoo-ghah-tree chch]
clothes dryer (drying stand)	lo stendibiancheria [loh stehn-dee-byah-keh-ree-ah]
cooker	fornello [fohr-neh-lloh]
current *(el)*	la corrente [lah koh-rrehn-teh]
day room	soggiorno [soh-djohr-noh]
dormitory	casa dello studente, dormitorio [kah-sah deh-lloh stoo-dehn-teh, dohr-mee-toh-ryoh]
drinking water	acqua potabile [ah-kwah poh-tah-bee-leh]
electrical outlet	presa di corrente [preh-sah dee koh-rrehn-teh]
farm	fattoria [fah-ttoh-ree-ah]
gas canister/tank	bombola di gas [bohm-boh-lah dee gahs]
gas cartridge	cartuccia del gas [kahr-too-chah dee gahs]
gas cooker	fornello a gas [fohr-neh-lloh ah gahs]
gas lamp	lampada a petrolio [lahm-pah-dah ah peh-troh-lyoh]
to lend	prestare [preh-stah-reh]
membership card	tessera di socio [teh-sseh-rah dee soh-choh]
outlet	presa [preh-sah]

plug	spina [spee-nah]
propane	propano [proh-pah-noh]
recreation room	sala per le attività ricreative comuni [sah-lah pehr leh ryoo-nyoh-nee]
rental charge	tariffa di noleggio, tassa per l'uso [tah-ree-ffah dee noh-leh-djoh, tah-ssah pehr loo-soh]
reservation	preavviso [preh-ah-vvee-soh]
room with several beds	camera a più letti [kah-meh-rah ah pee-oo leh-ttee]
sink	lavandino per i piatti [lah-vahn-dee-noh pehr ee pyah-ttee]
sleeping bag	sacco a pelo [sah-kkoh ah peh-loh]
tent	tenda [tehn-dah]
tent peg	paletto [pah-leh-ttoh]
tent pole	palo da tenda [pah-loh dah tehn-dah]
tent rope	laccio da tenda [lah-choh dah tehn-dah]
trailer	la roulotte [lah roo-loht]
washroom	stanzino da bagno [stahn-tsee-noh dah bah-nyoh]
water	acqua [ah-kwah]
youth group	gruppo giovanile [ghroo-ppoh joh-vah-nee-leh]
youth hostel	ostello della gioventù [oh-steh-lloh deh-llah joh-vehn-too]
youth hostel card	tessera per gli ostelli della gioventù [teh-sseh-rah pehr lyee oh-steh-llee deh-llah joh-vehn-too]
youth hostel director	il direttore dell'ostello [eel dee-reh-ttoh-reh deh-lloh-steh-lloh]

In Italy you'll find the following types of restaurants:

osteria — A wine tavern, serving primarily local wine. Sometimes you can get a bite to eat as well.

trattoria — An unassuming restaurant where homemade dishes are available, normally at modest prices. Usually these are family-operated establishments. In large cities, however, you have to be careful, because there the term trattoria often conceals an expensive restaurant where the food is not necessarily great. It's best to ask the locals to recommend a place to eat.

ristorante — A full-service restaurant serving a large range of foods. You need to keep in mind that in Italy it is customary to order a complete meal, consisting of a pasta dish, a rice dish, or a soup (the first course, or primo), fish or meat (the second course, or secondo), and fruit or a dessert. If all you want is a plate of spaghetti or the like, it's best to go to a...

tavola calda — Here you will find a variety of warm appetizers, although you usually have to eat them standing up.

bar — A café, in which at all times of the day Italians drink their espresso, macchiato, or aperitif and have a bite to eat, either standing at the counter or sitting at a table. Usually you first have to obtain a scontrino (receipt) from the cashier, and then you will be given your drink at the counter. It is a good idea to keep a supply of change on hand. The prices given in the price list (listino prezzi) apply only to foods and beverages consumed at the counter.

paninoteca — Similar to a bar. Warm and cold open-face sandwiches are available here, as well as nonalcoholic and low-alcohol beverages. This type of establishment is frequented mainly by young people.

Eating Out
Andare a mangiare

Excuse me, could you suggest...	Scusi, mi potrebbe indicare... [skoo-zee mee poh-treh-beh een-dee-kah-reh]
a good restaurant?	un buon ristorante? [oon bwoh ree-stoh-rahn-teh]
a restaurant with local specialties?	un locale tipico/una trattoria? [oon loh-kah-leh tee-pee-koh/oo-nah trah-ttoh-ree-ah]
an inexpensive restaurant?	un ristorante a buon mercato? [oon ree-stoh-rahn-teh ah bwohn mehr-kah-toh]
a fast-food restaurant/ delicatessen?	una tavola calda/rosticceria? [oo-nah tah-voh-lah kahl-dah/roh-stee-cheh-ree-ah]
Where can we go to eat around here and not spend a lot?	Dove si può andare a mangiare qui nelle vicinanze per non spendere molto? [doh-veh see poo-oh ahn-dah-reh ah mahn-jah-reh kwee neh-lleh vee-chee-nahn-tseh pehr nohn spehn-deh-reh mohl-toh]

At the Restaurant
Al ristorante

Would you reserve us a table for four this evening?	Può riservarci per stasera un tavolo per quattro persone? [poo-oh ree-sehr-vahr-chee pehr stah-seh-rah oon tah-voh-loh pehr kwah-ttroh pehr-soh-neh]
Is this table/seat free?	È libero questo tavolo/questo posto? [eh lee-beh-roh kweh-stoh tah-voh-loh]
A table for two/three, please.	Per favore, un tavolo per due/tre persone. [pehr fah-voh-roh, oon tah-voh-loh pehr doo-eh/treh pehr-soh-neh]

Excuse me, where is the restroom?	Mi può dire dov'è la toilette, per favore? [mee poo-<u>oh</u> <u>dee</u>-reh doh-<u>veh</u> lah twah-<u>leht</u> pehr fah-<u>voh</u>-reh]
This way, please.	Per di qui, prego. [pehr dee kwee <u>preh</u>-ghoh]

Ordering
Ordinazione

➤ *See also Chapter 4, Breakfast*

Waiter,…, please.	Cameriere,…, per favore. [kah-meh-<u>ryeh</u>-reh… pehr fah-<u>voh</u>-reh]
the menu	il menù [eel meh-<u>noo</u>]
the beverage list	la lista delle bevande [lah <u>lee</u>-sta <u>deh</u>-lleh beh-<u>vahn</u>-deh]
the wine list	la lista dei vini [lah <u>lee</u>-stah <u>deh</u>-ee <u>vee</u>-nee]
What do you recommend?	Che cosa mi consiglia? [keh <u>koh</u>-sah mee kohn-<u>see</u>-lyah]
Do you have vegetarian/dietary dishes?	Avete pietanze vegetariane/cibo dietetico? [ah-<u>veh</u>-teh pyeh-<u>tahn</u>-tseh veh-jeh-tah-<u>ryah</u>-neh/<u>chee</u>-boh dyeh-<u>teh</u>-tee-koh]
Can I order half portions for the children?	Si può avere la mezza porzione per i bambini? [see poo-<u>oh</u> ah-<u>veh</u>-reh lah <u>meh</u>-zah pohr-<u>tsyoh</u>-neh pehr ee bahm-<u>bee</u>-nee]
Have you decided?	Ha già scelto? [ah jah <u>shehl</u>-toh]
What would you like as an appetizer/for dessert?	Che cosa prende per antipasto/dessert? [keh <u>koh</u>-sah <u>prehn</u>-deh pehr ahn-tee-<u>pah</u>-stoh/deh-<u>ssehrt</u>]
I'll have…	Prendo… [<u>prehn</u>-doh]
For an appetizer/main dish/dessert I'll have…	Per antipasto/secondo/dessert prendo… [pehr ahn-tee-<u>pah</u>-stoh/seh-kohn-doh/deh-<u>ssehrt</u> <u>prehn</u>-doh]

I'm not having an appetizer, thank you.

L'antipasto non lo prendo, grazie. [lahn-tee-pah-stoh nohn loh prehn-doh ghrah-tsye]

I'm afraid we're out of...

Purtroppo il/la... è finito. [poor-troh-ppoh eel/lah...eh fee-nee-toh]

This dish must be ordered in advance.

Questa pietanza la serviamo solo su ordinazione. [kweh-stah pyeh-tahn-tsah lah sehr-vyah-moh soh-loh soo ohr-dee-nah-tsyoh-neh]

May I have... instead of...?

Al posto di... protrei avere...? [ahl poh-stoh dee... poh-treh-ee ah-veh-reh]

I don't like..., can you make the dish without...?

Non sopporto..., può preparare la pietanza senza...? [nohn soh-ppohr-toh..., poo-oh preh-pah-rah-reh lah pyeh-tahn-tsah sehn-tsah]

How do you like your meat?

Come vuole la carne? [koh-meh vwoh-leh lah kahr-neh]

well-done

ben cotta [behn koh-ttah]

medium

non troppo cotta [nohn troh-ppoh behn koh-ttah]

rare

all'inglese/al sangue [ah-lleen-ghleh-seh/ahl sahn-gweh]

What would you like to drink?

Che cosa desidera da bere? [keh koh-sah deh-see-deh-rah dah beh-reh]

A glass of..., please.

Per favore, un bicchiere di... [pehr fah-voh-reh oon bee-kkyeh-reh dee]

A (half) bottle of..., please.

Per favore, una (mezza) bottiglia di... [pehr fah-voh-reh oonah (meh-zah) boh-ttee-lyah dee]

With ice, please.

Con ghiaccio, per favore. [kohn ghyah-choh pehr fah-voh-reh]

Cheers!

Buon appetito! [bwohn ah-ppeh-tee-toh]

Would you like anything else?

Desidera altro? [deh-see-deh-rah ahl-troh]

Please bring us…	Ci porti, per favore… [chee pohr-tee pehr fah-<u>voh</u>-reh]
Could we please have some more bread/water/wine?	Ci può portare un altro po' di pane/d'acqua/di vino? [chee poo-oh pohr-<u>tah</u>-reh oon <u>ahl</u>-troh poh dee <u>pah</u>-neh/<u>dah</u>-kwah/dee <u>vee</u>-noh]

Complaints
Reclami

We need another…	Manca… [<u>mahn</u>-kah]
Did you forget my…?	Ha dimenticato il mio/la mia…? [ha dee-mehn-tee-<u>kah</u>-toh eel <u>mee</u>-oh/lah <u>mee</u>-ah]
I didn't order this.	Non ho ordinato questo. [nohn oh ohr-dee-<u>nah</u>-toh <u>kweh</u>-stoh]
The food is cold/too salty.	Il mangiare è freddo/troppo salato. [eel mahn-<u>jah</u>-reh eh <u>troh</u>-ppoh sah-<u>lah</u>-toh]
The meat is tough/too fatty.	La carne è dura/troppo grassa. [lah <u>kahr</u>-neh eh <u>doo</u>-rah/<u>troh</u>-ppoh <u>ghrah</u>-ssah]
The fish isn't fresh.	Il pesce non è fresco. [eel <u>peh</u>-sheh eh <u>freh</u>-skoh]
Take it back, please.	Lo porti indietro, per favore. [loh <u>pohr</u>-tee een-<u>dyeh</u>-troh pehr fah-<u>voh</u>-reh]
Please call the manager.	Mi chiami per favore il direttore/il proprietario! [mee <u>kyah</u>-mee pehr fah-<u>voh</u>-reh eel dee-reh-<u>ttoh</u>-reh/eel proh-pryeh-<u>tah</u>-ryoh]

The Check
Il conto

The check, please.	Il conto, per favore. [eel <u>kohn</u>-toh pehr fah-<u>voh</u>-reh]
We're in rather a hurry.	Abbiamo piuttosto fretta. [ah-<u>byah</u>-moh pyoo-<u>ttoh</u>-stoh <u>freh</u>-ttah]

All together.	Tutto insieme. [too-ttoh eon syeh-meh]
Separate checks, please.	Conti separati, per favore. [kohn-tee seh-pah-rah-tee pehr fah-voh-reh]
Is service included?	Il servizio/Il coperto è compreso? [eel sehr-vee-tsyoh/eel koh-pehr-toh eh kohm-preh-soh]

*On menus, a fixed charge for the **coperto** (cover) is usually stated. This amount is always included in your check, and is not affected by the size of your order. For the rolls and **grissini** that are on the table at every Italian meal, however, there is no charge.*

The check doesn't look right.	Il conto non mi pare esatto. [eel kohn-toh nohn mee pah-reh eh-sah-ttoh]
I didn't have this. I had...	Non ho mangiato questo. Ho mangiato... [nohn oh mahn-jah-toh kweh-stoh. oh mahn-jah-toh]
Did you enjoy your meal?	Era di Suo gradimento? [eh-rah dee soo-oh ghrah-dee-mehn-toh]

The food was excellent.	Il mangiare era eccellente. [eel mahn-<u>jah</u>-reh <u>eh</u>-rah eh-cheh-<u>lleh</u>n-teh]
That's for you.	Questo è per Lei. [<u>kweh</u>-stoh eh pehr <u>leh</u>-ee]
The rest is for you.	Il resto è per Lei. [eel <u>reh</u>-stoh eh pehr <u>leh</u>-ee]

As a Dinner Guest

Invito a pranzo o a cena/Mangiare in compagnia

Thank you very much for the invitation!	Mille grazie per l'invito! [mee-lleh <u>ghrah</u>-tsyeh pehr leen-<u>vee</u>-toh]
Help yourself!	Si serva pure! [see <u>sehr</u>-vah <u>poo</u>-reh]
Cheers!	Alla Sua salute! [<u>ah</u>-llah <u>soo</u>-ah sah-<u>loo</u>-teh]
Could you please pass me…?	Per favore, mi può passare…? [pehr fah-<u>voh</u>-reh mee poo-<u>oh</u> pah-<u>ssah</u>-reh]
Would you like some more…?	Un altro po' di…? [oon <u>ahl</u>-troh poh dee]
No, thank you. That was plenty!	Grazie, era sufficiente! [<u>grah</u>-tsye <u>eh</u>-rah soo-ffee-<u>chehn</u>-teh]
I'm full, thank you.	Sono sazio, grazie. [<u>soh</u>-noh sah-tsyoh <u>grah</u>-tsyeh]
May I smoke?	Posso fumare? [<u>poh</u>-ssoh foo-<u>mah</u>-reh]

Word List: Eating and Drinking ➤ See also Chapter 8, Word List: Groceries

appetizer	antipasto [ahn-tee-<u>pah</u>-stoh]
ashtray	il portacenere [eel pohr-tah-<u>cheh</u>-neh-reh]
bake	passare al forno, gratinare [pah-<u>ssah</u>-reh ahl <u>fohr</u>-noh, grah-tee-<u>nah</u>-reh]

bar	il bar [eel bahr]
bay leaf	alloro [ah-<u>lloh</u>-roh]
to be hungry	aver fame [ah-<u>vehr</u> <u>fah</u>-meh]
beef	la carne di manzo [lah <u>kahr</u>-neh dee <u>mahn</u>-zoh]
beer	birra [<u>bee</u>-rrah]
bitter	agro [<u>ah</u>-groh]
boiled/cooked	bollito, cotto [boh-<u>llee</u>-toh, <u>koh</u>-ttoh]
bone	osso [<u>oh</u>-ssoh]
bottle opener	l'apribottiglie *(m)* [lah-pree-boh-<u>ttee</u>-lyeh]
braised	brasato [brah-<u>zah</u>-toh]
bread	il pane [eel <u>pah</u>-neh]
breakfast	prima colazione [<u>pree</u>-mah koh-lah-<u>tsyoh</u>-neh]
butter	burro [<u>boo</u>-rroh]
carafe	caraffa [kah-<u>rah</u>-ffah]
chicken	pollo [<u>poh</u>-lloh]
cloves	i chiodi di garofani [ee <u>kyoh</u>-dee dee ghah-<u>roh</u>-fah-noh]
coffeepot	caffettiera [kah-ffeh-<u>ttyeh</u>-rah]
cold	freddo [<u>freh</u>-ddoh]
cook	cuoco/cuoca [<u>kwoh</u>-koh/<u>kwoh</u>-kah]
to cook	cuocere [<u>kwoh</u>-cheh-reh]
cooked/done	cotto [<u>koh</u>-ttoh]
corkscrew	il cavatappi [eel kah-vah-<u>tah</u>-ppee]
course	portata [pohr-<u>tah</u>-tah]
cover charge	coperto [koh-<u>pehr</u>-toh]
cumin	cumino [koo-<u>mee</u>-noh]
cup	tazza [<u>tah</u>-tsah]
cutlery	le posate [leh poh-<u>sah</u>-teh]

dessert	il dessert, il dolce [eel deh-<u>ssehr</u>, eel <u>dohl</u>-cheh]
diabetic	diab<u>e</u>tico [dyah-<u>beh</u>-tee-koh]
dietary meal	cibo diet<u>e</u>tico [<u>chee</u>-boh dyeh-<u>teh</u>-tee-koh]
dinner	cena [<u>cheh</u>-nah]
dish	piet<u>a</u>nza, pi<u>a</u>tto [pyeh-<u>tahn</u>-tsah, <u>pyah</u>-ttoh]
dish of the day	pi<u>a</u>tto del giorno [<u>pyah</u>-ttoh dehl <u>johr</u>-noh]
draft beer	birra alla spina [<u>bee</u>-rrah <u>ah</u>-llah <u>spee</u>-nah]
to dress (*salad*)	condire [kohn-<u>dee</u>-reh]
dressing	condimento per l'insalata [kohn-dee-<u>mehn</u>-toh pehr leen-sah-<u>lah</u>-tah]
drink	bevanda [beh-<u>vahn</u>-dah]
dry (*wine*)	(vino) secco [(<u>vee</u>-noh) <u>seh</u>-kkoh]
eggcup	il portau<u>o</u>va [eel pohr-tah-<u>woh</u>-vah]
fat	grasso [<u>grah</u>-ssoh]
fish	il pesce [eel <u>peh</u>-sheh]
fishbone	spina, lisca [<u>spee</u>-nah, <u>lee</u>-skah]
flavor	il sapore [eel sah-<u>poh</u>-reh]
fork	forchetta [fohr-<u>keh</u>-ttah]
french fries	le patate fritte [leh pah-<u>tah</u>-teh <u>free</u>-tteh]
fresh	fresco [<u>freh</u>-skoh]
fried	fritto, al tegame [<u>free</u>-ttoh, ahl teh-<u>ghah</u>-meh]
garlic	aglio [<u>ah</u>-lyoh]
glass	il bicchiere [eel bee-<u>kkyeh</u>-reh]
grilled	alla griglia [<u>ah</u>-llah <u>gree</u>-lyah]
grilled/roasted	griglia, grat<u>i</u>cola [<u>gree</u>-lyah, grah-<u>tee</u>-koh-lah]

half-portion	la mezza porzione [lah <u>meh</u>-zah pohr-<u>tsyoh</u>-neh]
hard, tough *(meat)*	duro [<u>doo</u>-roh]
herbs	le erbe [leh <u>ehr</u>-beh]
homemade	fatto in casa [<u>fah</u>-ttoh een <u>kah</u>-sah]
hot	caldo, bollente [<u>kahl</u>-doh boh-<u>llehn</u>-teh]
juicy	succoso [soo-<u>kkoh</u>-soh]
knife	coltello [kohl-<u>teh</u>-lloh]
lean	magro [<u>mah</u>-groh]
lemon	il limone [eel lee-<u>moh</u>-neh]
lunch	pranzo, il desinare [<u>prahn</u>-tsoh, deh-see-<u>nah</u>-reh]
main course	secondo (piatto) [seh-<u>kohn</u>-doh (<u>pyah</u>-ttoh)]
mayonnaise	la maionese [lah mah-yoh-<u>neh</u>-seh]
meat	la carne [lah <u>kahr</u>-neh]
menu	lista delle vivande, il menù [<u>lee</u>-stah deh-lleh vee-<u>vahn</u>-deh, eel meh-<u>noo</u>]
menu of the day	il menù del giorno [eel meh-<u>noo</u> dehl <u>johr</u>-noh]
mustard	la senape [lah <u>seh</u>-nah-peh]
napkin	tovagliolo [toh-vah-<u>lyoh</u>-loh]
nonalcoholic	analcolico [ah-nahl-<u>koh</u>-lee-koh]
nutmeg	la noce moscata [lah <u>noh</u>-che moh-<u>skah</u>-tah]
oil	olio [<u>oh</u>-lyoh]
olive oil	olio d'oliva [<u>oh</u>-lyoh doh-<u>lee</u>-vah]
olives	le olive [leh oh-<u>lee</u>-veh]
onion	cipolla [chee-<u>poh</u>-llah]
order	l'ordinazione *(f)* [lohr-dee-nah-<u>tsyoh</u>-neh]

to order	ordinare [ohr-dee-<u>nah</u>-reh]
parsley	prezz<u>e</u>molo [preh-<u>tseh</u>-moh-loh]
pasta	la pasta [lah <u>pah</u>-stah]
pepper *(spice)*	il pepe [eel <u>peh</u>-peh]
pepper *(vegetable)*	il peperone [eel peh-peh-<u>roh</u>-neh]
paprika	p<u>a</u>prica [<u>pah</u>-pree-kah]
pepper mill	pepar<u>o</u>la, pepai<u>o</u>la [peh-pah-<u>roh</u>-lah, peh-pah-<u>yoh</u>-lah]

plate	piatto [<u>pyah</u>-ttoh]
pork	la carne di maiale [lah <u>kahr</u>-neh dee mah-<u>yah</u>-leh]
portion	la porzione [lah pohr-<u>tsyoh</u>-neh]
potatoes	le patate [leh pah-<u>tah</u>-teh]
raw	crudo [<u>kroo</u>-doh]
rice	riso [<u>ree</u>-soh]
roasted	arrostito [ah-rroh-<u>stee</u>-toh]
salad	insalata [een-sah-<u>lah</u>-tah]
salad bar	il buffet delle insalate [el boo-<u>ffeh</u> <u>deh</u>-lleh een-sah-<u>lah</u>-teh]
salad bowl, tureen	terrina, insalati<u>e</u>ra [teh-<u>rree</u>-nah, een-sah-lah-<u>tyeh</u>-rah]
salt	il sale [eel <u>sah</u>-leh]
salted	salato [sah-<u>lah</u>-toh]
salt shaker	saliera [sah-<u>lyeh</u>-rah]
sauce	salsa [<u>sahl</u>-sah]
saucer	piattino [pyah-<u>ttee</u>-noh]
to season	condire [kohn-<u>dee</u>-reh]
seasonings/spices	le sp<u>e</u>zie [leh <u>speh</u>-tsyeh]
to serve/help yourself	servirsi [sehr-<u>veer</u>-see]
side dish	contorno [kohn-<u>tohr</u>-noh]
slice	fetta [<u>feh</u>-ttah]

smoked	affumicato [ah-ffoo-mee-<u>kah</u>-toh]
soft-boiled	tenero, morbido [<u>teh</u>-neh-roh, <u>mohr</u>-bee-doh]
soup bowl	piatto fondo, scodella [<u>pyah</u>-ttoh fohn-doh, skoh-<u>doh</u>-llah]
specialty	specialità [speh-chah-lee-<u>tah</u>]
spicy	piccante [pee-<u>kkahn</u>-teh]
spit-roasted	allo spiedo [<u>ah</u>-lloh <u>spyeh</u>-doh]
spoon	cucchiaio [koo-<u>kkyah</u>-yoh]
stain	macchia [<u>mah</u>-kkyah]
stain remover	lo smacchiatore [loh smah-kkyah-<u>toh</u>-reh]
steamed	cotto a vapore [<u>koh</u>-ttoh ahl vah-<u>poh</u>-reh]
stewed	stufato [stoo-<u>fah</u>-toh]
straw	cannuccia [kah-<u>nnoo</u>-chah]
stuffed	ripieno [ree-<u>pyeh</u>-noh]
sugar	zucchero [<u>zoo</u>-kkeh-roh]
sweet	dolce [<u>dohl</u>-cheh]
sweetener	dolcificante [leh-dool-koh-<u>rahn</u>-teh, (soh-<u>stahn</u>-tsah) dohl-chee-fee-<u>kahn</u>-teh]
tablecloth	tovaglia [toh-<u>vah</u>-lyah]
to taste	assaggiare [ah-ssah-<u>djah</u>-reh]
tasteless	insipido [een-<u>see</u>-pee-doh]
teapot	teiera [teh-yeh-rah]
teaspoon	cucchiaino [koo-kkyah-<u>ee</u>-noh]
tender	tenero [<u>teh</u>-neh-roh]
tip	mancia [<u>mahn</u>-chah]
toasted/roasted	tostato, arrostito [toh-<u>stah</u>-toh, ah-rroh-<u>stee</u>-toh]
toothpick	lo stuzzicadenti [loh stoo-tsee-kah-<u>dehn</u>-tee]

tough	duro [<u>doo</u>-roh]
to uncork	stappare [stah-<u>ppah</u>-reh]
veal	la carne di vitello [lah <u>kahr</u>-neh dee vee-<u>teh</u>-lloh]
vegetarian	vegetariano [veh-jeh-tah-<u>ryah</u>-noh]
vinegar	aceto [ah-<u>cheh</u>-toh]
waiter	il cameriere/la cameriera [eel kah-meh-<u>ryeh</u>-reh/lah kah-meh-<u>ryeh</u>-rah]

water	acqua [<u>ah</u>-kwah]
water glass	il bicchiere da acqua [eel bee-<u>kkyeh</u>-reh dah <u>ah</u>-kwah]
well-done	ben cotto [behn <u>koh</u>-ttoh]
wine	vino [<u>vee</u>-noh]
wineglass	il bicchiere da vino [eel bee-kkyeh-reh dah <u>vee</u>-noh]

Menu

Menù

Appetizers/Hors d'oeuvres	**Antipasti**

anchovies — acciughe [ah-<u>choo</u>-gheh]

cold cuts — affettato misto [ah-ffeh-<u>ttah</u>-toh <u>mee</u>-stoh]

cooked ham — prosciutto cotto [proh-<u>shoo</u>-ttoh <u>koh</u>-ttoh]

lobster — aragosta [ah-rah-<u>ghoh</u>-stah]

marinated artichokes — carciofini sott'olio [kahr-choh-<u>fee</u>-nee soh-<u>ttoh</u>-lyoh]

marinated mushrooms — funghi sott'olio [<u>foon</u>-ghee soh-<u>ttoh</u>-lyoh]

melon with prosciutto (cured ham) — melone e prosciutto [meh-<u>loh</u>-neh eh proh-<u>shoo</u>-ttoh]

prosciutto with fresh figs — prosciutto con fichi freschi [proh-<u>shoo</u>-ttoh kohn <u>fee</u>-kee <u>freh</u>-skee]

raw cured ham — prosciutto crudo [proh-<u>shoo</u>-ttoh <u>kroo</u>-doh]

shrimps — gamberi [<u>ghahrn</u>-beh-ree]

smoked eel — anguilla affumicata [ahn-<u>gwee</u>-llah ah-ffoo-mee-kah-tah]

tuna with beans — tonno con fagioli [<u>toh</u>-nnoh kohn fah-<u>joh</u>-lee]

Soups

Minestre

chicken or beef soup in broth with egg

stracciatella [strah-chah-<u>teh</u>-llah]

fish soup

zuppa di pesce [<u>zoo</u>-ppah dee <u>peh</u>-sheh]

pasta and bean soup

pasta e fagioli [<u>pah</u>-stah eh fah-<u>joh</u>-lee]

pasta in broth

pastina in brodo [pah-<u>stee</u>-nah een <u>broh</u>-doh]

rice soup

minestra di riso [mee-<u>neh</u>-strah dee <u>ree</u>-soh]

thick vegetable soup

minestrone [mee-neh-<u>stroh</u>-neh]

vegetable soup

minestra di verdure [mee-<u>neh</u>-strah dee vehr-<u>doo</u>-reh]

Main Dishes

Primi Piatti

cooked cornmeal mush served with melted cheese

polenta (alla valdostana) [poh-<u>lehn</u>-tah (<u>ah</u>-llah vahl-doh-<u>stah</u>-sauce nah)]

flat noodles

fettuccine/tagliatelle [feh-ttoo-<u>chee</u>-neh/ tah-lyah-<u>teh</u>-lleh]

flat pasta with meat filling

lasagne al forno [lah-<u>sah</u>-nyeh ahl <u>fohr</u>-noh]

green flat noodles

lasagne verdi [lah-sah-nyeh <u>vehr</u>-dee]

macaroni

maccheroni [mah-kkeh-<u>roh</u>-nee]

meat-filled tubular noodle, baked

cannelloni [kah-nneh-<u>lloh</u>-nee]

potato dumplings	gnocchi alla romana [nyoh-kkee ah-llah roh-mah-nah]
rice dish with mushrooms	risotto con funghi [ree-soh-ttoh kohn foon-ghee]
rice dish with saffron	risotto alla milanese [ree-soh-ttoh ah-llah mee-lah-neh-seh]
spaghetti	spaghetti [spah-gheh-ttee]

with butter	—al burro/in bianco [ahl boo-rroh/ een byahn-koh]
with clams	—alle vongole [ah-lleh vohn-ghoh-leh]
with cream	—alla panna [ah-llah pah-nnah]
with egg, bacon, oil, garlic, and cheese	—alla carbonara [ah-llah kahr-boh-nah-rah]
with meat and tomato sauce	—alla bolognese/al ragù [ah-llah boh-loh-nyeh-seh/ ahl rah-ghoo]
with tomato sauce	—alla napoletana/ al pomodoro [ah-llah nah-poh-leh-tah-nah/ahl poh-moh-doh-roh]
with tomatoes, olives, and spices	—alla puttanesca [ah-llah poo-ttah-neh-skah]
stuffed pasta	agnolotti/ravioli/ tortellini [ah-nyoh-loh-ttee/ rah-vyoh-lee/tohr-teh-llee-nee]
thin noodles	vermicelli [vehr-mee-cheh-llee]

Meats	Carni
beef	manzo/bue [mahn-zoh boo-eh]
beef stew	stufato [stoo-fah-toh]
boiled meats in rich broth	bollito misto [boh-llee-toh mee-stoh]
breaded veal cutlet	cotoletta alla milanese [koh-toh-leh-ttah ah-llah mee-lah-neh-seh]
calf's brains	cervello [chehr-veh-lloh]
chicken	pollo [poh-lloh]
chicken breast	petti di pollo [peh-ttee dee poh-loh]
duck	anatra [ah-nah-trah]
goat	capretto [kah-preh-ttoh]
goose	oca [oh-kah]
grilled meat	bistecca ai ferri [bee-steh-kkah ah-ee feh-rree]
hamburger	polpette (svizzere) [pohl-peh-tteh (svee-tseh-reh)]
hare	lepre [leh-preh]
kidney	rognoni [roh-nyoh-nee]
lamb	agnello [ah-nyeh-lloh]
liver	fegato [feh-ghah-toh]
mutton	montone [mohn-toh-neh]
pigeon	piccione [pee-choh-neh]
pork	maiale [mah-yah-leh]
pork chop	cotoletta di maiale [koh-toh-leh-ttah dee mah-yah-leh]
rabbit	coniglio [koh-nee-lyoh]
roast chicken	pollo arrosto [poh-lloh ah-rroh-stoh]

roast veal	arrosto di vitello [ah-rroh-stoh dee vee-<u>teh</u>-lloh]
sausage (pig's foot)	zampone [zahm-<u>poh</u>-neh]
small veal cutlets	scaloppine di vitello [skuh-loh-<u>ppee</u>-neh dee vee-<u>teh</u>-lloh]
stew with tomato	spezzatino [speh-tsah-<u>tee</u>-noh]
tongue	lingua [<u>leen</u>-gwah]
tripe	trippa [<u>tree</u>-ppah]
turkey	tacchino [tah-<u>kkee</u>-noh]
veal	vitello [vee-<u>teh</u>-lloh]
veal chop/cutlet	fesa di vitello [<u>feh</u>-sah dee vee-<u>teh</u>-lloh]
veal cutlet with ham and sage	saltimbocca alla romana [sahl-teem-<u>boh</u>-kkah <u>ah</u>-llah roh-<u>mah</u>-nah]
veal shank braised in white wine and tomato sauce	ossobuco [<u>oh</u>-ssoh <u>boo</u>-koh]
veal tenderloin	lombata di vitello [lohm-<u>bah</u>-tah dee vee-<u>teh</u>-lloh]

Fish

Pesce

eel	anguilla [ahn-<u>gwee</u>-llah]
fried fish	fritto di pesce [<u>free</u>-ttoh dee <u>peh</u>-sheh]
fried shrimp	scampi fritti [<u>skahm</u>-pee <u>free</u>-ttee]
mackerel	sgombro [<u>sghohm</u>-broh]
mussels/clams	cozze/vongole [<u>koh</u>-tseh/<u>vohn</u>-ghoh-leh]
prawn	gambero [<u>ghahm</u>-beh-roh]
razor clams	datteri di mare [<u>dah</u>-tteh-ree dee mah-reh]

red mullet	triglia [tree-lyah]
salmon	salmone [sahl-moh-neh]
seafood	frutti di mare [froo-ttee dee mah-reh]
sole	sogliola [soh-lyoh-lah]
spiny lobster	aragosta [ah-rah-ghoh-stah]
squid	calamari [kah-lah-mah-ree]
swordfish	pesce spada [peh-sheh spah-dah]
trout	trota [troh-ah]
tuna	tonno [toh-nnoh]

Vegetables and Side Dishes

Verdura e Contorni

artichokes	carciofi [kahr-choh-fee]
asparagus	asparagi [ah-spah-rah-jee]
broccoli	broccoli [broh-kkoh-lee]
carrot	carote [kah-roh-teh]
cauliflower	cavolfiore [kah-vohl-fyoh-reh]
celery	sedano [seh-dah-noh]
chicory	cicoria [chee-koh-ryah]
eggplant	melanzane [meh-lahn-zah-neh]
fennel	finocchi [fee-noh-kkee]
french fries	patatine fritte [pah-tah-tee-neh free-tteh]
green beans	fagiolini [fah-joh-lee-nee]
greens	bietola [byeh-toh-lah]

lentils	lenticchie [lehn-<u>tee</u>-kkyeh]
mashed potatoes	purè di patate [poo-<u>reh</u> dee pah-<u>tah</u>-teh]
mushrooms	funghi [<u>foon</u>-ghee]
peas	piselli [pee-<u>seh</u>-llee]
pepper (spicy)	peperoni [peh-peh-<u>roh</u>-nee]
potatoes	patate [pah-<u>tah</u>-teh]
radishes	ravanelli [rah-vah-<u>neh</u>-llee]
spinach	spinaci [spee-<u>nah</u>-chee]
tomatoes	pomodori [poh-moh-<u>doh</u>-ree]
white beans	fagioli [fah-<u>joh</u>-lee]
zucchini squash	zucchini [zoo-<u>kkee</u>-nee]

Salads   Insalate

green salad	insalata verde [een-sah-<u>lah</u>-tah <u>vehr</u>-deh]
mixed cooked vegetables with mayonnaise	insalata russa [een-sah-<u>lah</u>-tah <u>roo</u>-ssah]
mixed salad	insalata mista [een-sah-<u>lah</u>-tah <u>mee</u>-stah]
red lettuce	radicchio [rah-<u>dee</u>-kkyoh]

Eggs

Uova

fried egg

uova al tegame [woh-vah ahl teh-ghah-meh]

hard-boiled egg

uovo sode [woh-vah soh-deh]

omelet

frittata [free-ttah-tah]

scrambled eggs

uova strapazzate [woh-vah strah-pah-tsah-teh]

Cheese

Formaggi

cottage cheese

ricotta [ree-koh-ttah]

fresh buffalo milk cheese

mozzarella [moh-tsah-reh-llah]

mild soft cheese

stracchino [strah-kkee-noh]

mild white cheese

bel paese [behl pah-eh-seh]

parmesan cheese

parmigiano/grana [pahr-mee-jah-noh/ grah-nah]

sharp cheese

provolone (affumicato) [proh-voh-loh-neh (ah-ffoo-mee-kah-toh)]

sheep's milk cheese

pecorino [peh-koh-ree-noh]

Swiss cheese

groviera [groh-vyeh-rah]

Desserts and Fruit Dolci e Frutta

apple	mela [meh-lah]
apricot	albicocca [ahl-bee-koh-kkah]
caramel pudding	creme caramel [krehm kah-rah-mehl]
cherries	ciliegie [chee-lyeh-jch]
egg custard with Marsala wine	zabaione [zah-bah-yoh-neh]
figs	fichi [fee-kee]
fruit compote	frutta cotta [froo-ttah koh-ttah]
fruit salad	macedonia [mah-cheh-doh-nyah]
grapefruit	pompelmo [pom-pehl-moh]
grapes	uva [oo-vah]
honeydew melon	melone [meh-loh-nch]
ice cream with candied fruits	cassata [kah-ssah-tah]
orange	arancia [ah-rahn-chah]
peach	pesca [peh-skah]
pear	pera [peh-rah]
pineapple	ananas [ah-nah-nahs]
plum	prugna/susina [proo-nyah/soo-see-nah]
pudding	budino, lamponi [boo-dee-noh, lahm-poh-nee]
raspberries	mirtilli rossi [meer-tee-llee roh-ssee]
rich cake with cheese and rum	tiramisu [tee-rah-mee-soo]

strawberries	fragole [frah-ghoh-leh]
trifle	zuppa inglese [zoo-ppah een-gleh-seh]
watermelon	cocomero/anguria [koh-koh-meh-roh/ahn-ghoo-ryah]

Ice Cream
Gelati

apricot	albicocca [ahl-bee-koh-kkah]
chocolate	cioccolata [choh-kkoh-lah-tah]
cup of ice cream with cream	coppa con panna [koh-ppah kohn pah-nnah]
cup with assorted flavors	coppa assortita [koh-ppah ah-ssohr-tee-tah]
hazelnut	nocciola [noh-choh-lah]
lemon	limone [lee-moh-neh]
raspberry	mirtilli [meer-tee-llee]
strawberry	fragola [frah-ghoh-lah]
vanilla cream	fior di latte [fyohr dee lah-tteh]
vanilla flavors	vaniglia/crema [vah-nee-lyah/kreh-mah]
vanilla ice cream in chocolate shell	tartufo [tahr-too-foh]

Beverages	Lista delle Bevande
Wine	**Vini**
dry, light-bodied red	Bardolino [bahr-doh-<u>lee</u>-noh]
dry, light-bodied red	Valpolicella [vahl-poh-lee-<u>cheh</u>-llah]
dry, light-bodied white	Frascati [frah-<u>skah</u>-tee]
dry, light-bodied white (Latium)	Marino [mah-<u>ree</u>-noh]
dry, medium-bodied (Piedmont)	Grignolino [gree-nyoh-<u>lee</u>-noh]
dry, medium-bodied red (Tuscany)	Chianti [<u>kyahn</u>-tee]
dry, medium-bodied white (Umbria)	Orvieto [ohr-<u>vyeh</u>-toh]
nutmeg-flavored red dessert	Moscato [moh-<u>skah</u>-toh]
wine (Tuscan)	Ruffino [roo-ffee-noh]
robust red (Piedmont)	Barbera [bahr-<u>beh</u>-rah]
semidry red (Emilia Romagna)	Lambrusco [lahm-<u>broo</u>-skoh]
slightly sweet, medium-bodied red	Làcrima Christi [<u>lah</u>-kree-mah <u>kree</u>-stee]
sparkling wine (Piedmont)	Asti spumante [<u>ah</u>-stee spoo-<u>mahn</u>-teh]
sweet dessert wine (Sicily)	Marsala [mahr-<u>sah</u>-lah]
sweet red Tuscan wine	Aleatico [ah-leh-<u>ah</u>-tee-koh]

Beer	Birra
dark/light beer	birra scura/chiara [bee-rrah kyah-rah/skoo-rah]
draft beer	birra alla spina [bee-rah ah-llah spee-nah]
malt beer with low alcoholic content	birra al malto [bee-rrah ahl mahl-toh]
strong malt beer	birra forte [bee-rrah fohr-teh]

Nonalcoholic Beverages

Bevande Analcoliche

apple juice	succo di mele [soo-kkoh dee meh-leh]
black cherry soft drink	amarena [ah-mah-reh-nah]
fruit juice	succo di frutta [soo-kkoh dee froo-ttah]
grape juice	succo d'uva [soo-kkoh doo-vah]
lemonade (fresh)	spremuta di limone [spreh-moo-tah ahl lee-mohn-neh]
mineral water	acqua minerale [ah-kwah mee-neh-rah-leh]
orangeade	aranciata [ah-rahn-chah-tah]
seltzer	acqua di seltz [ah-kwah dee sehltz]
sparkling water	gassosa [ghah-ssoh-sah]
tomato juice	succo di pomodoro [soo-kkoh dee poh-moh-doh-roh]

Coffee and Tea	Caffetteria
cake	torta [<u>tohr</u>-tah]
camomile tea	camomilla [kah-moh-<u>mee</u>-llah]
espresso with frothed milk	cappuccino [kah-ppoo-<u>chee</u>-noh]
hot chocolate with cream	cioccolata con panna [choh-kkoh-<u>lah</u>-tah kohn <u>pah</u>-nnah]
small pastry	pasta [<u>pah</u>-stah]
strong black coffee with some milk	caffè macchiato [kah-<u>ffeh</u> mah-<u>kkyah</u>-toh]
strong black coffee without milk	caffè, espresso [kah-<u>ffeh</u>, eh-<u>spreh</u>-ssoh]
tea with milk/lemon	tè al latte/limone [teh ahl <u>lah</u>-tteh/lee-<u>moh</u>-neh]

Liqueurs/After Dinner Drinks

Liquori

bitters	amaro [ah-<u>mah</u>-roh]
Italian cognac	Vecchia Romagna [<u>veh</u>-kkyah roh-<u>mah</u>-nyah]
anisette liqueur	sambuca [sahm-<u>boo</u>-kah]
strong liqueur made from mashed grape skins	grappa [<u>grah</u>-ppah]

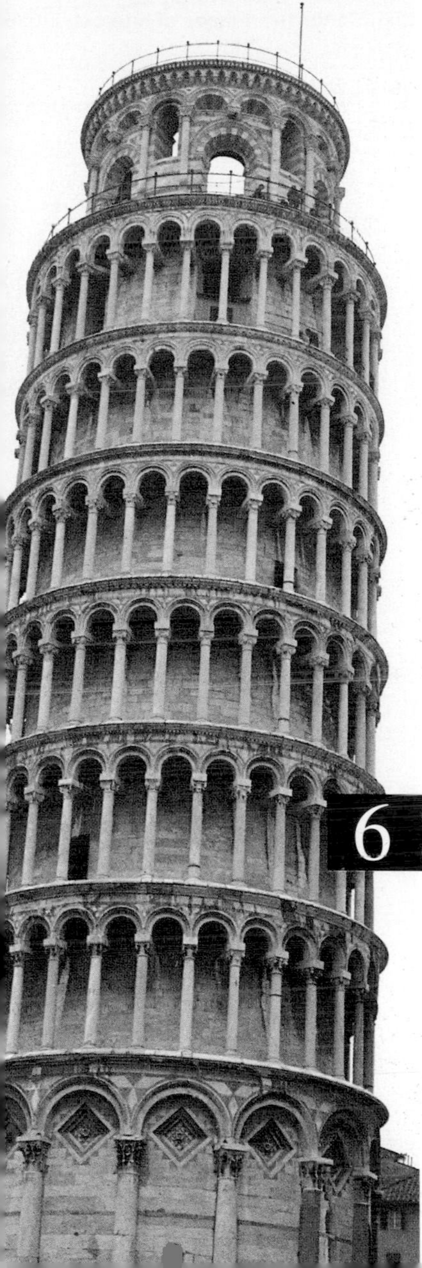

6 Culture and Nature
Cultura e natura

At the Visitor's (Tourist) Center
All'azienda di soggiorno

I'd like a map of the city of... Vorrei una pianta della città di... [voh-rreh-ee oo-nah pyahn-tah deh-llah chee-ttah dee]

Do you have any brochures of... ? Ha qualche depliant di... ? [ah kwahl-keh deh-plyahn dee]

Do you have a program of events for this week? Ha un programma delle manifestazioni di questa settimana? [ha oon proh-grah-mmah deh-lleh mah-nee-feh-stah-tzyoh-nee dee kweh-stah seh-ttee-mah-nah]

Are there any sightseeing tours of the city? Ci sono giri turistici della città organizzati? [chee soh-noh jee-ree too-ree-stee-chee deh-llah chee-ttah ohr-ghah-nee-zah-tee]

How much does the tour cost? Quanto costa il biglietto? [kwahn-toh koh-stah eel bee-lyeh-ttoh]

Places of Interest/Museums
Cose da vedersi/Musei

What is there to see here? Che cosa c'è da vedere qui? [keh koh-sah cheh dah veh-deh-reh kwee]

We'd like to see... Vorremmo visitare...[voh-rreh-mmoh vee-see-tah-reh]

When is the museum open? Quando è aperto il museo? [kwahn-doh eh ah-pehr-toh eel moo-seh-oh]

When does the tour start? Quando comincia la visita con la guida? [kwahn-doh koh-meen-chah lah vee-see-tah kohn lah gwee-dah]

Does the guide also speak English? La guida parla anche inglese? [lah gwee-dah pahr-lah een-gleh seh]

Is taking pictures permitted? È permesso fare fotografie? [eh pehr-meh-ssoh fah-reh foh-toh-grah-fee-eh]

What's the name of this square/church?	Come si chiama questa piazza/chiesa? [koh-meh see kyah-mah kweh-stah pyah-tza/kyeh-sah]

> Never wear shorts inside an Italian church because some people might find that offensive. If you're wearing a sleeveless dress, it's a good idea to put on a jacket.

Is that… ?	È questo il…/È questa la…? [eh kweh-stoh eel/ eh kweh-stah lah]
When was this palace built/restored?	Quando fu costruito/restaurato questo palazzo? [kwahn-doh foo koh-stroo-ee-toh/reh-stah-oo-rah-toh kweh-stoh pah-lah-tzoh]
What period does this building date back to?	A che epoca risale questo edificio? [ah keh eh-poh-kah ree-sah-leh kweh-stoh eh-dee-fee-choh]
Are there any other works by this architect in the city?	Ci sono altre opere di questo architetto nella città? [chee soh-noh ahl-treh oh-peh-reh dee kweh-stoh ahr-kee-teh-ttoh neh-llah chee-ttah]

Castle del Monte, built around 1340

Have they finished the excavation?	Sono terminati i lavori di scavo? [<u>soh</u>-noh tehr-mee-<u>nah</u>-tee ee lah-<u>voh</u>-ree dee <u>skah</u>-voh]
Where are the archeological findings shown?	Dove sono esposti i reperti archeol<u>og</u>ici? [<u>doh</u>-veh <u>soh</u>-noh eh-<u>spoh</u>-stee ee reh-<u>pehr</u>-tee ahr-keh-oh-<u>loh</u>-jee-chee]
Who did that painting?/Who did that sculpture?	Chi ha dipinto questo quadro?/Chi ha fatto questa scultura? [kee ah dee-<u>peen</u>-toh <u>kweh</u>-stoh <u>kwah</u>-droh/kee ah <u>fah</u>-ttoh <u>kweh</u>-stah skool-<u>too</u>-rah]
Is there an exhibition catalog?	Esiste un cat<u>a</u>logo dell'esposizione? [eh-<u>see</u>-steh oon kah-<u>tah</u>-loh-ghoh <u>deh</u>-lleh-spoh-see-<u>tzyoh</u>-neh]
Do you have a poster/postcard/any slides of… ?	Ha un poster/una cartolina/delle diapositive del quadro…? [ah oon <u>poh</u>-stehr/<u>oo</u>-nah kahr-toh-<u>lee</u>-nah/<u>deh</u>-lle dyah-poh-see-tee-veh dehl <u>kwah</u>-droh]

Word List: Places of Interest/Museums

abbey	abbaz<u>i</u>a [a-bah-<u>tzee</u>-ah]
act	atto [<u>ah</u>-ttoh]
altar	l'altare *(m)* [lahl-<u>tah</u>-reh]
amphitheater	anfiteatro [ahn-fee-teh-<u>ah</u>-troh]
ancient	antico [ahn-<u>tee</u>-koh]
antiquity	antichità [ahn-tee-kee-<u>tah</u>]
aqueduct	acquedotto [ah-kweh-<u>doh</u>-ttoh]
arch	arco [<u>ahr</u>-koh]
arch of triumph	arco di trionfo [<u>ahr</u>-koh dee tree-<u>ohn</u>-fyoh]
archway	arcata [ahr-<u>kah</u>-tah]
archeological finds	i reperti archeol<u>og</u>ici [ee reh-<u>pehr</u>-tee ahr-keh-oh-<u>loh</u>-jee-chee]

archeology	archeologia [ahr-keh-oh-loh-jee-ah]
architect	architetto [ahr-kee-teh-ttoh]
architecture	architettura [ahr-kee-teh-ttoo-rah]
area/corridor inside the apse	deambulatorio [deh-ahm-boo-lah-toh-ryoh]
arena	arena [ah-reh-nah]
art gallery	galleria (d'arte) [ghah-lleh-ree-ah (dahr-teh)]
arts and crafts	artigianato artistico [ahr-tee-jah-nah-toh ahr-tee-stee-koh]
balustrade	balaustra [bah-lah-oo-strah]
baroque	barocco [bah-roh-kkoh]
basilica	basilica [bah-see-lee-kah]
bell	campana [kahm-pah-nah]
Benedictine	benedettino [beh-neh-deh-ttee-noh]
birthplace	città natale [chee-ttah nah-tah-leh]
bridge	il ponte [eel ponh-teh]
bronze	bronzo [brohn-zoh]
Bronze Age	età del bronzo [eh-tah dehl brohn-zoh]
building	edificio, la costruzione [eh-dee-fee-choh, lah koh-stroo-tzyoh-neh]
to burn	bruciare [broo-chah-reh]
bust	busto [boo-stoh]
buttress	il contrafforte [eel kohn-trah-ffohr-teh]

Byzantine	bizantino [bee-zahn-tee-noh]
candelabra	candelabro [kahn-deh-lah-broh]
capital	capitello [kah-pee-teh-lloh]
castle	castello [kah-steh-lloh]
catacomb	le catacombe [leh kah-tah-kohm-beh]

Il Duomo, Florence

cathedral	la cattedrale [lah kah-tteh-<u>drah</u>-leh]
Catholic	cattolico [kah-<u>ttoh</u>-lee-koh]
ceiling	soffitto [soh-<u>ffee</u>-ttoh]
ceiling fresco	pittura del soffitto [pee-<u>ttoo</u>-rah dehl soh-<u>ffee</u>-ttoh]
cemetery	cimitero [chee-mee-<u>teh</u>-roh]
center	centro [<u>chehn</u>-troh]
century	secolo [<u>seh</u>-koh-loh]
ceramics	ceramica [cheh-<u>rah</u>-mee-kah]
changing of the guard	cambio della guardia [<u>kahm</u>-byoh <u>deh</u>-llah <u>gwahr</u>-dyah]
chapel	cappella [kah-<u>ppeh</u>-llah]
choir (chancel)	coro [<u>koh</u>-roh]
choir stall	stallo [<u>stah</u>-lloh]
Christian	cristiano [kree-<u>styah</u>-noh]
Christianity	cristianesimo [kree-styah-<u>neh</u>-see-moh]

church	chiesa [kyeh-sah]
Cistercians	i cistercensi *(pl)* [ee chee-stehr-chehn-see]
citadel	cittadella [chee-ttah-deh-llah]
city reduced to ruins	città ridotta in rovine [chee-ttah ree-doh-ttah een roh-vee-neh]
city walls	le mura della città [leh moo-rah deh-llah chee-ttah]
classicism	classicismo [klah-ssee-chee-smoh]
cloister	chiostro [kyoh-stroh]
column	colonna [koh-loh-nnah]
commercial center	città commerciale [chee-ttah koh-mmehr-chah-leh]
convent/monastery	convento, monastero [kon-vehn-toh, moh-nah-steh-roh]
copper engraving	l'incisione *(f)* su rame, calcografia [leen-chee-syoh-neh soo rah meh, kahl-koh-grah-foo ah]
copy	copia [koh-pyah]
Corinthian	corinzio [koh-reen-tzyoh]
courtyard	il cortile [eel kohr-tee-leh]
cross	la croce [lah kroh-cheh]
crucifix	crocifisso [kroh-chee-fee-ssoh]
crypt	cripta [kroop-tah]
cult of the dead	culto dei morti [kool-toh deh-ee mohr-tee]
cupola/dome	cupola [koo-poh-lah]
customs/traditions	gli usi e i costumi [lyee oo-see eh koh-stoo-mee]
denomination	la confessione, la religione [lah kohn-feh-ssyoh-neh, lah reh-lee-joh-neh]
design	il design [eel deh-sah-een]

1 *Il Duomo, Milan*
2 *Tower of Pisa, Pisa*
3 *i Truilli, Alberobello, Puglia*
4 *The Coliseum, Rome*
5 *S. Giorgio Maggiore, Rome*

diocese	diocesi [dee-oh-cheh-see]
dome	duomo [dwoh-moh]
domed building	la costruzione a cupola [lah koh-stroo-tzyoh-neh ah koo-poh-lah]
Doric	dorico [doh-ree-koh]
drawing	disegno [dee-seh-nyoh]
dynasty	dinastia [dee-nah-stee-ah]
early Christianity	protocristiano [proh-toh-kree-styah-noh]
early work	opera giovanile [oh-peh-rah joh-vah-nee-leh]
emblem	l emblema (m) [lehm-bleh-mah]
emperor/empress	imperatore/imperatrice [eem-peh-rah-toh-reh/eem-peh-rah-tree-cheh]
engraving	intaglio [een-tah-lyoh]
etching	l acquaforte (f) [lah-kwah-fohr-teh]
Etruscan	etrusco [eh-troo-skoh]
excavations	gli scavi [lyee skah-vee]
exhibit	mostra, l'esposizione (f) [moh-strah, eh-spoh-see-tzyoh-neh]
facade	facciata [fah-chah-tah]
folk museum	museo di tradizioni popolari [moo-seh-oh dee trah-dee-tzyoh-nee poh-poh-lah-ree]
font	il fonte battesimale [eel fohn-teh bah-tteh-see-mah-leh]
fortress	fortezza [fohr-teh-tzah]
forum	foro [foh-roh]
foundations	le fondamenta [leh fohn-dah-mehn-tah]
fountain	fontana [fohn-tah-nah]
Franciscan	francescano [frahn-cheh-skah-noh]
fresco	affresco [ah-ffreh-skoh]

frieze	fregio [freh-joh]
gate	il portone [eel pohr-toh-neh]
gold work	l'arte (f) orafa [lahr-teh oh-rah-fah]
Golden Age	periodo aureo [peh-ree-oh-doh ah-oo-reh-oh]
Gothic	gotico [ghoh-tee-koh]
governor's palace	palazzo del governo [pah-lah-tzoh dehl ghoh-vehr-noh]
graphic arts	l'arte (f) grafica [lahr-teh grah-fee-kah]
gravestone	monumento sepolcrale, la lapide [moh-noo-mehn-toh seh-pohl-krah-leh, lah lah-pee-deh]
Greek	greco [greh-koh]
Greeks	i greci [ee greh-chee]
ground plan, outline	la proiezione orizzontale [lah proh-yeh-tzyoh-neh oh-ree-zohn-tah-leh]
guided tour	visita guidata [vee-see-tah gwee-dah-tah]
Hebrew	ebraico [eh-brah-ee-koh]
historic district	centro storico [chehn-troh stoh-ree-koh]
history	storia [stoh-ryah]
houses with cone-shaped roof	i Trulli [ee troo-llee]
icon	icona [ee-koh-nah]
illustration	illustrazione (f) [ee-lloo-strah-tzyoh-neh]
impressionism	impressionismo [eem-preh-ssyoh-nee-smoh]
india ink	inchiostro, china [een-kyoh-stroh, kee-nah]
indoor/covered market	mercato coperto [mehr-kah-toh koh-pehr-toh]
influence	influenza [een-floo-ehn-tzah]

inlay	gli intarsi [lyee een-<u>tahr</u>-see]
inscription	l'iscrizione *(f)*, l'epigrafe *(f)* [lee-skree-<u>tzyoh</u>-neh, leh-<u>pee</u>-grah-feh]
interior court	cortile *(m)* interno [kohr-<u>tee</u>-leh een-<u>tehr</u>-noh]
Ionic	ionico [<u>yoh</u>-nee-koh]
king/queen	re/regina [reh/reh-<u>jee</u>-nah]
landscape	pittura di paesaggi [pee-<u>ttoo</u>-rah dee pah-ch-<u>sah</u>-djee]
late Gothic	tardo gotico [<u>tahr</u>-doh <u>ghoh</u>-tee-koh]
latest work	opera dell'ultimo periodo [<u>oh</u>-peh-rah deh-<u>llool</u>-tee-moh peh-ree-<u>oh</u>-doh]
library	biblioteca [bee-blyoh-<u>teh</u>-kah]
lithography	litografia [lee-toh-grah-<u>fee</u>-ah]
mannerism	manierismo [mah-nyeh-<u>ree</u>-smoh]
mannerist	manicristico [mah-nyeh-<u>ree</u>-stee-koh]
marble	marmo [<u>mahr</u>-moh]
market	mercato [mer-<u>kah</u>-toh]
mass	messa, la funzione sacra [<u>meh</u>-ssah foon-<u>tzyoh</u>-neh <u>sah</u>-krah]
material	il materiale [eel mah-teh-<u>ryah</u>-leh]
mausoleum	mausoleo [mah-oo-soh-<u>leh</u>-oh]
mayor	sindaco [<u>seen</u>-dah-koh]
medieval	medioevale [meh-dyoh-eh-<u>vah</u>-leh]
memorial	monumento commemorativo [moh-noo-<u>mehn</u>-toh koh-mmeh-moh-rah-<u>tee</u>-voh]
Middle Ages	Medioevo [meh-dyoh-<u>eh</u>-voh]
model	modello [moh-<u>deh</u>-lloh]
modern	moderno [moh-<u>dehr</u>-noh]
monument	monumento [moh-noo-<u>mehn</u>-toh]

mosaic	mosaico [moh-<u>sah</u>-ee-koh]
mural	pittura murale [pee-<u>ttoo</u>-rah moo-<u>rah</u>-leh]
museum	museo [moo-<u>seh</u>-oh]
museum piece	pezzo d'esposizione [<u>peh</u>-tzoh deh-spoh-see-<u>tzyoh</u>-neh]

nave	la nave [lah <u>nah</u>-veh]
neoclassicism	neoclassicismo [<u>neh</u>-oh-klah-ssee-<u>chee</u>-smoh]
Norman	normanno [nohr-<u>mah</u>-nnoh]
obelisk	obelisco [oh-beh-<u>lee</u>-skoh]
oil painting	pittura ad olio [pee-<u>ttoo</u>-rah ahd <u>oh</u>-lyoh]
order *(rel)*	l'<u>ordine</u> *(m)* [<u>lohr</u>-dec-neh]
organ	organo [<u>ohr</u>-ghah-noh]
original	l'originale *(m)* [loh-ree-jee-<u>nah</u>-leh]

Ponte Vecchio, Florence

ornament	ornamento [ohr-nah-mehn-toh]
pagan	pagano [pah-ghah-noh]
painted	dipinto [dee-peen-toh]
painter	pittore/pittrice [pee-ttoh-reh/pee-ttree-cheh]
painting	pittura, quadro [pee-ttoo-rah, kwah-droh]
painting collection	raccolta di dipinti [rah-kkohl-tah dee dee-peen-tee]
painting on glass	pittura su vetro, vetrocromia [pee-ttoo-rah soo veh-troh, veh-troh-kroh-mee-ah]
palace	palazzo [pah-lah-tzoh]
panel	dipinto su tavola [dee-peen-toh soo tah-voh-lah]
parchment	pergamena [pehr-ghah-meh-nah]
pastel	pastello [pah-steh-lloh]

patrician's home	casa patrizia [kah-sah pah-tree-tzyah]
pavilion	il padiglione [eel pah-dee-lyoh-neh]
period/era	epoca [eh-poh-kah]
photo montage	fotomontaggio [foh-toh-mohn-tah-djoh]
photograph	fotografia [foh-toh-grah-fee-ah]
pilgrimage	pellegrinaggio [peh-lleh-gree-nah-djoh]
pilgrim	pellegrino/pellegrina [peh-lleh-gree-noh/peh-lleh-gree-nah]
pillar	pilastro [pee-lah-stroh]
places of interest	le cose da vedersi [leh koh-seh dah veh-dehr-see]
plunder/pillage	saccheggio [sah-kkeh-djoh]
pointed arch	arco ogivale [ahr-koh oh-jee-vah-leh]
porcelain	porcellana [pohr-cheh-llah-nah]
portal	il portale [eel pohr-tah-leh]
portrait	ritratto [ree-trah-ttoh]
poster/placard	manifesto [mah-nee-feh-stoh]
pottery	l'arte *(f)* di vasaio [lahr-teh dee vah-sah-yoh]
prehistoric	preistorico [preh-ee-stoh-ree-koh]
priest/clergyman	il sacerdote, il prete [eel sah-chehr-doh-teh, eel preh-teh]
protection of monuments	tutela dei monumenti [too-teh-lah deh-ee moh-noo-mehn-tee]
Protestant	il/la protestante [eel/lah proh-teh-stahn-teh]
pulpit	pulpito [pool-pee-toh]
realism	realismo [reh-ah-lee-smoh]
rebuild	ricostruire [ree-koh-stroo-ee-reh]

relief	rilievo [ree-<u>lyeh</u>-voh]
religion	la religione [lah reh-lee-<u>joh</u>-neh]
remnants	i resti [ee <u>reh</u>-stee]
Renaissance	rinascimento [ree-nah-shee-<u>mehn</u>-toh]
restoration	restauro [reh-<u>stah</u>-oo-roh]
rococo	rococò [roh-koh-<u>koh</u>]
Roman	romano [roh-mah-noh], *(pl)* i romani [ee roh-<u>mah</u>-nee]
Romanesque	romanico [roh-<u>mahn</u>-tee-koh]
romanticism	romanticismo [roh-mahn-tee-<u>chee</u>-smoh]
roof	tetto [<u>teh</u>-ttoh]
rosette	il rosone [eel roh-<u>zoh</u>-neh]
round arch	arco a tutto sesto [<u>ahr</u>-koh ah <u>too</u>-ttoh <u>seh</u>-stoh]
ruins	rovina [roh-<u>vee</u>-nah]
sacred cult site	luogo consacrato ad un culto [<u>lwoh</u>-ghoh kohn-sah-<u>krah</u>-toh ahd oon <u>kool</u>-toh]
sanctuary	santuario [sahn-<u>twah</u>-ryoh]
sandstone	pietra arenaria [<u>pyeh</u>-trah ah-reh-<u>nah</u>-ryah]
sarcophagus	sarcofago [sahr-<u>koh</u>-fah-ghoh]
school	scuola [<u>skwoh</u>-lah]
sculptor	lo scultore [loh skool-<u>toh</u>-reh]
sculpture	scultura [skol-<u>too</u>-rah]
silkscreen	serigrafia [seh-ree-grah-<u>fee</u>-ah]
square	piazza, quadrato [<u>pyah</u>-tzah, kwah-<u>drah</u>-toh]
statue	statua [<u>stah</u>-twah]
steeple	il campanile [eel kahm-pah-<u>noc</u>-leh]

stele	la stele [lah steh-leh]
still life	natura morta [nah-too-rah mohr-tah]
Stone Age	età della pietra [eh-tah deh-llah pyeh-trah]
stucco	stucco [stoo-kkoh]
style	lo stile [loh stee-leh]
surrealism	surrealismo [soo-rre-ah-lee-smoh]
symbolism	simbolismo [seem-boh-lee-smoh]
tapestry	arazzo, tappeto [ah-rah-tzoh, tah-ppeh-toh]

temple	tempio [tehm-pyoh]
terracotta	terracotta [teh-rrah-koh-ttah]
theater	teatro [teh-ah-troh]
thermal baths	le terme [leh tehr-meh]
tomb/grave	tomba [tohm-bah]
torso	torso [tohr-soh]
tour	giro [jee-roh]
tourist guide	guida turistica, il cicerone [gwee-dah too-ree-stee-kah, eel chee-cheh-roh-neh]
tower	la torre [lah toh-rreh]
town hall	municipio [moo-nee-chee-pyoh]
transept	transetto [trahn-seh-ttoh]
treasure	tesoreria [teh-soh-reh-ree-ah]
tympanum	timpano [teem-pah-noh]
university	università [oo-nee-vehr-see-tah]
vase	vaso [vah-soh]
vault	volta [vohl-tah]
vestry	sagrestia [sah-greh-stee-ah]
Visigoth	visigotico [vee-see-goh-tee-koh]
visit	visita [vee-see-tah]

wall	muro [moo-roh]
watercolor	acquerello [ah-kweh-reh-lloh]
weaving/weaving industry	tessitura, industria tessile [teh-ssee-too-rah, een-doo-stryah teh-ssee-leh]
window	finestra [fee-neh-strah]
wing	ala [ah-lah]
women's gallery (*arch*)	matroneo [mah-troh-neh-oh]
woodcarving	intaglio in legno [een-tah-lyee een leh-nyoh]
woodcut	silografia [see-loh-ghrah-fee-ah]
work	opera [oh-peh-rah]

Excursions

Gite

Can you see... from here?	Di qui si può vedere...? [dah kwee see poo-oh veh-deh-reh]
In what direction is... ?	In che direzione è situato/a...? [een keh dee-reh-tzyoh-neh eh see-too-ah-toh/ah]
Will we pass... ?	Passiamo da...? [pah-ssyah-moh dah]
Are we also going to see... ?	Si va anche a vedere...? [see vah ahn-keh ah veh-deh-reh]
How much free time do we have at...?	Quanto tempo a disposizione abbiamo a...? [kwahn-toh tehm-poh ah dee-spoh-see-tzyoh-neh ah-byah-moh ah]
When are we going back?	Quando si parte per il viaggio di ritorno? [kwahn-doh see pahr-teh pehr eel vyah-djoh dee ree-tohr-noh]
What time will we get back?	A che ora saremo di ritorno? [ah keh oh-rah sah-reh-moh dee ree-tohr-noh]

Word List: Excursions

amusement park	parco divertimenti [pahr-koh dee-vehr-tee-mehn-tee]
bird sanctuary	zona di protezione degli uccelli [zoh-nah proh-teh-tzyoh-neh oo-cheh-llee]
botanical garden	giardino botanico [jahr-dee-noh boh-tah-nee-koh]
cave	grotta, caverna [groh-ttah, kah-vehr-nah]
cave dwelling	l'abitazione (f) troglodita [lah-bee-tah-tzyoh-neh troh-gloh-dee-tah]
cavern with stalactites and stalagmites	grotta con stalattiti e stalagmiti [groh-ttah kohn stah-lah-ttee-tee eh stah-lahg-mee-tee]
cliff	scogliera [skoh-lyeh-rah]
country house	residenza di campagna [reh-see-dehn-tzah dee kahm-pah-nyah]
countryside	paesaggio [pah-eh-sah-djoh]
day trip	gita di un giorno [jee-tah dee johr-noh]
environs	i dintorni [ee deen-tohr-nee]
excursion	gita [jee-tah]
fishing port	porto di pesca [pohr-toh dee peh-skah]
fishing region	il paese di pescatori [eel pah-eh-seh dee peh-skah-toh-ree]
forest fire	incendio forestale [een-chehn-dyoh foh-reh-stah-leh]
forest/wood	bosco [boh-skoh]
gorge	gola [ghoh-lah]
inland	il retroterra [eel reh-troh-teh-rrah]
island tour	giro dell'isola [jee-roh deh-llee-soh-lah]

lake	lago [<u>lah</u>-ghoh]
lava	lava [<u>lah</u>-vah]
market	mercato [mehr-<u>kah</u>-toh]
mountain	montagna [mohn-<u>tah</u>-nyah]
mountain village	villaggio di montagna [vee-<u>llah</u>-djoh dee mohn-<u>tah</u>-nyah]
national park	parco nazionale [<u>pahr</u>-koh nah-tzyoh-<u>nah</u>-leh]
nature park	parco naturale [<u>pahr</u>-koh nah-too-<u>rah</u>-leh]
nature preserve	riserva naturale [ree-<u>sehr</u>-vah nah-too-<u>rah</u>-leh]
observatory	osservatorio astronomico [oh-ssehr-vah-<u>toh</u>-ryoh ah-stroh-<u>noh</u>-mee-koh]
outdoor museum	museo all'aperto [moo-<u>seh</u>-oh ah-llah-<u>pehr</u>-toh]
panorama	vista panoramica [<u>vee</u>-stah pah-noh-<u>rah</u>-mee-kah]
pass	passo [<u>pah</u>-ssoh]
pilgrimage site	luogo di pellegrinaggio [<u>lwoh</u>-ghoh dee peh-lleh-gree-<u>nah</u>-djoh]
planetarium	planetario [plah-neh-<u>tah</u>-ryoh]
reef	scoglio [<u>skoh</u>-lyoh]
square	piazza [<u>pee</u>-tzah]
suburb	sobborgo [soh-<u>bohr</u>-ghoh]
tour	giro [<u>jee</u>-roh]
valley	la valle [lah <u>vah</u>-lleh]
vantage point	il belvedere [eel behl-veh <u>deh</u>-reh]
volcano	vulcano [vool-<u>kah</u>-noh]
waterfall	cascata [kah-<u>skah</u>-tah]

Events/Entertainment

Manifestazioni/Divertimenti

Theater/Concert/Movies	Teatro/Concerto/Cinema

What's playing at the theater tonight?

Che cosa c'è al teatro stasera? [keh koh-sah cheh ahl teh-ah-troh stah-seh-rah]

What's playing at the movies tomorrow night?

Che cosa c'è al cinema domani sera? [keh koh-sah cheh ahl chee-neh-mah doh-mah-nee seh-rah]

In most Italian movie theaters, there are no fixed starting times for the showings. You can enter the theater at any time and stay until you have seen the film in its entirety. Since the idea of possibly seeing the end of a film first and then the beginning doesn't appeal to everyone, you can also ask what time the next show will start at the box office.

Are there concerts in the cathedral?

Danno concerti in chiesa? [dah-nnoh kohn-chehr-tee een kyeh-sah]

Can you recommend a good play?

Mi può consigliare una buona rappresentazione teatrale? [mee poo-oh kohn-see-lyah-reh oo-nah bwoh-nah rah-ppreh-seh-tah-tzyoh-neh teh-ah-trah-leh]

When does the performance start?

Quando comincia lo spettacolo? [kwahn-doh koh-meen-chah loh speh-ttah-koh-loh]

Where do you get tickets?

Dove si prendono i biglietti? [doh-veh see prehn-doh-noh ee bee-lyeh-ttee]

Two tickets for tonight/tomorrow night, please.

Due biglietti per stasera/domani sera, per favore. [doo-eh bee-lyeh-ttee pehr stah-seh-rah/doh-mah-nee seh-rah pehr fah-voh-reh]

Two tickets at... lire, please.

Per favore due biglietti da... lire. [pehr fah-voh-reh doo-eh bee-lyeh-ttee dah...lee-reh]

Two adults and a child.

Due adulti e un bambino. [doo-eh ah-dool-tee eh oon bahm-bee-noh]

May I please have a program?	Mi può dare un programma, per favore? [mee poo-<u>oh</u> <u>dah</u>-reh oon proh-<u>grah</u>-mmah pehr fah-<u>voh</u>-reh]
What time does the performance end?	Quando finisce lo spettacolo? [<u>kwahn</u>-doh fee-<u>nee</u>-sheh loh speh-<u>ttah</u>-koh-loh]
Where is the cloakroom?	Dov'è il guardaroba? [doh-<u>veh</u> eel <u>gwahr</u>-dah-<u>roh</u>-bah]

Word List: Theater/Concert/Movies

accompaniment	accompagnamento [ah-kkohm-pah-nyah-<u>mehn</u>-toh]
act	atto [<u>ah</u>-ttoh]
actor/actress	l'attore *(m)*/l'attrice *(f)* [lah-<u>ttoh</u>-reh/lah-<u>tree</u>-che]
advance booking	prevendita [preh-<u>vehn</u>-dee-tah]
ballet	balletto [bah-<u>llch</u>-ttoh]
box (seat)	palco [<u>pahl</u>-koh]
box office	cassa [<u>kah</u>-ssah]
cabaret	il cabaret [eel kah-bah-<u>reh</u>]
calendar of events	calendario delle manifestazioni [kah-lehn-<u>dah</u>-ryoh <u>deh</u>-lleh mah-nee-feh-stah-<u>tzyoh</u>-nee]
chamber music concert	concerto da camera [kohn-<u>chehr</u>-toh dah <u>kah</u>-meh-rah]
choir	coro [<u>koh</u>-roh]
circus	circo [<u>cheer</u>-koh]
cloakroom	il guardaroba [eel <u>gwahr</u>-dah-<u>roh</u>-bah]
comedy	commedia [koh-<u>mmeh</u>-dyah]
composer	compositore [kohm-poh-see-<u>toh</u>-reh]
concert	concerto [kohn-<u>chehr</u>-toh]
conductor	il direttore d'orchestra [eel dee-reh-<u>ttoh</u>-reh dohr-<u>keh</u>-strah]

curtain	tenda, sipario [tehn-dah see-pah-ryoh]
dancer	ballerino/a [bah-lleh-ree-noh/ah]
direction	regia [reh-jee-ah]
drama	il dramma [eel drah-mmah]
festival	il féstival [eel feh-stee-vahl]
film	il film [eel feelm]
gallery *(theater)*, balcony *(cinema)*	galleria [ghah-lleh-ree-ah]
intermission	intervallo [een-tehr-vah-lloh]
jazz concert	concerto di jazz [kohn-chehr-toh dee jazz]
leading role	ruolo principale [rwoh-loh preen-chee-pah-leh]
movie actor/actress	l'attore *(m)*/l'attrice *(f)* di cinema [lah-ttoh-reh/lah-ttree-che dee chee-neh-mah]
movies	il cinema [eel chee-neh-mah]
musical	il musical, commedia musicale [eel myoo-see-kohl, koh-mmeh-dyah moo-see-kah-leh]
opera	opera [oh-peh-rah]
opera glasses	binócolo [bee-noh-koh-loh]
operetta	operetta [oh-peh-reh-ttah]
orchestra	orchestra [ohr-keh-strah]
original version	la versione originale [lah vehr-syoh-neh o-ree-jee-nah-leh]
outdoor movies	il cinema all'aperto [eel chee-neh-mah ah-llah-pehr-toh]
outdoor theater	teatro all'aperto [teh-ah-troh ah-llah-pehr-toh]
performance/show	spettacolo [speh-ttah-koh-loh]
play	opera teatrale [oh-peh-rah teh-ah-trah-leh]

pop concert	concerto di musica pop [kohn-chehr-toh dee moo-see-kah pohp]
premiere	prima [pree-mah]
program	il programma [eel proh-grah-mmah]
program booklet	opuscolo del programma [oh-poo-skoh-loh dehl proh-grah-mmah]
religious music concert	concerto di musica sacra [kohn-chehr-toh dee moo-see-kah sah-krah]
role	ruolo [rwoh-loh]
show	spettacolo [speh-ttah-koh-loh]
singer	il/la cantante [eel/lah kahn-tahn-teh]
soloist	il/la solista [eel/lah soh-lee-stah]
stage	palcoscenico [pahl-koh-sheh-nee-koh]
staging/direction	messa in scena [meh-ssah een sheh-nah]
stalls	platea [plah-teh-ah]
subtitle	sottotitolo [soh-ttoh-tee-toh-loh]
symphony concert	concerto sinfonico [kohn-chehr-toh seen-foh-nee-koh]
theater	teatro
ticket	biglietto [bee-lyeh-ttoh]
tragedy	tragedia [trah-jeh-dyah]
variety show	il varietà [eel vah-ryeh-tah]

Bar/Discotheque/Nightclub	**Bar/Discoteca/Nightclub**
What type of show do they have here at night?	Che manifestazioni tipiche hanno luogo qui la sera? [keh mah-nee-feh-stah-tzyoh-nee tee-pee-keh ah-nnoh lwoh-ghoh kwee lah seh-rah]
Is there a nice café around here?	C'è una trattoria accogliente da queste parti? [cheh oo-nah trah-ttoh-ree-ah ah-kkoh-lyehn-teh dah kwoh-ste pahr-tee]

Where can we go dancing? — Dove si può andare a ballare? [<u>doh</u>-veh see poo-<u>oh</u> ahn-<u>dah</u>-reh ah bah-<u>llah</u>-reh]

What's the crowd like, young or old? — Com'è il pubblico, giovane o meno? [koh-<u>meh</u> eel <u>poo</u>-blee-koh, joh-<u>vah</u>-neh oh meh-noh]

Is evening dress required? — È richiesto l'abito da sera? [eh ree-<u>kyeh</u>-stoh <u>lah</u>-bee-toh dah <u>seh</u>-rah]

One drink is included in the admission price. — Il biglietto d'ingresso comprende una consumazione. [eel bee-<u>lyeh</u>-ttoh deen-<u>greh</u>-ssoh kohm-<u>prehn</u>-deh <u>oo</u>-nah kohn-soo-mah-<u>tzyoh</u>-neh]

A beer, please. — Una birra, per favore. [<u>oo</u>-nah <u>bee</u>-rrah pehr fah-<u>voh</u>-reh]

Another, please. — Un'altra/Un altro, per favore. [oo-<u>nahl</u>-trah/oon <u>ahl</u>-troh pehr fah-<u>voh</u>-reh]

This round is on me. — Stavolta offro io. [stah-<u>vohl</u>-tah oh-ffroh <u>ee</u>-oh]

Shall we dance (again)? — Balliamo (ancora)? [bah-<u>llyah</u>-moh (ahn-<u>koh</u>-rah)]

Shall we go for a walk? — Vogliamo fare una passeggiatina? [voh-<u>lyah</u>-moh <u>fah</u>-reh <u>oo</u>-nah pah-sseh-<u>djah</u>-tah]

Word List: Bar/Discotheque/Nightclub

band	complesso [kohm-<u>pleh</u>-ssoh]
bar	il bar [eel bahr]
bouncer	il portiere [eel pohr-<u>tyeh</u>-reh]
casino	casinò, sala giochi [kah-see-<u>noh</u>, <u>sah</u>-lah <u>joh</u>-kee]
to dance	ballare [bah-<u>llah</u>-reh]
dance band	orchestra [ohr-<u>keh</u>-strah]
dance music	musica da ballo [<u>moo</u>-see-kah dah <u>bah</u>-lloh]

disco	discoteca [dee-skoh-<u>teh</u>-kah]
disk jockey	il/la discjockey [eel/lah deesk <u>joh</u>-kee]
evening of folk dancing	serata folcloristica [seh-<u>rah</u>-tah fohl-kloh-<u>ree</u>-stee-kah]
fashion show	sfilata di moda [sfee-<u>lah</u>-tah dee <u>moh</u>-dah]
folk dancing	il folclore [eel fohl-<u>kloh</u>-reh]
to go out	uscire [oo-<u>shee</u>-reh]
live music	musica dal vivo [<u>moo</u>-see-kah dahl <u>vee</u>-voh]
nightclub	il night-club [eel <u>nah</u>-eet clahb]
pub	osteria, trattoria [oh-steh-<u>ree</u>-ah, trah-ttoh-<u>ree</u>-ah]
show	lo show [lo shoh]

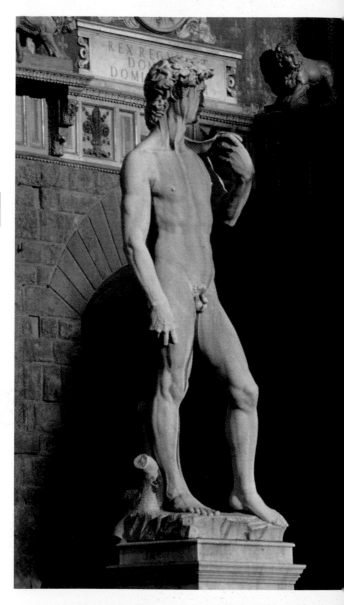

7 **At the Beach/Sports**
Sulla spiaggia/Sport

At the Swimming Pool/At the Beach
In piscina/Sulla spiaggia

Is there...	C'è...In piscina/Sulla spiaggia [cheh... een pee-shee-nah/soo-llah spyah-djah]
an outdoor pool?	una piscina all'aperto? [oo-nah pee-shee-nah ah-llah-pehr-toh? cheh]
an indoor pool?	una piscina coperta? [oo-nah pee-shee-nah koh-pehr-tah]
a thermal bath?	un bagno termale? [oon bah-nyoh tehr-mah-leh]
An admission ticket, please.	Un biglietto d'ingresso (con cabina), per favore [oon bee-lyeh-ttoh deen-greh-ssoh (kohn kah-bee-nah), pehr fah-voh-reh]
Swimmers only!	Per soli nuotatori! [pehr soh-lee nwoh-tah-toh-ree]
No diving!	Vietato tuffarsi! [vyeh-tah-toh too-ffahr-see]
No swimming!	Vietato bagnarsi! [vyeh-tah-toh bah-nyahr-see]
Is the beach sandy/rocky?	La spiaggia è di sabbia/sassi? [lah spyah-djah eh dee sah-byah/sah-ssee]
Is there any algae?	Ci sono scogli? [chee soh-noh skoh-lyee]
Are there sea urchins/jellyfish?	Ci sono ricci/meduse? [chee soh-noh ree-chee/meh-doo-seh]
How far out can we swim?	Fin dove si può nuotare? [feen doh-veh see poo-oh nwoh-tah-reh]
Is the current very strong?	È molto forte la corrente? [eh mohl-toh fohr-teh lah koh-rreh-teh]
Is it dangerous for children?	È pericoloso per i bambini? [eh peh-ree-koh-loh-soh pehr ee bahm-bee-neh]

When is low/high tide?	Quando viene la bassa/l'alta marea? [kwahn-doh vyeh-neh lah bah-ssah/lahl-tah mah-reh-ah]
I'd like to rent...	Vorrei noleggiare... [voh-rreh-ee noh-leh-djah-reh]
a boat.	una barca. [oo-nah bahr-kah]
a pair of water skis.	un paio di sci nautici. [oon pah-yoh dee shee nah-oo-tee-chee]
How much is it per hour/day?	Quanto costa all'ora/al giorno? [kwahn-toh koh-stah ahl jorh-noh]

Sports
Gli Sport

What sporting events are there here?	Quali manifestazioni sportive ci sono qui? [kwah-lee mah-nee-feh-stah-tzyoh-nee spohr-tee-veh chee soh-noh kwee]
What sports facilities do they have here?	Quali sport si possono praticare qui? [kwah-lee spohrt see poh-ssoh-noh prah-tee-kah-reh kwee]
Is there a golf course/tennis court/race course?	C'è un campo da golf/un campo da tennis/un ippodromo? [cheh oon kahm-poh dah ghohlf/oon kahm-poh dah teh-nnees/oon ee-ppoh-droh-moh]
Where can I go fishing?	Dove si può pescare? [doh-veh see poo-oh peh-skah-reh]
I would like to see a soccer match/horse race.	Vorrei vedere una partita di calcio/una corsa ippica. [voh-rreh-ee veh-deh-reh oo-nah pahr-tee-tah dee kahl-choh/oo-nah kohr-sah ee-ppee-kah]
When/Where is it?	Quando/Dove ha luogo? [kwahn-doh/doh-veh ah lwoh-ghoh]
How much does it cost to get in?	Quanto costa l'ingresso? [kwahn-toh koh-stah leen-greh-ssoh]

Are there some good ski runs on the mountains?	Sui monti, ci sono delle buone piste da sci? [soo-ee mohn-tee chee soh-noh deh-lleh bwoh-neh pee-steh dah shee]
What time is the last trip up/down the mountain on the ski lift?	A che ora c'è l'ultima salita a monte/discesa a valle della cabi novia? [ah keh oh-rah cheh lool-tee-mah sah-lee-tah/dee-sheh-sah ah vah-lleh deh-llah kah-bee-noh-vee-ah]
I'd like to go for a hike in the mountains.	Vorrei fare una gita in montagna. [voh-rreh-ee fah-reh oo-nah jee-tah een monh-tah-nyah]
Can you show me an interesting route on the map?	Mi può indicare un itinerario interessante sulla carta? [mee poo-oh een-dee-kah-reh oon ee-tee-neh-rah-ryoh een-teh-reh-ssahn-teh soo-llah kahr-tah]

Where can I rent...?	Dove posso noleggiare...? [doh-veh poh-ssoh noh-leh-djah-reh]
I'd like to take a course in...	Vorrei fare un corso di... [voh-rreh-ee fah-reh oon kohr-soh dee]
What sports do you do?	Che sport pratica Lei? [keh spohrt prah-tee-kah leh-ee]
I play...	Io gioco a... [ee-oh joh-koh ah]
I love...	Sono appassionato di... [soh-noh ah-ppah-ssyoh-nah-toh dee]
I like to go...	Mi piace andare... [mee pyah-cheh ahn-dah-reh]
May I play too?	Posso giocare anch'io? [poh-ssoh joh-kah-reh ahn-kee-oh]

The coast near Gargano

Word List: Beach/Sports

active vacation	vacanza attiva [vah-kahn-tzah ah-ttee-vah]
aerobics	aerobica [ah-eh-roh-bee-kah]
archery	tiro a segno con i dardi [tee-roh ah seh-nyoh kohn ee dahr-dee]
athletic	sportivo/sportiva [spohr-tee-voh/spohr-tee-vah]
athletics	atletica leggera [ah-tleh-tee-kah leh-djeh-rah]
badminton	il badminton, gioco del volano [eel bahd-meen-tohn, joh-koh dehl voh-lah-noh]
ball (small)	palla [pah-llah]
basketball	il basket, pallacanestro [eel bah-skeht, pah-llah-kah-neh-stroh]
bath house	stabilimento balneare [stah-bee-lee-mehn-toh bahl-neh-ah-reh]
bath towel	telo da bagno [teh-loh dah bah-nyoh]

bathing inlet	insenatura ideale per bagnanti [een-seh-nah-<u>too</u>-rah ee-deh-<u>ah</u>-leh pehr bah-<u>nyahn</u>-tee]
beach umbrella	l'ombrellone *(m)* [lohm-breh-<u>lloh</u>-neh]
beginner	il principiante [eel preen-chee-<u>pyahn</u>-teh]
bet	pari [<u>pah</u>-ree]
bicycle racing	corsa ciclistica [<u>kohr</u>-sah chee-<u>klee</u>-stee-kah]
bicycle tour	gita in bicicletta [<u>jee</u>-tah een bee-chee-<u>kleh</u>-ttah]
bicycling	ciclismo [chee-<u>klee</u>-smoh]
boat racing	motociclismo [moh-toh-chee-<u>klee</u>-smoh]
boat rental	noleggio di barche [noh-<u>leh</u>-djoh dee <u>bahr</u>-keh]
bocce (Italian game)	(gioco delle) bocce [(<u>joh</u>-koh <u>deh</u>-lleh) <u>boh</u>-cheh]
bowling	il bowling [eel <u>boh</u>-leen]
cable car	funivia, la funicolare [foo-nee-<u>vee</u>-ah, lah foo-nee-koh-<u>lah</u>-reh]
canoe	canoa (canadese) [kah-<u>noh</u>-ah (kah-nah-<u>deh</u>-seh)]
chair lift	seggiovia [seh-djoh-<u>vee</u>-ah]
chaise lounge	sedia a sdraio [<u>seh</u>-dyah ah <u>sdrah</u>-yoh]
championship	campionato [kahm-pyoh-<u>nah</u>-toh]
competition	gara [<u>ghah</u>-rah]
course	rotta, corso [<u>roh</u>-ttah <u>kohr</u>-soh]
cross-country ski trail	pista di fondo [<u>pco</u>-stah dee <u>fohn</u>-doh]
cross-country skiing	lo sci di fondo [loh shee dee <u>fonh</u>-doh]
to cycle	andare in bicicletta [ahn-<u>dah</u>-reh een bee-chee-<u>kleh</u>-ttah]

daily pass	(abbonamento) giornaliero [(ah-boh-nah-<u>mehn</u>-toh) johr-nah-<u>lyeh</u>-roh]
deep-sea fishing	pesca d'alto mare [<u>peh</u>-skah <u>dahl</u>-toh <u>mah</u>-reh]
defeat	sconfitta [skohn-<u>fee</u>-ttah]
to dive	nuotare sott'acqua [nwoh-<u>tah</u>-reh soh-<u>ttah</u>-kwah]
diving gear	attrezzatura da palombaro [ah-treh-tzah-<u>too</u>-rah dah pah-lom-<u>bah</u>-roh]
diving mask	gli occhiali da immersione [lyee oh-<u>kkyah</u>-lee dah ee-mmehr-<u>syoh</u>-neh]
doubles (tennis)	doppio [<u>doh</u>-ppyoh]
dune	duna [<u>doo</u>-nah]
figure skating	pattinaggio artistico [pah-ttee-<u>nah</u>-djoh]
to fish	pescare [peh-<u>skah</u>-reh]
fishing license	licenza di pesca [lee-<u>chehn</u>-tzah dee <u>peh</u>-skah]
fitness center	centro ginnico [<u>chen</u>-troh jee-nee-koh]
fitness training	allenamento per migliorare la forma [ah-lleh-nah-<u>mehn</u>-toh pehr mee-lyoh-<u>rah</u>-reh lah <u>fohr</u>-mah]
flippers	le pinne [leh <u>pee</u>-nneh]
footbridge	passerella per bagnanti [pah-sseh-<u>reh</u>-llah pehr bah-<u>nyahn</u>-tee]
gliding	volo a vela [<u>voh</u>-loh ah <u>veh</u>-lah]
to go sledding	andare in slitta [ahn-<u>dah</u>-reh een <u>slee</u>-ttah]
goal (post)	porta, il goal [pohr-<u>tah</u>, eel gohl]
goalee	il portiere [eel pohr-<u>tyeh</u>-reh]
golf	il golf [eel gohlf]
golf course	mazza da golf [<u>mah</u>-tzah dah gohlf]

gymnastics	ginnastica [jee-nnah-stee-kah]
half-time	primo/secondo tempo [pree-moh/seh-kohn-doh tehm-poh]
handball	palla a mano [pah-llah ah mah-noh]
to hang glide	praticare lo sport del deltaplano [prah-tee-kah-reh loh spohrt dehl dehl-tah-plah-noh]
hang glider	il/la deltaplanista [eel/lah dehl-tah-plah-nee-stah]
hang gliding	il paragliding [eel pah-rah-glah-deen]
hiking	escursionismo [eh-skoor-syoh-nee-smoh]
horse	cavallo [kah-vah-lloh]
horse racing	corsa di cavalli [kohr-sah dee kah-vah-llee]
horseback riding	l'equitazione (f); ippica [leh-kwee-tah-tzyoh-neh, ee-ppee-kah]
ice hockey	l'hockey su ghiaccio (m) [loh-kee soo ghyah-choh]
ice skates	i pattini [ee pah-ttee-nee]
ice skating	pattinaggio su ghiaccio [pah-ttee-nah-djoh soo ghyah-choh]
ice skating rink	pista per pattinaggio su ghiaccio [pee-stah pehr pah-ttee-nah-djoh soo ghyah-choh]
inflatable mattress	materasso pneumatico [mah-teh-rah-ssoh pneh-oo-mah-tee-koh]
intermediate (nonbeginner)	progredito, non principiante [proh-greh-dee-toh, nohn preen-chee-pyahn-teh]
jazz dancing	danza jazz [dahn-tzah jahzz]
to jog	fare jogging [fah-reh joh-ggheen]
jogging	il jogging [eel joh-ggheen]

judo	judo [joo-doh]
karate	il karatè [eel kah-rah-teh]
life preserver	il salvagente [eel sahl-vah-jehn-teh]
lifeguard	bagnino [bah-nyee-noh]
to lose	perdere [pehr-deh-rch]
lower station	la stazione a valle [lah stah-tzyoh-neh ah vah-lleh]
match	partita [pahr-tee-tah]
middle station	la stazione a mezza quota [lah stah-tzyoh-neh ah meh-zah kwoh-tah]
minigolf	il minigolf [eel mee-nee-ghohlf]
motorboat	motoscafo [moh-toh-skah-foh]
mountain climbing, hiking, rock climbing	alpinismo [ahl-pee-nee-smoh]
mountain station	la stazione a monte [lah stah tzyoh-nch ah mohn-teh]
net	la rete [lah roh teh]
nine pins (game)	gioco dei birilli [joh-koh deh-ee bee-ree-llee]
nonswimmer	non nuotatore [nohn nwoh-tah-toh-rh]
nudist beach	spiaggia per nudisti [spyah-djah pehr noo-dee-stee]
outdoor pool	piscina all'aperto [pee-shee-nah ah-llah-pehr-toh]
parachuting	paracadutismo [pah-rah-kah-doo-tee-smoh]
pebble	ciottolo [choh-ttoh-loh]
pedal boat	pattino a pedali [pah-ttee-noh ah peh-dah-lee]
Ping-Pong	il ping-pong [eel peeng-pohng]
polo	polo [poh-loh]

pool	piscina [pee-<u>shee</u>-nah]
private beach	spiaggia privata [<u>spyah</u>-djah pree-<u>vah</u>-tah]
program	il programma [eel proh-<u>grah</u>-mmah]
racing	corsa [kohr-sah]
racket	racchetta [rah-<u>kkeh</u>-ttah]
rafting	il rafting [eel <u>rahf</u>-teen]
referee	arbitro [<u>ahr</u>-bee-troh]
regatta	regata [reh-<u>ghah</u>-tah]
result	risultato [ree-sool-<u>tah</u>-toh]
ride (horseback)	cavalcata [kah-vahl-<u>kah</u>-tah]
to ride horseback	cavalcare [kah-vahl-<u>kah</u>-reh]
rowboat	barca a remi [<u>bahr</u>-kah ah <u>reh</u>-mee]
rowing	canottaggio [kah-noh-<u>ttah</u>-djoh]
rubber boat/dinghy	canotto pneumatico [kah-<u>noh</u>-ttoh pneh-oo-<u>mah</u>-tee-koh]
rugby	rugby [<u>rahg</u>-bee]
sail	vela [<u>veh</u>-lah]
sailboat	barca a vela [<u>bahr</u>-kah ah <u>veh</u>-lah]
saltwater pool	piscina d'acqua salata [pee-<u>shee</u>-nah <u>dah</u>-kwah sah-<u>lah</u>-tah]
sand	sabbia [<u>sah</u>-bbyah]
sauna	sauna [<u>sah</u>-oo-nah]
shower	doccia [<u>doh</u>-chah]
singles (tennis)	singolo [<u>seen</u>-ghoh-loh]
skateboard	lo skate-board [loh <u>skeh</u>-eet bohrd]
to ski	sciare [shee-<u>ah</u>-reh]
ski binding	attacco [ah-<u>ttah</u>-kkoh]

ski goggles	gli occhiali da sci [lyee oh-kkyah-lee dah shee]
skiing	lo sci (alpino) [loh shee (ahl-pee-noh)]
ski lift	sciovia, lo ski-lift [shee-oh-vee-ah, loh skee leeft]
ski poles	i bastoni da sci [ee bah-stoh-nee dah shee]
ski pro	maestro di sci [mah-eh-stroh dee shee]
ski run	corso di sci [kohr-soh dee shee]
sled	slitta [slee-ttah]
snorkel	il respiratore di superficie [eel reh-spee-rah-toh-reh dee soo-pehr-fee-cheh]
soccer	calcio [kahl-choh]
soccer field	campo da gioco (del calcio) [kahm-poh dah joh-koh (dehl kahl-choh)]
soccer match	partita di calcio [pahr-lee-tah dee kahl-choh]
soccer team	squadra di calcio [skwah-drah dee kahl-choh]
solarium	solario [soh-lah-ryoh]
sports	campo sportivo [kahm-poh spohr-tee-voh]
squash	lo squash [loh skwoh-sh]
start	partenza [pahr-tehn-tzah]
surf	il surf [eel sehrf]
to surf	praticare il surfing [prah-tee-kah-reh eel sehr-feen]
surfboard	tavoletta per il surf [tah-voh-leh-ttah pehr eel sehrf]
swimmer	il nuotatore [eel nwoh-tah-toh-reh]

swimming	nu<u>o</u>to [<u>nwoh</u>-toh]
team	squadra [<u>skwah</u>-drah]
tennis	il tennis [eel <u>teh</u>-nnees]
ticket	biglietto d'ingresso [bee-<u>lyeh</u>-ttoh deen-<u>greh</u>-ssoh]
ticket office	cassa [<u>kah</u>-ssah]
trainer	allenamento [ah-lleh-nah-<u>mehn</u>-toh]
trampoline	trampolino [trahm-poh-<u>lee</u>-noh]
victory	vitt<u>o</u>ria [vee-<u>ttoh</u>-ryah]
volleyball	la pallavolo [lah pah-llah-<u>voh</u>-loh]
to walk	camminare [kah-mmee-<u>nah</u>-reh]
walking path	sentiero per escursioni [sehn-<u>tyeh</u>-ree pehr eh-skoor-<u>syoh</u>-nee]

water	pallanuoto [<u>pah</u>-llah-<u>nwoh</u>-toh]
water wings	i bracciali salvagente [ee brah-<u>chah</u>-lee sahl-vah-<u>jehn</u>-teh]
weekly pass	abbonamento settimanale [ah-boh-nah-<u>mehn</u>-toh seh-ttee-mah-<u>nah</u>-leh]
whirlpool	vasca per cura idroter<u>a</u>pica [<u>vah</u>-ska pehr <u>koo</u>-rah ee-droh-teh-<u>rah</u>-pee-kah]
to win	v<u>i</u>ncere [<u>veen</u>-cheh-reh]
windbreak	frangivento [frahn-jee-<u>vehn</u>-toh]
wrestling	lotta [<u>loh</u>-ttah]

8

Shopping/Stores
Facendo la spesa/Negozi

Questions/Prices
Domande/Prezzi

opening	orari d'apertura [oh-<u>rah</u>-ree dah-pehr-<u>too</u>-rah]
open/closed/closed for holidays	aperto/chiuso/chiuso per ferie [ah-<u>pehr</u>-toh/<u>kyoo</u>-soh/<u>kyoo</u>-soh pehr <u>feh</u>-ryeh]
Where can I find...?	Dove si può trovare…? [<u>doh</u>-veh see poo-oh troh-<u>vah</u>-reh]
Can you recommend a... shop?	Mi può indicare un negozio di…? [mee poo-<u>oh</u> een-dee-<u>kah</u>-reh oon neh-<u>ghoh</u>-tzyoh dee]
Are you being served?	La servono già? [lah <u>sehr</u>-voh-noh jah]
Thank you, I'm just looking.	Grazie, vorrei solo dare un'occhiata. [<u>grah</u>-tzye voh-<u>rreh</u>-ee <u>soh</u>-loh <u>dah</u>-reh oo-noh-<u>kkyah</u>-tah]

I'd like...	Vorrei… [voh-<u>rreh</u>-ee]
Do you have...?	Ha…? [ah]
Could you please show me...?	Mi mostri per favore…? [mee <u>moh</u>-stree pehr fah-<u>voh</u>-reh]
Please give me...	Mi dia per favore… [mee <u>dee</u>-ah pehr fah-<u>voh</u>-reh]
Please,...	Per favore,… [pehr fah-<u>voh</u>-reh]
a pair of...	un paio di… [oon <u>pah</u>-yoh dee]
a piece of...	un pezzo di… [oon <u>peh</u>-tzoh dee]
Could you please show me another...?	Per favore mi può mostrare un altro/un'altra…? [pehr fah-<u>voh</u>-reh mee poo-<u>oh</u> moh-<u>strah</u>-reh oo-<u>nahl</u>-troh/oo-<u>nahl</u>-trah]
Have you anything cheaper?	Ha qualcosa di meno caro? [ah kwahl-<u>koh</u>-sah dee <u>meh</u>-noh <u>kah</u>-roh]
I like it. I'll take it.	Mi piace. Lo prendo. [mee <u>pyah</u>-cheh loh <u>prehn</u>-doh]

How much is it?	Quanto costa? [kwahn-toh koh-stah]
Do you accept...	Accetta... [ah-cheh-ttah]
Eurochecks?	eurocheques? [eh-oo-roh-chek]
credit cards?	carte di credito? [kahr-teh dee kreh-dee-toh]
traveler's checks	assegni turistici, traveller's cheques? [ah-sseh-nyee too-ree-stee-chee, trah-vehls chek]
Could you please wrap it for me?	Me lo può incartare? [meh loh poo-oh een-kahr-tah-reh]
I'd like to exchange this.	Lo vorrei cambiare. [loh voh-rreh-ee kahm-byah-reh]

Bills and sales slips that you receive in restaurants, bars, movie theaters, hair dressing salons and barbershops, and stores have to be carefully saved and presented to government revenue officers in case an examination or check is conducted. Such examinations can take place within a radius of 100 meters of the place the bill or sales slip was issued. It is very important, therefore, to always ask for an invoice and keep it.

Word List: Stores

antique store	negozio di antichità [neh-ghoh-tzyoh dee ahn-tee-kee-tah]
art dealer	il commerciante in oggetti d'arte [eel koh-mmehr-chahn-teh een oh-djeh-ttee dahr-teh]
arts and crafts store	artigianato artistico, arti decorative [ahr-tee-jah-nah-toh ahr-tee-stee-koh, ahr-tee deh-koh-rah-tee-veh]
bakery	panificio [pah-nee-fee-choh]
bazaar	il bazar [eel bah-zahr]
beauty salon	il salone di bellezza [eel sah-loh-neh dee beh-lleh-tzah]

boating equipment	attrezzatura nautica [ah-ttreh-tzah-too-rah nah-oo-tee-kah]
bookstore	libreria [lee-breh-ree-ah]
boutique	la boutique [lah boo-teek]
butcher	macelleria [mah-cheh-lleh-ree-ah]
camera shop	gli articoli fotografici [lyee ahr-tee-koh-lee foh-toh-grah-fee-chee]
dairy	latteria [lah-tteh-ree-ah]
department store	il grande magazzino [eel grahn-deh mah-ghah-zee-noh]
dry cleaner	lavanderia a secco, tintoria [lah-vahn-deh-ree-ah ah seh-kkoh]
electrician	l'elettricista (m) [leh-leh-ttree-chee-stah]
fish store	pescheria [peh-skeh-ree-ah]
flea market	mercato delle pulci [mehr-kah-toh deh-lleh pool-chee]
florist	fioraio [fyoh-rah-yoh]
food store	negozio di generi alimentari [neh-ghoh-tzyoh dee jeh-neh-ree ah-lee-mehn-tah-ree]
fruit store	fruttivendolo [froo-ttee-vehn-doh-loh]
furniture store	(negozio di) mobili [(neh-ghoh-tzyoh dee) moh-bee-lee]
furrier's	pellicceria [peh-llee-cheh-ree-ah]
gourmet foods store	negozio di specialità gastronomiche [neh-ghoh-tzyoh dee speh-chah-lee-tah ghah-stroh-noh-mee-keh]
grocery/greengrocer	erbivendolo [ehr-bee-vehn-doh-loh]
hardware store	negozio di ferramenta [neh-ghoh-tzyoh dee feh-rrah-mehn-tah]
health food store	negozio di prodotti dietetici [neh-ghoh-tzyoh dee proh-doh-ttee dyeh-teh-tee-chee]

housewares store	negozio di casalinghi [neh-<u>ghoh</u>-tzyoh dee kah-sah-<u>leen</u>-ghee]
jeweler	gioielleria [joh-yeh-lleh-<u>ree</u>-ah]
laundromat	lavanderia a gettone [lah-vahn-deh-<u>ree</u>-ah ah jeh-<u>ttoh</u>-neh]
laundry	lavanderia [lah-vahn-deh-<u>ree</u>-ah]
leather goods shop	pelletteria [peh-lleh-tteh-<u>ree</u>-ah]
liquor store	rivendita di prodotti alcolici [ree-<u>vehn</u>-dee-tah dee proh-<u>doh</u>-ttee ahl-<u>koh</u>-lee-chee]
market	mercato [mehr-<u>kah</u>-toh]
music store	negozio di articoli musicali [neh-<u>ghoh</u>-tzyoh dee ahr-<u>tee</u>-koh-lee moo-see-<u>kah</u>-lee]
newsdealer	giornalaio [johr-nah-<u>lah</u>-yoh]
optician	ottico [<u>oh</u>-ttee-koh]
pastry shop	pasticceria [pah-stee-cheh-<u>ree</u>-ah]
perfumery	profumeria [proh-foo-meh-<u>ree</u>-ah]
pharmacy	farmacia [fahr-mah-<u>chee</u>-ah]
record store	negozio di dischi [neh-<u>ghoh</u>-tzyoh dee <u>dee</u>-skee]
secondhand book dealer	antiquariato [ahn-tee-kwah-<u>ryah</u>-toh]
secondhand shop	negozio dell'usato, il rigattiere [neh-<u>ghoh</u>-tzyoh deh-<u>lloo</u>-sah-toh, eel ree-ghah-<u>ttyeh</u>-reh]
self-service	il self-service [eel sehlf <u>sehr</u>-vees]
shoe store	negozio di calzature [neh-<u>ghoh</u>-tzyoh dee kahl-tsah-too-reh]
shoemaker	calzolaio [kahl-tzoh-<u>lah</u>-yoh]
souvenir shop	i souvenirs [ee soo-veh-<u>neer</u>]
sporting goods store	gli articoli sportivi [lyee ahr-<u>tee</u>-koh-lee spohr-<u>tee</u>-vee]

stationery	cartoleria [kahr-toh-leh-<u>ree</u>-ah]
supermarket	supermercato [soo-pehr-mehr-<u>kah</u>-toh]
tailor	sarto/sarta [sahr-toh/<u>sahr</u>-tah]
tobacconist	tabaccaio [tah-bah-<u>kkah</u>-yoh]
toy store	negozio di giocattoli [neh-<u>ghoh</u>-tzyoh dee joh-<u>kah</u>-ttoh-lee]
travel agency	agenzia viaggi [ah-jehn-<u>tzee</u>-ah <u>vyah</u>-djee]
watchmaker	orologiaio [oh-roh-loh-<u>jah</u>-yoh]
wig store	il parrucchiere [eel pah-rroo-<u>kkyeh</u>-reh]
wine store	negozio di vini [neh-<u>ghoh</u>-tzyoh dee <u>vee</u>-nee]

Groceries
Generi alimentari

What can I get you?	Cosa desidera? [<u>koh</u>-sah deh-<u>see</u>-deh-rah]
I'd like...	Mi dia…, per favore. [mee <u>dee</u>-ah pehr fah-<u>voh</u>-reh]
a kilo of...	un chilo di… [oon <u>kee</u>-loh dee]
100 grams of...	un etto di… [oon <u>eh</u>-ttoh dee]
ten slices of...	10 fette di… [<u>dyeh</u>-chee <u>feh</u>-tteh dee]
a piece of...	un pezzo di… [oon <u>peh</u>-tzoh dee]
a package of...	un pacco di… [oon <u>pah</u>-kkoh dee]
a jar of...	un bicchiere di… [oon bee-<u>kkyeh</u>-reh dee]
a can of...	una scatola di… [<u>oo</u>-nah <u>skah</u>-toh-lah dee]

a bottle of...	una bottiglia di... [oo-nah boh-ttee-lyah dee]
a bag.	un sacchetto, una busta. [oon sah-kkeh-ttoh, oo-nah boo-stah]
More of the same?	È un po' di più, è lo stesso? [eh oon poh dee pyoo eh loh steh-ssoh]
Can I get you anything else?	Altro? [ahl-troh]
Could I please try some of this?	Ne posso assaggiare un po'? [neh poh-ssoh ah-ssah-djah-reh oon poh]
Nothing else, thank you.	Nient'altro, grazie. [nyehn-tahl-troh grah-tzyeh]

Word List: Groceries

almonds	le mandorle [leh mahn-dohr-leh]
apples	le mele [leh meh-leh]
apricots	le albicocche [leh ahl-bee-koh-kkeh]
artichokes	i carciofi [ee kahr-choh-fee]
asparagus	gli asparagi [lyee ah-spah-rah-jee]
avocado	l'avocado *(m)* [lah-voh-kah-doh]
baby food	l'alimentazione *(f)* infantile [lah-lee-mehn-tah-tzyoh-neh een fahn-tee-leh]

bananas	**banane** [leh bah-<u>nah</u>-neh]
basil	**bas<u>i</u>lico** [bah-<u>see</u>-lee-koh]
beans	**i fagioli** [ee fah-<u>joh</u>-lee]
beef	**la carne di manzo** [lah <u>kahr</u>-neh dee <u>mahn</u>-zoh]
beer	**birra** [<u>bee</u>-rrah]
Belgian endive	**ind<u>i</u>via del Belgio** [een-<u>dee</u>-vyah dehl <u>behl</u>-joh]
black (Russian) bread	**il pane nero** [eel <u>pah</u>-neh <u>neh</u>-roh]
blackberries	**le more** [leh <u>moh</u>-reh]
bread	**il pane** [eel <u>pah</u>-neh]
butter	**burro** [boo-rroh]
cabbage	**cavolo** [<u>kah</u>-voh-loh]
cake	**torta** [<u>tohr</u>-tah]
Camembert cheese	**il Camembert** [eel kah-mehm-<u>behr</u>]
canned foods	**le conserve, lo scatolame** [leh kohn-<u>sehr</u>-veh loh skah-toh-<u>lah</u>-meh]
carrots	**le carote** [leh kah-<u>roh</u>-teh]
cauliflower	**il cavolfiore** [eel kah-vohl-<u>fyoh</u>-reh]
celery	**sedano** [<u>seh</u>-dah-noh]
champagne	**lo champagne** [loh shahm-<u>pah</u>-nye]
cheese	**form<u>a</u>ggio** [fohr-<u>mah</u>-djoh]
cherries	**le ciliegie** [leh chee-<u>lyeh</u>-jeh]
chestnuts	**le castagne** [leh kah-<u>stah</u>-nyeh]
chick peas	**i ceci** [ee <u>cheh</u>-chee]
chicken	**pollo** [<u>poh</u>-lloh]
chocolate	**cioccolata** [choh-kkoh-<u>lah</u>-tah]
chocolate bar	**barra di cioccolata** [<u>bah</u>-rrah dee choh-kkoh-<u>lah</u>-tah]

chopped meat	la carne tritata [lah kahr-neh tree-tah-tah]
clams	le vongole [leh vohn-ghoh-leh]
coconut	la noce di cocco [lah noh-cheh dee koh-kkoh]
coffee	il caffè [eel kah-ffeh]
cold cuts	affettato misto, i salumi [ah-ffeh-ttah-toh mee-stoh, ee sah-loo-mee]
cooked ham	prosciutto cotto [proh-shoo-ttoh koh-ttoh]
corn	il mais, granturco [eel mah-ees, grahn-toor-koh]
crabs	i granchi [ee grahn-kee]
crackers	i biscotti [ee bee-skoh-ttee]
cream	panna [pah-nnah]
cucumber	cetriolo [cheh-tryoh loh]
cutlet	cotoletta [koh-toh-leh-ttah]
cuttlefish	seppia [seh-ppyah]
dates	i datteri [ee dah-tteh-ree]
eel	anguilla [ahn-gwee-llah]
eggplant	le melanzane [leh meh-lahn-zah-neh]
eggs	le uova [leh woh-vah]
fennel	finocchio [fee-noh-kkyoh]
figs	i fichi [ee fee-kee]
fish	il pesce [eel peh-sheh]
flour	farina [fah-ree-nah]
free-range eggs	le uova di galline ruspanti [leh woh-vah dee ghah-llee-neh roo-spahn-tee]
fresh	fresco [freh-skoh]
fruit	la frutta [lah froo-ttah]

garlic	aglio [ah-lyoh]
gilthead (fish)	orata [oh-rah-tah]
goat cheese	formaggio di capra [fohr-mah-djoh dee kah-prah]
goat meat	la carne di capra [lah kahr-neh dee kah-prah]
grape, grapes	l'uva (f) [loo-vah]
grapefruit	pompelmo [pohm-pehl-moh]
green beans	i fagiolini [ee fah-joh-lee-nee]
ham	prosciutto [proh-shoo-ttoh]
herring	aringa [ah-reen-ghah]
homegrown vegetables	verdura di coltivazione propria [vehr-doo-rah dee kohl-tee-vah-tzyoh-neh proh-pryah]
honey	il miele [eel myeh-leh]
ice cream	gelato [jeh-lah-toh]
lamb	la carne d'agnello [lah kahr-neh dah-nyeh-lloh]
leeks	porro [poh-rroh]
lemon	il limone [eel lee-moh-neh]
lemonade (fresh)	limonata [lee-moh-nah-tah]
lentils	le lenticchie [leh lehn-tee-kkyeh]
lettuce	insalata verde, lattuga [een-sah-lah-tah vehr-deh, lah-ttoo-ghah]
licorice	liquirizia [lee-kwee-ree-tzyah]
liver pâté	pasticcio di fegato [pah-stee-choh dee feh-ghah-toh]
liver sausage	salsiccia di fetato [sahl-see-chah dee feh-ghah-toh]
low-fat milk	il latte magro [eel lah-tteh mah-groh]
mackerel	sgombro [sghohm-broh]

mandarin orange	mandarino [mahn-dah-ree-noh]
margarine	margarina [mahr-ghah-ree-nah]
marmalade	marmellata [mahr-meh-llah-tah]
mayonnaise	maionese [mah-yoh-neh-seh]
meat	la carne [lah kahr-neh]
melon	melone [meh-loh-neh]
milk	il latte [eel lah-tteh]
mineral water	acqua minerale [ah-kwah mee-neh-rah-leh]
mixed grains bread (rye and wheat)	il pane misto di segala e frumento [eel pah-neh mee-stoh dee seh-ghah-lah eh froo-mehn-toh]
mulberry	le more di gelso [leh moh-reh dee jehl-soh]
mussels	i mitili, le cozze [ee mee-tee-lee, leh koh-tzeh]
mustard	la senape [lah seh-nah-peh]
mutton	la carne di montone/castrato [lah kahr-neh dee monh-toh-neh/kah-strah-toh]
nonalcoholic beer	birra analcolica [bee-rrah ah-nahl-koh-lee-kah]
nonalcoholic wine	vino analcolico [vee-noh ah-nahl-koh-lee-koh]
oat flakes	i fiocchi d'avena [ee fyoh-kkee dah-veh-nah]
oil	olio [oh-lyoh]
olives	le olive [leh oh-lee-veh]
onion	cipolla [chee-poh-llah]
orange drink, orangeade	aranciata [ah-rahn-chah-tah]
orange juice	succo d'arancia [soo-kkoh dah-rahn-chah]

oranges	le arance [leh ah-<u>rahn</u>-cheh]
oregano	origano [oh-<u>ree</u>-ghah-noh]
ostrich	le <u>o</u>striche [leh <u>oh</u>-stree-keh]
paprika	paprica [<u>pah</u>-pree-kah]
parsley	prezzemolo [preh-<u>tzeh</u>-moh-loh]
pasta/noodles	pasta [<u>pah</u>-stah]
peaches	le pesche [leh <u>peh</u>-skeh]
pears	le pere [leh <u>peh</u>-reh]
peas	i piselli [ee pee-<u>seh</u>-llee]
pepper	il pepe [eel <u>peh</u>-peh]
pepperoni	salsiccia [sahl-<u>see</u>-chah]
perch	il pesce p<u>e</u>rsico [eel <u>peh</u>-sheh <u>pehr</u>-see-koh]

pineapple	l'ananas *(m)* [<u>lah</u>-nah-nahs]
plums	le prugne [leh <u>proo</u>-nyeh]
pork	la carne di maiale [lah <u>kahr</u>-neh dee mah-<u>yah</u>-leh]
potatoes	le patate [leh pah-<u>tah</u>-teh]
pumpkin	zucca [<u>zoo</u>-kkah]
rabbit	coniglio [koh-<u>nee</u>-lyoh]
raw ham	prosciutto crudo [proh-<u>shoo</u>-ttoh <u>kroo</u>-doh]
red wine	vino rosso [<u>vee</u>-noh <u>roh</u>-ssoh]
rice	riso [<u>ree</u>-soh]
roll	panino [pah-<u>nee</u>-noh]
rolled oats cereal (uncooked)	pappa di fiocchi d'avena [<u>pah</u>-ppah dee <u>fyoh</u>-kkee dah-<u>veh</u>-nah]
saffron	zafferano [zah-ffeh-<u>rah</u>-noh]
salad	insalata [een-sah-<u>lah</u>-tah]
salami	il salame [eel sah-<u>lah</u>-meh]

saffron	zafferano [zah-ffeh-<u>rah</u>-noh]
salad	insalata [een-sah-<u>lah</u>-tah]
salami	il salame [eel sah-<u>lah</u>-meh]
salt	il sale [eel <u>sah</u>-leh]
sandwiches	i panini imbottiti [ee pah-<u>nee</u>-nee eem-boh-<u>ttee</u>-tee]
sausage	salsiccia [sahl-<u>see</u>-chah]
semolina	semolino [seh-moh-<u>lee</u>-noh]
shrimp	i gamberetti [ee gham-beh-<u>reh</u>-ttee]
smoked meat	la carne affumicata
soft cheese	formaggio molle [fohr-<u>mah</u>-djoh <u>moh</u>-lleh]
soft roll	i maritozzi [ee mah-ree-<u>toh</u>-tzee]
sole	sogliola [<u>soh</u>-lyoh-lah]
soup	minestra [mee-<u>neh</u>-strah]
sour cream	panna acida [<u>pah</u>-nnah <u>ah</u>-chee-dah]
spaghetti	gli spaghetti [lyee spah-<u>gheh</u>-ttee]

strawberries	le fragole [leh frah-ghoh-leh]
sugar	zucchero [zoo-kkeh-roh]
sweet cream	panna dolce [pah-nnah dohl-cheh]
sweets	i dolciumi [ee dohl-choo-mee]
swordfish	il pesce spada [eel peh-sheh spah-dah]
tea	il tè [eel teh]
teabag	bustina di tè [boo-stee-nah dee teh]
thyme	timo [tee-moh]
toast	il toast [eel tohst]
tomatoes	i pomodori [ee poh-moh-doh-ree]
treated with pesticides	trattato con pesticidi [trah-ttah-toh kohn ahn-tee-kree-ttoh-ghah-mee-chee]
tuna	tonno [toh-nnoh]
veal	la carne di vitello [lah kahr-neh dee vee-teh-lloh]
vegetables	verdura [vehr-doo-rah]
vinegar	aceto [ah-cheh-toh]
wafers	le cialde [leh chahl-deh]
walnuts	le noci [leh noh-chee]
watermelon	cocomero, anguria [koh-koh-meh-roh, ahn-ghoo-ryah]
wax beans	i fagioli bianchi [ee fah-joh-lee byahn-kee]
whipped cream	panna montata [pah-nnah mohn-tah-tah]
white bread	il pane bianco [eel pah-neh byahn-koh]
white wine	vino bianco [vee-noh byahn-koh]

wine	vino [vee-noh]
yogurt	lo yogurt [loh yoh-ghoort]

Drugstore Items
Articoli di profumeria

Word List: Drugstore Items

after-shave lotion	la lozione dopobarba [lah loh-tzyoh-neh doh-poh-bahr-bah]
anti-dandruff shampoo	lo shampoo contro la forfora [loh shahm-poh kohn-troh lah fohr-foh-rah]
baby bottle	il biberon [eel bee-beh-rohn]
blush	il rouge [eel rooj]
bobby pins	le mollette (per capelli) [loh moh-lleh-tteh (pehr kah-peh-llee)]
body lotion	crema per il corpo [kreh-mah pehr eel kohr-poh]
brush	spazzola [spah-tzoh-lah]
bubble bath	schiuma (fissante) [skyoo-mah (fee-ssahn-teh)]
cleansing milk	il latte detergente [eel lah-tteh deh-tehr-jehn-teh]
clothesbrush	spazzola per vestiti [spah-tzoh-lah pehr veh-stee-tee]
cologne	acqua di Colonia [ah-kwah dee koh-loh-nyah]
comb	il pettine [eel peh-ttee-neh]
condom	preservativo [preh-sehr-vah-tee-voh]
cotton swabs	cotton fioc [koh-ttohn fyohk]
cotton wool	il cotone idrofilo [eel koh-toh-neh ee-droh-fee-loh]

cream	crema [kreh-mah]
cream for dry/normal/oily skin	crema per pelle secca/normale/grassa [kreh-mah pehr peh-lleh seh-kkah/nohr-mah-leh/grah-ssah]
curlers	i bigodini [ee bee-ghoh-dee-nee]
deodorant	il deodorante [eel deh-oh-doh-rahn-teh]
detergent	la lozione detergente, detersivo [lah loh-tzyoh-neh deh-tehr-jehn-teh, deh-tehr-see-voh]
diapers	i pannolini [ee pah-nnoh-lee-nee]
dishwashing brush	spazzolino per le stoviglie [spah-tzoh-lee-noh pehr leh stoh-vee-lyeh]
dishwashing liquid	il sapone per le stoviglie [eel sah-poh-neh pehr leh stoh-vee-lyeh]
electric razor	rasoio (elettrico) [rah-zoh-yoh eh-leh-ttree-koh]
eyebrow pencil	il lapis per sopracciglia [eel lah-pees pehr leh soh-prah-chee-lyah]
eyeliner	l'eye-liner (m) [lah-ee lah-ee-nehr]
eyeshadow	ombretto [ohm-breh-ttoh]
face powder	cipria [chee-pryah]
hair gel	il gel per capelli [eel jehl pehr ee kah-peh-llee]
hair remover	crema depilatoria [kreh-mah deh-pee-lah-toh-ryah]
hairband	elastico per capelli [eh-lah-stee-koh pehr ee kah-peh-llee]
hairbrush	spazzola per i capelli [spah-tzoh-lah pehr ee kah-peh-llee]
hairspray	lacca [lah-kkah]
hand cream	crema per le mani [kreh-mah pehr leh mah-nee]

lipstick	rossetto [roh-__sseh__-ttoh]
mascara	il mascara [eel mah-__skah__-rah[
mirror	specchio [__speh__-kkyoh]
moisturizing cream	crema idratante [__kreh__-mah ee-drah-__tahn__-teh]
mouthwash	collutorio [koh-lloo-__ttoh__-ryoh]
nail file	limetta [lee-__meh__-ttah]
nail polish	smalto [__smahl__-toh]
nail polish remover	l'acetone *(m)*, il solvente per smalto [lah-cheh-__toh__-neh, eel sohl-__vehn__-teh pehr __smahl__-toh]
nail scissors	forbicine per le unghie [foh-bee-__chee__-neh pehr leh __oon__-ghyeh]
nailbrush	spazzolino per le unghie [spah-tzoh-__lee__-noh pehr leh __oon__-ghyeh]
pacifier	ciuccio, succhietto [__choo__-cchoh, soo-__kkyeh__-ttoh]
perfume	profumo [proh-__foo__-moh]
plaster	cerotto [cheh-__roh__-ttoh]
razor blade	la lametta [lah lah-__meh__-ttah]
safety pin	spilla da balia [__spee__-llah dah __bah__-lyah]
sanitary napkins	gli assorbenti [lyee ah-ssohr-__behn__-tee]
setting lotion	la frizione [lah free-__tzyoh__-nch]
shampoo	lo shampoo [loh __shahm__-poh]
shampoo for oily/normal/ dry hair	lo shampoo per capelli grassi/nor mali/secchi [loh-__shahm__-poh pehr kah-__peh__-llee __grah__-ssee/nohr-__mah__-lee/__seh__-kkee]
shaving brush	pennello da barba [peh-__nneh__-lloh dah __bahr__-bah]

shaving soap	il sapone da barba [eel sah-<u>poh</u>-neh dah <u>bahr</u>-bah]
shower gel	il gel per la doccia [eel jehl pehr lah <u>doh</u>-chah]
shower glove	guanto di spugna, manopola [<u>gwahn</u>-toh dee <u>spoo</u>-nyah, mah-<u>noh</u>-poh-lah]
soap	il sapone [eel sah-<u>poh</u>-neh]
sponge	spugna [<u>spoo</u>-nyah]
stain remover	lo smacchiatore [loh smah-kkyah-<u>toh</u>-reh]
sunscreen (lotion)	crema solare [eel fah-<u>ttoh</u>-reh proh-teh-<u>ttee</u>-voh]
suntan lotion	crema solare [<u>kreh</u>-mah soh-<u>lah</u>-reh]
suntan oil	<u>o</u>lio solare [<u>oh</u>-lyoh soh-<u>lah</u>-reh]
talcum powder	borotalco [boh-roh-<u>tahl</u>-koh]
tampons	i tamponi [ee tahm-<u>poh</u>-nee]
tissues	i fazzoletti di carta [ee fah-tzoh-<u>leh</u>-ttee dee kahr-tah]
toilet paper	carta igienica [<u>kahr</u>-tah ee-<u>jeh</u>-nee-kah]
toothbrush	spazzolino da denti [spah-tzoh-<u>lee</u>-noh dah <u>dehn</u>-tee]
toothpaste	dentifricio [dehn-tee-<u>free</u>-choh]
towelette	i fazzolettini rinfrescanti [ee fah-tzoh-leh-<u>ttee</u>-nee reen-freh-<u>skahn</u>-tee]
travel necessities	il necessaire da viaggio [eel neh-cheh-<u>ssehr</u> dah <u>vyah</u>-djoh]
tweezers	le pinzette [leh peen·<u>tzeh</u>-tteh]

Tobacco Products
Tabacchi

A pack/carton of... filtered/ nonfiltered, please.

Un pacchetto/Una stecca di... [oon pah-kke-ttoh/oo-nah steh-kkah dee] con/senza filtro, per favore. [kohn/ sehn-tzah feel-troh, pehr fah-voh-reh]

Do you have American/ menthol cigarettes?

Ha delle sigarette americane/al mentolo? [ah deh-lleh see-ghah-reh-tteh ah-meh-ree-kah-neh/ahl mehn-toh-loh]

Which brand (of light/strong cigarettes) do you recommend?

Quale marca (di sigarette leggere/forti) mi consiglia? [kwah-leh mahr-kah (dee see-ghah-reh-tteh leh-djeh-reh/fohr-tee) mee kohn-see-lyah]

Ten cigars/cigarillos, please.

Dieci sigari/sigarillos, per favore. [dyeh-chee see-ghah-ree/see-ghah-ree-lyoh pehr fah-voh-reh]

A package/can of cigarette/ pipe tobacco, please.

Un pacchetto/Una scatola di tabacco per sigarette/per la pipa, per favore. [oon pah-kkeh-ttoh/oo-nah skah-toh-lah dee tah-bah-kkoh pehr see-ghah-reh-tteh/pehr lah pee-pah pehr fah-voh-reh]

A box of matches/A lighter, please.

Una scatola di fiammiferi/Un accendino, per favore. [oo-nah skah-toh-lah dee fyah-mmee-feh-ree/oo-nah-chen-dee-noh pehr fah-voh-reh]

Clothing/Leather Goods/Dry Cleaning
Abbigliamento/Pelletteria/Lavanderia a secco
See also Chapter 1, Colors

Can you please show me...?

Mi può mostrare...? [mee poo-oh moh-strah-reh]

What color do you have in mind?

Che colore desidera? [keh koh-loh-reh deh-see-deh-rah]

Something in...	Qualcosa in… [kwahl-<u>koh</u>-sah een]
I'd like something to match this.	Vorrei qualcosa che vada bene con questo. [voh-<u>rreh</u>-ee kwahl-<u>koh</u>-sah keh <u>vah</u>-dah <u>beh</u>-neh kohn <u>kweh</u>-stoh]
May I try it on?	Posso provarlo? [<u>poh</u>-ssoh proh-<u>vahr</u>-loh]
What size do you wear?	Che taglia porta? [keh <u>tah</u>-lyah <u>pohr</u>-tah]
It's too...	Questo mi è troppo… [<u>kweh</u>-stoh mee eh <u>troh</u>-ppoh]
tight/big.	stretto/largo. [<u>streh</u>-ttoh/<u>lahr</u>-ghoh]
short/long.	corto/lungo. [<u>kohr</u>-toh/<u>loon</u>-ghoh]
small/large.	piccolo/grande. [<u>pee</u>-kkoh-loh/<u>grahn</u>-deh]
This is fine. I'll take it.	Va bene. Lo prendo. [vah <u>beh</u>-neh loh <u>prehn</u>-doh]
It's not exactly what I wanted.	Non è proprio quello che volevo. [nohn eh <u>proh</u>-pryoh <u>kweh</u>-lloh keh voh-<u>leh</u>-voh]
I'd like a pair of... shoes.	Vorrei un paio di scarpe... [voh-<u>rreh</u>-ee oon <u>pah</u>-yoh dee <u>skahr</u>-peh]
I wear a size...	Ho il numero… [oh eel <u>noo</u>-meh-roh]
They don't fit well.	Mi fanno male. [mee <u>fah</u>-nnoh <u>mah</u>-leh]
They're too narrow/wide.	Sono troppo strette/larghe. [<u>soh</u>-noh <u>troh</u>-ppoh <u>streh</u>-tteh/<u>lahr</u>-gheh]
Also a tube of shoe cream/ a pair of laces, please.	Anche un lucido da scarpe/un paioa di laccetti, per favore. [<u>ahn</u>-keh oon <u>loo</u>-chee-doh dah <u>skahr</u>-peh/oon <u>pah</u>-yoh dee lah-<u>cheh</u>-ttee pehr fah-<u>voh</u>-reh]
I'd like these shoes resoled, please.	Vorrei far risolare queste scarpe. [voh-<u>rreh</u>-ee fahr ree-soh-<u>lah</u>-reh leh <u>skahr</u>-peh]

Can you put new heels on, please?	Può rifare i tacchi, per favore? [poo-<u>oh</u> ree-<u>fah</u>-reh ee <u>tah</u>-kkee pehr fah-<u>voh</u>-reh]
I'd like to have these clothes dry cleaned/washed.	Vorrei far lavare a secco/lavare questa roba. [voh-<u>rreh</u>-ee fahr lah-<u>vah</u>-reh ah <u>seh</u>-kkoh/lah-<u>vah</u> roh <u>kwch</u>-stah <u>roh</u>-bah]
When will they be ready?	Quando sarà pronta? [<u>kwahn</u>-doh sah-<u>rah</u> <u>prohn</u>-tah]

Word List: Clothing/Leather Goods/Dry Cleaning

bathing cap	cuffia [<u>koo</u>-ffyah]
bathing shoes/beach shoes	scarpe di gomma [skahr-peh dee ghoh-<u>mmah</u>]
bathing suit	il costume da bagno [eel koh-<u>stoo</u>-meh dah <u>bah</u>-nyoh]
bathrobe	accappatoio [ah-kkah-ppah-toh-yoh]
belt	cintura [cheen-<u>too</u>-rah]
bikini	il bikini [eel bee-<u>kee</u>-nee]
blazer	il blazer [eel <u>blah</u>-zehr]
blouse	camicetta [kah-mee-<u>cheh</u>-ttah]
boots	gli stivali [lyee stee-<u>vah</u>-lee]
bow tie	il papillon, farfalla [eel pah-pee-<u>lyohn</u>, fahr-<u>fah</u>-llah]
bra	reggiseno [reh-djee-<u>seh</u>-noh]
briefs	lo slip [loh sleep]
button	il bottone [eel boh-<u>ttoh</u>-neh]
cap	berretto [beh-<u>rreh</u>-ttoh]
cardigan	giacca di lana, il golf [<u>jah</u>-kkah dee <u>lah</u>-nah, eel ghohlf]
checked	a quadri [ah <u>kwah</u>-dree]

children's shoes	le scarpe da bambini [leh skahr-peh dah bahm-bee-nee]
coat	cappotto, soprabito [kah-ppoh-ttoh, soh-prah-bee-toh]
collar	il colletto [eel koh-lleh-ttoh]
color	tinta, il colore [teen-tah eel koh-loh-reh]
cotton	il cotone [eel koh-toh-neh]
dress	vestito [veh-stee-toh]
drip-dry/wash and wear	non-stiro [nohn stee-roh]
to dry-clean	lavare/pulire a secco [lah-vah-reh/poo-lee-reh ah seh-kkoh]
evening dress	abito da sera [ah-bee-toh dah seh-rah]
fur coat	pelliccia [peh-llee-chah]
fur jacket	giacca di pelliccia [jah-kkah dee peh-llee-chah]
gloves	i guanti [ee gwahn-tee]
gym shoes	le scarpe da ginnastica [leh skahr-peh dah jee-nnah-stee-kah]
handkerchief	fazzoletto [fah-tzoh-leh-ttoh]
hat	cappello [kah-ppeh-lloh]
housecoat	vestaglia [veh-stah-lyah]
to iron	tirare [stee-rah-reh]
jacket	giacca [jah-kkah]
jeans	i jeans [ee jeens]
jumpsuit	tuta [too-tah]
knapsack	lo zaino [loh zah-ee-noh]
knee socks	i calzettoni [ee kahl-tzeh-ttoh-nee]
leather coat	cappotto di pelle [kah-ppoh-ttoh dee peh-lleh]

leather jacket	giacca di pelle [jah-kkah dee peh-lleh]
leather pants	i pantaloni di pelle [ee pahn-tah-loh-nee dee peh-lleh]
linen	lino [lee-noh]
lingerie	biancheria intima [byan-keh-ree-ah een-lee-mah]
lining	fodera [foh-deh-rah]
low-heeled shoes	le scarpe basse [leh skahr-peh bah-sseh]
machine washable	lavabile in lavatrice [lah-vah-bee-leh een lah-vah-tree-cheh]
miniskirt	minigonna [mee-nee-ghoh-nnah]
nightshirt	camicia da notte [kah-mee-chah dah noh-tteh]
pajamas	il pigiama [eel pee-jah-mah]
practical	pratico [prah-tee-koh]
pullover	il pullover, il maglione [eel poo-lloh-vchr, eel mah-lyoh-neh]
raincoat	l'impermeabile *(m)* [leem-pchr-meh-ah-bee-leh]
rubber boots	gli stivali di gomma [lyee stee-vah-lee dee ghoh-mmah]
sandals	i sandali [ee sahn-dah-lee]
scarf	il foulard, lo scialle, sciarpa [eel foo-lahr, loh sha-lleh, shar-pah]
shirt	camicia [kah-mee-chah]
shoe brush	spazzola da scarpe [spah tzoh-lah dah skahr-peh]
shoe polish	lucido per scarpe [loo-chee-doh pehr skahr-peh]
shoes	le scarpe [leh skahr-peh]
shoe size	numero di scarpe [noo-meh-roh dee skahr-peh]

shorts	i pantaloncini, gli shorts [ee pahn-tah-lohn-<u>chee</u>-nee, lyee shohrt]
shoulder bag	borsa a tracolla [<u>bohr</u>-sah ah trah-<u>koh</u>-llah]
silk	seta [<u>seh</u>-tah]
silk stockings	le calze di seta [leh <u>kahl</u>-tzeh dee <u>seh</u>-tah]
ski boots	gli scarponi da sci [lyee skahr-<u>poh</u>-nee dah shee]
ski pants	i pantaloni da sci [ee pahn-tah-<u>loh</u>-nee dah shee]
skirt	gonna [<u>ghoh</u>-nnah]
sleeve	m<u>a</u>nica [<u>mah</u>-nee-kah]
slip	la sottoveste [lah soh-ttoh-<u>veh</u>-steh]
slippers	le pant<u>o</u>fole [leh pahn-<u>toh</u>-foh-leh]

snap	(bottone) autom<u>a</u>tico [(boh-<u>ttoh</u>-neh) ah-oo-toh-<u>mah</u>-tee-koh]
socks	i calzini [ee kahl-<u>tzee</u>-nee]
sole	su<u>o</u>la [<u>swoh</u>-lah]
stockings	le calze [leh <u>kahl</u>-tzeh]
striped	a righe [ah <u>ree</u>-gheh]
suede coat	soprabito di pelle scamosciata [soh-<u>prah</u>-bee-toh dee <u>peh</u>-lleh skah-moh-<u>shah</u>-tah]
suede jacket	giacca di pelle scamosciata [<u>jah</u>-kkah dee <u>peh</u>-lleh skah-moh-<u>shah</u>-tah]
suit (men's)	vestito da uomo [veh-<u>stee</u>-toh dah <u>woh</u>-moh]
suit (women's)	il tailleur [eel tah-<u>lyehr</u>]
summer dress	vestito estivo [veh-<u>stee</u>-toh eh-<u>stee</u>-voh]

sun hat	**cappello da sole** [kah-<u>ppeh</u>-lloh dah <u>soh</u>-leh]
sweatpants	**i pantaloni della tuta** [ee pahn-tah-<u>loh</u>-nee <u>deh</u>-llah <u>too</u>-tah]
synthetic fiber	**fibra sintetica** [<u>fee</u>-brah seen-<u>teh</u>-tee-kah]
T-shirt	**maglietta** [mah-<u>lyeh</u>-ttah]
terrycloth	**spugna** [<u>spoo</u>-nyah]
tie	**cravatta** [krah-<u>vah</u>-ttah]
tights/panty hose	**il collant, calzamaglia** [eel koh-<u>llahnt</u>, kahl-tzah-<u>mah</u>-lyah]
tracksuit/sweatsuit	**tuta da ginnastica/tuta sportiva** [<u>too</u>-tah dah jee-<u>nnah</u>-stee-kah/<u>too</u>-tah spohr-<u>tee</u>-vah]
travel bag	**borsa da viaggio** [<u>bohr</u>-sah dah <u>vyah</u>-djoh]
trousers/pants	**i pantaloni, i calzoni** [ee pahn-tah-<u>loh</u>-nee, ee kahl-<u>tzoh</u>-nee]
umbrella	**ombrello** [ohm-<u>breh</u>-lloh]
undershirt	**maglietta, canottiera** [mah-<u>lyeh</u>-ttah, kah-noh-ttyeh-rah]
underwear	**le mutande** [leh moo-<u>tahn</u>-deh]
vest	**il golf, il gilè** [eel ghohlf, eel jee-<u>leh</u>]
windbreaker	**giacca a vento** [<u>jah</u>-kkah ah <u>vehn</u>-toh]
wool	**lana** [<u>lah</u>-nah]
zipper	**chiusura lampo** [kyoo-<u>soo</u>-rah <u>lahm</u>-poh]

Books and Stationery
Libri e articoli di cartoleria

I'd like...	Vorrei... [voh-<u>rreh</u>-e]
an American newspaper.	un giornale americano. [oon johr-<u>nah</u>-leh ah-meh-ree-<u>kah</u>-noh]

a magazine. una rivista. [oo-nah ree-<u>vee</u>-stah]

a tourist guide. una guida turistica. [oo-<u>nah</u> <u>gwee</u>-dah too-<u>ree</u>-stee-kah]

Word List: Books and Stationery

ballpoint pen	la biro [lah <u>bee</u>-roh]
city map	pianta della città [<u>pyahn</u>-tah <u>deh</u>-llah chee-<u>ttah</u>]
colored pencil	matita colorata [mah-<u>tee</u>-tah koh-loh-<u>rah</u>-tah]
coloring book	l'album *(m)* da colorare [<u>lahl</u>-boom dah koh-loh-<u>rah</u>-reh]
envelope	busta [<u>boo</u>-stah]
eraser	gomma [<u>ghoh</u>-mmah]
felt-tip pen	pennarello [peh-nnah-<u>reh</u>-lloh]
fountain pen	penna stilografica [<u>peh</u>-nnah stee-loh-<u>grah</u>-fee-kah]
glue	colla [<u>koh</u>-llah]
magazine	rivista, rotocalco [ree-<u>vee</u>-stah, roh-toh-<u>kahl</u>-koh]
map	carta geografica [<u>kahr</u>-tah jeh-oh-<u>grah</u>-fee-kah]
mystery novel	(romanzo) giallo [(roh-<u>mahn</u>-zoh) <u>jah</u>-lloh]
newspaper	il giornale [eel johr-<u>nah</u>-leh]
notebook	taccuino [tah-kkoo-<u>ee</u>-noh]
notepad	il blocco per appunti, bloc-notes [eel <u>bloh</u>-kkoh pehr ah-<u>ppoon</u>-tee, blohk <u>noh</u>-tehs]
novel	romanzo [roh-<u>mahn</u>-zoh]
paper	carta [<u>kahr</u>-tah]
paperback	libro tascabile [<u>lee</u>-broh tah-<u>skah</u>-bee-leh]

pencil	matita [mah-<u>tee</u>-tah]
pencil sharpener	il temperamatite [eel <u>tehm</u>-peh-rah-mah-<u>tee</u>-teh]
periodical	periodico [peh-<u>ryoh</u>-dee-koh]
picture postcard	cartolina illustrata [kahr-toh-<u>lee</u>-nah ee-lloo-<u>strah</u>-tah]
playing cards	carte da gioco [<u>kahr</u>-teh dah <u>joh</u>-koh]
road map	carta automobilistica [<u>kahr</u>-tah ah-oo-toh-moh-bee-<u>lee</u>-stee-kah]
Scotch tape	lo scotch, nastro adesivo [loh sko-htch, <u>nah</u>-stroh ah-deh-<u>see</u>-voh]
sketchbook	album da disegno [<u>ahl</u>-boom dah dee-<u>seh</u>-nyoh]
stamp	francobollo [frahn-koh-<u>boh</u>-lloh]
stationery	carta da lettera [<u>kahr</u>-tah dah <u>leh</u>-tteh-rah]
wrapping paper/gift wrap	carta da regalo [<u>kahr</u>-tah dah reh-<u>ghah</u>-loh]

Housewares
Articoli casalinghi

Word List: Housewares

aluminum foil	foglio di alluminio [<u>foh</u>-lyoh dee ah-lloo-<u>mee</u>-nyoh]
bottle opener	l'apribottiglie *(m)* [lah-pree-boh-<u>ttee</u>-lyeh]
broom	scopa [<u>skoh</u>-pah]
brush	scopetta [skoh-<u>peh</u>-ttah]
bucket	secchio [<u>seh</u>-kkyoh]
can opener	l'apriscatole *(m)* [lah-pree-<u>skah</u>-toh-leh]
candles	le candele [leh kahn-<u>deh</u>-leh]

charcoal	carbonella [kahr-boh-neh-llah]
clothesline	corda per stendere il bucato [kohr-dah pehr eel boo-kah-toh]
clothespin	molletta (per stendere la biancheria) [moh-lleh-ttah (pehr stehn-deh-reh ee pah-nnee)]
corkscrew	il cavatappi [eel kah-vah-tah-ppee]
cutlery	le posate [leh poh-sah-teh]
dustpan	paletta [pah-leh-ttah]
firelighter	il combustibile solido [eel kohm-boo-stee-bee-leh soh-lee-doh]
folding chair	seggiola da campeggio [seh-djoh-lah dah kahm-peh-djoh]
folding table	tavolo da campeggio [tah-voh-loh dah kahm-peh-djoh]
garbage bag	sacco delle immondizia [sah-kkoh deh-llee-mmohn-dee-tzyah]
glass	il bicchiere [eel bee-kkyeh-reh]
grill	griglia [gree-lyah]
ice pack	piastra refrigerante [pyah-strah re-free-jeh-rahn-teh]
methyl alcohol	alcol metilico [alh-kohl meh-tee-lee-koh]
oil	petrolio [peh-troh-lyoh]
paper napkins	i tovagliolini di carta [ee toh-vah-lyoh-lee dee kahr-tah]
plastic bag	sacchetto di plastica [sah-kkeh-ttoh dee plah-stee-kah]
plastic wrap	pellicola (per la conservazione dei cibi) [peh-llee-koh-lah (pehr lah proh-teh-tzyoh-neh dch ce chee-bee]
pocketknife	temperino, coltello tascabile [tehm-peh-ree-noh, kohl-teh-lloh tah-skah-bee-leh]

saucepan	p**e**ntola [pehn-<u>toh</u>-lah]
suntan lotion	l'ombrellone *(m)* [lohm-breh-<u>lloh</u>-neh]
thermos	il termos [eel <u>tehr</u>-mohs]

Electrical Goods and Photographic Supplies
Articoli elettrici e fotografici

I'd like...	Vorrei... [voh-<u>rreh</u>-ee]
film for this camera.	un rullino per questa m**a**cchina. [oon roo-<u>llee</u>-noh pehr <u>kweh</u>-stah <u>mah</u>-kkee-nah]
color (slide) film.	un rullino a colori (per diaposi-tive). [oon roo-<u>llee</u>-noh ah koh-<u>loh</u>-ree (pehr dyah-poh-see-<u>tee</u>-veh]
film with 36/24/12 exposures.	un rullino da 36/24/12. [oon roo-<u>llee</u>-noh dah <u>trehn</u>-tah-<u>seh</u>-ee/<u>vehn</u>-tee-<u>kwah</u>-ttroh/<u>doh</u>-dee-chee]
Could you please load the camera?	Mi può inserire il rullino, per favore? [mee poo-<u>oh</u> een-seh-<u>ree</u>-reh eel roo-<u>llee</u>-noh pehr fah-<u>voh</u>-reh]
Would you please develop this film for me?	Mi potrebbe sviluppare questo rullino, per favore? [mee poh-<u>treh</u>-bbeh svee-loo-<u>ppah</u>-reh <u>kweh</u>-stoh roo-<u>llee</u>-noh pehr fah-<u>voh</u>-reh]
One print of each of these negatives, please.	Una foto di ciascuno di questi nega-tivi, per favore. [<u>oo</u>-nah <u>foh</u>-toh dee chah-<u>skoo</u>-noh dee <u>kweh</u>-stee neh-ghah-<u>tee</u>-vee pehr fah-<u>voh</u>-reh]
What size?	Che formato? [keh fohr-<u>mah</u>-toh]
seven by ten/nine by nine (centimeters) = 2.8 × 4/3.6 × 3.6 inches	Sette per dieci/Nove per nove [<u>seh</u>-tteh pehr <u>dyeh</u>-chee/<u>noh</u>-veh pehr <u>noh</u>-veh]
Glossy or matte?	Lucido o opaco? [<u>loo</u>-chee-doh oh oh-<u>pah</u>-koh]
When can I pick up the photos?	Quando posso venire a pr**e**ndere le foto? [<u>kwahn</u>-doh poh-<u>ssoh</u>-veh-<u>nee</u>-reh ah <u>prehn</u>-deh-reh leh <u>foh</u>-toh]

The viewfinder/shutter doesn't work.	Il mirino/Lo scatto non funziona. [eel mee-_ree_-noh/loh _skah_-ttoh nohn foon-_tzyoh_-nah]
This is broken; can you please fix it?	Questo non funziona; me lo può riparare per favore? [_kweh_-stoh nohn foon-_tzyoh_-nah meh loh poo-_oh_ ree-pah-_rah_-reh pehr fah-_voh_-reh]

Word List: Electrical Goods and Photographic Supplies

adapter	l'addattore *(m)* [lah-dah-ttah-_toh_-reh]
aperture (setting)	il diaframma [eel dyah-_frah_-mmah]
automatic release	autoscatto [_ah_-oo-toh-_skah_-ttoh]
battery	batteria [bah-tteh-_ree_-ah]
black and white film	rullino in bianco e nero [roo-_llee_-noh een _byahn_-koh eh _neh_-roh]
bulb	lampadina (ad incandescenza) [lahm-pah-_dee_-nah (ahd een-kahn-deh-_shehn_-tzah)]
cassette	cassetta, il caricatore [kah-_sseh_-tah, kah-ree-kah-_toh_-reh]
CD/compact disc	il CD, il compact disc [eel chee dee, eel kohm-_pahkt_ deesk]
extension cord	cavo di prolungamento, prolunga [_kah_-voh dee proh-loon-ghah-_mehn_-toh, proh-_loon_-ghah]
film speed	sensibilità del film [sehn-see-bee-lee-_tah_ dehl feelm]
flash	il flash [eel flehsh]
flashcube	il cubo (flash) [eel _koo_-boh (flehsh)]
hair dryer	l'asciugacapelli *(m)* [lah-_shoo_-ghah-kah-_peh_-llee]
headphone	cuffia [_koo_-ffyah]

lens	obiettivo, la lente [oh-byeh-ttee-voh, lehn-teh]
light meter	esposimetro [eh-spoh-see-meh-troh]
movie camera	cinepresa [chee-neh-preh-sah]
passport photo	fotografia formato tessera [foh-toh-grah-fee-ah fohr-mah-toh teh-sseh-rah]
pen light	lampadina tascabile [lahm-pah-dee-nah tah-skah-bee-leh]
plug	spina [spee-nah]
portable calculator	il calcolatore tascabile [eel kahl-ko-lah-toh-reh tah-skah-bee-leh]
record	disco [dee-skoh]
release	scatto [skah-ttoh]
shutter	l'otturatore (m) [loh-ttoo-rah-toh-reh]
speaker	l'altoparlante (m) [lahl-toh-pahr-lahn teh]
Super 8 film	il film in super-8 [eel feelm een soo-pehr oh-ttoh]
telephoto lens	teleobiettivo [teh-leh-oh-byeh-ttee-voh]
tripod	il treppiedi [eel treh-ppyeh-dee]
video camera	videocamera [vee-deh-oh-kah-meh-rah]
video film	videofilm (m) [vee-deh-oh-feelm]
videocassette	videocassetta [vee-deh-oh-kah-sseh-ttah]
videocassette recorder (VCR)	il videoregistratore [eel vee-deh-oh-reh-jee-strah-toh-reh]
viewfinder	mirino [mee-ree-noh]
walkman	il walkman [eel wohlk-mehn]

At the Optician
Dall'ottico

Could you please fix these glasses/the frame?	Mi potrebbe aggiustare questi occhiali/la montatura, per favore? [mee poh-treh-bbeh ah-djoo-stah-reh kweh-stee oh-kkyah-lee/lah mohn-tah-too-rah pehr fah-voh-reh]
One of the lenses is broken.	Mi si è rotta una lente degli occhiali. [mee see eh roh-ttah oo-nah lehn-teh deh-lyee oh-kkyah-lee]
I'm nearsighted/farsighted.	Sono miope/presbite. [soh-noh mee-oh-peh/preh-sbee-teh]
What is your eye prescription?	Che capacità visiva ha? [keh kah-pah-chee-tah vee-see-vah ah]
plus/minus... in the right eye... in the left eye	destra più/meno…, sinistra… [deh-strah pee-oh/meh-noh... see-nee-strah]
When can I pick up the glasses?	Quando posso venire a prendere gli occhiali? [kwahn-doh poh-ssoh veh-nee-reh ah prehn-deh-reh lyee oh-kkyah-lee]
I need...	Ho bisogno di… [oh bee-soh-nyoh dee]
some cleansing solution...	soluzione detergente/soluzione per la conservazione... [soh-loo-tzyoh-neh deh-tehr-jehn-teh/soh-loo-tzyoh-neh pehr lah kohn-sehr-vah-tzyoh-neh]
for hard/soft contact lenses.	per lenti a contatto rigide/morbide. [pehr lehn-tee ah kohn-tah-ttoh ree-jee-deh/mohr-bee-deh]
I'd like...	Vorrei… [voh-rreh-ee]
a pair of sunglasses.	un paio di occhiali da sole… [oon pah-yoh dee oh-kkyah-lee dah soh-leh]
a pair of binoculars.	un cannocchiale. [oon kah-nnoh-kyah-leh]

At the Watchmaker/Jeweler
Dall'orologiaio/Dal gioielliere

My watch isn't working. Could you take a look?	Il mio orologio non va più. Potrebbe darci un'occhiata? [eel mee-oh oh-roh-loh-joh nohn vah pee-oo poh-treh-beh dahr-chee oo-noh-kkyah-tah]
I'd like a nice souvenir/present.	Vorrei un bel ricordo/regalo. [voh-rre-ee oon behl ree-kohr-doh/reh-ghah-loh]
How much do you want to spend?	Quanto vuole spendere? [kwahn-toh vwoh-leh spehn-deh-reh]
I'd like something that's not too expensive.	Vorrei qualcosa di non troppo caro. [voh-rreh-ee kwahl-koh-sah dee nohn troh-ppoh kah-roh]

Word List: Watchmaker/Jeweler

bracelet	braccialetto [brah-chah-leh-ttoh]
brooch	spilla [spee-llah]
coral	corallo [koh-rah-lloh]
crystal	cristallo [kree-stah-lloh]
earrings	gli orecchini [lyee oh-reh-kkee-nee]
gold	oro [oh-roh]
jewelry	gioiello [joh-yeh-lloh]
necklace	collana, catenina [koh-llah-nah, kah-teh-nee-nah]
pearl	perla [pehr-lah]
pendant	ciondolo [chohn-doh-loh]
ring	anello [ah-neh-lloh]
silver	argento [ahr-jehn-toh]
turquoise	il turchese [eel toor-keh-seh]
wristwatch	orologio da polso [oh-roh-loh-joh dah pohl-soh]

At the Hairdresser/Barber

Dal parrucchiere

May I make an appointment for tomorrow?	Posso prendere un appuntamento per domani? [poh-ssoh prehn-deh-reh oon ah-ppoon-tah-mehn-toh pehr doh-mah-nee]
How would you like your hair done?	Come desidera i capelli? [koh-meh deh-see-deh-rah ee kah-peh-llee]
Shampoo and blow-dry/set.	Shampoo e phon/messa in piega. [shahm-poh eh fohn/meh-ssah een pyeh-ghah]
Wash and cut/Dry cut.	Tagliare e lavare/Tagliare senza lavare. [tah-lyah-reh eh lah-vah-reh/tah-lyah-reh sehn-tzah lah-vah-reh]
I'd like…	Vorrei… [voh-rreh-ee]
a perm.	una permanente. [oo-nah pehr-mah-nehn-teh]

to have my hair dyed/tinted.	farmi tingere i capelli. [fahr-mee teen-jeh-reh ee kah-peh-llee]
to have my hair highlighted.	farmi i colpi di sole. [fahr-mee ee kohl-pee dee soh-leh]
to have my hair toned down.	farmi le mèche. [fahr-mee leh mehsh]
Leave it long, please.	Li lasci lunghi, per favore. [lee lah-shee loon-ghee pehr fah-voh-reh]
Just trim the ends.	Solo le punte. [soh-loh leh poon-teh]
Not too short/Very short/A little shorter, please.	Non troppo corti/Molto corti/Un po' più corti, per favore. [nohn troh-ppoh kohr-tee/mohl-toh kohr-tee/oon poh pee-oh kohr-tee pehr fah-voh-reh]
A bit more off the back/front/top/sides.	Tagli un po' di dietro/davanti/sopra/ai lati. [tah-lyee oon poh dee dyeh-troh/soh-prah/ah-ee lah-tee]
Cut above/below the ears.	Le orecchie devono essere scoperte/coperte. [leh oh-reh-kkyeh deh-voh-noh eh-sseh-reh skoh-pehr-teh/koh-pehr-teh]

Please make the part on the left/right.	Faccia la riga a sinistra/a destra, per favore. [fah-chah lah ree-ghah ah see-nee-strah/ah deh-stra pehr fah-voh-reh]
A razor cut, please.	Tagli col rasoio, per favore. [tah-lyee kohl rah-zoh-yoh pehr fah voh-reh]
Would you please tease it?	Me li cotoni, per favore. [meh lee koh-toh-nee pehr fah-voh-reh]
No/Not too much hairspray, please.	Niente lacca/Poca lacca, per favore. [nyehn-teh lah-kkah/poh-kah lah-kkah pehr fah-voh-reh]
A shave, please.	La barba, per favore. [lah bahr-bah pehr fah-voh-reh]
Would you please trim my beard?	Mi spunti la barba, per favore? [mee spoon-tee lah bahr-bah pehr fah-voh-reh]
Could you give me a manicure?	Mi può fare le mani? [mee poo-oh fah-reh leh mah-nee]
Thank you. That's fine.	Grazie. Va bene così. [grah-tzyeh vah beh-neh koh-see]

Word List: Hairdresser/Barber

bangs	frangetta [frahn-jeh-ttah]
beard	barba [bahr-bah]
blond	biondo [byohn-doh]
to blow-dry	asciugare con il phon [ah-shoo-ghah-reh kohn eel fohn]
to comb	pettinare [peh-ttee-nah-reh]
curlers	i bigodini [ee bee-ghoh-dee-nee]
curls	i ricci [ee ree-chee]
dandruff	forfora [fohr-foh-rah]
dry hair	i capelli secchi [ee kah-peh-llee seh-kkee]
to dye	tingere [teen-jeh-reh]

eyebrows	le sopracciglia [leh soh-prah-<u>chee</u>-lyah]
hair	i capelli [ee kah-<u>peh</u>-llee]
hair treatment	trattamento curativo per capelli [trah-ttah-<u>mehn</u>-toh koo-rah-tee-<u>voh</u> pehr ee kah-<u>peh</u>-llee]
haircut	taglio [<u>tah</u>-lyoh]
hairspray	lacca [<u>lah</u>-kkah]
hairstyle	pettinatura [peh-ttee-nah-<u>too</u>-rah]
to have a shave	farsi fare la barba [<u>fahr</u>-see <u>fah</u>-reh lah <u>bahr</u>-bah]
layered cut	taglio scalato [<u>tah</u>-lyoh skah-<u>lah</u>-toh]
loss of hair	caduta dei capelli [kah-<u>doo</u>-tah <u>deh</u>-ee kah-<u>peh</u>-llee]
mustache	i baffi [ee <u>bah</u>-ffee]
oily hair	i capelli grassi [ee kah-<u>peh</u>-llee <u>grah</u>-ssee]
permanent	la permanente [lah pehr-mah-<u>nehn</u>-teh]
to pluck the eyebrows	correggere le sopracciglia [koh-<u>rreh</u>-djeh-reh leh soh-prah-<u>chee</u>-lyah]
to set	mettere in piega [<u>meh</u>-tteh-reh een <u>pyeh</u>-ghah]
set/permanent	messa in piega [<u>meh</u>-ssah een <u>pyeh</u>-ghah]
shampoo	lo shampoo [loh <u>shahm</u>-poh]
sideburns	le basette [leh bah-<u>seh</u>-tteh]
to tint	tingere [<u>teen</u>-jeh-reh]
toupee	il toupet [eel too-<u>peh</u>]
to trim	tagliare, spuntare [tah-<u>lyah</u>-reh spoon-<u>tah</u>-reh]
wig	parrucca [pah-<u>rroo</u>-kkah]

9 Services
I servizi

Money Matters
Questioni di denaro

Excuse me, where can I find a bank/currency exchange office?

Scusi, dove posso trovare una banca/un'agenzia di cambio? [skoo-zee doh-veh poh-ssoh troh-vah-reh oo-nah bahn-kah/oo-nah-jehn-tzee-ah dee kahm-byoh]

When does the bank open/close?

Quando apre/chiude la banca? [kwahn-doh ah-preh/kyoo-deh lah bahn-kah]

I'd like to change these dollars into lire.

Vorrei cambiare questi dollari in lire. [voh-rreh-ee kahm-byah-reh kweh-stee doh-llah-ree (mahr-kee. sheh-llee-nee, frahn-kee svee-tzeh-ree) een lee-reh]

What is the current exchange rate?

Quant'è oggi il cambio? [kwahn-teh oh-djee eel kahm-byoh]

How many lire do I get for $100?

A quante lire corrispondono $100? [ah kwahn-teh lee-reh koh-rree-spohn-doh-noh chen-toh doh-llah-ree]

I'd like to change this traveler's check/Eurocheck/money order.

Vorrei riscuotere questo tra-veller's cheque/eurocheque/vaglia postale. [voh-rreh-ee ree-skwoh-teh-reh kweh-stoh trah-vehl chek/eh-oo-roh-chek/vah-lyah poh-stah-leh]

What is the maximum I can cash on one check?

Qual è l'importo massimo per la riscossione dell'assegno? [kwah-leh leem-pohr-toh mah-ssee-moh pehr lah ree-skoh-ssyoh-neh deh-llah-sseh-nyoh]

Your check card, please.

La carta assegni, per favore. [lah kahr-tah ah-sseh-nyee pehr fah-voh-reh]

May I please see your passport/ID card?

Posso vedere il Suo passaporto/la Sua carta d'identità? [poh-ssoh veh-deh-reh eel soo-oh pah-ssah-pohr-toh/lah soo-ah kahr-tah dee-dehn-tee-tah]

Sign here, please.

Firmi qui, per favore. [feer-mee kwee pehr fah-voh-reh]

I'd like to withdraw... dollars/lire from my account.

Vorrei prelevare...dollari/lire dal mio conto. [voh-rreh-ee preh-leh-vah-reh ...doh-llah-ree/lee-reh dahl mee-oh lee-breh-ttoh poh-stah-leh dee ree-spahr-myoh]

Has any money been transferred to my account?

Sono stati versati soldi sul mio conto/per me? [soh-noh stah-tee vehr-sah-tee sohl-dee sool mee-oh kohn-toh/pehr meh]

Please go to the cashier.

Si accomodi alla cassa, per favore. [see ah-kkoh-moh-dee ah-llah kah-ssah pehr fah-voh-reh]

How would you like the money?

Che tagli preferisce? [keh tah-lyee preh-feh-ree-sheh]

Bills only, please.

Solo banconote, per favore. [soh-loh bahn-koh-noh-teh]

Some small bills and some change, please.

Banconote di piccolo taglio e spiccioli per favore. [bahn-koh-noh-teh dee pee-kkoh-loh tah-lyoh eh spee-choh-lee pehr fah-voh-reh]

Please give me three bills of 1000 lire and the rest in change.

Mi dia tre banconote da 1000 lire e il resto in spiccioli, per favore. [mee dee-ah treh bahn-koh-noh-teh dah mee-lleh lee-reh eh eel reh-stoh een spee-choh-lee]

I lost my traveler's checks. What should I do now?

Ho perso i miei traveller's cheque. Che cosa devo fare ora? [oh pehr-soh ee mee-eh-ee trah-vehl chek keh koh-sah deh-voh fah-reh oh-rah]

Word List: Money Matters

amount	**importo** [eem-<u>pohr</u>-toh]
automatic teller machine	**cassa automatica prelievi, il bancomat, sportello automatico** [kah-ssah ah-oo-toh-<u>mah</u>-too kah pre-<u>lyeh</u>-vee, eel <u>bahn</u>-koh-maht, spohr-<u>teh</u>-llo ah-oo-toh-<u>mah</u>-tee-koh]
bank	**banca** [<u>bah</u>-kah]
bank account	**conto bancario, conto corrente** [<u>kohn</u>-toh bahn-<u>kah</u>-ryoh, <u>kohn</u>-toh koh-<u>rrehn</u>-teh]
bank code number	**numero guida bancario** [<u>noo</u>-meh-roh <u>gwee</u>-dah bahn-<u>kah</u>-ryoh]
banknote/bill	**banconota** [bahn-koh-<u>noh</u>-tah]
cash	**in contanti** [een kohn-<u>tahn</u>-tee]
to cash a check	**riscuotere un assegno** [ree-<u>skwoh</u>-teh-reh oo-<u>nah</u>-<u>seeh</u>-nyoh]
change	**gli spiccioli, moneta** [lyee <u>spee</u>-choh-lee, moh-<u>neh</u>-tah]
to change/to exchange	**cambiare** [kahm-<u>byah</u>-reh]
check	**assegno** [ah-sseh-nyoh]
check card	**carta assegni** [<u>kahr</u>-tah ah-<u>sseh</u>-nyee]
checkbook	**libretto degli assegni** [lee-<u>breh</u>-ttoh <u>deh</u>-lyee ah-<u>sseh</u>-nyee]
coin	**moneta** [moh-<u>neh</u>-tah]
commission	**la provvigione** [lah proh-vve'e-<u>joh</u>-neh]
counter	**sportello** [spohr-<u>teh</u>-lloh]
currency	**valuta** [vah-<u>loo</u>-tah]
currency exchange office	**agenzia di cambio** [ah-jen-<u>tzee</u>-ah dee <u>kahm</u>-byoh]

to deposit	versare [vehr-<u>sah</u>-reh]
deposit slip	modulo di versamento [moh-doo-loh dee vehr-sah-<u>mehn</u>-toh]
Eurocheck	l'eurocheque *(m)* [<u>leh</u>-oo-roh-chek]
exchange rate	(corso del) cambio [(<u>kohr</u>-soh dehl) <u>kahm</u>-byoh]
foreign currency	la valuta estere [lah vah-<u>loo</u>-tah <u>eh</u>-steh-rah]
form	modulo [<u>moh</u>-doo-loh]
money	denaro [deh-<u>nah</u>-roh]
money order	il vaglia, assegno, il vaglia postale [eel <u>vah</u>-lyah, ah-<u>sseh</u>-nyoh, eel <u>vah</u>-lyah poh-<u>stah</u>-leh]
notice of reimbursement/ refund	bollettino di rimborso [boh-lleh-<u>ttee</u>-noh dee reem-<u>bohr</u>-soh]
to pay	pagare [pah-<u>ghah</u>-reh]
payment	pagamento [pah-ghah-<u>mehn</u>-toh]
PIN number	numero segreto [<u>noo</u>-meh-roh seh-<u>greh</u>-toh]
receipt	ricevuta [re-cheh-<u>voo</u>-tah]
remittance/transfer	rimessa, trasferimento [ree-<u>meh</u>-ssah, trah-sfeh-ree-<u>mehn</u>-toh]
savings account	conto di risparmio [<u>kohn</u>-toh dee ree-<u>spahr</u>-myoh]
savings bank	cassa di risparmio [<u>kah</u>-ssah dee ree-<u>spahr</u>-myoh]
savings book	libretto di risparmio [lee-<u>breh</u>-ttoh dee ree-<u>spahr</u>-myoh]
to sign	firmare [feer-<u>mah</u>-reh]
signature	firma [<u>feer</u>-mah]
Swiss franc	franco svizzero [<u>frah</u>-koh <u>svee</u>-tzeh-roh]

telegraph money order	vaglia telegrafico [vah-lyah teh-leh-grah-fee-koh]
traveler's check	assegno turistico, il traveller's chèque [ah-sseh-nyoh too-ree-stee-koh, eel trah-vehl chehk]
to withdraw	ritirare [ree-tee-rah-roh]
to write a check	rilasciare un assegno [ree-lah-shah-reh oo-nah-sseh-nyoh]

At the Post Office
All'ufficio postale

Where is the nearest post office/ mailbox?	Per favore, dov'è l'ufficio postale più vicino/la cassetta postale più vicina? [pehr fah-voh-reh doh-veh loo-ffee-choh poh-stah-leh pee-oo vee-chee-noh/lah kah-sseh-tta poh-stah-leh pee-oo vee-chee-nah]
How much does a letter/ postcard cost to ...	Quanto costa una lettera/una cartolina illustrata per... [kwahn-toh koh-stah oo-nah leh-tteh-rah/oo-nah kahr-toh-lee-nah ee-llo-strah-tah pehr]
the United States?	gli Stati Uniti?... [lyee stah-tee oo-nee-tee]

Canada?	il Canada? [eel <u>kah</u>-nah-dah]
Three... lire stamps, please.	Tre francobolli da...lire, per favore. [treh frahn-koh-<u>boh</u>-llee dah ... lee-re pehr fah-<u>voh</u>-reh]
(I'd like to send) this letter ...,	Questa lettera…, per favore. [kweh-stah <u>leh</u>-tteh-rah... pehr fah-<u>voh</u>-reh]
registered	raccomandata [rah-kkoh-mahn-<u>dah</u>-tah]
air mail	posta aerea [<u>poh</u>-stah ah-<u>eh</u>-reh-ah]
express	per espresso [pehr eh-<u>spreh</u>-ssoh]
How long does a letter to the United States take?	Quanto tempo impiega una lettera per gli Stati Uniti? [<u>kwahn</u>-toh <u>tehm</u>-poh eem-<u>pyeh</u>-ghah <u>oo</u>-nah <u>leh</u>-tteh-rah pehr lyee <u>stah</u>-tee oo-<u>nee</u>-tee]
Do you also have any special issue stamps?	Ha anche delle emissioni speciali? [ah <u>ahn</u>-keh <u>deh</u>-lleh eh-mee-<u>ssyoh</u>-nee speh-<u>chah</u>-lee]
This set/One stamp of each, please.	Questa serie/Un francobollo di ciascuna, per favore. [<u>kweh</u>-stah <u>seh</u>-ryeh/oon frah-koh-<u>boh</u>-lloh dee chah-<u>skoo</u>-nah pehr fah-<u>voh</u>-reh]

Held Mail

Fermo Posta

Is there any mail for me? My name is...	C'è posta per me? Il mio nome è … [cheh <u>poh</u>-stah pehr meh? eel <u>mee</u>-oh <u>noh</u>-meh eh]
No, there's nothing for you.	No, non c'è niente. [noh, nohn cheh <u>nyehn</u>-teh]
Yes there's something for you. Your passport (ID), please.	Sì, c'è qualcosa. Ha un documento, per favore? [see cheh kwahl-<u>koh</u>-sah. ah oon doh-koo-<u>mehn</u>-toh pehr fah-<u>voh</u>-reh]

Telegrams/Faxes	Telegrammi/Telefax

I'd like to send a telegram.

Vorrei spedire un telegramma.
[voh-<u>rreh</u>-ee speh-<u>dee</u>-reh oon teh-leh-<u>grah</u>-mmah]

Would you please help me fill it out?

Per favore, mi potrebbe aiutare a compilarlo? [pehr fah-<u>voh</u>-reh mee poh-<u>treh</u>-bbeh ah-yoo-<u>tah</u>-reh ah kohm-pee-<u>lahr</u>-loh]

How much does it cost per word?

Quanto costa a parola? [<u>kwahn</u>-toh <u>koh</u>-stah ah pah-<u>roh</u>-lah]

Up to 10 words it costs...; beyond that ...

Fino a 10 parole costa...; ogni ulteriore parola [<u>fee</u>-noh ah <u>dyeh</u>-chee pah-<u>roh</u>-leh <u>koh</u>-stah...; <u>oh</u>-nyee ool-teh-<u>ryoh</u>-reh pah-<u>roh</u>-lah]

Will the telegram arrive in... the same day (today)?

Il telegramma arriverà oggi stesso a…? [eel teh-leh-<u>grah</u>-mmah ah-rree-veh-<u>rah</u> <u>oh</u>-djee <u>steh</u>-ssoh]

May I send a fax from here?

Posso spedire da qui un telefax a …? [<u>poh</u>-ssoh speh-<u>dee</u>-reh dah kwee oon <u>teh</u>-leh-fax ah]

Word List: Post Office	➤ See also Word List: Money Matters

address

indirizzo [een-dee-<u>ree</u>-tzoh]

addressee

destinatario [deh-stee-nah-<u>tah</u>-ryoh]

airmail

via aerea [<u>vee</u>-ah ah-<u>eh</u>-rehah]

all other destinations

per tutte le altre destinazioni [pehr <u>too</u>-tteh leh <u>ahl</u>-treh deh-stee-nah-<u>tzyoh</u>-nee]

city

per la città

collection

levata [leh-<u>vah</u>-tah]

counter

sportello [spohr-<u>teh</u>-lloh]

countersign (COD)

contr'assegno [kohn-trah-<u>sseh</u>-nyoh]

customs declaration	la dichiarazione doganale [lah dee-kyah-rah-<u>tzyoh</u>-neh doh-ghah-<u>nah</u>-leh]
declared value	il valore dichiarato [eel vah-<u>loh</u>-reh dee-kyah-<u>rah</u>-toh]
destination	la destinazione [lah deh-stee-nah-<u>tzyoh</u>-neh]
envelope	busta [<u>boo</u>-stah]
express	espresso [eh-<u>spreh</u>-ssoh]
fax	il telefax [eel <u>teh</u>-leh-fahx]
fee	tariffa [tah-<u>ree</u>-ffah]
to fill out	compilare [kohm-pee-<u>lah</u>-reh]
form	modulo [<u>moh</u>-doo-loh]
to forward	recapitare [reh-kah-pee-<u>tah</u>-reh]
general delivery	fermo posta [<u>fehr</u>-moh <u>poh</u>-stah]
letter	lettera [<u>leh</u>-tteh-rah]
letter carrier	il/la portalettere [eel/lah <u>pohr</u>-tah-<u>leh</u>-tteh-reh]
mailbox	cassetta postale [kah-<u>sseh</u>-ttah poh-<u>stah</u>-leh]
mailing form	bollettino di spedizione dei pacchi postali [boh-lleh-<u>ttee</u>-noh dee speh-dee-<u>tzyoh</u>-neh <u>deh</u>-ee pah-kkee poh-<u>stah</u>-lee]
main post office	posta centrale [<u>poh</u>-stah chehn-<u>trah</u>-leh]
package (small)	pacchetto [pah-<u>kkeh</u>-ttoh]
parcel	pacco [<u>pah</u>-kkoh]
post office	ufficio postale [oo-<u>ffee</u>-choh poh-<u>stah</u>-leh]

postage	affrancatura [ah-ffrah-kah-<u>too</u>-rah]
postcard	cartolina postale [kahr-toh-<u>lee</u>-nah poh-<u>stah</u>-leh]
printed matter	le stampe *(pl)* [leh <u>stahm</u>-peh]
receipt	ricevuta di consegna/di scarico [ree-cheh-<u>voo</u>-tah dee kohn-<u>seh</u>-nyah/dee <u>skah</u>-ree-koh]
registered	raccomandata [rah-kkoh-mahn-<u>dah</u>-tah]
to send	spedire [speh-<u>dee</u>-reh]
sender	il mittente [eel mee-<u>ttehn</u>-teh]
special issue stamp	l'emissione *(f)* speciale [leh-mee-<u>ssyoh</u>-neh speh-<u>chah</u>-leh]
stamp	francobollo [frahn-koh-<u>boh</u>-lloh]
to stamp	affrancare [ah-ffrahn-<u>kah</u>-reh]
stamp machine	il distributore automatico per francobolli [eel dee-stree-boo-<u>toh</u>-reh ah-oo-toh-<u>mah</u>-tee-koh pehr frahm-koh-<u>boh</u>-llee]
telegram	il telegramma [eel teh-leh-<u>grah</u>-mmah]
telex	il telex [eel <u>tch</u> lchx]
weight	peso [<u>peh</u>-soh]
window hours	orario per il pubblico [oh-<u>rah</u>-ryoh pehr eel <u>poo</u>-blee-koh]
zip code	CAP (codice di avviamento postale) [kahp (<u>koh</u>-dee-che dee ah-vvyah-<u>mehn</u>-toh poh-<u>stah</u>-leh)]

Telephoning
Telefonare

May I use your phone?

Potrei usare il Suo telefono? [poh-treh-ee oo-sah-reh eel soo-oh teh-leh-foh-noh]

Where is the nearest phone booth?

Dov'è la cabina telefonica più vicina? [doh-veh lah kah-bee-nah pee-oo vee-chee-nah]

Could I please have a phone card/token?

Mi potrebbe dare una carta telefonica/un gettone? [mee poh-treh-bbeh dah-reh oo-nah kahr-tah teh-leh-foh-nee-kah/oon jeh-ttoh-neh]

Could you change this, please? I need change for the telephone.

Mi potrebbe cambiare, per favore? Mi serve una moneta per il telefono. [mee poh-treh-bbe kahm-byah-reh pehr fah-voh-reh?mee sehr-veh oo-nah moh-neh-tah pehr eel teh-leh-foh-noh]

Do you have a... telephone directory?

Ha un elenco telefonico di...? [ah oon eh-lehn-koh teh-leh-foh-nee-koh]

What is the prefix/national code for...?

Qual è il prefisso di/per...? [kwah-leh eel pre-fee-ssoh dee/pehr]

Hello, information? I'd like the number for...

Pronto, servizio informazioni? Vorrei il numero di... [prohn-toh, sehr-vee-tzyoh een-fohr-mah-tzyoh-nee? voh-rreh-ee eel noo-meh-roh dee]

I'd like to make a collect call.

Vorrei annunciare una telefonata a carico del ricevente. [voh-rreh-ee ah-nnoon-chah-reh oo-nah teh-leh-foh-nah-tah ah kah-ree-koh dehl ree-cheh-vehn-teh]

Can you put me through to..., please?

Mi può mettere in comunicazione con..., per favore? [mee poo-oh meh-tteh-reh een koh-moo-nee-kah-tzyoh-neh kohn... peh fah-voh-reh]

In Italy, you can use coins, phone cards, or phone tokens to make a telephone call. Phone tokens are given automatically as change in stores and upon request in stand-up cafés, at newsstands, and in most restaurants. In addition, there are token dispensers in phone booths, train stations, and other places. Of course, you need to keep small change on hand to purchase tokens from the dispensers.

Go to booth...	Vada nella cabina numero... [vah-dah ah-llah kah-bee-nah noo-meh-roh]
The line is busy.	La linea è occupata. [lah lee-neh-ah eh oh-kkoo-pah-tah]
There's no reply.	Non risponde nessuno. [nohn ree-spohn-deh neh-ssoo-noh]
Please stay on the line.	Resti all'apparecchio. [reh-stee ah-llah-ppah-reh-kkyoh]
This is... speaking.	Qui parla... [kwee pahr-lah]

Hello, with whom am I speaking?…	Pronto, con chi parlo? [prohn-toh kohn kee pahr-loh]
May I please speak to Mr./Mrs./Miss... ?	Scusi, potrei parlare con il signor/la signora/la signorina\…? [skoo-zee poh-treh-ee pahr-lah-reh kohn eel see-nyohr/lah see-nyoh-rah/lah see-nyoh-ree-nah]
Speaking.	Sono io. [soh-noh ee-oh]
I'll get him/her.	Glielo/La passo. [lyeh-loh/lah pah-ssoh]
I'm sorry, but he/she is not at home.	Mi dispiace, ma non c'è/è a casa. [mee dee-spyah-cheh mah nohn cheh/eh ah kah-sah]
When will he/she be back?	Quando sarà di ritorno? [kwahn-doh sah-rah dee ree-tohr-noh]
May I call back?	La posso far richiamare? [lah poh-ssoh fahr kyah-mah-reh]
Yes, my number is ...	Sì, il mio numero è… [see eel mee-oh noo-meh-roh eh]
Would you like to leave a message?	Vuol lasciar detto qualcosa? [vwohl lah-shah-reh deh-ttoh kwahl-koh-sah]
Would you please tell him/her that I called?	Gli/Le potrebbe dire che ho chiamato, per favore? [lyee/leh poh-treh-bbeh dee-reh keh oh kyah-mah-toh pehr fah-voh-reh]
Could I leave him/her a message?	Gli/Le posso lasciar detto qual cosa? [lyee/leh poh-ssoh lah-shahr deh-ttoh kwahl-koh-sah]
I'll call back later.	Richiamo più tardi. [ree-kyah-moh pyoo tahr-dee]
You have the wrong number.	Ha sbagliato numero. [ah sbah-lyah-toh noo-meh-roh]

You have dialed a nonworking number.

È stata raggiunta una numerazione inesistente. [eh <u>stah</u>-tah rah-<u>djoon</u>-tah oo-nah noo-meh-rah-<u>tzyoh</u>-neh ee-neh-see-<u>stehn</u>-teh]

Word List: Telephoning

to answer the phone	rispondere al tel<u>e</u>fono [ree-<u>spohn</u>-deh-reh]
answering machine	segreteria telef<u>o</u>nica [seh-greh-teh-<u>ree</u>-ah teh-leh-<u>foh</u>-nee-kah]
area/national code	prefisso [preh-<u>fee</u>-ssoh]
busy	occupato [oh-kkoo-<u>pah</u>-toh]
busy signal	il segnale d'occupato [eel seh-<u>nyah</u>-leh doh-kkoo-<u>pah</u>-toh]
to call	telefonare [teh-leh-foh-<u>nah</u>-reh]
change machine	il cambiamonete automatico [eel <u>kahm</u>-byah-moh-<u>neh</u>-teh ah-oo-toh-<u>mah</u>-tee-koh]
collect call	la comunicazione telef<u>o</u>nica a carico del ricevente [lah koh-moo-nee-kah-<u>tzyoh</u>-neh teh-leh-<u>foh</u>-nee-kah ah <u>kah</u>-ree-koh dehl ree-cheh-<u>vehn</u>-teh]
conversation	la conversazione [lah kohn-vehr-sah-<u>tzyoh</u>-neh]
customer service	ufficio guasti [oo-<u>ffee</u>-choh <u>gwah</u>-stee]
to dial direct	raggiungere in teleselezione [rah-<u>djoon</u>-jeh-reh een toh leh-seh-leh-<u>tzyoh</u>-neh]
to dial the number	formare il n<u>u</u>mero [fohr-<u>mah</u>-reh eel <u>noo</u>-meh-roh]

dial tone	il segnale di libero [eel seh-<u>nyah</u>-leh dee <u>lee</u>-beh-roh]
fee	tariffa [tah-<u>ree</u>-ffah]
information	informazioni [een-fohr-mah-<u>tzyoh</u>-nee]
international call	la comunicazione internazionale [lah koh-moo-nee-kah-<u>tzyoh</u>-neh een-tehr-nah-<u>tzyoh</u>-nah-leh]
local call	telefonata urbana [teh-leh-foh-<u>nah</u>-tah oor-<u>bah</u>-nah]
long distance call	interurbana [een-teh-roor-<u>bah</u>-nah]
notice	preavviso [preh-ah-<u>vvee</u>-soh]
operator	centralino [chehn-trah-<u>lee</u>-noh]
pay phone	telefono a gettone [teh-<u>leh</u>-foh-noh ah jeh-ttoh-neh]
receiver	il ricevitore [eel ree-cheh-vee-<u>toh</u>-reh]
telephone	telefono [teh-<u>leh</u>-foh-noh]
telephone book	elenco telefonico [eh-<u>lehn</u>-koh teh-leh-<u>foh</u>-nee-koh]
telephone booth	cabina telefonica [kah-<u>bee</u>-nah teh-leh-<u>foh</u>-nee-kah]
telephone call	la comunicazione, telefonata [lah koh-moo-nee-kah-<u>tzyoh</u>-neh, teh-leh-foh-<u>nah</u>-tah]
telephone number	numero telefonico [<u>noo</u>-meh-roh teh-leh-<u>foh</u>-nee-koh]
telephone office	ufficio telecomunicazioni [oo-<u>ffee</u>-choh teh-leh-koh-moo-nee-kah-<u>tzyoh</u>-nee]
telephone token	il gettone telefonico [eel jeh-<u>ttoh</u>-neh teh-leh-<u>foh</u>-nee-koh]
unit	scatto [<u>skah</u>-ttoh]

yellow pages	le pagine gialle [leh pah-jee-neh jah-lleh]

At the Police Station
Al commissariato di Polizla

➤ *See also* **Chapter 3, Car/Motorcycle/Bicycle**

Where is the nearest police station?	Dov'è il commissariato di polizia più vicino? [doh-veh ool kōh-mmee-ssah-ryah-toh dee poh-lee-tzee-ah pyoo vee-chee-noh]
I'd like to report a theft/something lost/an accident.	Vorrei denunciare un furto/uno smarrimento/un incidente. [voh-rreh-ee deh-noon-chah-reh oon foor-toh/oo-noh smah-rree-mehn-toh/oon een-chee-dehn-teh]
My... was stolen.	Mi è stata/o rubata/o... [mee eh stah tah/toh roo-bah-tah/oh]
purse	la borsa. [lah bohr-sah]
wallet	il portafoglio. [eel pohr-tah-foh-lyoh]
camera	la macchina fotografica. [lah mah-kkee-nah foh-toh-grah-fee-kah]
car/bike	la macchina/la bicicletta. [lah mah-kkee-nah/lah bee-chee-kleh-ttah]
My car was broken into.	La mia macchina è stata forzata. [lah mee-ah mah-kkee-nah eh-stah-tah fohr-tzah-tah]
...was stolen from my car.	Dalla mia macchina è stato ruba-to... [dah-llah mee-ah mah-kkee-nah eh stah-toh roo-bah-toh]
I lost...	Ho perso...[oh pehr-soh]

My son/daughter has been missing since ...	Mio figlio/Mia figlia è scomparso/a da... [mee-oh fee-lyoh/mee-ah fee-lyah eh skohm-pahr-soh/ah dah]
This man is bothering me.	Quest'uomo mi infastidisce. [kweh-stwoh-moh mee een-fah-stee-dee-sheh]
Can you help me, please?	Mi può aiutare, per favore? [mee poo-oh ah-yoo-tah-reh pehr fah-voh-reh]
When exactly did it happen?	Quando è successo esattamente? [kwahn-doh eh soo-cheh-ssoh eh-sah-ttah-mehn-teh]
We'll look into the matter.	Ce ne occuperemo. [cheh neh oh-kkoo-peh-reh-moh]
I've got nothing to do with this.	Non ho niente a che fare con questa faccenda. [nohn oh nyehn-teh ah keh fah-reh kohn kweh-stah fah-chehn-dah]
Your name and address, please.	Il Suo nome e indirizzo, per favore. [eel soo-oh noh-meh eh een-dee-ree-tzoh pehr fah-voh-reh]
Get in touch with the American/British/Canadian consulate, please.	Per favore, si rivolga al consolato americano/inglese/canadese. [pehr fah-voh-reh see ree-vohl-ghah ahl kohn-soh-lah-toh ah-meh-ree-kah-noh/een-gleh-seh/kah-nah-deh-seh]

Word List: Police

to arrest	arrestare [ah-rreh-stah-reh]
attack/assault	l'aggressione *(f);* assalto [lah-greh-ssyoh-neh, lah-ssahl-toh]
to beat up	picchiare [pee-kkyah-reh]
to break into	forzare, scassinare [fohr-tzah-reh, skah-ssee-nah-reh]

car keys	la chiave della macchina [lah kyah-veh deh-llah mah-kkee-nah]
car radio	l'autoradio *(f)* [lah-oo-toh-rah-dyoh]
to confiscate	sequestrare [seh-kweh-strah-reh]
contraband	contrabbando [kohn-trah-bahn-doh]
court	il tribunale [eel tree-boo-nah-leh]
crime	delitto [deh-lee-ttoh]
to denounce	denunciare [deh-noon chah-reh]
documents, papers	i documenti [ee doh-koo-mehn-tee]
drugs	gli stupefacenti [lyee stoo-peh-fah-chehn-tee]
guilt	colpa [kohl-pah]
to harass	infastidire [een-fah-stee-dee-reh]
identity card	carta d'identità [kahr-tah dee-dehn-tee-tah]
judge	il giudice [eel joo-dee-cheh]
keys	la chiave [lah kyah-veh]
lawyer	avvocato [ah-vvoh-kah-toh]
log book	libretto di circolazione [lee-breh-ttoh dee cheer-koh-lah-tzyoh-neh]
to lose	perdere [pehr-deh-reh]
passport	passaporto [pah-ssah-pohr-toh]
pickpocket	borsaiolo, lo scippatore [bohr-sah-yoh-loh, loh shee-ppah-toh-reh]
police	polizia [poh-lee-tzee-ah]
police car	auto della polizia [ah-oo-toh deh-llah poh-lee-tzee-ah]
police officer	l'agente *(m/f);* il vigile/la vigilessa [lah-jehn-teh, eel vee-jee-leh/lah vee-jee-leh-ssah]
preventive	la detenzione preventiva [lah deh-tehn-tzyoh-neh preh-vehn-tee-vah]

prison	**la prigione** [lah pree-<u>joh</u>-neh]
purse	**borsellino** [bohr-seh-<u>llee</u>-noh]
rape	**violenza (carnale), stupro** [vyoh-<u>lehn</u>-tzah (kahr-<u>nah</u>-leh) <u>stoo</u>-proh]
theft	**furto** [foor-toh]
thief	**ladro** [<u>lah</u>-droh]

Lost and Found
Ufficio oggetti smarriti

Where is the lost and found office, please?	**Per favore, dov'è l'ufficio oggetti smarriti?** [pehr fah-<u>voh</u>-reh doh-veh loo-<u>ffee</u>-choh oh-<u>djeh</u>-ttee smah-<u>rree</u>-tee]
I lost...	**Ho perso...** [oh <u>pehr</u>-soh]
I left my purse on the train.	**Ho lasciato la (mia) borsa sul treno.** [oh lah-<u>shah</u>-toh lah (<u>mee</u>-ah) <u>bohr</u>-sah sool <u>treh</u>-noh]
Please let me know if it is handed in.	**Per favore, se vengono riconsegnati/ritrovati, me lo faccia sapere.** [pehr fah-<u>voh</u>-reh seh <u>vehn</u>-ghoh-noh ree-kohn-seh-<u>nyah</u>-tee/ree-troh-<u>vah</u>-tee meh loh <u>fah</u>-chah sah-<u>peh</u>-reh]
Here's the address of my hotel/my home address.	**Ecco l'indirizzo del mio albergo/l'indirizzo di casa.** [<u>eh</u>-kkoh leen-dee-<u>ree</u>-tzoh dehl <u>mee</u>-oh ahl-<u>behr</u>-ghoh/leen-dee-<u>ree</u>-tzoh dee <u>kah</u>-sah]

10 **Health**
Salute

At the Pharmacy
In farmacia

Where is the nearest pharmacy?	Dov'è la farmacia (di turno) più vicina? [doh-veh lah fahr-mah-chee-ah (dee toor-noh) pyoo vee-chee-nah]
Please give me something for…	Mi dia qualcosa contro…, per favore. [mee dee-ah kwahl-koh-sah kohn-troh… pehr fah-voh-reh]
You need a prescription for this medicine.	Ci vuole una ricetta per questa medicina. [chee vwoh-leh oo-nah ree-cheh-ttah pehr kweh-stah meh-dee-chee-nah]
Can I wait?	Posso aspettare? [poo-oh ah-speh-ttah-reh]
When can I pick it up?	Quando posso venire a prenderla? [kwahn-doh poh-ssoh veh-nee-reh ah prehn-dehr-lah]

Word List: Pharmacy

➤ *See also* **Word List: Doctor/Dentist/Hospital**

after meals	dopo i pasti [doh-poh ee pah-stee]
antibiotic	antibiotico [ahn-tee-byoh-tee-koh]
antidote	antidoto [ahn-tee-toh-doh]
aspirin	aspirina [ah-spee-ree-nah]
before meals	prima dei pasti [pree-mah deh-ee pah-stee]
camomile	camomilla [kah-moh-mee-llah]
charcoal tablets	l'astringente *(m)* intestinale a base di caolino carbone [lah-streen-jehn-toh een-teh-stee-nah-leh ah bah-seh dee kah-oh-lee-noh kahr-boh-neh]
condom	preservativo [preh-sehr-vah-tee-voh]
cotton wool	il cotone idrofilo [eel koh-toh-neh ee-droh-fee-loh]

cough syrup	sciroppo (contro la tosse) [shee-<u>roh</u>-ppoh (<u>kohn</u>-troh lah <u>toh</u>-sseh)]
decongestant	le pillole anticoncezionali [leh pee-<u>lloh</u>-leh ahn-tee-kohn-cheh-<u>tzyoh</u>-nah-lee]
disinfectant	il disinfettante [eel dee-seen-feh-<u>ttahn</u>-teh]
to dissolve in the mouth	far sciogliere in bocca [fahr <u>shoh</u>-lyeh-reh een <u>boh</u>-kkah]
drops	le gocce [leh <u>ghoh</u>-cheh]
eardrops	le gocce per gli orecchi [leh <u>ghoh</u>-cheh pehr lyee oh-<u>reh</u>-kkee]
elastic bandage	benda elastica [<u>behn</u>-dah eh-<u>lah</u>-stee-kah]
eyedrops	le gocce per gli occhi, collirio [leh <u>ghoh</u>-cheh pehr lyee <u>oh</u>-kkee, koh-<u>llee</u>-ryoh]
for external use	per uso esterno [pehr <u>oo</u>-soh eh-<u>stehr</u>-noh]
for internal use	per uso interno [pehr <u>oo</u>-soh een-<u>tehr</u>-noh]
gauze	fascia di garza [<u>fah</u>-shah dee <u>ghahr</u>-zah]
glucose	glucosio [gloo-<u>koh</u>-syoh]
headache tablets	le compresse contro il mal di testa [leh kohm-<u>preh</u>-sseh <u>kohn</u>-troh eel mahl dee <u>teh</u>-stah]
heart medicine	medicamento per disturbi circolatori [meh-dee-kah-<u>mehn</u>-toh pehr dee-<u>stoor</u>-bce cheer-koh-<u>lah</u>-ree]
insect repellent	l'insetticida *(m)* [leen-seh-ttee-<u>chee</u>-dah]
insulin	insulina [een-soo-<u>lee</u>-nah]
iodine	tintura di iodio [teen-<u>too</u>-rah dee <u>yoh</u>-dyoh]

laxative	lassativo [lah-ssah-<u>tee</u>-voh]
medication/medicine	medicina, farmaco [meh-dee-<u>chee</u>-nah, <u>fahr</u>-mah-koh]
medicine (science)	medicina [meh-dee-<u>chee</u>-nah]
medicine for relief of upset stomach	digestivo in gocce [dee-jeh-<u>stee</u>-voh een <u>ghoh</u>-cheh]
mouthwash	la soluzione per gargarismi [lah soh-loo-<u>tzyoh</u>-neh pehr ee ghahr-ghah-<u>ree</u>-smee]
ointment for burns	pomata per le scottature [poh-<u>mah</u>-tah pehr leh skoh-ttah-<u>too</u>-reh]
on an empty stomach	a stomaco vuoto [ah <u>stoh</u>-mah-koh <u>vwoh</u>-toh]
painkillers/analgesics	le compresse contro il dolore, gli analgesici [leh kohm-<u>preh</u>-sseh <u>kohn</u>-troh eel doh-<u>loh</u>-reh, lyee ah-nahl-<u>jeh</u>-see-chee]
plaster	cerotto [cheh-<u>roh</u>-ttoh]
powder	cipria, borotalco [<u>chee</u>-pryah boh-roh-<u>tahl</u>-koh]
prescription	ricetta [ree-<u>cheh</u>-ttah]
salve/ointment	pomata [poh-<u>mah</u>-tah]
sedative	il calmante [eel kahl-<u>mahn</u>-teh]
side effects	le reazioni secondarie [leh reh-ah-<u>tzyoh</u>-nee seh-kohn-<u>dah</u>-ryeh]
sleeping pills	i sonniferi [ee soh-<u>nnee</u>-feh-ree]
sunburn	scottatura (solare) [skoh-ttah-<u>too</u>-rah (soh-<u>lah</u>-reh)]
suppository	supposta [soo-<u>ppoh</u>-stah]
tablet	compressa [kohm-<u>preh</u>-ssah]
to take	prendere [<u>prehn</u>-deh-reh]
thermometer	termometro [tehr-moh-meh-tro]

throat lozenges	le pastiglie per la gola [leh pah-stee-lyeh pehr lah ghoh-lah]

At the Doctor
Dal medico

Can you recommend a good...	Mi può consigliare un buon... [mee poo-oh kohn-see-lyah-reh oon bwohn]
doctor?	medico? [meh-dee-koh]
eye specialist?	oculista? [oh-koo-lee-stah]
gynecologist?	ginecologo? [jee-neh-koh-loh-ghoh]
ear, nose, and throat doctor?	otorinolaringoiatra? [oh-toh-ree-noh-la-reen-ghoh-yah-trah]
dermatologist?	dermatologo? [dehr-mah-toh-loh-ghoh]
internist?	internista? [een-tehr-nee-stah]
pediatrician?	pediatra? [peh-dyah-trah]
neurologist?	neurologo? [neh-oo-roh-loh-ghoh]
general practitioner?	medico generico? [meh-dee-koh jeh-neh-ree-koh]
urologist?	urologo? [oo-roh-loh-ghoh]
dentist?	dentista? [dehn-tee-stah]
Where is his/her practice?	Dov'è il suo ambulatorio? [doh-veh eel soo-oh ahm-boo-lah-toh-ryoh]
What are his/her office hours?	Quando riceve? [kwahn-doh ree-cheh-veh]
What's the trouble?	Che disturbi ha? [keh dee-stoor-bee ah]
I don't feel well.	Non mi sento bene. [nohn mee senh-toh beh-neh]
I have a fever.	Ho la febbre. [oh lah feh-breh]

I can't sleep.	Non riesco a dormire. [nohn ree-eh-skoh ah dohr-mee-reh]
I often feel sick/nauseated.	Spesso mi sento male/mi gira la testa. [speh-ssoh mee sehn-toh mah-leh/mee jee-rah lah teh-stah]
I fainted.	Sono svenuto/a. [soh-noh sveh-noo-toh/ah]
I have a bad cold.	Sono molto raffreddato/a. [soh-noh mohl-toh rah-ffreh-ddah-toh/ah]
I have ...	Ho… [oh]
a headache.	mal di testa. [mahl dee teh-stah]
a sore throat.	mal di gola. [mahl dee ghoh-lah]
a cough.	la tosse. [lah toh-sseh]
I got stung/bitten.	Sono stato punto/a/morso/a. [soh-noh stah-toh poon-toh/ah/mohr-soh/ah]
I have indigestion/an upset stomach.	Ho fatto un'indigestione. [oh fah-ttoh oo-neen-dee-jeh-styoh-neh]
I have diarrhea./I'm constipated.	Soffro di diarrea/stitichezza. [soh-ffroh dee dee-ah-reh-ah/stee-tee-keh-tzah]
Food doesn't agree with me./I can't stand the heat.	Digerisco male./Non sopporto il caldo. [dee-jeh-ree-skoh mah-leh/nohn soh-ppohr-toh eel kahl-doh]
I hurt myself.	Mi sono fatto/a male. [mee soh-noh fah-ttoh/ah mah-leh]
I fell.	Sono caduto/a. [soh-noh kah-doo-toh/ah]
I think I sprained ...	Credo di essermi rotto/a/slogato/a... [kreh-doh dee eh-ssehr-mee sloh-ghah-toh/ah]
Where does it hurt?	Dove fa male? [doh-veh fah mah-leh]
It hurts here.	Ho dei dolori qui. [oh doh-loh-ree kwee]

Does that hurt? | Fa male qui? [fah mah-leh kwee]

I have high/low blood pressure. | Ho la pressione alta/bassa. [oh lah preh-ssyoh-neh ahl-tah/bah-ssah]

I am a diabetic. | Sono diabetico/a. [soh-noh dyah-beh-tee-koh/ah]

I'm pregnant. | Sono incinta. [soh-noh een-cheen-tah]

I had... recently. | Poco tempo fa ho…[poh-koh tehm-poh fah oh]

Get undressed, please./ Uncover your arm. | Si spogli, per favore./Si scopra il braccio. [see spoh-lyee pehr fah-voh-reh/see skoh-prah eel brah-choh]

Take a deep breath. Hold your breath, please. | Respiri profondamente. Tratten ga il respiro, per favore. [reh-spee-ree proh-fohn-dah-mehn-teh.trah-ttehn-ghah eel reh-spee-roh]

Open your mouth. | Apra la bocca. [ah-prah lah boh-kkah]

Let me see your tongue. | Mi faccia vedere la lingua. [mee fah-chah veh-deh-reh lah leen-gwah]

Cough, please. | Tossisca. [toh-ssee-skah]

How long have you been feeling like this? | Da quanto tempo si sente male? [dah kwahn-toh tehm-poh see sehn-teh mah-leh]

Do you have an appetite? | Ha appetito? [ah ah-ppeh-tee-toh]

I have no appetite. | Non ho appetito. [nohn oh ah-ppeh-tee-toh]

Do you have a vaccination certificate? | Ha un certificato di vacci nazione? [ah oon chehr tce-fee-kah-toh dee vah-chee-nah-tzyoh-neh]

I've been vaccinated against ... | Sono vaccinato contro… [soh-noh vah-chee-nah-toh kohn-troh]

You need to have an X-ray. | Bisogna fare una radiografia. [bee-soh-nyah fah-reh oo-nah rah dyoh-grah-fee-ah]

I need to do a blood test/urinalysis.

Ho bisogno dell'esame del sangue/dell'urina. [oh bee-<u>soh</u>-nyoh <u>deh</u>-lleh-<u>sah</u>-meh dehl sahn-gweh/deh-lloo-<u>ree</u>-nah]

I'm sending you to a specialist.

La mando da uno specialista. [lah <u>mahn</u>-doh dah <u>oo</u>-noh speh-chah-<u>lee</u>-stah]

You need to have an operation.

Deve essere operato/a. [<u>deh</u>-veh eh-sseh-reh oh-peh-<u>rah</u>-toh/ah]

You need to stay in bed for a few days.

Deve stare a letto per qualche giorno. [<u>deh</u>-veh <u>stah</u>-reh ah <u>leh</u>-ttoh pehr <u>kwahl</u>-keh <u>johr</u>-noh]

It's nothing serious.

Non è niente di grave. [nohn eh <u>nyehn</u>-teh dee grah-veh]

Can you give me/prescribe something for... ?

Mi può dare/prescrivere qual cosa contro…? [mee poo-<u>oh</u> dah-reh/preh-<u>skree</u>-veh-reh kwahl-<u>koh</u>-sah <u>kohn</u>-troh]

I usually take ...

Di solito prendo… [dee <u>soh</u>-lee-toh <u>prehn</u>-doh]

Take one tablet/pill at...

Prenda una compressa prima di andare a letto... [<u>prehn</u>-dah <u>oo</u>-nah kohm-<u>preh</u>-ssah <u>pree</u>-mah dee ahn-<u>dah</u>-reh ah <u>leh</u>-ttoh]

Here is my international medical insurance card.

Ecco la mia tessera dell'assicu razione medica internazionale. [<u>eh</u>-kkoh lah <u>mee</u>-ah <u>teh</u>-sseh-rah deh-<u>llah</u>-ssee-koo-rah-<u>tzyoh</u>-neh <u>meh</u>-dee-kah een-tehr-nah-tzyoh-<u>nah</u>-leh]

Can you give me a doctor's certificate?

Mi può rilasciare un certificato medico? [mee poo-<u>oh</u> ree-lah-<u>shah</u>-reh oon chehr-tee-fee-<u>kah</u>-toh <u>meh</u>-dee-koh]

At the Dentist
Dal dentista

I have a (terrible) toothache.	Ho (un forte) mal di denti. [oh (oon fohr-teh) mahl dee <u>dehn</u>-tee]
This (top/bottom/front/back) tooth hurts.	Questo dente (di sopra/di sotto/davanti/in fondo) fa male. [<u>kweh</u>-stoh <u>dehn</u>-teh (dee <u>soh</u>-prah/dee <u>soh</u>-ttoh/dah-<u>vahn</u>-tee/een <u>fohn</u>-doh) fah <u>mah</u>-leh]
The filling fell out.	La piombatura è andata via. [lah pyohm-bah-<u>too</u>-rah eh ahn-<u>dah</u>-tah <u>vee</u>-ah]
I broke a tooth.	Mi si è rotto un dente. [mee see eh <u>roh</u>-ttoh oon <u>dehn</u>-toh]
I need to fill it.	Lo devo otturare. [loh <u>deh</u>-voh oh-ttoo-<u>rah</u>-reh]
I'll only do a temporary job.	Faccio soltanto un trattamento provvisorio. [<u>fah</u>-choh sohl-<u>tahn</u>-toh oon trah-ttah-<u>mehn</u>-toh proh-vvee-<u>soh</u>-ryoh]
I have to pull it out.	Devo estrarlo. [<u>deh</u>-voh eh-<u>strahr</u>-loh]
This tooth needs a crown.	A questo dente bisogna fare una corona. [ah <u>kweh</u>-stoh <u>dehn</u>-teh bee-<u>soh</u>-nyah <u>fah</u>-reh <u>oo</u>-nah koh-<u>roh</u>-nah]
Please give me a shot./Please do not give me a shot.	Mi faccia una puntura./Non mi faccia la puntura. [mee <u>fah</u>-chah <u>oo</u>-nah poon-<u>too</u>-rah/nohn mee <u>fah</u>-chah <u>oo</u>-nah poon-<u>too</u>-rah]
Rinse out your mouth.	Si sciacqui la bocca. [see <u>shah</u>-kwee lah <u>boh</u>-kkah]
Can you fix these dentures?	Mi può riparare questa protesi? [mee poo-<u>oh</u> ree-pah-<u>rah</u>-reh <u>kweh</u>-stah <u>proh</u>-teh-see]

Come back in three days for a checkup.

Torni fra due giorni per il con trollo. [tohr-nee frah doo-eh johr-nee pehr eel kohn-troh-lloh]

When you get home, go straight to your dentist.

Quando torna a casa, vada subito dal Suo dentista. [kwahn-doh tohr-nah ah kah-sah vah-dah soo-bee-toh dahl soo-oh dehn-tee-stah]

At the Hospital
In ospedale

How long do I have to stay here?

Per quanto tempo devo stare qui? [pehr kwahn-toh tehm-poh deh-voh stah-reh kwee]

I'm in pain/I can't sleep. Please give me some painkillers/sleeping pills.

Ho dolore/Non riesco ad addor mentarmi. Per favore mi dia un analgesico/un sonnifero. [oh doh-loh-reh/nohn ryeh-skoh ahd ah-ddohr-mehn-tahr-mee. pehr fah-voh-reh mee dee-ah oon ah-nahl-jeh-see-koh/oon soh-nnee-feh-roh]

When can I get up?

Quando potrò alzarmi? [kwahn-doh poh-troh ahl-tzahr-mee]

Please give me a certificate stating how long I was in the hospital along with the diagnosis.

Per favore, mi rilasci un certifi cato con la specificazione della durata della degenza ospedaliera e della diagnosi. [pehr fah-voh-reh mee ree-lah-shee oon chehr-tee-fee-kah-toh kohn lah speh-chee-fee-kah-tzyoh-neh deh-llah doo-rah-tah deh-llah deh-jehn-tza oh-speh-dah-lyeh-rah eh deh-llah dee-ah-nyoh-see]

Word List: Doctor/Dentist/Hospital

abdomen	l'addome *(m)* [lah-<u>ddoh</u>-meh]
abscess	ascesso [ah-<u>sheh</u>-ssoh]
AIDS	AIDS [<u>ah</u>-eeds]
allergy	allergia [ah-llehr-<u>jee</u>-ah]
anesthesia	anestesia [ah-neh-steh-<u>see</u>-ah]
angina	angina [<u>ahn</u>-jee-nah]
appendicitis	l'appendicite *(f)* [lah-ppehn-dee-<u>chee</u>-teh]
appendix	l'appendice *(f)* [lah-ppehn-<u>dee</u>-cheh]
arm	braccio [<u>brah</u>-choh]
artificial limb	la protesi [lah <u>proh</u>-teh-see]
asthma	l'asma *(m/f)* [<u>lah</u>-smah]
attack/fit	attacco [ah-<u>ttah</u>-kkoh]
back	schiena [<u>skyeh</u>-nah]
backache	il dolore alla schiena [eel doh-<u>loh</u>-reh <u>ah</u>-llah <u>skyeh</u>-nah]
bladder	vescica [veh-<u>shee</u>-kah]
to bleed	sanguinare [sahn-gwee-<u>nah</u>-reh]
bleeding/hemorrhage	emorragia [eh-moh-rrah-<u>jee</u>-ah]
blood	il sangue, gruppo sanguigno [eel <u>sahn</u>-gweh, <u>groo</u>-ppoh sahn-<u>gwee</u>-nyoh]
blood poisoning	setticemia [seh-ttee-cheh-<u>mee</u>-ah]
blood pressure (high/low)	la pressione sanguigna (alta/bassa) [lah preh-<u>ssyoh</u>-neh sahn-<u>gwee</u>-nyah (<u>ahl</u>-tah/<u>bah</u>-ssah)]
blood test	l'esame *(m)* del sangue [<u>leh</u>-sah-meh dehl <u>sahn</u>-gweh]

blood transfusion	la trasfusione del sangue [lah trah-sfoo-<u>syoh</u>-neh dehl <u>sahn</u>-gweh]
bone	osso [<u>oh</u>-ssoh]
bowel movement	l'evacuazione *(f)* [leh-vah-kwah-<u>tzyoh</u>-neh]
brain	cervello [chehr-<u>veh</u>-lloh]
break/fracture	frattura (ossea) [frah-ttoo-rah (<u>oh</u>-sseh-ah)]
breast/chest	petto [<u>peh</u>-ttoh]
to breathe	respirare [reh-spee-<u>rah</u>-reh]
broken	rotto [<u>roh</u>-ttoh]
bronchial tubes	i bronchi [ee <u>brohn</u>-kee]
bronchitis	la bronchite [lah brohn-<u>kee</u>-teh]
bruise	ematoma [eh-mah-<u>toh</u>-mah]
burn	l'ustione *(f)* [loo-<u>styoh</u>-neh]
bypass	bypass [<u>bah</u>-ee pahss]
cancer	cancro [<u>kahn</u>-kroh]
cardiologist	cardiologo [kahr-<u>dyoh</u>-loh-ghoh]
to catch a cold	pr<u>e</u>ndere freddo, raffreddarsi [<u>prehn</u>-deh-reh <u>freh</u>-ddoh, rah-ffreh-<u>ddahr</u>-see]
cavity	la carie [lah <u>kah</u>-ryeh]
certificate	certificato [chehr-tee-fee-<u>kah</u>-toh]
chest	cassa tor<u>a</u>cica [<u>kah</u>-ssah toh-<u>rah</u>-chee-kah]
chicken pox	varicella [vah-ree-<u>cheh</u>-llah]
chills	i br<u>i</u>vidi [ee <u>bree</u>-vee-dee]
cholera	il col<u>e</u>ra [eel koh-<u>leh</u>-rah]
circulatory disorders	disturbi circolatori [dee-<u>stoor</u>-bee chee-koh-lah-<u>toh</u>-ree]

cold	il raffreddore [eel rah-ffreh-ddoh-reh]
colic	colica [koh-lee-kah]
collarbone	clavicola [klah-vee-koh-lah]
concussion	la commozione cerebrale [lah koh-mmoh-tzyoh-neh cheh-reh-brah-leh]
constipation	la costipazione, stitichezza [lah koh-stee-pah-tzyoh-neh, stee-tee-keh-tzah]
contagious	contagioso [kohn-tah-joh-soh]
contusion	la contusione [lah kohn-too-syoh-neh]
cough	la tosse [lah toh-sseh]
cramp	crampo [krahm-poh]
crown (tooth)	corona [koh-roh-nah]
cut	ferita da taglio [feh-ree-tah dah tah-lyoh]
department	reparto [reh-pahr-toh]
diabetes	il diabete [eel dyah-beh-teh]
diagnosis	la diagnosi [lah dyah-nyoh-see]
diarrhea	diarrea [dyah-rreh-ah]
diet	il regime, la dieta [eel reh-jee-meh, lah dyeh-tah]
difficulty breathing	difficoltà di respirazione [dee-ffee-kohl-tah dee reh-spee-rah-tzyoh-neh]
digestion	la digestione [lah dee-jeh-styoh-neh]
diphtheria	la difterite [lah deef-teh-ree-teh]
to disinfect	disinfettare [dee-seen-feh-ttah-reh]
dislocated	slogato [sloh-ghah-toh]
dizziness	le vertigini [leh vehr-tee-jee-nee]
to dress (wound)	fasciare [fah-shah-reh]

ear	orecchio [oh-<u>reh</u>-kkyoh]
eardrum	membrana del timpano [mehm-<u>brah</u>-nah dehl <u>teem</u>-pah-noh]
elbow	gomito [<u>ghoh</u>-mee-toh]
esophagus	esofago [eh-<u>soh</u>-fah-ghoh]
examination	l'esame *(m)* [leh-<u>sah</u>-meh]
to extract (tooth)	togliere, estrarre [<u>toh</u>-lyeh-reh, eh-<u>strah</u>-rreh]
eye(s)	l'occhio, *(pl)* gli occhi [<u>loh</u>-kkyoh, lyee <u>oh</u>-kkee]
face	faccia [<u>fah</u>-chah]
fainting	privo di sensi, svenimento [<u>pree</u>-voh dee <u>sehn</u>-see, sveh-nee-<u>mehn</u>-toh]
fever	la febbre [lah <u>feh</u>-breh]
filling	piombatura [pyohm-bah-<u>too</u>-rah]
finger	dito [<u>dee</u>-toh]
first aid supplies	il materiale di pronto soccorso [eel mah-teh-<u>ryah</u>-leh dee <u>prohn</u>-toh soh-<u>kkohr</u>-soh]
flu	influenza [een-floo-<u>ehn</u>-zah]
food poisoning	l'intossicazione *(f)* da alimenti [leen-toh-ssee-kah-<u>tzyoh</u>-neh dah ah-lee-<u>mehn</u>-tee]
foot	il piede [eel <u>pyeh</u>-deh]
gallbladder	la cistifellea [lah chee-stee-<u>feh</u>-lleh-ah]
gas	flatulenza [flah-too-<u>lehn</u>-zah]
German measles	rosolia [roh-soh-<u>lee</u>-ah]
gland	ghiandola [<u>ghyahn</u>-doh-lah]
gum	gengiva [jehn-<u>jee</u>-vah]
hand	la mano [lah <u>mah</u>-noh]

to have a cold	raffreddato [rah-ffreh-<u>ddah</u>-toh]
to have a sore throat	avere la voce rauca [ah-<u>veh</u>-reh lah <u>voh</u>-cheh <u>rah</u>-oo-kah]
hay fever	il raffreddore da fieno [eel rah-ffreh-<u>ddoh</u>-reh dah <u>fyeh</u>-noh]
head	testa [<u>teh</u>-stah]
headache	il mal di testa [mahl dee teh-stah]
hearing	udito [oo-<u>dee</u>-toh]
heart	il cuore, infarto [eel <u>kwoh</u>-reh, leen-<u>fahr</u>-toh]
heart attack	attacco cardiaco [ah-ttah-kkoh kahr-<u>dee</u>-ah-koh]
heart defect	difetto cardiaco [dee-<u>feh</u>-ttoh kahr-<u>dee</u>-ah-koh]
heart trouble	i disturbi cardiaci [ee dee-<u>stoor</u>-bee kahr-<u>dee</u>-ah-chee]
heartburn	acidità di stomaco [ah-chee-dee-<u>tah</u> dee <u>stoh</u>-mah-koh]
hemorrhoids	le emorroidi [leh eh-moh-<u>rroh</u>-ee-dee]
hernia	l'ernia (inguinale) [<u>lehr</u>-nyah (een-gwee-<u>nah</u>-leh]
hip	anca [<u>ahn</u>-kah]
hospital	l'ospedale *(m)* [loh-speh-<u>dah</u>-leh]
to hurt	far male [fahr <u>mah</u>-leh]
incisor	il dente incisivo [eel <u>dehn</u>-teh een-chee-<u>see</u>-voh]
indigestion	l'indigestione *(f)* [leen-dee-jeh-<u>styoh</u>-neh]
infection	l'infezione *(f)* [leen-feh-<u>tzyoh</u>-neh]
inflammation	l'infiammazione *(f)* [leen-fyah-mmah-<u>tzyoh</u>-neh]

infusion	la fleboclisi, l'ipodermoclisi *(f)* [lah fleh-<u>boh</u>-see, lee-poh—dehr-<u>moh</u>-see]
injection/shot	l'iniezione *(f),* puntura [ee-nyeh-<u>tzyoh</u>-neh, poon-<u>too</u>-rah]
to injure	ferire [feh-<u>ree</u>-reh]
injury/wound	ferita [feh-<u>ree</u>-tah]
insomnia	insonnia [een-<u>soh</u>-nnyah]
intestine	intestino [een-teh-<u>stee</u>-noh]
jaundice	itterizia [ee-tteh-ree-tzyah]
jaw	mascella [mah-<u>sheh</u>-llah]
joint	l'articolazione *(f)* [lahr-tee-koh-lah-<u>tzyoh</u>-neh]
kidney	il rene [eel <u>reh</u>-neh]
kidney disease	la nefrite [lah neh-<u>free</u>-teh]
kidney stone	calcolo renale [kahl-<u>koh</u>-loh reh-<u>nah</u>-leh]
knee	ginocchio [jee-<u>noh</u>-kkyoh]
knuckle	malleolo *(foot)*; nocella *(hand)* [mah-<u>lleh</u>-oh-loh, noh-<u>cheh</u>-llah]
leg	gamba [<u>ghahm</u>-bah]
limbs	le membra [leh <u>mehm</u>-brah]
lip	labbro [<u>lah</u>-broh]
liver	fegato [<u>feh</u>-ghah-toh]
loss of appetite	mancanza d'appetito [mahn-<u>kahn</u>-tzah dah-ppeh-<u>tee</u>-toh]
lumbago	la lombaggine [lah lohm-<u>bah</u>-djee-neh]
lung	il polmone [eel pohl-<u>moh</u>-noh]
malaria	malaria [mah-<u>lah</u>-ryah]
measles	morbillo [mohr-<u>bee</u>-lloh]

medical insurance	cassa malattia [kah-ssah mah-lah-ttee-ah]
medical insurance form	buono per le cure mediche [bwoh-noh pehr leh koo-reh meh-dee-keh]
medical office	ambulatorio [ahm-boo-lah-toh-ryoh]
menstruation	la mestruazione [lah meh-stroo-ah-tzyoh-neh]
middle ear infection	l'otite *(f)* [loh-tee-teh]
migraine	emicrania [eh-mee-krah-nyah]
miscarriage	aborto [ah-bohr-toh]
molar	il dente molare [eel dehn-teh moh-lah-reh]
mouth	bocca [boh-kkah]
mumps	gli orecchioni [lyee oh-reh-kkyoh-nee]
muscle	muscolo [moo-skoh-loh]
nausea	nausea [nah-oo-seh-ah]
neck	collo [koh-lloh]
nerve	nervo [nehr-voh]
nervous	nervoso [nehr-voh-soh]
nose	naso [nah-soh]
nosebleed	emorragia nasale [eh-moh-rrah-jee-ah nah-sah-leh]
nurse	infermiera [een-fehr-myeh-rah]
operation	l'operazione *(f)* [loh-peh-rah-tzyoh-neh]
pacemaker	il cardiostimolatore, il pacemaker [eel kahr-dyoh-stee-moh-lah-toh-reh, eel peh-ees-meh-kehr]
pains	i dolori [ee doh-loh-ree]
paralysis	la paralisi [lah pah-rah-lee-see]

to perspire	sudare [soo-<u>dah</u>-reh]
perspiration	il sudore [eel soo-<u>doh</u>-reh]
pneumonia	la polmonite [lah pohl-moh-<u>nee</u>-teh]
poisoning	avvelenamento [ah-vveh-leh-nah-<u>mehn</u>-toh]
polio	la polio (melite) [lah <u>poh</u>-lyoh (meh-<u>lee</u>-teh)]
pregnancy	gravidanza [grah-vee-<u>dahn</u>-tzah]
to prescribe	prescrivere [preh-<u>skree</u>-veh-reh]
pulled ligament/muscle	stiramento [stee-rah-<u>mehn</u>-toh]
pulse	polso [<u>pohl</u>-soh]
pus	il pus [eel poos]
rash	l'eruzione f cutanea, l'esantema *(m)* [leh-roo-<u>tzyoh</u>-neh koo-<u>tah</u>-neh-ah, leh-sah-<u>teh</u>-mah]
rheumatism	i reumatismi [ee reh-mah-oo-<u>tee</u>-smee]
rib	costola [<u>koh</u>-stoh-lah]
salmonella	la salmonellosi [lah sahl-moh-neh-<u>lloh</u>-see]
scar	la cicatrice [lah chee-kah-<u>tree</u>-cheh]
scarlet fever	scarlattina [skahr-lah-<u>ttee</u>-nah]
sciatica	sciatica *(f)* [<u>shah</u>-tee-kah]
to sew	cucire [koo-<u>chee</u>-reh]
sex organs	gli organi genitali [lyee <u>ohr</u>-ghah-nee jeh-nee-<u>tah</u>-lee]
sharp pain (side or back)	le fitte al fianco [leh <u>fee</u>-tteh ahl fyahn-koh]
shin	tibia [<u>tee</u>-byah]
shoulder	spalla [<u>spah</u>-llah]

sick	malato [mah-<u>lah</u>-toh]
sickness	malattia [mah-lah-<u>ttee</u>-ah]
sinus	la sinusite [lah see-noo-<u>see</u>-teh]
skin	la pelle [lah <u>peh</u>-lleh]
skin disease	malattia della pelle [mah-lah-<u>ttee</u>-ah <u>deh</u>-llah <u>peh</u>-lleh]
skull	cranio [<u>krah</u>-nyoh]
smallpox	vaiolo [vah-<u>yoh</u>-loh]
sore throat	mal di gola [mahl dee <u>ghoh</u>-lah]
specialist	lo specialista [loh speh-chah-<u>lee</u>-stah]
spinal column	spina dorsale, colonna vertebrale [<u>spee</u>-nah dohr-<u>sah</u>-leh, koh-<u>loh</u>-nnah vehr-teh-<u>brah</u>-leh]
splint	stecca [<u>steh</u>-kkah]
stitch	punto [<u>poon</u>-toh]
stomach	stomaco [<u>stoh</u>-mah-koh]
stomachache	il mal di stomaco [eel mahl dee <u>stoh</u>-mah-koh]
stroke	apoplessia cerebrale [ah-poh-pleh-<u>sse</u>-ah cch-reh-<u>brah</u>-leh]
stroke (apoplexy)	colpo apoplettico [<u>kohl</u>-poh ah-poh-<u>pleh</u>-ttee-koh]
sunlamp	lampada solare [<u>lahm</u>-pah-dah soh-<u>lah</u>-reh]
sunstroke	colpo di sole [<u>kohl</u>-poh dee <u>soh</u>-leh]
surgeon	chirurgo [kee-<u>roor</u>-ghoh]
swelling	il gonfiore, la tumefazione [eel ghohn-<u>fyoh</u>-reh, lah too-meh-fah-<u>tzyoh</u>-neh]
syringe	siringa [see-<u>reen</u>-ghah]

tetanus	tetano [teh-tah-noh]
throat	gola [ghoh-lah]
to be allergic to	essere allergico a [eh-sseh-reh ah-llehr-jee-koh ah]
toe	dito del piede [dee-toh dehl pyeh-deh]
tongue	lingua [leen-gwah]
tonsillitis	la tonsillite [lah tohn-see-llee-teh]
tonsils	le tonsille [leh tohn-see-lleh]
tooth	il dente [eel dehn-teh]
toothache	il mal di denti [eel mahl dee dehn-tee]
torn ligament	strappo dei legamenti [strah-ppoh deh-ee leh-ghah-mehn-tee]
tumor	il tumore [eel too-moh-reh]
typhus	tifo [tee-foh]
ulcer	ulcera [ool-cheh-rah]
ultrasound	l'esame (m) con ultrasuoni [leh-sah-neh kohn ool-trah-swoh-nee]
urine	urina [oo-ree-nah]
to vaccinate	vaccinare [vah-chee-nah-reh]
vaccination	la vaccinazione [lah vah-chee-nah-tzyoh-neh]
vein	vena [veh-nah]
venereal disease	malattia venerea [mah-lah-ttee-ah veh-neh-reh-ah]
virus	il virus [eel vee-roos]
visiting hours	orario di visita [oh-rah-ryoh dee vee-see-tah]
to vomit	vomitare [voh-mee-tah-reh]
waiting room	sala d'aspetto [sah-lah dah-speh-ttoh]

whooping cough	la pertosse [lah pehr-<u>toh</u>-sseh]
X-ray	radiografia [rah-dyoh-grah-<u>fee</u>-ah]
to X-ray	radiografare [rah-dyoh-grah-<u>fah</u>-reh]
yellow fever	la febbre gialla [lah <u>feh</u>-breh jah-llah]

At a Health Resort

In cura

What is your doctor's diagnosis?	Che cosa ha diagnosticato il Suo medico? [keh <u>koh</u>-sah ah dyah-nyoh-stee-<u>kah</u>-toh eel <u>soo</u>-oh meh-dee-koh]
How many more treatments do I have?	Quante applicazioni ho ancora? [<u>kwahn</u>-teh ah-pplee-kah-<u>tzyoh</u>-nee oh ahn-<u>koh</u>-rah]
I'd like to have some more...	Vorrei ancora alcune...in più. [voh-<u>rreh</u>-ee anh-<u>koh</u>-rah ahl-<u>koo</u>-neh...een pyoo]
Would you make another appointment for me?	Mi potrebbe dare un altro appuntamento? [mee poh-<u>treh</u> beh <u>dah</u>-reh oo-<u>nahl</u>-troh ah-ppoon-tah-<u>mehn</u>-toh]

Word List: Health Resort

1000-calorie diet	la dieta delle 1000 calorie [lah <u>dyeh</u>-tah <u>deh</u>-lleh <u>mee</u>-lleh kah-loh-<u>ree</u>-eh]
bath	bagno [<u>bah</u>-nyoh]
cell therapy	terapia cellulare [teh-rah-<u>pee</u>-ah cheh-lloo-<u>lah</u>-reh]
cure/treatment	cura, trattamento [<u>koo</u>-rah trah-ttah-<u>mehn</u> toh]
diet	il regime, la dieta [eel reh-<u>jee</u>-meh lah <u>dyeh</u>-tah]
to eliminate	eliminare le scorie [eh-lee-mee-<u>nah</u>-reh leh <u>skoh</u>-ryeh]

follow-up	cura di consolidamento [koo-rah dee kohn-soh-lee-dah-mehn-toh]
foot bath	pediluvio [peh-dee-loo-vyoh]
health spa	la stazione termale [lah stah-tzyoh-neh tehr-mah-leh]
hot air	aria calda [ah-ryah kahl-dah]
hydrotherapy treatment	cura idroterapica [koo-rah ee-droh-teh-rah-pee-kah]
hydrotherapy tub	vasca per la cura idroterapica [vah-skah pehr lah koo-rha ee-droh-teh-rah-pee-kah]
inhalation	l'inalazione (f) [lee-nah-lah-tzyoh-nee]
inhalation therapy	inalare, fare inalazioni [ee-nah-lah-reh, fah-reh ee-nah-lah-tzyoh-nee]
level of treatment	piano di cura [pyah-noh dee koo-rah]
liposuction	drenaggio linfatico [dreh-nah-djoh leen-fah-tee-koh]
massage	massaggio [mah-ssah-djoh]
to massage	massaggiare [mah-ssah-djah-reh]
masseur/masseuse	massaggiatore/massaggiatrice [mah-ssah-djah-toh-reh/mah-ssah-djah-tree-cheh]
medicine	farmaco [fahr-mah-koh]
mineral bath	bagno d'acque minerali, bagno idrominerale [bah-nyoh dah-kweh mee-neh-rah-lee, bah-nyoh ee-droh-mee-neh-rah-leh]
mineral spring	la sorgente d'acqua minerale [lah sohr-jehn-teh dah-kwah mee-neh-rah-leh]
mud	fango [fahn-ghoh]

mudbath(s)	i fanghi, fangatura [ee <u>fahn</u>-ghee, fahn-ghah-<u>too</u>-rah]
natural therapy	terapia naturalista [teh-rah-<u>pee</u>-ah nah-too-rah-<u>lee</u>-stah]
nursing home	casa di cura [<u>kah</u>-sah dee <u>koo</u>-rah]
pain therapy	terapia analgesica [teh-rah-<u>pee</u>-ah ah-nahl-<u>jeh</u>-see-kah]
physical therapy	ginnastica medica [jee-nnah-stee-kah meh-dee-kah]
physiotherapy	fisioterapia [fee-syoh teh-rah-<u>pee</u>-ah]
rate of stay	tassa di soggiorno [<u>tah</u>-ssah dee soh-<u>djohr</u>-noh]
reflex massage	massaggio delle zone riflesse [mah-<u>ssah</u>-djoh <u>deh</u>-lleh <u>zoh</u>-neh ree-<u>fleh</u>-sseh]
respiratory therapy	terapia respiratoria [teh-rah-<u>pee</u>-ah reh-spee-rah <u>toh</u>-ryah]
sanatorium	sanatorio, casa di cura [sah-nah-<u>toh</u>-ryoh, <u>kah</u>-sah dee <u>koo</u>-rah]
seabath	bagno di mare [<u>bah</u>-nyoh dee <u>mah</u>-reh]
self-training	il training autogeno [eel treh-<u>ee</u>-neeng ah-oo-<u>toh</u>-jeh-noh]
sunlamp	lampada solare [<u>lahm</u>-pah-dah soh-<u>lah</u>-reh]
therapeutic bath	bagno terapeutico [<u>bah</u>-nyoh teh-rah-<u>peh</u>-oo-tee-koh]
thermal bath	bagno termale [<u>bah</u>-nyoh tehr-<u>mah</u>-leh]
thermal pool	piscina termale [pee-<u>shee</u>-nah tehr-<u>mah</u>-leh]
thermal treatment	medico termale [<u>meh</u>-dee-koh tehr-<u>mah</u>-leh]

treatment	cura medica, l'applicazione *(f)* [koo-rah meh-dee-kah, lah-pplee-kah-tzyoh-neh]
Turkish bath	bagno turco [bah-nyoh toor-koh]
ultrasound	gli ultrasuoni [lyee ool-trah-swoh-nee]
underwater massage	massaggio sott'acqua [mah-ssah-djoh soh-ttah-kwah]
X-rays	i raggi, l'irradiazione *(f)* [ee rah-djee, lee-rah-dyah-tzyoh-neh]
yoga	lo yoga [loh yoh-ghah]

On the Way to a Business Meeting
Il lungo viaggio per raggiungere il socio d'affari

Which is the street to…? Qual è la strada per…? [kwah-<u>leh</u> lah <u>strah</u>-dah pehr]

Where is the main entrance? Dov'è l'ingresso principale? [doh-<u>veh</u> leen-<u>greh</u>-ssoh preeh-chee-<u>pah</u>-leh]

My name is... I'm from... Il mio nome è… Sono della ditta … [eel <u>mee</u>-oh <u>noh</u>-meh eh… <u>soh</u>-noh <u>deh</u>-llah <u>dee</u>-ttah]

May I please speak to…? Posso parlare con…, per favore? [<u>poh</u>-ssoh pahr-<u>lah</u>-reh kohn… pehr fah-<u>voh</u>-reh]

Would you please tell…that I'm here? Per favore mi prenda un appuntamento con… [pehr fah-<u>voh</u>-reh mee <u>prehn</u>-dah oon ah-ppon-tah-<u>mehn</u>-toh kohn]

I have an appointment with... Ho un appuntamento con… [oh oon ah-ppoon-tah-<u>mehn</u>-toh kohn]

… is expecting you. … La sta aspettando. [lah stah ah-speh-<u>ttahn</u>-doh]

He/She is still in a meeting. È ancora ad una riunione. [eh ahn-<u>koh</u>-rah ahd <u>oo</u> nah ryoo-<u>nyoh</u>-neh]

I'll take you… La accompagno da… [lah ah-kkohm-<u>pah</u>-nyoh dah]

I'm sorry I'm late. La prego di scusare il ritardo. [lah <u>preh</u>-ghoh dee skoo-<u>sah</u>-reh eel ree-<u>tahr</u>-doh]

Please sit down. Si accomodi, prego. [see ah-<u>kkoh</u>-moh-dee <u>preh</u>-ghoh]

May I offer you something to drink?	Le posso offrire qualcosa da bere? [leh poh-ssoh oh-ffree-reh kwahl-koh-sah dah beh-reh]
Did you have a good trip?	Ha fatto buon viaggio? [ah fah-ttoh bwohn vyah-djoh]
How much time do we have?	Quanto tempo abbiamo? [kwahn-toh tehm-poh ah-byah-moh]
When does your plane leave?	Quando parte il Suo aereo? [kwahn-doh pahr-teh eel soo-oh ah-eh-reh-oh]
I need an interpreter.	Ho bisogno di un interprete. [oh bee-soh-nyoh dee oon een-tehr-preh-teh]

Word List: Business Meeting

appointment	appuntamento [ah-ppoon-tah-mehn-toh]
building	edificio [eh-dee-fee-choh]
conference center	centro conferenze [chehn-troh kohn-feh-rehn-tzeh]
conference room	sala delle conferenze [sah-lah kohn-feh-rehn-tzeh]
department/division	reparto [reh-pahr-toh]
doorman	il portiere [eel pohr-tyeh-reh]
entrance	ingresso [een-greh-ssoh]
firm/company	ditta [dee-ttah]
floor	piano [pyah-noh]

interpreter	l'interprete *(m/f)* [leen-tehr-preh-teh
meeting	seduta [seh-doo-tah]
office	ufficio [oo-ffee-choh]
reception	la ricezione, ricevimento [lah ree-cheh-tzyoh-neh ree-cheh-vee-mehn-toh]
secretary	segretario/a [seh-greh-tah-ryoh/ah]
secretary's office	segreteria [seh-greh-teh-ree-ah]

Negotiations/Conferences/Trade Fairs
Trattativa/Conferenza/Fiera

I'm looking for the ... booth.	Cerco lo stand della ditta... [chehr-koh loh stehnd deh-llah dee-ttah]
Go to hall... booth (number)...	Vada nel padiglione..., Stand numero... [vah-dah nehl pah-dee-lyoh-neh...stehnd noo-meh-roh]
We manufacture ...	Siamo produttori di... [syah-moh proh-doo-ttoh-ree dee]
We deal in/handle ...	Noi commerciamo con... [noh-ee koh-mmehr-chyah-moh kohn]
Do you have information on... ?	Ha del materiale informativo su...? [ah dehl mah-teh-ryah-leh een-fohr-mah-tee-voh soo]
We can send you detailed information on ...	Le possiamo inviare materiale informativo dettagliato su... [leh poh-ssyah-moh een-vee-ah-reh mah-teh-ryah-leh]
Who is the contact person for...?	Chi è l'interlocutore per...? [kee eh leen-tehr-loh-koo-toh-reh pehr]
Could you give us a quote/ an offer?	Ci può far pervenire un'offerta? [chee poo-oh fahr pehr-veh-nee-reh oo-noh-ffehr-tah]

We should arrange a meeting date.	Dovremmo fissare la data di un incontro. [doh-vreh-mmoh fee-ssah-reh lah dah-tah dee oon een-kohn-troh]
Here is my business card.	Ecco il mio biglietto da visita. [eh-kkoh eel mee-oh bee-lyeh-ttoh dah vee-see-tah]

Word List: Negotiations/Conferences/Trade Fairs

advertising	pubblicità [poo-blee-chee-tah]
advertising campaign	campagna pubblicitaria [kahm-pah-nyah poo-blee-chee-tah-ryah]
advertising material	il materiale pubblicitario [eel mah-teh-ryah-leh poo-blee-chee-tah-ryoh]
agenda	l'ordine (m) del giorno [lohr-dee-neh dehl johr-noh]
agent	concessionario [kohn-ceh-ssyoh-nah-ryoh]
agreement/contract	contratto [kohn-trah-ttoh]
to be interested in	essere interessato allo stand delle informazioni [eh-sseh-reh een-teh-reh-ssah-toh ah-lloh stehnd deh-lleh een-fohr-mah-tzyoh-nee]
bill of sale	contratto d'acquisto [kohn-trah-ttoh dah-kwee-toh]
booth	cabina [kah-bee-nah]
business card	biglietto da visita [bee-lyeh-ttoh dah vee-see-tah]
business concern	complesso industriale [kohm-pleh-ssoh een-doo-stryah-leh]
business connections	relazioni d'affari [reh-lah-tzyoh-nee dah-ffah-ree]
business partner	la parte contraente [lah pahr-teh kohn-trah-ehn-teh]

catalog	catalogo [kah-<u>tah</u>-loh-ghoh]
central/head office	la centrale [lah chehn-<u>trah</u>-leh]
commercial agent	il/la rappresentante commerciale, l'agente *(m/f)* di commercio [eel/lah rah-ppreh-sehn-<u>tahn</u>-teh koh-mmehr-<u>chah</u>-leh, lah-<u>jehn</u>-teh dee koh-<u>mmehr</u>-choh]
condition	la condizione [lah kohn-dee-<u>tzyoh</u>-neh]
conference	conferenza [kohn-feh-<u>rehn</u>-tzah]
confirmation order	conferma d'<u>o</u>rdine [kohn-<u>fehr</u>-mah <u>dohr</u>-dee-neh]
contact person	l'interlocutore *(m)* [leen-tehr-loh-koo-<u>toh</u>-reh]
cooperation	la cooperazione [lah koh-oh-peh-rah-<u>tzyoh</u>-neh]
costs	i costi, le spese [ee <u>kohn</u>-tee, leh <u>speh</u>-seh]
customer	il/la cliente [eel/lah klee-<u>ehn</u>-teh]
delivery	consegna [kohn-<u>seh</u>-nyah]
delivery time/date	il t<u>e</u>rmine di consegna [eel <u>tehr</u>-mee-neh dee kohn-<u>seh</u>-nyah]
discount	sconto [<u>skohn</u>-toh]
distribution network	la rete di distribuzione [lah <u>reh</u>-teh dee see-stree-boo-<u>tzyoh</u>-neh]
encounter/meeting	incontro [een-<u>kohn</u>-troh]
estimate	preventivo di spesa [preh-vehn-<u>tee</u>-voh dee <u>speh</u>-sah]
exhibit(ion) catalog	cat<u>a</u>logo dell'esposizione [kah-<u>tah</u>-loh-ghoh deh-<u>lleh</u>-spoh-see-<u>tzyoh</u>-neh]
exhibition booth	lo stand in fiera [loh stehnd een <u>fyeh</u>-rah]

exhibition discount	sconto in fiera [skohn-toh een fyeh-rah]
exhibition hall	centro fieristico, il capannone [chehn-troh fyeh-ree-stee-koh, eel kah-pah-nnoh-neh]
exhibition management	la direzione della fiera [lah dee-reh-tzyoh-neh deh-llah fyeh-rah]
exhibition pass	tesserino fieristico [teh-sseh-ree-noh fyeh-ree-stee-koh]
exhibition service	servizio fieristico [sehr-vee-tzyoh fyeh-ree-stee-koh]
exhibitor	espositore [eh-spoh-see-toh-reh]
export	l'esportazione (f) [leh-spohr-tah-tzyoh-neh]
exporter	l'esportatore (m) [leh-spoh-see-toh-reh]
fair	fiera [fyeh-rah]
financing	finanziamento [fee-nahn-tzyah-mehn-toh]
floor plan	pianta del padiglione [pyahn-tah dehl pah-dee-lyoh-neh]
freight/transport	trasporto [trah-spohr-toh]
guarantee	garanzia [ghah-rahn-tzee-ah]
import	l'importazione (f) [leem-pohr-tah-tzyoh-neh]
importer	l'importatore (m) [leem-pohr-tah-toh-reh]
industrial fair	fiera industriale [fyeh-rah een-doo-stryah-leh]
information	il materiale informativo [eel mah-teh-ryah-leh een-fohr-mah-tee-voh]
information booth	lo stand delle informazioni [loh stehnd deh-lleh een-fohr-mah-tzyoh-nee]

insurance	l'assicurazione *(f)* [lah-ssee-koo-rah-<u>tzyoh</u>-neh]
invoice	fattura, conto [fah-<u>ttoo</u>-rah, <u>kohn</u>-toh]
joint venture	impresa comune [eem-<u>preh</u>-sah koh-<u>moo</u>-neh]
leasing	il leasing [eel <u>lee</u>-seeng]
license (licensing agreement)	(contratto di) licenza [(kohn-<u>trah</u>-ttoh dee) lee-<u>chehn</u>-tzah]
manufacturer	il produttore [eel proh-doo-<u>ttoh</u>-reh]
marketing	il marketing [eel <u>mahr</u>-keh-teen]
meeting	convegno [cohn-<u>veh</u>-nyoh]
merchandise/product	la merce [lah <u>mehr</u>-cheh]
minutes	il verbale [eel vehr-<u>bah</u>-leh]
offer/quote	offerta [oh-<u>ffehr</u>-tah]
order	l'ordine *(f)* [<u>lohr</u>-dee-neh]
packaging	imballaggio [eem-bah-<u>llah</u>-djoh]
price	prezzo [<u>preh</u>-tzoh]
price list	listino prezzi [lee-<u>stee</u>-noh <u>preh</u>-tzee]
price reduction	la riduzione di prezzo [lah ree-doo-<u>tzyoh</u>-neh dee <u>preh</u>-tzoh]
pro forma invoice	fattura pro forma [fah-<u>ttoo</u>-rah proh <u>fohr</u>-mah]
production	la produzione [lah proh-doo-<u>tzyoh</u>-neh]
prospectus/brochure	op<u>u</u>scolo, prospetto [oh-<u>poo</u>-skoh-loh, proh-<u>speh</u>-ttoh]
public relations	le pubbliche relazioni [leh <u>poo</u>-blee-keh reh-lah-<u>tzyoh</u>-nee]
representative	l'agente *(m/f)*, il/la rappresentante [lah-<u>jehn</u>-teh, eel/lah rah-ppreh-sehn-<u>tahn</u>-teh]

retailer	il/la commerciante al minuto (al dettaglio) [eel/lah koh-mmehr-chahn-teh ahl mee-noo-toh (ahl deh-ttah-lyoh]
sale/distribution	smercio, distribuzione *(f)* [smehr-choh, dee-stree-boo-tzyoh-neh]
sales promotion	la promozione delle vendite [lah proh-moh-tzyoh-neh deh-lleh vehn-dee-teh]
sales tax	imposta generale sull'entrata [eem-poh-stah jeh-neh-rah-leh soo-llehn-trah-tah]
salesperson	il venditore/la venditrice [eel vehn-dee-toh-reh/lah vehn-dee-tree-cheh]
sample	il campione [eel kahm-pyoh-neh]
shipping/transport	trasporto [trah-spohr-toh]
sole agent/agency	rappresentanza generale [rah-ppreh-sehn-tahn-tzah jeh-neh-rah-leh]
stock list	distinta di merci [dee-steen-tah dee mehr-chee]
subsidiary	società affiliata [soh-cheh-tah ah-ffee-lyah-tah]
supplier	il fornitore [eel fohr-nee-toh-reh]
talk/lecture	conferenza [kohn-feh-rehn-tzah]
terms of delivery	le condizioni di consegna [leh kohn-dee-tzyoh-nee dee kohn-seh-nyah]
terms of payment	le condizioni di pagamento [leh kohn-dee-tzyoh-nee dee pah-ghah-mehn-toh]
terms of the contract	le condizioni contrattuali [leh konh-dee-tzyoh-nee kohn-trah-ttwah-lee]
trade fair	fiera settoriale [fyeh-rah seh-ttoh-ryah-leh]

training	addestramento [ah-ddah-eh-strah-<u>mehn</u>-toh]
value-added tax	IVA (Imposta sul valore aggiunto) [ee-vah (eem-<u>poh</u>-stah sool vah-<u>loh</u>-reh ah-<u>djoon</u>-toh)]
wholesaler (commercial)	il/la grossista, il/la commerciante all'ingrosso [eel/lah groh-<u>ssee</u>-stah, eel/lah koh-mmehr-<u>chahn</u>-teh ah-lleen-<u>groh</u>-ssoh]

Business Equipment
Attrezzatura

Do you need any copies of this?	Avrei bisogno di alcune copie di questo? [ah-<u>vreh</u>-ee bee-<u>soh</u>-nyoh dee ahl-<u>koo</u>-neh <u>koh</u>-pyeh dee <u>kweh</u>-stoh]
I will need an overhead projector for my talk.	Per la conferenza mi serve una lavagna luminosa. [pehr lah kohn-feh-<u>rehn</u>-tzah mee <u>sehr</u>-veh <u>oo</u>-nah lah-<u>vah</u>-nyah loo-mee-<u>noh</u>-sah]
Could you get me... please?	Mi potrebbe procurare…, per favore? [mee poh-<u>treh</u>-bbeh proh-koo-<u>rah</u>-reh... pehr fah-<u>voh</u>-reh]

Word List: Business Equipment

catalog	cat<u>a</u>logo [kah-<u>tah</u>-loh-ghoh]
color copier	la fotocopiatrice a colori [lah foh-toh-koh-pyah-<u>tree</u>-cheh ah koh-<u>loh</u>-ree]
copy	c<u>o</u>pia [<u>koh</u>-pyah]
darkening	oscuramento [oh-skoo-rah-<u>mehn</u>-toh]
diskette	dischetto magn<u>e</u>tico [dee-<u>skeh</u>-toh mah-<u>nyeh</u>-tee-koh]

display material	il materiale d'esposizione [eel mah-teh-<u>ryah</u>-leh deh-spoh-see-<u>tzyoh</u>-neh]
extension cord	prolunga [proh-<u>loon</u>-ghah]
fax	il telefax [eel teh-leh-<u>fahx</u>]
felt-tip pen	penna in fibra [<u>peh</u>-nnah een <u>fee</u>-brah]
flip chart	il flip chart
microphone	microfono [mee-<u>kroh</u>-foh-noh]
modem	il modem [eel <u>moh</u>-dehm]
notepad	blocco per appunti [<u>bloh</u>-kkoh pehr ah-<u>ppoon</u>-tee]
overhead projector	lavagna luminosa [lah-<u>vah</u>-nyah loo-mee-<u>noh</u>-sah]
PC	PC [pee-see]
pen for overhead transparencies	pennarello per i lucidi [peh-nnah-<u>reh</u>-lloh pehr loo-chee dee]
pencil	matita [mah-<u>tee</u>-tah]
photocopy machine	la fotocopiatrice [lah foh-toh-koh-pyah-<u>tree</u>-cheh]
podium	podio dell'oratore [<u>poh</u>-dyoh deh-lloh-rah-<u>toh</u>-reh]
printer	la stampante [lah stahm-<u>pahn</u>-teh]
telephone	telefono [teh-<u>leh</u>-foh-noh]
telex	il telex [eel <u>teh</u>-lehx]
VCR	il videoregistratore [eel <u>vee</u>-deh-oh-reh-jee-strah-<u>toh</u>-reh]
word processor	il sistema di elaborazione del testo [eel see-<u>steh</u>-mah dee eh-lah-boh-rah-tzyoh-neh dehl teh-stoh]

A Short Grammar

Articles

Singular and Plural Definite Article (the)

	Sing.	Plur.	
Feminine	la	le	before consonants ex.: la bambina/le bambine
	l'	le	before vowels in the singular ex.: l'amica/le amiche
Masculine	il	i	before consonants, except **s** followed by another consonant, or **a**, **gn**, or **ps** ex.: il treno/i treni
	l'	gli	before a vowel ex.: l'amico/gli amici
	lo	gli	before **s** followed by another consonant, **z**, **gn**, or **ps**, ex.: lo zaino/gli zaini

- The definite article is used
  — before a title + name: Dov'è **il signor Neri**? Where is Mr. Neri?
  (It is not used when directly addressing someone: Buongiorno, signor Neri.)
  — before names of countries: Conosce **l'Italia**? Do you know Italy?
  (To express in a country, use in + name of country: in Italia/in Italy.)
  — before the hour: È **l'una**. It is one o'clock. Sono **le due**. It is two o'clock.
  — generally before a noun:
  La benzina costa molto in Italia. Gas is expensive in Italy.

- Examples with the definite article:
  ciuso il lunedì/il martedì closed Mondays/Tuesdays
  l'anno prossimo next year

fare il bagno to bathe
fare il pieno to fill up the tank
fare il biglietto to buy a ticket

● Examples without the definite article:
partire lunedì/martedì to leave (on) Monday/Tuesday
in aprile/maggio in April/May
andare in città to go to the city/downtown
andare in treno/macchina to go on the train/in the car

Indefinite Article (a, an)

Feminine	una	before a consonant ex.: una ragazza
	un'	before a vowel ex.: un'amica
Masculine	un	before a vowel or a consonant except **s** + consonant, **z**, or **gn**
	uno	before **s** + consonant, **z**, or **gn** ex.: uno sciopero

Nouns

Singular and Plural Nouns

In Italian there are:
1. masculine nouns ending in -o (plural -i)
   -e (plural -i)
   a (plural -i)
2. feminine nouns ending in -a (plural -e)
   -e (plural -i)
   -o (plural -I)

	Singular		Plural	
Masculine	il	ragazzo	i	ragazzi
	il	padre	i	padri
	il	problema	i	problemi
Feminine	la	ragazza	le	ragazze
	la	madre	le	madri
	la	mano	le	mani

- Nouns ending in *-ista* and *-ente* denoting people can be masculine or feminine. The article specifies the gender
  ex.: il cliente/la cliente il turista/la turista
- Nouns that are always singular are: la gente the people, la roba clothes
- Nouns that are always plural are: gli occhiali (eye)glasses, i pantaloni pants, i soldi pocket money/change

Some special rules for the formation of the plural:

- Feminine nouns ending in *-ca* and *-ga* end in *-che* and *-ghe* in the plural (an *h* is added):
  l'amica (female) friend—le amiche; la riga ruler—le righe
- Nouns ending in *-co* end in *-chi* if preceded by a consonant:
  il disco record—i di**schi**
  But: l'amico friend—gli amici; il medico doctor—i medici
  (*-ci* is preceded by a vowel)
- Nouns ending in *-cia* and *-gia* change to *-ce* and *-ge* if the *-i* is not stressed:
  l'arancia orange—le arance; la spiaggia beach—le spiagge
  But: la farmacia pharmacy—le farmacie (the *-i* is stressed)
- Nouns ending in *-cio* or *-gio* change to *-ci* and *-gi:*
  l'edificio building—gli edifici; il viaggio/i viaggi, il figlio/i figli
- Some nouns have irregular plural forms: l'uomo man—gli uomini; un paio a pair—due paia; l'uovo egg—le uova

Nouns whose ending does not change in the plural

- Nouns ending in a consonant. These are usually masculine: il bar/i bar; il film/i film; il sport/gli sport
- Nouns ending with an accented vowel: la città/le città; il caffè/i caffè
- Abbreviated nouns: la moto/le moto, l'auto/le auto; il cinema/i cinema; la radio/le radio
- Feminine or masculine nouns ending in *-i:* la crisi/le crisi; il brindisi/brindisi

Adjectives

Formation of the Adjective

In Italian there are
1. Adjectives ending in -o; the feminine form ends in -a;
2. Adjectives ending in -e. These have the same form in the feminine.
In the plural, adjectives have the same endings as nouns: $o \rightarrow i$, $a \rightarrow e$, $e \rightarrow i$.

	Singular	Plural
1. Masculine Feminine	il ragazzo contento la ragazza contenta	i ragazzi contenti le ragazze contente
2. Masculine and Feminine	il ragazzo gentile la ragazza gentile	i ragazzi gentili le ragazze gentili

● Most adjectives ending in -co and -go add an h in the plural:
  ricco rich—ric**ch**i, ric**ch**e; lungo long—lun**gh**i, lun**gh**e
  But: simp**a**tico—simpatici, simpati**ch**e

Adjectives agree in number and gender with the noun they modify.

The Position of Adjectives

Adjectives usually follow the noun they modify:

la valigia **nera/pesante** the black/heavy suitcase
un giornale **italiano/inglese** an Italian/English newspaper

● Some adjectives precede the noun. They are:
  bello beautiful, handsome   buono good   grande big
  lungo long   brutto ugly   cattivo bad   piccolo little
  Buono has the same forms as the definite article when it precedes the noun:
  Buon viaggio! Have a good trip!
  Buona fortuna! Good luck!
  buon'amica good friend (f)

● *Bello* follows the same forms as the definite article:
—before a consonant (except before *z, gn,* or *s* + consonant):
  bel viso handsome/beautiful face; **bei** visi
  bella donna beautiful woman; **belle donne**
—before a vowel:
  bell'uomo handsome man; **begli** uomini
—Before *z, gn* or *s* + consonant:
  una **bella** statua; **belle** statue
  un **bello** scherzo; **begli** scherzi

Comparison of Adjectives

bello	più bello	il più bello	bellissimo
beautiful	more beautiful	the most beautiful	very beautiful

The comparative is expressed by using *più* (more) or *meno* (less). The English *than* is expressed by *di* when comparing two different things or people or numbers, and by *che* in other cases.

Il Po è più lungo **dell'A**dige.	Noun	The Po is longer than the Danube.
Questo fiume è più (meno) lungo **di** quello.	Pronoun	This river is longer than that one.
Tacere è più difficile **che** parlare.	Verb	Keeping quiet is harder than talking.

The superlative is formed with the definite article, and *più* or *meno* are followed by the adjective.

Roma è la più bella città del mondo.	Rome is the most beautiful city in the world.

When the superlative follows the noun the definite article is not repeated:

La città più bella del mondo è Roma.	The most beautiful city in the world is Rome.

The ending *-issimo/a* expresses the highest possible degree or quality:

Roma è bellissima.	Rome is very beautiful.
Roma è una città bellissima.	Rome is a very beautiful city.

- Irregular comparative and superlative forms:

buono	migliore	il migliore	ottimo/buonissimo
good	better	the best	very good
cattivo	peggiore	il peggiore	pessimo/cattivissim
bad	worse	the worst	very bad
grande	maggiore	il maggiore	massimo
big	bigger	the biggest	very big
piccolo	minore	il minore	minimo
small	smaller	the smallest	very small

Adverbs

Some adverbs have an original form, for example, *tardi* (late). Some are formed by adding *-mente* to the feminine form of adjectives that end in *-o*. If the adjective ends in *-e*, add *-mente* to the word.

lento, lenta:	Parla **lentamente**.	He/She speaks slowly.
veloce:	Corre **velocemente**.	He/She runs fast.

- With adjectives ending in *-le, -are,* or *-ile,* drop the *-e* before adding *-mente:*
  facile—facilmente *easily;* familiare —familiarmente *familiarly;* commerciale—commercialmente *commercially*
- The adjectives *buono* and *cattivo* correspond to *bene* and *male*: Lavora **bene/male**. He/She works well/poorly.
- Many adverbs have comparative and superlative forms; for

example:	tardi	più tardi	al più tardi	tardissimo
	late	later	at the latest	very late

- *Bene* and *male* have irregular forms:

Paolo canta…bene	meglio	il meglio	benissimo
Paul sings… well	better	the best	very well
male	peggio	il peggio	malissimo
badly	worse	the worst	very badly

Prepositions

The Prepositions di and a:

The preposition *di* is equivalent to *of, from; a* means *to:*

A chi scrivi? Scrivo a mio padre.	To whom are you writing? I am writing to my father.
È di Roma la signora Curti?	Is Mrs. Curti from Rome?

Di is used to express possession:

Dov'è la borsa di Maria?	Where is Maria's purse?

The prepositions *a, di, da, in, su* + the definite article:

The prepositions *a, di, da, in, su* contract with the definite article to become a single word, e.g., *a + il* = al mare at/to the sea.

		il	lo	la	l'	i	gli	le
a	at, to	al	allo	alla	all'	ai	agli	alle
di	of, some	del	dello	della	dell'	dei	degli	delle
da	from	dal	dallo	dalla	dall'	dai	dagli	dalle
in	in	nel	nello	nella	nell'	nei	negli	nelle
su	on	sul	sullo	sulla	sull'	sui	sugli	sulle

The Partitive di

The combination of *di* + the definite article expresses the idea of *some, any,* or *a few.*

Mi dia dell'acqua, per favore. Please give me some water. Vorrei del vino rosso. I'd like some red wine. Ha preso delle foto? Do you have any photos?

Di alone is used to specify contents or specific amounts:

un litro di vino	a liter of wine
una tazza di caffè	a cup of coffee
due chili di arance	two kilos of oranges
un milione di lire	a million lire

● Other useful expressions to express quantity are:
 un po' di vino (pane) a little/some wine (bread)
 un paio di scarpe a pair of shoes

Pronouns

Personal Pronouns

	Singular					Plural			
(who?)	io	tu	lui	lei	Lei	noi	voi	loro	Loro
	I	you	him	her	you	we	you	them	you

● Personal pronouns are not used as much in Italian as they are in English because the verb ending indicates the person and number of the subject: Partiamo oggi. We are leaving today. They are used for emphasis or clarification after the verb: Ordino io? Am I ordering?
● There are formal and informal forms for you:
 —*tu* is used to address family, friends, pets, and small children.
 —*lei* and *loro* (*Lei, Loro* when written) are used to address people you do not know well and older people. *Loro* is used only in *very* formal situations, and is seldom used in everyday conversation.
 —*voi* is used to address groups of people in formal and informal situations.

Direct and Indirect Object Pronouns (*whom, to whom*)

	Singular					Plural					
o?	mi	ti	lo	la	La	ci	vi	li	le	Li	Le
	me	you	him, it	her, it	you, pol.	us	you, inf.	them (m)	them (f)	you (m)	you (f)
om?	mi	ti	gli	le	Le	ci	vi	Loro	loro (gli)	loro (gli)	
	to me	to you	to him	to her	to you, pol.	to us	to you, inf.	to you, pol.	to them (m)	to them (f)	

Ex.: Vedi Maria? Sì, la vedo. Do you see Maria? Yes, I see her.
Stasera incontro Maria e le do il libro. Tonight I will meet Maria and give the book to her.

● Object pronouns are placed near the verb on which they depend. They precede a conjugated verb:
Hai comprati i libri? Sì, li ho comprati. Did you buy the books? Yes, I bought them.

Lo and *la* are often elided before a verb that begins with a vowel or silent *h:*
Ex.: Vuole ascoltare la radio? Si, L'accendo io. Do you want to listen to the radio? I'll turn it on.
Hai visto Mario? No, non l'ho visto. Did you see Mario? No, I didn't see him.

● Object pronouns are attached:

Siamo contenti di veder**la**. We are happy to see her.	to the end of infinitives.
Compra**lo**! Buy it! Comprate**glielo**! Buy it for him! But it precedes the verb in the polite imperative: **Lo** compri! Buy it!	to the informal imperative.
Ecco**lo**! There it is! Ecco**li**! There they are!	to the expression **ecco** *(there is, there are).*

Stressed pronouns are used as objects of prepositions and for emphasis. They are placed after the verb.

me	te	lui	lei	Lei
me	you	him	her	you, pol.
noi	voi	loro/Loro		
us	you	them		

Ex.: Chi vedi? Lui. Whom do you see? Him.
Vado a Roma con loro. I'm going to Rome with them.
Paolo chiama te, non me. Paul is calling me, not you.

Ci and Ne

ci there	ne of it/them
Va spesso a Roma/in Italia?	Vuole delle arance ?
—Sì, **ci** vado ogni anno.	—Sì, me **ne** dia un chilo, per favore.
Do you often go to Rome/to Italy?	Do you want some oranges?
—Yes, I go there every year.	—Yes, give me a kilo, please.

Double Object Pronouns

When a verb has both a direct and an indirect object pronoun, the pronouns change form. With *ne,* the indirect object pronouns undergo the same changes.

—Mi/ti/ci/vi/si → me/te/ce/ve/se: **Me lo** dia. Give it to me.
—Gli/le → glie-: **Gliene** parlerò. I will speak to him about it.

Reflexive Pronouns and Verbs

Reflexive verbs refer back to the subject: Reflexive pronouns *(myself, yourself, etc.)* come before the verb.
Reflexive verbs are conjugated like other verbs. They are always conjugated with *essere* in compound tenses. The past participle agrees with the subject. (See section on the present perfect and conjugation of essere, page 298.)
Ci siamo alzati alle nove. We got up at nine.

alzarsi to get up

Present	Present Perfect
mi alzo	mi sono alzato, -a
I get up	I got up
ti alzi	ti sei alzato, -a
you get up	you got up
si alze	si è alzato, -a
he/she gets up	he/she/you (pol.) got up
ci alziamo	ci siamo alzati, -e
we get up	we got up
vi alzate	vi siete alzati, -e
you get up	you got up
si alzano	si sono alzati, -e
they/you (pol.) get up	they/you (pol.) got up

Reflexive pronouns are attached to the verb.

rallegrar**si** to be glad fermar**si** to stop	in the infinitive
ferma**ti** stop! *But:* si fermi stop!	in the affirmative imperative (except in the *lei* form)

The impersonal **si**

Si + third-person form of a verb is used when the action of a sentence is performed by an indefinite or unknown subject. It is equivalent to the English *one, people,* or *you, we, they,* when used impersonally.

si + third-person singular verb	Da qui si vede il lago. You/One can see the lake from here. In questo negozio si parla tedesco. English is spoken in this store.
si + third-person plural verb	Da qui si vedono le Alpi. You/One can see the Alps from here. Non si accettano assegni. Checks are not accepted.

The Relative Pronoun che

The relative pronoun *che* can mean *who, whom, that,* or *which.* It is invariable; in other words, it has only one form. It can refer to persons or things. *Che* is never the object of a preposition.

Who/What	il signore/la signora **che** ha telefonato... the man/woman who called...
Which/That	i guanti/le valigie **che** cerco... the gloves/suitcases that I am looking for...

After a preposition the following are used instead of *che:*

il quale, la quale, i quali, le quali *or* cui (invariable)	
Masc. sing.	È il paese nel quale (in cui) sono nato. It is the country where (in which) I was born.
Masc. pl.	Conosce i ragazzi con i quali (con cui) ho parlato? Do you know the boys with whom I spoke?
Fem. sing.	Firenze è la città nella quale (in cui) abito. Florence is the city in which I live.
Fem. pl.	Ecco le ragazze delle quali (di cui) parlo. Here are the girls whom I am speaking about.

Possessive Pronouns

	Singular		Plural	
	Masculine	Feminine	Masculine	Feminine
Singular Possessive	il mio my il tuo your (inf.) il suo his il Suo your (pol.)	la mia la tua la sua la Sua	i miei i tuoi i suoi i Suoi	le mie le tue le sue le Sue
Plural Possessive	il nostro our il vostro your il Loro your (pol.) il loro their	la nostra la vostra la Loro la loro	i nostri i loro le nostre le loro	i vostri i Loro le vostre le Loro

● Possessive pronouns agree with the object possessed, not the possessor. They agree with it in gender and number and are usually preceded by the definite article: Dov'è la mia borsa? Where is my purse?

They are not used
—before a singular noun referring to a family member:
  mio zio my uncle
    —in certain fixed expressions, such as: a casa **mia** my house

Demonstrative Pronouns

Masculine	Singular	Feminine	Masculine	Plural	Feminine
questo	this	questa	questi	these	queste
quello	that	quella	quelli	those	quelle
Preferisce queste scarpe o quelle?			Do you prefer these shoes or those?		

When used as demonstrative pronouns, *questo* has the same forms, but *quello* follows the same pattern as *bello:*

Singular		Plural	
quel parco	that park	quei parchi	those parks
quello studente	that student (m)	quegli studenti	those students
quell'uomo	that man	quegli uomini	those men
quella donna	that woman	quelle donne	those women

Questa borsa mi piace.
I like this purse.

Quest'anno andremo a Roma.
This year we are going to Rome.

Conosce **quel** signore?
Do you know that man?

Question (Interrogative) Words

who? whom? to whom?	**Chi** è venuto? Who came? **Chi** cerca? Whom are you looking for? **A chi** scrive? To whom are you writing?
what?	**Che cosa** desidera? What do you want?
what?	**Che** libro è questo? What book is this?
which?	**Quale** strada? Which street? **Qual** è la sua macchina? Which is your car?
how much? how many?	**Quanto** costa? How much does it cost? **Quanti** chilometri? How many kilometers?

where?	**Dove** si trova…? Where is…?
	Dove va? Where are you going?
from where	**Da dove** viene? Where are you coming from?
when?	**Quando** aprono i negozi? When do the stores open?
at what time?	**A che ora** partiamo? At what time are we leaving?
how long?	**Quanto** devo aspettare? How long must I wait?
how?	**Come** funziona? How does it work?
why?	**Perché** non funziona? Why isn't it working?

Verbs

The Present Indicative Tense

- Verb forms indicate the person and number of the subject, so subject pronouns are usually omitted (see. p. 289): **Abbiamo** tempo. We have time.
- To address someone formally, or someone you do not know well, use
  —the third person singular: **Ha** tempo, signor Neri? Do you have time, Mr. and Mrs. Neri?
  —and the second person or third person plural. Note that the *loro* form is used only in very formal situations:
  Avete tempo?/**Hanno** tempo, signori? Do you have time?/Do you have time, sirs?

avere, essere

	av**e**re	to have	essere	to be
io	ho	I have	sono	I am
tu	hai	you have	sei	you are
lui/lei	ha	he/she/it has; you (pol.) have	è	he/she/it is; you (pol.) are
noi	abbiamo	we have	si**a**mo	we are
voi	avete	you have	si**e**te	you are; you (pol.) are
loro	hanno	they have; you (pol.) have	sono	they are; you (pol.) are

- ci sono there are   c'è there is

Regular Verbs

Italian has three verb conjugations, according to their infinitive ending.

	Verbs ending in -are		-ere	-ire	
	parlare to speak		vendere to sell	partire to leave	capire to understand
io	parlo	I speak	vendo	parto	capisco
tu	parli	you speak	vendi	parti	capisci
lui lei lei	parla	he/she/it speaks; you (pol.) speak	vende	parte	capisce
noi	parliamo	we speak	vendiamo	partiamo	capiamo
voi	parlate	you speak	vendete	partite	capite
loro	parlano	they speak	vendono	partono	capiscono

- Other verbs like *capire (-isc-* is inserted before all endings except the *noi* and *voi* forms): finire to finish, preferire to prefer, construire to build, spedire to send, ubbidire to obey, pulire to clean.

- Other verbs like *partire:* dormire to sleep, sentire to hear, to smell, aprire to open.

- Verbs that end in *-care* and *-gare* add an *h* in the *tu* and *noi* forms to keep the hard sound of the *c* and *g:* cercare to look for: cerco, cherchi, cerca, cerchiamo, cecarte, cercano.

The Imperative

	Familiar Form		Polite Form	
	Singular	Plural	Singular	Plural
avere to have essere to be	abbi sii	abbiate siate	abbia sia	abbiate/abbiano siate/siano
parlare to speak	parla	parlate	parli	parlate/parlino
prendere to take sentire to hear, to smell finire to finish	prendi senti finisci	prendete sentite finite	prenda senta finisca	prendete/prendano sentite/sentano finite/finiscano

Ex.: Abbia pazienza! Be patient!/Prendi la medicina! Take the medicine!

- Direct object pronouns and reflexive pronouns are attached to the familiar forms of the imperative to form one word. In the polite form, the pronoun precedes the imperative and is kept separate:
  Compra**lo**! Buy it! Prendi**lo**! Take it!
  Ferma**ti**! Stop!
  But: **Lo** compri! Buy it! **Si** fermi! Stop!

- The negative is formed by placing *non* before all forms except the 2nd person singular: **Non aspettate!** Don't wait!
  –**Bambini, non parlare!** Children, don't talk!

The Past Tense

The Past Participle

Auxiliary verbs		Regular verbs ending in		
		-are	-ere	-ire
avere **avuto** had	essere **stato** was	parl**are** parl**ato** spoken	vend**ere** vend**uto** sold	cap**ire** cap**ito** understood
Past participle ending		-ato	-uto	-ito

● The following have irregular past participles:

accendere to light	acceso
aprire to open	aperto
chiedere to ask	chiesto
chiudere to close	chiuso
correre to run	corso
fare to make, to do	fatto
leggere to read	letto
mettere to put	messo
offrire to offer	offerto
rompere to break	rotto
scendere to go down	sceso
scrivere to write	scritto
spegnere to turn off	spento
spendere to spend	speso
vedere to see	visto
vivere to live	vissuto

The Simple Past with avere and essere

The past tense is a compound tense made up of two parts: the auxiliary verb and the past participle. The formation of the past participle is shown above.

—Most verbs are conjugated with *avere* as the auxiliary: ho avuto I had

—Some verbs are conjugated with *essere*. In these cases, the past participle agrees in gender and number with the subject: *Le mie amiche* sono state a Roma. My friends (f) have been to Rome. *Signor Rossi* è partito ieri. Mr. Rossi left yesterday.

Perfect with *avere*	Perfect with *essere*
ho capito	sono andato/andata
I understood	I went
hai capito	sei andato/andata
you understood	you went
ha capito	è andato/andata
he/she understood;	he/she went; you
you (pol.) understood	(pol.) went
abbiamo capito	siamo andati/andate
we understood	we went

avete capito	siete andati/andate
you understood	you went
hanno capito	sono andati/andate
they understood;	they went
you (pol.) understood	

● When the subject is plural and includes a masculine noun (or male person), use the *-i* ending. If the plural subject is comprised of all female nouns (or females), use the *-e* ending:

Maria e Toni sono andat**i** al parco.
Mary and Tony went to the park.
But: Sara e Anna sono andat**e** al parco.
Sara and Anna went to the park.

● Reflexive verbs also take *essere* as the auxiliary (see p. 291).

● Most verbs that take avere as the auxiliary take a direct object: Ha mangiato la pasta? Some verbs that do not take a direct object are also conjugated with *avere*. A few of these are: dormire to sleep; viaggiare to travel; nuotare to swim; passeggiare to stroll; sciare to ski.

Abbiamo viaggiato molto. We have traveled a lot.

● Modal verbs *(potere, dovere, volere)* are conjugated with essere or *avere:*
Non ho voluto mangiare. I didn't want to eat.
Pietro è voluto andare a Roma. Peter wanted to go to Rome.

The Future and the Conditional

The Future

	-are	-ere	-ire
	comprare	vendere	partire
io	comprerò I will buy, etc.	venderò	partirò
tu	comprerai	venderai	partirai
lui/lei	comprerà	venderà	partirà
noi	compreremo	venderemo	partiremo
voi	comprerete	venderete	partirete
loro	compreranno	venderanno	partiranno

The Conditional

io	comprer**ei**	vender**ei**	partir**ei**
	I would buy, etc.	I would sell, etc.	I would leave, etc.
tu	comprer**esti**	vender**esti**	partir**esti**
lui/lei	comprer**ebbe**	vender**ebbe**	partir**ebbe**
noi	comprer**emmo**	vender**emmo**	partir**emmo**
voi	comprer**este**	vender**este**	partir**este**
loro	comprer**ebbero**	vender**ebbero**	partir**ebbero**

● The conditional is used to convey wishes politely:
Vorrei una camera singola. I would like a single room.
Avrebbe un fiammifero? Do (Might) you have a match?
Mi potrebbe aiutare? Could you help me?

● Verbs that end in *-care* and *-gare* require an *h* to keep the hard
-c and *-g* sound: cercheremo we will look for.

Irregular Verbs

andare to go—andato

Present	vado	vai	va	andiamo	andate	vanno
Imperative		va'	vada		andate	vadanno
Future	andrò, etc.			*Conditional:* andrei, etc.		

av<u>e</u>re to have—avuto

Present	ho	hai	ha	abbiamo	avete	hanno
Imperative		abbi	abbia		abbiate	abbiano
Future	avrò, etc.			*Conditional:* avrei, etc.		

bere to drink—bevuto

Present	bevo	bevi	beve	beviamo	bevete	bevono
Imperative		bevi	beva		bevete	bevano
Future	berrò, etc.			*Conditional:* berrei, etc.		

dare to give—dato

Present	do	dai	da	diamo	date	danno
Imperative		da'	dia		date	diano
Future	darò, etc.			*Conditional:* darei, etc.		

dire to say, to tell—detto

Present	dico	dici	dice	diciamo	dite	dicono
Imperative		di'	dica		dite	dicano
Future	dirò, etc.			*Conditional:* direi, etc.		

dovere to have to, must, should—dovuto

Present	devo	devi	deve	dobbiamo	dovete	devono
Future	dovrò, etc.			*Conditional:* dovrei, etc.		

● Ha dovuto pagare. I had to pay.
   È dovuto venire. He had to come.

essere to be—stato

Present	sono	sei	è	siamo	siete	sono
Imperative		sii	sia		siate	siano
Future	sarò etc.			*Conditional:* sarei, etc.		

fare to do, to make—fatto

Present	faccio	fai	fa	facciamo	fate	fanno
Imperative		fa'	faccia		fate	facciano
Future	farò, etc.			*Conditional:* farei, etc.		

potere to be able to, can—potuto

Present	posso	puoi	può	possiamo	potete	possono
Future	potrò, etc			*Conditional:* potrei, etc.		

● Andrea non ha potuto vedere Maria. Andrea couldn't see Maria.
   Non è potuto venire. He couldn't come.
   Mi potrebbe dire…? Could you tell me…?

rimanere to remain, to stay—rimasto

Present	rimango	rimani	rimane	rimaniamo	rimanete	rimangono
Imp.		rimani	rimanga		rimanete	rimangono
Future	rimarrò, etc			*Conditional:* rimarrei, etc.		

sal<u>i</u>re to get on—salito

Present	salgo	sali	sale	saliamo	salite	salgano
Imperative		sali	salga		salite	salgano

sap<u>e</u>re to know, to know how to—saputo

Present	so	sai	sa	sappiamo	sapete	sanno
Future	saprò, etc.			*Conditional:* saprei, etc.		

sc<u>e</u>gliere to choose—scelto

Present	scelgo	scegli	sceglie	scegliamo	scegliete	scelgono
Imperative		scelgi	scelga		scegliete	scelgono

stare to stay, to stand: to be—stato

Present	sto	stai	sta	stiamo	state	stanno
Imperative		sta'	stia		state	stiano
Future	starò, etc.			*Conditional:* starei, etc.		

ten<u>e</u>re to have, to hold—tenuto

Present	tengo	tieni	tiene	teniamo	tenete	tengono
Imperative		tieni	tenga		tenete	tengano

usc<u>i</u>re to go out—uscito

Present	esco	esci	esce	usciamo	uscite	escono
Imperative		esci	esca		uscite	escano

ven<u>i</u>re to come—venuto

Present	vengo	vieni	viene	veniamo	venite	vengono
Imperative		vieni	venga		venite	vengano
Future	verrò, etc.			*Conditional:* verrei, etc.		

vol<u>e</u>re to want—voluto

Present	voglio	vuoi	vuole	vogliamo	volete	vogliono
Future	vorrò, etc.			*Conditional:* vorrei, etc.		

● Non ha voluto parlare. He/She did not want to speak.
  Non siamo voluti venire. We did not want to come.
  Vorrei un gelato. I'd like ice cream.

Verb + Object

In Italian some verbs take a direct object, whereas in English the same verb may take an indirect object. Examples of these are: **aspettare** to wait for, **ascoltare** to listen to, and **cercare** to look for:

Non vuole ascoltare la radio?
Don't you want to listen to the radio?
La ragazza cerca il suo cane.
The girl is looking for her dog.

Other verbs require an indirect object, whereas in English the verb takes a direct object. Examples of these are: **chiedere/domandare** to ask; **parlare** to speak; **telefonare** to telephone:

Ho telefonato alla mia amica. I phoned my friend.
Chiede la strada a un passante. Ask a passerby the way.

Word Order

Normal word order in a declarative sentence is:

Subject	Verb	Complement	
Carla	compra	la borsa.	Carla buys the bag.
Oggi Carla	ha comprato	la borsa.	Today Carla bought the bag.

The subject, however, is placed after the verb:

Oggi è arrivata Carla. Today Carla arrived.	if special emphasis is being placed on the subject.
Dov' è la mia borsa? Where's my bag?	in questions.

● Questions that do not contain an interrogative word usually follow the normal word order for declarative sentences:
Ha visto il signor Neri? Have you seen Mr. Neri?

The Negative

no *(no)*
È stanco?—Are you tired?—**No**, signora.—No.
Pioverà?—Is it going to rain?—Speriamo **di no**.—We hope not.

non *(not)*

	non	verb	
Perché	**non**	sei venuto/a?	Why didn't you come?
Gina	**non**	ha tempo.	Gina doesn't have time.

● *ci* (there) and *ne* (some, of it, them) follow *non* and precede the verb:
Non ne vedo. I don't see any.
Non ci sono panini. There are no rolls.

non... nessuno/nulla/niente/mai, etc.

Non c'è nessuno.	No one is there.
Non voglio nulla/niente.	I don't want anything.
Non fumo mai.	I never smoke.
Non fumo più.	I don't smoke anymore.
Non beve né vino né birra.	He drinks neither wine nor beer.

ENGLISH–ITALIAN DICTIONARY

A

a (an) un/uno/una [oon, oo noh, oo-nah]

a little un po' [oon poh]

abbreviation abbreviazione *(f)* [ah-bbreh-vyah-tzyoh-neh]; **shortcut** scorciatoia [skohr-chah-toh-yah]

able to, to be *(v)* potere [poh-teh-reh]

about circa, quasi [cheer-kah, kwah-see]

above sopra, sù [soh-prah, suu]; **up there** lassù [lah-ssoo]

above all soprattutto, anzitutto [soh-prah-ttoo-ttoh, ahn-tzee-too-ttoh]

absent assente [ah-ssehn-teh]

absolutely assolutamente [ah-ssoh-loo-tah-mehn-teh]

abuse *(v)* abusare [ah-boo-sah-reh]

abuse abuso [ah-boo-soh]

accelerate *(v)* accelerare [ah-cheh-leh-rah-reh]

accent accento [ah-chehn-toh]

accept *(v)* accettare [ah-cheh-ttah-reh]

accident contrattempo, incidente *(m)* [kohn-trah-ttehm-poh, een-chee-dehn-teh]

accompaniment accompagnamento, compagnia [ah-kkohm-pah-nyah-mehn-toh, kohm-pah-nyee-ah]

accompany *(v)* accompagnare [ah-kkohm-pah-nyah-reh]

accuracy accuratezza [ah-kkoo-rah-teh-tzah]

accurate accurato [ah-kkoo-rah-toh]

acid(ic) acido [ah-chee-doh]

acquaintance conoscente *(m/f)* [koh-noh-shehn-teh]; conoscenza [koh-noh-shehn-tzah]

across attraverso [ah-ttrah-vehr-soh]

action azione *(f)* [ah-tzyoh-neh]

activity attività [ah-ttee-vee-tah]

add *(v)* aggiungere, sommare, addizionare [ah-djoon-jeh-reh, soh-mmah-reh, ah-ddee-tzyoh-nah-reh]

additional supplementare, in più [soo-ppleh-mehn-tah-reh, een pyoo]

address *(v)* indirizzare [een-dee-ree-tzah-reh]

address indirizzo [enn-dee-ree-tzoh]

administration amministrazione *(f)* [ah-mmee-nee-strah-tzyoh-neh]

admire *(v)* ammirare [ah mmee-rah-reh]

admittance accesso [ah-cheh-ssoh]

Adriatic Adriatico [ah-dryah-tee-koh]

adult adulto/adulta [ah-dool-toh/ah-dool-tah]

advantage vantaggio [vahn-tah-djoh]

advantageous vantaggioso [vahn-tah-djoh-soh]

advertisement annuncio [ah-nnoon-choh]

advice suggerimento, consiglio [soo-djeh-ree-mehn-toh, kohn-see-lyoh]

advise *(v)* consigliare [kohn-see-lyah-reh]

aerate *(v)* areare, dare aria [ah-reh-ah-reh, dah-reh ah-ryah]

affirm *(v)* affermare [ah-ffehr-mah-reh]

after dopo [doh-poh]

afternoon pomeriggio [poh-meh-ree-djoh]; **in the afternoon** di pomeriggio [dee poh-meh-ree-djoh]

again ancora, di nuovo, ancora una volta [ahn-koh-rah, dee nwoh-voh, ahn-koh-rah oo-nah vohl-tah]; **not yet** non ancora [nohn ahn-koh-rah]

against contro [kohn-troh]

age età [eh-tah]

agency agenzia [ah-jehn-tzyah]

agree *(v)* essere d'accordo, accordarsi [eh-sseh-reh dah-kkohr-doh]

agree (on) *(v)* accordarsi su [ah-kkohr-dahr-see soo]

agreement accordo [ah-kkohr-doh]

ahead avanti [ah-vahn-tee]

aid aiuto [ah-yoo-toh]; **first aid** pronto soccorso [prohn-toh soh-kkohr-soh]

air aria [ah-ryah]; **current of air, draft** corrente *(f)* d'aria [koh-rrehn-teh dah-ryah]

alarm clock sveglia [zveh-lyah]

alcohol spirito, alcool [spee-ree-toh, ahl-kohl]; **alcohol stove** fornello a spirito [fohr-neh-lloh ah spee-ree-toh]

algae alghe *(pl)* [ahl-gheh]

all tutti, tutte [too-ttee, too-ttoh]; **every day** tutti i giorni [too-ttee ee johr-nee]; **every two days** ogni due giorni [oh-nyee doo-eh johr-nee]

all tutto *(adj)* [too-ttoh]

alliance alleanza [ah-lleh-<u>ahn</u>-zah]
allow (v) permettere [pehr-<u>meh</u>-tteh-reh]
almost quasi [<u>kwah</u>-see]
alone solo [<u>soh</u>-loh]
already già [<u>jah</u>]
also anche, pure [<u>ahn</u>-keh, <u>poo</u>-reh]
although benché [behn-<u>keh</u>]
always sempre [<u>sehm</u>-preh]
ambiance ambiente (m) [ahm-<u>byehn</u>-teh]
ambulance autoambulanza [ah-oo-tohm-
  boo-<u>lahn</u>-tzah]
among tra, fra [trah, frah]
amount somma [<u>soh</u>-mmah]
amusing divertente [dee-vehr-<u>tehn</u>-teh]
ancient antico [ahn-<u>tee</u>-koh]
and e [eh]; **and so on** e così via, eccetera
  [eh koh-<u>see</u> <u>vee</u>-ah, eh-cheh-<u>teh</u>-rah]
anger rabbia [<u>rah</u>-byah]
angle (v) pescare con l'amo (la lenza)
  [peh-<u>skah</u>-reh kohn <u>lah</u>-moh (lah <u>lehn</u>-
  tsah)]
angry arrabbiato, infuriato, in collera
  [ah-rrah-<u>byah</u>-toh, een-foo-<u>ryah</u>-toh, een
  <u>koh</u>-lleh-rah]; **get angry about** (v)
  arrabbiarsi [ah-rrah-<u>byahr</u>-see]
animal animale (m) [ah-nee-<u>mah</u>-leh]
announce (v) annunciare [ah-nnoon-
  <u>chah</u>-reh]
annoy (v) infastidire [een-fah-stee-<u>dee</u>-
  reh]
annoying noioso, seccante [noh-<u>yoh</u>-
  soh, seh-<u>kkahn</u>-teh]
annually annuale [ah-<u>nnwah</u>-leh]
another un altro [oo-<u>nahl</u>-troh]; **another
  time** un'altra volta [oo-<u>nahl</u>-trah <u>vohl</u>-
  tah]
answer (v) rispondere [ree-<u>spohn</u>-deh-
  reh]
answer risposta [ree-<u>spoh</u>-stah]
apartment appartamento [ah-ppahr-tah-
  <u>mehn</u>-toh]; **furnished apartment**
  appartamento ammobiliato [ah-ppahr-
  tah-<u>mehn</u>-toh ah-mmoh-bee-<u>lyah</u>-toh]
apparently apparentemente [ah-ppah-
  rehn-teh-<u>mehn</u>-teh]
appear (v) apparire [ah-ppah-<u>ree</u>-reh]
appearance apparenza [ah-ppah-<u>rehn</u>-
  tzah]
appetite appetito [ah-ppeh-<u>tee</u>-toh]
applause applauso [ah-<u>pplah</u>-oo-soh]
appointment appuntamento [ah-ppoon-
  tah-<u>mehn</u>-toh]; **make an appointment**
  (v) darsi appuntamento [<u>dahr</u>-see oo-
  nah-ppoon-tah-<u>mehn</u>-toh]
approach (v) avvicinarsi [ah-vve-chee-
  <u>nahr</u>-see]

around (time) circa [<u>cheer</u>-kah]
arrive (v) arrivare [ah-rree-<u>vah</u>-reh]
article articolo [ahr-<u>tee</u>-koh-loh]
as come, poiché [<u>ko</u>-meh, poh-ee-<u>keh</u>];
  as if come se [<u>ko</u>-meh seh]
ask (v) chiedere [<u>kyeh</u>-deh-reh]
association associazione (f) [ah-ssoh-
  chah-<u>tzyoh</u>-neh]
assumption supposizione (f) [soo-ppoh-
  see-<u>tzyoh</u>-neh]
at a [ah]
at least almeno [ahl-<u>meh</u>-noh]
at that very moment proprio in quel
  momento [<u>proh</u>-pryoh een kwehl moh-
  <u>mehn</u>-toh]
attack (v) attaccare, aggredire [ah-tah-
  <u>kkah</u>-reh, ah-ghreh-<u>dee</u>-reh]
attempt (v) tentativo [tehn-tah-<u>tee</u>-voh]
attempt prova [<u>proh</u>-vah]
attentive attento [ah-<u>tten</u>-toh]
aunt zia [<u>tzee</u>-ah]
authorized autorizzato [ah-oo-toh-ree-
  <u>zah</u>-toh]
automatic automatico [ah-oo-toh-mah-
  <u>tee</u>-koh]
avoid (v) evitare [eh-vee-<u>tah</u>-reh]

B

backwards all'indietro [ah-lleen-<u>dyeh</u>-
  troh]
bad cattivo (adj), villano [kah-<u>ttee</u>-voh,
  vee-<u>llah</u>-noh]; (weather) brutto [<u>broo</u>-
  ttoh]; male (adv) [<u>mah</u>-leh]; **worse**
  peggio [<u>peh</u>-djoh]; **the worst** il pessimo [eel <u>peh</u>-ssee-moh]
bag sacco [<u>sah</u>-kkoh]
balance bilancia [bee-<u>lahn</u>-chah]
ball palla, pallone (m) [<u>pah</u>-llah, pah-<u>lloh</u>-
  neh]; (party) ballo [<u>bah</u>-lloh]
bandaging (med) fasciatura [fah-shah-
  <u>too</u>-rah]
bank banca [<u>bahn</u>-kah]
banknote banconota [bahn-koh-<u>noh</u>-tah]
basket cesto [<u>cheh</u>-stoh]
bath bagno [<u>bah</u>-nyoh]
bathe (v) fare il bagno [<u>fah</u>-reh eel <u>bah</u>-
  nyoh]
battery batteria [bah-<u>tteh</u>-<u>ree</u>-ah]; (for
  flashlight) pila [<u>pee</u>-lah]
be able to, can (v) potere [poh-<u>teh</u>-reh]
be fit (v) essere in forma [<u>eh</u>-sseh-reh
  een <u>fohr</u>-mah]
be friends (v) essere in amicizia [eh-
  <u>sseh</u>-reh een ah-mee-<u>chee</u>-tzyah]

beach spiaggia [spyah-djah]
beach resort località marittima [loh-kah-lee-tah mah-ree-ttee-mah]
beach umbrella ombrellone (m) [ohm-breh-lloh-neh]
beautiful bello [beh-lloh]
beauty bellezza [beh-lleh-tzah]
become (v) diventare [dee-vehn-tah-reh]
bed letto; **go to bed** (v) andare a letto [ahn-dah-reh ah leh-ttoh]
bedroom camera da letto [kah-meh-rah dah leh-ttoh]
bee ape (f) [ah-peh]
before prima di [pree-mah dee]
begin (v) cominciare, iniziare [koh-meen-chah-reh, ee-nee-tzyah-reh]
beginning inizio [ee-nee-tzyoh]
behavior comportamento [kohm-pohr-tah-mehn-toh]
behind dietro, indietro [dyeh-troh, een-dyeh-troh]
believe (v) credere [kreh-deh-reh]
bell campanello [kahm-pah-neh-lloh]
belong (v) appartenere [ah-ppahr-teh-neh-reh]
belt cinghia [cheen-ghyah]
bench panchina [pahn-kee-nah]
benevolent benevolo [beh-neh-voh-loh]
besides inoltre [ee-nohl-treh]
best migliore (m/f) [mee-lyoh-reh]
bet (v) scommettere [skoh-mmeh-tteh-reh]
bet scommessa [skoh-mmeh-ssah]
better meglio [meh-lyoh]; **better than** meglio di/che [meh-lyoh dee/keh]
between (time) entro [ehn-troh]
big grande [grahn-deh]
bill conto [kohn-toh]
binoculars binocolo [bee-noh-koh-loh]
bird uccello [oo-cheh-lloh]
birth nascita [nah-shee-tah]; **birthplace** luogo di nascita [lwoh-ghoh dee nah-shee-tah]
birthday compleanno [kohm-pleh-ah-nnoh]
bite (v) mordere [mohr-deh-reh]
bitter amaro, aspro, acerbo [ah-mah-roh, ah-sproh, ah-chehr-boh]
blanket coperta [koh-pehr-tah]
blind cieco [cheh-koh]
blink (v) (car lights) lampeggiare [lahm-peh-djah-reh]
bloom (v) fiorire [fyoh-ree-reh]
blow colpo [kohl-poh]
board (v) andare a bordo [ahn-dah-reh a bohr-doh]

boat barca [bahr-kah]
body corpo [kohr-poh]
boil (v) bollire [boh-llee-reh]
book libro [lee-broh]
booth cabina [kah-bee-nah]
border frontiera, confine (m) [frohn-tyeh-rah, kohn-fee-neh]
born nato [nah-toh]
boss padrone (m) [pah-droh-neh]
both tutti e due [too-ttee eh doo-eh]
bottle bottiglia [boh-ttee-lyah]
boy ragazzo [rah-gha-tzoh]
branch office filiale (f) [fee-lyah-leh]
brand marca [mahr-kah]
break (v) rompere [rohm-peh-reh]
breath respiro [reh-spee-roh]
breathing respirazione (f) [reh-spee-rah-tzyoh-neh]
bright chiaro, brillante [kyah-roh, bree-llahn-teh]
broadcast trasmissione (f) [trah-zmee-ssyoh-neh]
broken rotto [roh-ttoh]
brother fratello [frah-teh-lloh]
brown marrone [mah-rroh-neh]
brush (v) spazzolare [spah-tsoh-lah-reh]
brush spazzola [spah-tzoh-lah]
build (v) costruire [koh-stroo-ee-roh]
building edificio [eh-dee-fee-choh]
bunch mazzo [mah-tzoh]
burn (v) bruciare [broo-chah-reh]
bush cespuglio [cheh-spoo-lyoh]
business affare (m) [ah-ffah-reh]
business/visiting hours orario d'apertura (al pubblico) [oh-rah-ryoh dah-pehr-too-rah (ahl poo-blee-koh)]
busy occupato [oh-kkoo-pah-toh]
busy with, to be (v) occuparsi di [oh-kkoo-pahr-see dee]
but ma, però [mah, peh-roh]
button bottone (m) [boh-ttoh-neh]
buy (v) comprare [kohm-prah-reh]

C

café, coffee caffè (m) [kah-feh]
calculate (v) calcolare [kahl-koh-lah-reh]
call (v) chiamare [kyah-mah-reh]
called, to be (v) chiamarsi [kyah-mahr-see]; **mi chiamo ...** my name is ... [mee kyah-moh]
calm down (v) tranquillizzarsi [trahn-kwee-llee-zahr-see]
camera macchina fotografica [mah-kkee-nah foh-toh-grah-fee-kah]

can barattolo, scatola [bah-rah-ttoh-loh, skah-toh-lah]; **can opener** apriscatole *(m)* [ah-pree-skah-toh-leh]

canal canale *(m)* [kah-nah-leh]

candle candela [kahn-deh-lah]

capable capace, bravo, abile [kah-pah-cheh, brah-voh, ah-bee-leh]

capable, to be *(v)* essere capace di [eh-sseh-reh kah-pah-che dee]

capital capitale *(f)* [kah-pee-tah-leh]

car auto *(f)*, macchina [ah-oo-toh, mah-kkee-nah]; **car** *(train)* vagone *(m)* [vah-ghoh-neh]

card cartolina [cahr-toh-lee-nah]

care cura [koo-rah]

careful attento, cauto, prudente, diligente [ah-ttehn-toh, kah-oo-toh, proo-dehn-teh, dee-lee-jehn-teh]

careful! attenzione! [ah-ttehn-tzyoh-neh]

careless imprudente [eem-proo-dehn-teh]

carry *(v)* portare, portare con sé [pohr-tah-reh kohn seh]

carry out *(v)* eseguire, svolgere, svolgersi [eh-seh-gwee-reh, zvohl-jeh-reh, zvohl-jehr-see]

case caso [kah-soh]; **in case** casomai [kah-soh-mah-ee]

cash register cassa [kah-ssah]

castle castello [kah-steh-lloh]

cat gatta/gatto [ghah-ttah/ghah-ttoh]

cause *(v)* causare [kah-oo-sah-reh]

cause causa [kah-oo-sah]

ceiling soffitto [soh-ffee-ttoh]

center centro [chehn-troh]

central centrale [chehn-trah-leh]

ceramics ceramica [cheh-rah-mee-kah]

certain certo *(adj, adv)* [chehr-toh]

certainly certamente, certo, sì [chehr-tah-mehn-teh, chehr-toh, see]

certificate certificato [chehr-tee-fee-kah-toh]

certify *(v)* certificare [chehr-tee-fee-kah-reh]

chain catena [kah-teh-nah]

chalk gesso [jeh-ssoh]

champion campione *(m)* [kahm-pyoh-neh]

change *(v)* cambiare, modificare [kahm-byah-reh, moh-dee-fee-kah-reh]

change cambiamento [kahm-byah-mehn-toh]

change *(money)* moneta [moh-neh-tah]; **money exchange** cambio [kahm-byoh]

chapel cappella [kah-ppeh-llah]

charge *(v)* denunciare [deh-noon-chah-reh]

charge denuncia [deh-noon-chah]

cheap non caro, economico, a buon mercato [nohn kah-roh, eh-koh-noh-mee-koh, ah bwohn mehr-kah-toh]

check *(v)* verificare, controllare [veh-ree-fee-kah-reh, kohn-troh-llah-reh]

cheerful allegro [ah-lleh-groh]

chef capo [kah-poh]

chewing gum gomma da masticare [ghoh-mmah dah mah-stee-kah-reh]

child bambino [bahm-bee-noh]

choice scelta [shehl-tah]

choir coro [koh-roh]

choose *(v)* scegliere [sheh-lyeh-reh]

cigar sigaro [see-ghah-roh]

cigarette sigaretta [see-ghah-reh-ttah]

city città [chee-ttah]

class classe *(f)* [klah-sseh]

clean *(v)* pulire [poo-lee-reh]

clean pulito [poo-lee-toh]

clear chiaro [kyah-roh]

climate clima *(m)* [klee-mah]

close *(v)* chiudere [kyoo-deh-reh]

closed chiuso [kyoo-soh]

cloth panno, straccio, stoffa, tessuto [pah-nnoh, strah-choh, stoh-ffah, teh-ssoo-toh]

clothes iron ferro da stiro [feh-rroh dah stee-roh]

clothing abbigliamento [ah-bbe-lyah-mehn-toh]

coal carbone *(m)* [kahr-boh-neh]

coast costa [koh-stah]

cockroach scarafaggio [skah-rah-fah-djoh]

coffee caffè *(m)* [kah-ffeh]

coin moneta [moh-neh-tah]

cold (to be) *(v)* aver freddo [ah-veh-reh freh-ddoh]

cold freddo [freh-ddoh]

colleague collega *(m/f)* [koh-lleh-gah]

collision scontro, collisione *(f)* [skohn-troh, koh-llee-syoh-neh]

color colore *(m)* [koh-loh-reh]

colored a colori, multicolore [ah koh-loh-ree, mool-tee-koh-loh-reh]

come *(v)* venire [veh-nee-reh]

come from *(v)* derivare, provenire, discendere [deh-ree-vah-reh, proh-veh-nee-reh, dee-shehn-deh-reh]

comfort comodità [koh-moh-dee-tah]

common comune [koh-moo-neh]

communicate *(v)* comunicare [koh-moo-nee-kah-reh]

company ditta, società, associazione
(f), compagnia [dee-ttah, soh-cheh-tah,
ah-sso-chah-tzyoh-neh, kohm-pah-nyee-
ah]

compare (v) comparare, confrontare
[kohm-pah-rah-reh, kohn-frohn-tah-reh]

comparison paragone (m), confronto
[pah-rah-ghoh-neh, kohn-frohn-toh]

compass bussola [boo-ssoh-lah]

compassion compassione (f) [kohm-
pah-ssyoh-neh]

compensation compenso, retribuzione
(f) [kohm-pehn-soh, reh-tree-boo-tzyoh-
neh]

competent competente [kohm-peh-tehn-te]

competition concorso [kohn-kohr soh]

complain (about) (v) lamentarsi (di),
reclamare (per) [lah-mehn-tahr-see
(dee) reh-klah-mah-reh (pehr)]

complaint reclamo [reh-klah-moh]

concerning concernente [kohn-chehr-
nehn-teh]

condition condizione (f) [kohn-dee-
tzyoh-neh]

condolences condoglianze (pl) [kohn-
doh-lyahn-tzeh]

condom preservativo, profilattico
[preh-sehr-vah-tee-voh proh-fee-lah-ttee
koh]

conductor conduttore (m) [kohn-doo-
ttoh-reh]

confirm (v) confermare [kohn-fehr-mah-
reh]

congratulate (v) congratularsi, fare gli
auguri [kohn-grah-too-lahr-see, fah-reh
lyee al-oo-goo-ree]

connection (tel) comunicazione (f)
[koh moo-nee-kah-tzyoh-neh]

conscientious coscienzioso [koh-shehn-
tzyoh-soh]

conscious cosciente [koh-shehn-teh]

consent (v) acconsentire [ah-kkohn-
sehn-tee-reh]

considerable considerevole [kohn-see-
deh-reh-voh-leh]

consulate consolato [kohn-soh-lah-toh]

consult (v) consultare [kohn-sool-tah-reh]

consume (v) consumare [kohn-soo-mah-
reh]

consumption consumo [kohn-soo-moh]

contact contatto [kohn-tah-ttoh]

container recipiente (m) [reh-chee-
pyehn-teh]

contemporaneous, contemporary
contemporaneo [kohn-tehm-poh-rah-neh-
oh]

content contento [kohn-tehn-toh]

contents contenuto [kohn-teh-noo-toh]

continue (v) continuare [kohn-tee-nwah-
reh]

contraceptive anticoncezionale (m)
[ahn-tee-kohn-cheh-tzyoh-nah-leh]

contract (v) contrattare [kohn-trah ttah-
reh]

contract contratto [kohn-trah ttoh]

contrary contrario [kohn-trah-ryoh]; **on
the contrary** al contrario [ahl kohn-
trah-ryoh]

control (v) controllare [kohn-troh-llah-reh]

conversation conversazione (f) [kohn-
vehr-sah-tzyoh-neh]

converse (v) conversare [kohn-vehr-sah-
reh]

cook (v) cucinare [koo-chee-nah-reh]

cooked cotto [koh-ttoh]

cooking pot pentola [pehn-toh-lah]

cool fresco [freh-skoh]

copy copia [koh-pya]

cordiality cordialità [kohr-dyah-lee-tah]

cordially cordialmente [kohr-dyahl-mehn-
teh]

corner angolo [ahn-goh-loh]

correct corretto [koh-rreh-ttoh]

correspondance corrispondenza [koh-
rree-spohn-dehn-tzah]

cost (v) costare [koh-stah-reh]

cough (v) tossire [toh-ssee-reh]

count (v) contare [kohn-tah-reh]

counter sportello [spohr-teh-lloh]

country paese (m), patria [pah-eh-seh,
pah-tryah]

coupon tagliando [tah-lyahn-doh]

course corso [kohr-soh]

courteous cortese [kohr-teh-seh]

courtesy cortesia [kohr-teh-see-ah]

courtyard cortile (m) [kohr-tee-leh]

cousin cugino/cugina [koo-jee-noh/koo-
jee-nah]

cover (v) coprire [koh-pree-reh]

cow mucca [moo-kkah]

creative creativo [kreh-ah-tee-voh]

credit credito [kreh-dee-toh]

crew equipaggio [eh-kwee-pah-djoh]

criticize (v) criticare [kree-tee-kah-reh]

cross (v) attraversare [ah-ttrah-vehr-sah-
reh]

crossing (street) incrocio [een-kroh-
choh]

crowd folla [foh-llah]

crowded affollato [ah-ffoh-llah-toh]

cry (v) piangere [pyahn-jeh-reh]

culture cultura [kool-too-rah]

cunning furbo [foor-boh]
cup tazza [tah-tzah]
curious curioso [koo-ryoh-soh]
current *(el)* corrente *(f)* (elettrica) [koh-rrehn-teh eh-leh-ttree-kah]
curse *(v)* imprecare [eem-preh-kah-reh]
curve curva [koor-vah]
custom costume *(m)* [koh-stoo-meh]
customer cliente *(m)* [klyehn-teh]
customs dogana [doh-ghah-nah]; **customs office** ufficio doganale [oo-ffee-choh doh-ghah-nah-leh]; **customs officer** il doganiere [eel doh-ghah-nyeh-reh]; **duty** *(taxes)* i diritti doganali [ee dee-ree-ttee doh-ghah-nah-lee]
cut *(v)* tagliare [tah-lyah-reh]

D

damage *(v)* danneggiare [dah-nneh-djah-reh]
damage danno [dah-nnoh]; **compensation for damages** risarcimento dei danni [ree-sahr-chee-mehn-toh deh-ee dah-nnee]
dance ballo, danza [bah-lloh, dahn-tszah]
danger pericolo [peh-ree-koh-loh]
dangerous dannoso, malsano, pericoloso [dah-nnoh-soh, mahl-sah-noh, peh-ree-koh-loh-soh]
dare *(v)* osare [oh-sah-reh]
dark scuro [skoo-roh]
darn *(v)* rammendare [rah-mmehn-dah-reh]
date data [dah-tah]
daughter figlia [fee-lyah]
day giorno [johr-noh]
dead morto [mohr-toh]
dear caro, gentile, amabile [kah-roh, jehn-tee-leh, ah-mah-bee-leh]
death morte *(f)* [mohr-teh]
debt debito [deh-bee-toh]
deceit inganno [een-ghah-nnoh]
decide *(v)* decidere [deh-chee-deh-reh]; **make up one's mind** *(v)* decidersi [deh-chee-dehr-see]; **be decided, resolute** *(v)* essere deciso [eh-sseh-reh deh-chee-soh]
decision risoluzione *(f)* [ree-soh-loo-tzyoh-neh]; decisione *(f)* [deh-chee-syoh-neh]
declare *(v)* dichiarare [dee-kyah-rah-reh]
deed fatto [fah-ttoh]
deep profondo [proh-fohn-doh]

defect difetto [dee-feh-tto]
defective difettoso [dee-feh-ttoh-soh]
definite definitivo *(adj)* [deh-fee-nee-tee-voh]
definitely definitivamente [deh-fee-nee-tee-vah-mehn-teh]
delay *(v)* ritardare, tardare [ree-tahr-dah-reh, tahr-dah-reh]
delay dilazione *(f)* [dee-lah-tsyoh-neh]
deliberately apposta [ah-ppoh-stah]
delicate morbido, tenue [mohr-bee-doh, teh-nweh]
deliver *(v)* consegnare [kohn-seh-nyah-reh]
deny *(v)* negare [neh-ghah-reh]
department stores i grandi magazzini [ee grahn-dee mah-ghah-zee-nee]
departure partenza [pah-rtehn-tzah]
deposit *(v)* depositare [deh-poh-see-tah-reh]
describe *(v)* descrivere [deh-skree-veh-reh]
description descrizione [deh-skree-tzyoh-neh] *(f)*; **detailed description** descrizione dettagliata [deh-skree-tzyoh-neh deh-ttah-lyah-tah]
deserve *(v)* meritare [meh-ree-tah-reh]
desire desiderio, voglia [deh-see-deh-ryoh, voh-lyah]
despite malgrado [mahl-grah-doh]
destroy *(v)* distruggere [dee-stroo-djeh-reh]
detail dettaglio, particolare *(m)* [deh-ttah-lyoh, pahr-tee-koh-lah-reh]
develop *(v)* sviluppare [svee-loo-ppah-reh]
development sviluppo [svee-loo-ppoh]
diagnosis diagnosi *(f)* [dyah-nyoh-see]
dial *(v)* formare il numero [fohr-mah-reh eel noo-meh-roh]
die *(v)* morire [moh-ree-reh]
difference differenza [dee-ffeh-rehn-tzah]
different diverso *(adj)* [dee-vehr-soh]
difficult difficile [dee-ffee-chee-leh]
difficulty difficoltà [dee-ffee-kohl-tah]
direct diretto *(adj)* [dee-reh-ttoh]
direction direzione *(f)*, indicazione *(f)* [dee-reh-tzyoh-neh, een-dee-kah-tzyoh-neh]
directly direttamente [dee-reh-ttah-mehn-teh]
director direttore/direttrice *(m/f)* [dee-reh-ttoh-reh/dee-reh-ttree-cheh]
dirt immondizia [ee-mmohn-dee-tzyah]
dirty sporco [spohr-koh]
disadvantage svantaggio, inconveniente *(m)* [zvahn-tah-djoh, een-kohn-veh-nyehn-teh]

disappear *(v)* sparire [spah-<u>ree</u>-reh]
disappointed deluso [deh-<u>loo</u>-soh]
discotheque discoteca [dee-skoh-<u>teh</u>-kah]
discount sconto [<u>skohn</u>-toh]
discover *(v)* scoprire [skoh-<u>pree</u>-reh]
discuss *(v)* discorrere, parlare [dee-skoh-<u>rreh</u>-reh, pahr-<u>lah</u>-reh]
dish *(meal, eating)* piatto, pietanza, portata [<u>pyah</u>-ttoh, pyeh-<u>tahn</u>-tzah, pohr-<u>tah</u>-tah]
disorder disordine *(m)* [dee-<u>sohr-dee</u>-neh]
dispute *(v)* litigare, bisticciare [lee-tee-<u>ghah</u>-reh, bee-stee-<u>chah</u>-reh]
dispute lite *(f)*, disputa [<u>lee</u>-teh, dee-<u>spoo</u>-tah]
distance distanza, lontananza [dee-<u>stahn</u>-tsah, lohn-tah-<u>nahn</u>-tzah]
distinct distinto [dee-<u>steen</u>-toh]
distinguish *(v)* distinguere [dee-<u>steen</u>-gweh-reh]; **distinguish oneself from** *(v)* distinguersi da [dee-<u>steen</u>-gwehr-see]
distribute *(v)* distribuire [dee-stree-boo-<u>eeh</u>-re]
distribution distribuzione *(f)* [dee-stree-boo-<u>tzyoh</u>-neh]
district quartiere *(m)* [kwahr-<u>tyeh</u>-reh]
distrust (someone/something) *(v)* diffidare [dee-ffee-<u>dah</u>-reh]
disturb *(v)* disturbare [dee-stoor-<u>bah</u>-roh]
disturbance disturbo, interruzione *(f)* [dee-<u>stoor</u>-boh, een-teh-rroo-<u>tzyoh</u>-neh]
divide *(v)* dividere [dee-<u>vee</u>-deh-reh]; **split up with someone** *(v)* dividere con qlcu [dee-<u>vee</u>-deh-reh kohn kwahl-<u>koo</u>-noh]
do the shopping *(v)* fare la spesa [<u>fah</u>-reh lah <u>speh</u>-sah]
doctor dottore *(m)* [doh-<u>ttoh</u>-reh]
document *(paper)* documento [doh-koo-<u>mehn</u>-toh]
dog cane *(m)* [<u>kah</u>-neh]
doll bambola [<u>bahm</u>-boh-lah]
donkey asino [<u>ah</u>-see-noh]
double doppio *(adj)* [<u>doh</u>-ppyoh]
doubt *(v)* dubitare di qlcu [doo-bee-<u>tah</u>-reh dee kwahl-<u>koo</u>-noh]; **without a doubt** senza dubbio [<u>sehn</u>-tzah doo byoh]
doubt dubbio [<u>doo</u>-byoh]
doubtful dubbioso, incerto [doo-<u>byoh</u>-soh, een-<u>chehr</u>-toh]
down in giù, in discesa [een <u>joo</u>, een dee-<u>sheh</u>-sah]
down there laggiù [lah-<u>djoo</u>]

downstairs di sotto [dee <u>soh</u>-ttoh]
draft sorso [<u>sohr</u>-soh]
draw *(v)* disegnare [dee-seh-<u>nyah</u>-reh]
dream *(v)* sognare [soh-<u>nyah</u>-reh]
dream sogno [<u>soh</u>-nyoh]
dress (oneself) *(v)* vestirsi [veh-<u>steer</u>-see]
drink *(v)* bere [<u>beh</u>-reh]
drinkable potabile [poh-<u>tah</u> bee-leh]
drive *(v)* guidare [gwee-<u>dah</u>-reh]
driver autista *(m)*, conducente *(m)* [ah-oo-<u>tee</u>-stah, kohn-doo-<u>chehn</u>-teh]
drop goccia [<u>ghoh</u>-chah]
drunk ubriaco, brillo [oo-<u>bryah</u>-koh, <u>bree</u>-lloh]
dry *(v)* asciugare [ah-shoo-<u>ghah</u>-reh]
dry secco, asciutto [<u>seh</u>-kkoh, ah-<u>shoo</u>-ttoh]
dry cleaner lavanderia a secco [lah-vahn-deh-<u>ree</u>-ah ah <u>seh</u>-kkoh]
duration durata [doo-<u>rah</u>-tah]
dust polvere *(f)* [<u>pohl</u>-veh-re]
duty dovere *(m)* [doh-<u>veh</u>-reh]
dyed colorato [koh-loh-<u>rah</u>-toh]

E

each ogni *(adj)*, ognuno, ciascuno *(pron)*, [<u>oh</u>-nyee, oh-<u>nyoo</u>-noh, chah-<u>skoo</u>-noh]
early in anticipo [een ahn-<u>tee</u>-chee-poh]
earn *(v)* guadagnare [gwah-dah-<u>nyah</u>-reh]
earnings guadagno [gwah-<u>dah</u>-nyoh]
earth terra [<u>teh</u>-rrah]
east est *(m)* [ehst]
easy facile [<u>fah</u>-chee-leh]
eat *(v)* mangiare [mahn-<u>jah</u>-reh]
edge orlo [<u>ohr</u>-loh]
edible commestibile [koh-mmeh-<u>stee</u>-bee-leh]
effect effetto [eh-<u>ffeh</u>-ttoh]
effective efficace [eh-fee-<u>kah</u>-cheh]
effort sforzo [<u>sfohr</u>-tzoh]; **try hard** *(v)* sforzarsi [sfohr-<u>tzahr</u>-see]
egg uovo [<u>woh</u>-voh]
either… or o… o… [oh… oh]
electric elettrico [eh-<u>leh</u>-ttree-koh]
elevator ascensore *(m)* [ah-shehn-<u>soh</u>-reh]
embassy ambasciata [ahm-bah-<u>shah</u>-tah]
embers brace *(f)* [<u>brah</u>-cheh]
embrace *(v)* abbracciare [ah-brah-<u>chah</u>-reh]
employment impiego [eem-<u>pye</u>-ghoh]
empty vuoto [<u>vwoh</u>-toh]

enchanted incantato [een-kahn-tah-toh]

enchanting incantevole [een-kahn-teh-voh-leh]

enclosure *(letter)* allegato [ah-lleh-gah-toh]

end fine *(f)*, finale *(m)* [fee-neh, fee-nah-leh]; **at/in the end** alla fine [ah-llah fee-neh]

engaged to, to be *(v)* fidanzarsi con [fee-dahn-tzahr-see kohn]

English inglese [een-gleh-seh]

enjoyment godimento [ghoh-dee-mehn-toh]

enough abbastanza, sufficiente [ah-bah-stahn-tzah, soo-ffee-chehn-teh]

enroll *(v)* iscriversi [ee-skree-vehr-see]

enter (in) *(v)* entrare [ehn-trah-reh]

enterprise impresa [eem-preh-sah]

enthusiastic (about) entusiasta (di) [ehn-too-syah-stah (dee)]

entrance entrata, ingresso, ingresso principale, porta d'ingresso [ehn-trah-tah, een-greh-ssoh, een-greh-sso preen-chee-pah-leh, pohr-tah deen-greh-ssoh]

equal uguale [oo-gwah-leh]

equipment corredo, dotazione *(f)* [koh-rreh-doh, doh-tah-tzyoh-neh]

equivalent equivalente *(m)* [eh-kwee-vah-lehn-teh]

errand commissione *(f)* [koh-mmee-ssyoh-neh]

esteem pregio [preh-joh]

Europe Europa [eh-oo-roh-pah]

European europeo/europea [e-oo-roh-peh-oh, eh-oo-roh-peh-ah]

evening sera [seh-rah]

event avvenimento [ah-vvyah-mehn-toh]

eventually eventualmente [eh-vehn-twahl-mehn-teh]

every tutto [too-ttoh]

every time ogni volta [oh-nyee vohl-tah]

everywhere dappertutto [dah-ppehr-too-ttoh]

exact preciso [preh-chee-soh]; **both… and** tanto… quanto [tahn-toh… kwahn-toh]

exam esame *(m)* [eh-zah-meh]

examine *(v)* esaminare; [eh-sah-mee-nah-reh] *(med)* visitare [vee-see-tah-reh]

example esempio [eh-sehm-pyoh]; **for example** per esempio [pehr eh-sehm-pyoh]

exceed *(v)* sorpassare [sohr-pah-ssah-reh]

excellent eccellente [eh-cheh-llehn-teh]

except eccetto, tranne [eh-cheh-ttoh, trah-nneh]

excepted escluso [eh-skloo-soh]

exception eccezione *(f)* [eh-cheh-tzyoh-neh]

exchange *(v)* scambiare [skahm-byah-reh]

exchange scambio [skahm-byoh]

excursion gita, giro [jee-tah, jee-roh]

excuse *(v)* scusare, perdonare [skoo-zah-reh, pehr-doh-nah-reh]; **excuse oneself** *(v)* scusarsi [skoo-zahr-see]

excuse scusa [skoo-zah]; **I beg your pardon!** chiedo scusa! [kyeh-doh skoo-sah]

exercise *(v)* esercitare [eh-sehr-chee-tah-reh]

exercise esercizio [eh-sehr-chee-tzyoh]

exhibition manifestazione *(f)* [mah-nee-feh-stah-tzyoh-neh]

exit uscita [oo-schee-tah]

exorbitant esagerato, eccessivo [eh-sah-jeh-rah-toh, eh-cheh-ssee-voh]

expenses spese *(pl)* [speh-seh]

expensive costoso, caro [coh-stoh-soh, kah-roh]

experience esperienza [eh-speh-ryehn-tzah]

expert esperto *(adj)* [eh-spehr-toh]

explain *(v)* spiegare [spyeh-gah-reh]

export *(v)* esportare [eh-spohr-tah-reh]

expression espressione *(f)* [eh-spreh-ssyoh-neh]

expressly espressamente [eh-spreh-ssah-mehn-teh]

exterior esterno, esteriore [eh-steh-rnoh, eh-steh-ryoh-reh]

extinguish *(v)* spegnere [speh-nyeh-reh]

extraordinary straordinario [strah-ohr-dee-nah-ryoh]

eye occhio, occhi *(pl)* [oh-kkyoh, oh-kkee]

F

faith fede *(f)* [feh-deh]

faithful fedele [feh-deh-leh]

fake falso [fahl-soh]

fall *(v)* cadere [kah-deh-reh]

family famiglia [fah-mee-lyah]; **family name** cognome *(m)* [koh-nyoh-meh]

famous famoso [fah-moh-soh]

far lontano [lohn-tah-noh]

farm fabbrica, fattoria [fah-bree-kah, fah-ttoh-ree-ah]

farmer contadino [kohn-tah-dee-noh]

fashion moda [moh-dah]

fat grasso [grah-ssoh]

father padre *(m)* [pah-dreh]

fatten (v) ingrassare [een-ghras-ssah-reh]
faucet rubinetto [roo-bee-neh-ttoh]
favor favore (m) [fah-voh-reh]
favorable favorevole [fah-voh-reh-voh-leh]
fear (v) aver paura di, temere [ah-veh-reh pah-oo-rah, teh-meh-reh]
fear paura [pah-oo-rah]
feather penna [peh-nnah]
feeling sentimento [sehn-tee-mehn-toh]
feminine femminile [feh-mmee-nee-leh]
fiancé/fiancée fidanzato, fidanzata [fee-dahn-tza-toh, fee-dahn-tza-tah]
field campo [kahm-poh]
fill (v) riempire [ryehm-pee-reh]
fill out (v) compilare [kohm-pee-lah-reh]; **fill out a form** (v) compilare un modulo [kohm-pee-lah-reh oon moh-doo-loh]
film pellicola [peh-llee-koh-lah]; **movie** film (m) [feelm]
filter filtro [feel-troh]
filth sporcizia [spohr-chee-tzyah]; fango [fahn-ghoh]
finally finalmente [fee-nahl-mehn-teh]
find (v) trovare [troh-vah-reh]
fine multa, sottile [mool-tah, soh-ttee-leh]
fingertip punta del dito [poon-tah dehl dee-toh]
finish (v) finire [fee-nee-reh]
finish off (v) sbrigare [sbree-gah-reh]
fire fuoco, incendio [fwoh-koh, een-chehn-dyoh]
fire alarm segnalatore (m) d'incendio [seh-nyah-lah-toh-reh deen-chehn-dyoh]
fire extinguisher estintore (m) [eh-steen-toh-reh]
firefighter vigili (pl) del fuoco, pompieri (pl) [vee-jee-lee dehl fwoh-koh, pohm-pyeh-ree]
firewood legna [leh-nyah]
fireworks fuochi (pl) d'artificio [fwoh-kee dahr-tee-fee-choh]
first primo/prima [pree-moh, pree-mah]; **in the first place** primo, in primo luogo [een pree-moh lwoh-ghoh]; **of top quality** di prima qualità [dee pree-mah kwah-lee-tah]
fish (v) pescare [peh-ska-reh]
fish pesce (m) [peh-sheh]
fishmonger pescivendolo [peh-schee-vehn-doh-loh]
flame fiamma [fyah-mmah]
flat piano, piatto [pyah-noh, pyah-ttoh]
flirt flirt (m) [flehrt]
flower fiore (m) [fyoh-reh]
fly (v) volare [voh-lah-reh]
fly mosca [moh-skah]

fodder foraggio, fodera [foh-rah-joh, foh-deh-rah]
foggy nebbioso [neh-byoh-soh]
fold up (v) piegare [pyeh-ghah-reh]
follow (v) seguire [seh-gwee-reh]
food alimento, alimentari (pl), alimentazione (f), cibo, prodotto alimentare, vitto [ah-lee-mehn-toh, ah-lee-mehn-tah-ree, ah-lee-mehn-tah-tzyoh-neh, cheeboh, proh-doh-ttoh ah-lee-mehn-tah-reh, vee-ttoh]
fool (v) ingannare [een-ghah-nnah-reh]
for per [pehr]
forbidden vietato [vyeh-tah-toh]; **no admittance** vietato l'ingresso [vyeh-tah-toh leen-greh-ssoh]; **no smoking** vietato fumare [vyeh-tah-toh foo-mah-reh]
force (v) costringere, forzare [koh-streen-jeh-reh, fohr-tzah-reh]
foreign estero [eh-steh-roh]; **abroad** all'estero [ah-leh-steh-roh]
foreigner forestiero, forestiera, straniero/a [foh-reh-styeh-roh, foh-reh-styeh-rah, strah-nyeh-roh/ah]
forget (v) dimenticare [dee-mehn-tee-kah-reh]
form formulario, modulo [fohr-moo-lah-ryoh, moh-doo-loh]; (shape) forma [fohr-mah]
forward (v) inviare [een-vee-ah-reh]
fountain fontana [fohn-tah-nah]
fragile fragile [frah-jee-leh]
free libero, gratis [lee-beh-roh, grah-tees]; (gratis) gratuito [grah-too-ee-toh]; **tax-free** esente da dazio [eh-sehn-teh dah dah-tzyoh]
freight nolo [noh-loh]
French francese [frahn-cheh-seh]
friend amico/amica [ah-mee-koh/ah-mee-kah]
friendly amichevole [ah-mee-keh-voh-leh]
friendship amicizia [ah-mee-chee-tzyah]
frighten (v) spaventare [spah-vehn-tah-reh]
from da, di [dah, dee]; **he/she is from Rome** è di Roma [eh dee roh-mah] **a letter from Rome** una lettera da Roma [oo-nah leh-tteh-rah dah roh-mah]
front davanti [dah-vahn-tee]; **in front of** davanti a [dah-vahn-tee ah]
front door portone (m) [pohr-toh-neh]
fry (v) friggere [free-djeh-reh]
full pieno [pyeh-noh]; **no vacancy** pieno, al completo [ahl kohm-pleh-toh]

fur pelo, pelliccia [peh-loh, peh-llee-chah]
furnish (v) ammobiliare [ah-mmoh-bee-lyah-reh]
furniture (piece) mobile (m) [moh-bee-leh]
future futuro [foo-too-roh]

G

game (animals) selvaggina [sehl-vah-djee-nah]
garage garage (m) [ghah-rahj]
garbage bidone (m) (delle immondizie), spazzatura [bee-doh-neh deh-lleh ee-mmohn-dee-tzyeh, spah-zzah-too-rah]
garden giardino [jahr-dee-noh]
gasoline benzina [behn-zee-nah]; **fill up the tank** (v) far benzina [fahr behn-zee-nah]
gate cancello [kahn-cheh-lloh]
gather (v) raccogliere [rah-kkoh-lyeh-reh]
gear (auto) marcia [mahr-chah]
general generale [jeh-neh-rah-leh]; **usually** in generale [een jeh-neh-rah-leh]
get (v) procurare [proh-koo-rah-reh]
get away (v) togliersi [toh-lyehr-see]
get drunk (v) ubriacarsi [oo-bryah-kahr-see]
get lost (v) smarrirsi [smah-rreer-see]
get on (v) andare su, salire [ahn-dah-reh soo, sah-lee-reh]
get up (v) (from bed) alzarsi [ahl-tzahr-see]
gift regalo [reh-ghah-loh]
girl ragazza [rah-gha-tzah]
give (v) (gift) regalare, dare [reh-ghah-lah-reh, dah-reh]
give back (v) ridare, restituire, rendere [ree-dah-re, reh-stee-too-ee-reh, rehn-deh-reh]
give directions (v) dare delle indicazioni [dah-reh deh-lleh een-dee-kah-tzyoh-nee]
give in (v) concedere, cedere [kohn-cheh-deh-reh, cheh-deh-reh]
glance sguardo [sgwahr-doh]
glass (window) vetro [veh-troh]; (drink) bicchiere (m) [bee-kkyeh-reh]
go (v) andare; **go straight** (v) andare diritto; **go ahead** (v) andare avanti; **go back** (v) tornare indietro [ahn-dah-reh dee-ree-ttoh, ah-vahn-tee, tohr-nah-reh een-dyeh-troh]
go abroad (v) partire (per l'estero) [pahr-tee-reh pehr leh-steh-roh]

go ahead (v) andare avanti [ahn-dah-reh ah-vahn-tee]
go around (v) circolare [cheer-koh-lah-reh]
go away (v) andar via [ahn-dahr vee-ah]
go down (v) scendere [shehn-deh-reh]
go get (v) andare a prendere [ahn-dah-reh ah prehn-deh-reh]
go on vacation (v) andare in ferie [ahn-dah-reh een feh-ryeh]
go out (v) uscire [oo-schee-reh]
go to sleep (v) addormentarsi [ah-ddohr-mehn-tahr-see]
God Dio [dee-oh]; **thank God!** grazie a Dio! [grah-tzye ah dee-oh]
good buono (adj) [bwoh-noh]; bene (adv) [beh-neh]
good-bye ciao [chah-oh]
government governo [ghoh-vehr-noh]
grand grandioso [grahn-dyoh-soh]
grandfather nonno [noh-nnoh]
grandmother nonna [noh-nnah]
grateful grato [grah-toh]
greatness grandezza [grahn-deh-tzah]
greet (v) salutare [sah-loo-tah-reh]
ground terreno [teh-rreh-noh]
ground floor pianoterra, pianterreno [pyah-noh-teh-rrah, pyahn-teh-rreh-noh]
group gruppo [groo-ppoh]
grow (v) crescere [kreh-sheh-reh]
guarantee garanzia [ghah-rahn-tzee-ah]
guest ospite (m) [oh-spee-teh]
guide guida (m) [gwee-dah]
guitar chitarra [kee-tah-rrah]
gulf golfo [ghohl-foh]

H

habit abitudine (f) [ah-bee-too-dee-neh]; **as usual** come d'abitudine [koh-meh dah-bee-too-dee-neh]
half metà, mezzo [meh-tah, meh-zoh]
hammer martello [mahr-teh-lloh]
hand mano (f) [mah-noh]
handkerchief fazzoletto [fah-tzoh-leh-ttoh]
handle impugnatura [eem-poo-nyah-too-rah]
handmade fatto a mano [fah-ttoh ah mah-noh]
handwriting calligrafia [kah-llee-grah-fee-ah]
hang (v) appendere [ah-ppehn-deh-reh]

happen *(v)* accadere, succedere [ah-kkah-<u>deh</u>-reh, soo-<u>cheh</u>-deh-reh]; **what happened?** cosa è successo? [<u>koh</u>-sah eh soo-<u>cheh</u>-ssoh]

happiness felicità [feh-lee-chee-<u>tah</u>]

happy felice [feh-<u>lee</u>-cheh]

happy (to) lieto (di) [<u>lyeh</u>-toh (dee)]

hard duro [<u>doo</u>-roh]

hardly appena [ah ppeh-nah]

hardness durezza [doo-<u>reh</u>-tzah]

harm *(v)* nuocere [<u>nwoh</u>-cheh-reh]

harvest raccolta [rah-<u>kkoh</u>l-tah]

have *(v)* avere, tenere [ah-<u>veh</u>-reh, teh-<u>neh</u>-reh]

have an accident *(v)* avere un incidente [ah-<u>veh</u>-reh oon een-chee-<u>dehn</u>-teh]

have fun *(v)* divertirsi [dee-vehr-<u>teer</u>-see]

have to, must *(v)* dovere [doh-<u>veh</u>-reh]

he lui [loo-ee]

headlight faro [<u>fah</u>-roh]

health salute *(f)*, benessere *(m)* [sah-<u>loo</u>-teh, beh-<u>neh</u>-sseh-reh]

healthy sano [<u>sah</u>-noh]

hear *(v)* udire, sentire [oo-<u>dee</u>-reh, sehn-<u>tee</u>-reh]

heart cuore *(m)* [<u>kwoh</u>-reh]

heavy pesante [peh-<u>sahn</u>-teh]

heel *(shoe)* tacco [tah-<u>kkoh</u>]

height altezza [ahl-<u>teh</u>-tzah]

hello *(tel)* pronto [<u>prohn</u>-toh]; *(greeting)* ciao [<u>chah</u>-oh]

help aiuto, appoggio [ah-<u>yoo</u>-toh, ah-<u>ppoh</u>-djoh]

help someone *(v)* aiutare qlcu [ah-yoo-<u>tah</u>-reh kwahl-<u>koo</u>-noh]

here qui [kwee]

herring aringa [ah-<u>reen</u>-gah]

hesitate *(v)* esitare [eh-see-<u>tah</u>-reh]

hide *(v)* nascondere, celare [nah-<u>skohn</u>-deh-reh, cheh-<u>lah</u>-reh]

hill collina [koh-<u>llee</u>-nah]

hire *(v)* assumere [ah-<u>ssoo</u>-meh-reh]

history storia [<u>stoh</u>-ryah]

hobby hobby *(m)* [<u>oh</u>-bee]

hold *(v)* contenere [kohn-teh-<u>neh</u>-reh]

hold oneself back *(v)* trattenersi [trah-tteh-<u>nehr</u>-see]

hole buco [<u>boo</u>-koh]

holiday giorno festivo [<u>johr</u>-noh feh-<u>stee</u>-voh]

holidays ferie *(pl)* [<u>feh</u>-ryeh]

homeland patria [<u>pah</u>-tryah]

honor onore *(m)* [oh-<u>noh</u>-reh]

hook uncino, gancio [oon-<u>chee</u>-noh, <u>gahn</u>-choh]

hope *(v)* sperare [speh-<u>rah</u>-reh]

hors-d'oeuvre *(appetizer)* antipasto [ahn-tee-<u>pah</u>-stoh]

hospitality ospitalità [oh-spee-tah-lee-<u>tah</u>]

host/hostess ospite *(m/f)* [<u>oh</u>-spee-teh]; padrone/padrona di casa [pah-<u>droh</u>-ne/pah-<u>droh</u>-nah dee <u>kah</u>-sah]

hot caldo [<u>kahl</u>-doh]

hotel hotel *(m)* [oh-tehl]

hour ora [<u>oh</u>-rah]; **a half hour** una mezz'ora [oo-nah meh-<u>zoh</u>-rah]; **a quarter of an hour** un quarto d'ora [oon <u>kwahr</u>-toh <u>doh</u>-rah]

house casa [<u>kah</u>-sah]

how come [<u>koh</u>-meh]

human umano [oo-<u>mah</u>-noh]

humid umido [<u>oo</u>-mee-doh]

hundred cento [<u>chehn</u>-toh]; **a hundred times** cento volte [<u>chehn</u>-toh <u>vohl</u>-teh]

hunger fame *(f)* [<u>fah</u>-meh]; **be hungry** *(v)* avere fame [ah-<u>veh</u>-reh <u>fah</u>-meh]

hungry affamato [ah-ffah-<u>mah</u>-toh]

hurried frettoloso [freh-ttoh-<u>loh</u>-soh]; **be in a hurry** *(v)* aver fretta [ah-veh-reh <u>freh</u>-ttah]

hurry *(v)* affrettarsi [ah-ttreh-<u>ttahr</u>-see]

hurry fretta [<u>freh</u>-ttah]

hurt *(v)* far male (a) [fahr <u>mah</u>-leh (ah)]

husband marito [mah-<u>ree</u>-toh]

hut capanna [kah-<u>pah</u>-nnah]; *(mountain)* baita [<u>bah</u>-ee-tah]

I

I io [<u>ee</u>-oh]

ice ghiaccio [<u>ghyah</u>-choh]

ice cream gelato [jeh-<u>lah</u>-toh]

idea idea [ee-<u>deh</u>-ah]

identification card carta d'identità [kahr-tah dee-dehn-tee-<u>tah</u>]

if se [seh]

illustration illustrazione *(f)* [ee-lloo-strah-<u>tzyoh</u>-neh]; **picture** quadro [<u>kwah</u>-droh]

immediate immediato [ee-mmeh-<u>dyah</u>-toh]

immediately immediatamente [ee-meh-dyah-tah-<u>mehn</u>-teh]

impede *(v)* impedire [eem-peh-dee-reh]

impolite scortese [skohr-<u>teh</u>-seh]

import importazione *(f)* [eem-pohr-tah-<u>tzyoh</u>-neh]

importance importanza [eem-pohr-tahn-tzah]

important importante [eem-pohr-tahn-teh]

impossible impossibile [eem-poh-ssee-bee-leh]

impractical poco pratico [poh-koh prah-tee-koh]

imprecise impreciso [eem-preh-chee-soh]

impression impressione *(f)* [eem-preh-ssyoh-neh]

improbably improbabile [eem-proh-bah-bee-leh]

improve *(v)* migliorare [mee-lyoh-rah-reh]

impudent sfacciato [sfah-chah-toh]

in in [een]

in every case in ogni caso [een oh-nyee kah-soh]

in Italian in italiano [een ee-tah-lyah-noh]

in the first place in primo luogo [een pree-moh lwoh-ghoh]

in front (of) di fronte [dee frohn-teh]

incapable incapace [een-kah-pah-cheh]

include *(v)* includere, comprendere [een-kloo-deh-reh, kohm-prehn-deh-reh]

included compreso [kohm-preh-soh]

incomplete incompiuto, incompleto [een-kohm-pyoo-toh, een-kohm-pleh-toh]

incredible incredibile [een-kreh-dee-bee-leh]

indecent indecente [een-deh-chehn-teh]

indeed anzi [ahn-tzee]

indemnity indennizzo [een-deh-nnee-tzoh]

indispensible indispensabile [een-dee-spehn-sah-bee-leh]

inevitable inevitabile [ee-neh-vee-tah-bee-leh]

inexpensive non caro, economico, a buon mercato [nohn kah-roh, eh-koh-noh-mee-koh, ah bwon mehr-kah-toh]

inexperienced inesperto [ee-neh-spehr-toh]

inflammable infiammabile [een-fyah-mmah-bee-leh]

inflate *(v)* gonfiare [gohn-fyah-reh]

inform *(v)* informare [een-fohr-mah-reh]

information informazione *(f)* [een-fohr-mah-tzyoh-neh]; **ask for information** *(v)* chiedere un'informazione [kyeh-deh-reh oon-een-fohr-mah-tzyoh-neh]

information bureau ufficio informazioni [oo-ffee-choh een-fohr-mah-tzyoh-nee]

inhabitant abitante *(m/f)* [ah-bee-tahn-teh]

injured ferito/ferita [feh-ree-toh/feh-ree-tah]

innocent innocente [ee-nnoh-chehn-teh]

inquire *(v)* informarsi [een-fohr-mahr-see]

insect insetto [een-seh-ttoh]

insecure insicuro [een-see-koo-roh]

inside dentro [dehn-troh]

insist (on) *(v)* insistere su [een-see-steh-reh]

instant istante *(m)* [ee-stahn-teh]

instead of invece di [een-veh-cheh dee]

insufficient insufficiente [een-soo-ffee-chehn-teh]

insurance assicurazione *(f)* [ah-sse-koo-rah-tsyoh-neh]

insure *(v)* assicurare [ah-sse-koo-rah-reh]

intelligence intelligenza [een-teh-llee-jehn-tzah]

intelligent intelligente [een-teh-llee-jehn-teh]

intend (to do something) *(v)* avere l'intenzione, intendere [ah-veh-reh leen-tehn-tzyoh-neh]

intention intenzione *(f)* [een-tehn-tzyoh-neh]

interest interesse *(m)* [een-teh-reh-sseh]

interest oneself (in) *(v)* interessarsi (di) [een-teh-reh-ssahr-see dee]

interesting interessante [een-teh-reh-ssahn-teh]

interior interno [een-tehr-noh]

international internazionale [een-tehr-nah-tzyoh-nah-leh]

interrupt *(v)* interrompere [een-teh-rrohm-peh-reh]

intimidate *(v)* intimidire [een-tee-mee-dee-reh]

intolerable insopportabile [een-soh-ppohr-tah-bee-leh]

invalid non valido [nohn vah-lee-doh]

invent *(v)* inventare [een-vehn-tah-reh]

invitation invito [een-vee-toh]

invite *(v)* invitare [een-vee-tah-reh]

iron ferro [feh-rroh]

irregular irregolare [ee-rreh-ghoh-lah-reh]

island isola [ee-soh-lah]

Italian *(n/adj)* italiano/italiana [ee-tah-lyah-noh/ee-tah-lyah-nah]

Italy Italia [ee-tah-lyah]

itch *(v)* prudere [proo-deh-reh]

itinerary itinerario [ee-tee-neh-rah-ryoh]

J

jellyfish medusa [meh-<u>doo</u>-sah]
job posto [<u>poh</u>-stoh]
joke barzelletta, scherzo [bahr-zeh-<u>lleh</u>-ttah, <u>skehr</u>-tzoh]
joy gioia [<u>joh</u>-yah]
judge (v) giudicare [joo-dee-<u>kah</u>-reh]
judgment giudizio [joo-<u>dee</u>-tzyoh]
just proprio [<u>proh</u>-pryoh]

K

kindness gentilezza, cortesia, amabilità [jehn-tee-<u>leh</u>-tzah, kohr-teh-<u>see</u>-ah, ah-mah-bee-lee-<u>tah</u>]
kiosk edicola (dei giornali) [eh-<u>dee</u>-koh-lah (<u>deh</u>-ee johr-<u>nah</u>-lee)]
kiss (v) baciare [bah-<u>chah</u>-reh]
kiss bacio [<u>bah</u>-choh]
kitchen cucina [koo-<u>chee</u>-nah]
knapsack zaino [<u>zah</u>-ee-noh]
knock (v) bussare [boo-<u>ssah</u>-reh]
knot nodo [<u>noh</u>-doh]
know (v) sapere (m) [sah-<u>peh</u>-reh]
know (someone) (v) conoscere [koh-noh-<u>sheh</u>-reh]
knowledge conoscenza [koh-noh-<u>shehn</u>-tzah]

L

lace laccio [<u>lah</u>-choh]
lack mancanza [mahn-<u>kahn</u>-tzah]
lamp lampada [<u>lahm</u>-pah-dah]
landlord/landlady padrone/parona di casa [pah-<u>droh</u>-neh/ pah-<u>droh</u>-nah dee <u>kah</u>-sah]
language lingua [<u>leen</u>-gwah]
last (v) durare [doo-<u>rah</u>-reh]
last ultimo/ultima [<u>ool</u>-tee-moh/<u>ool</u>-tee-mah]
latch chiavistello [kyah-vee-<u>steh</u>-lloh]
late tardi [<u>tahr</u>-dee]
later più tardi [pyoo <u>tahr</u>-dee]
laugh (v) ridere [<u>ree</u>-deh-reh]
lazy pigro [<u>pee</u>-groh]
leaf foglia [<u>foh</u>-lyah]
learn (v) imparare [eem-pah-<u>rah</u>-reh]
leather pelle (f), cuoio [<u>peh</u>-lleh, <u>kwoh</u>-yoh]
leave (v) lasciare, abbandonare, partire, prendere il via [lah-<u>shah</u>-reh, ah-bahn-doh-<u>nah</u>-reh, pahr-<u>tee</u>-reh, <u>prehn</u>-deh-reh eel <u>vee</u>-ah]

leave (for) (v) partire (per) [pahr-<u>tee</u>-reh pehr]
leave (from) (v) partire (da) [pahr-<u>tee</u>-reh]
left sinistra [see-<u>nee</u>-strah]; **to the left** a sinistra [ah see-<u>nee</u>-strah]
lend (v) prestare [preh-<u>stah</u>-reh]
length lunghezza [loon-<u>gheh</u>-tzah]
lengthen (v) allungare [ah-lloon-<u>ghah</u>-roh]
less meno [<u>moh</u>-noh]; **at the least** per lo meno [pehr loh <u>meh</u>-noh]
lessen (v) diminuire [dee-mee-noo-<u>ee</u>-reh]
letter lettera [<u>leh</u>-tteh-rah]
lie bugia [boo-<u>jee</u>-ah]
life vita [<u>vee</u>-tah]
light (v) accendere [ah <u>ohehn</u> deh reh]
light luce (f) [<u>loo</u>-cheh]; **to turn on/off the light** accendere/spegnere la luce [ah-<u>chehn</u>-deh-reh/<u>speh</u>-nyeh-reh lah <u>loo</u>-cheh]
light (color) chiaro [<u>kyah</u>-roh]
light bulb lampadina [lahm-pah-<u>dee</u>-nah]
lighter accendino [ah-chehn-<u>dee</u>-noh]
like, to be (v) assomigliare [ah-ssoh-mee-<u>lyah</u>-reh]
likewise altrettanto [ahl-treh-<u>ttahn</u>-toh]
line (tel) linea [<u>lee</u>-neh-ah]
linen biancheria (per il letto) [byahn-keh-<u>ree</u>-ah (pehr eel <u>leh</u>-ttoh)]; **laundry** bucato [boo-<u>kah</u>-toh]
lingerie biancheria intima [byahn-keh-<u>ree</u>-ah <u>een</u>-tee-mah]
liquid liquido [<u>lee</u>-kwee-doh]
list elenco, lista [eh-<u>lehn</u>-koh, <u>lee</u>-stah]
listen (to someone) (v) ascoltare (qlcu) [ah-skohl-<u>tah</u>-reh (kwahl-<u>koo</u>-noh)]
lit (up) illuminato [ee-lloo-mee-<u>nah</u>-toh]
live (v) vivere, abitare [<u>vee</u>-veh-reh, ah-bee-<u>tah</u>-reh]
lively vivace [vee-<u>vah</u>-cheh]
living room soggiorno [soh-<u>djohr</u>-noh]
living vivente [vee-<u>vehn</u>-teh]
load (v) (camera) caricare [kah-ree-<u>kah</u>-reh]
local indigeno, del posto [een-<u>dee</u>-jeh-noh, dehl <u>poh</u>-stoh]
lock (v) chiudere a chiave [<u>kyoo</u>-deh-reh ah <u>kyah</u>-veh]
lock chiusura [kyoo-<u>soo</u>-rah]
lodging alloggio [ah-<u>lloh</u>-djoh]
logical logico [<u>loh</u>-jee-koh]
lonely solitario [soh-lee-<u>tah</u>-ryoh]
long lungo [<u>loon</u>-ghoh]
look after (v) custodire [koo-stoh-<u>dee</u>-reh]
look at (v) guardare [gwahr-<u>dah</u>-reh]

lose (v) perdere [pehr-deh-reh]

lose weight (v) dimagrire [dee-mah-gree-reh]

lost perdita [pehr-dee-tah]

loudspeaker altoparlante (m) [ahl-toh-pahr-lahn-teh]

love (v) amare [ah-mah-reh]

love amore (m) [ah-moh-reh]

loving tenero, affettuoso [teh-neh-roh, ah-ffeh-ttwo-soh]

low basso [bah-ssoh]

lower (v) (price) abbassare [ah-bah-ssah-reh]

loyal leale [leh-ah-leh]

lunch pranzo (f) [prahn-tzoh]; have lunch (v) pranzare [pran-tzah-reh]

luxurious lussuoso [loo-sswoh-soh]

luxury lusso [loo-ssoh]

M

magazine rivista [ree-vee-stah]

magnificent magnifico, splendido [mah-nyee-fee-koh, splehn-dee-doh]

mail (v) imbucare [eem-boo-kah-reh]

make (v) fare, produrre [fah-reh, proh-doo-rreh]

make a mistake (v) sbagliare [sbah-lyah-reh]

make possible (v) render possibile [rehn-dehr poh-ssee-bee-leh]

make someone's acquaintance (v) fare la conoscenza di qlcu [fah-reh lah koh-noh-shehn-tzah dee kwahl-koo-noh]

man uomo [woh-moh]

management direzione (f) [dee-reh-tzyoh-neh]

manner modo, maniera [moh-doh, mah-nyeh-rah]

map cartina [kahr-tee-nah]

map (street) pianta della città [pyahn-tah deh-llah chee-ttah]

mark (v) contrassegnare [kohn-trah-sseh-nyah-reh]

marriage matrimonio [mah-tree-moh-nyoh]

marry (v) sposare [spoh-sah-reh]

marsh palude (f) [pah-loo-deh]

marvel at (v) meravigliarsi di [meh-rah-vee-lyahr-see]

masculine maschile [mah-sskee-leh]

mass (rel) messa [meh-ssah]

maximum massimo [mah-ssee-moh]; at the maximum al massimo [ahl mah-ssee-moh]

match fiammifero [fyah-mmee-feh-roh]

matchbox scatola di fiammiferi [skah-toh-lah dee fyah-mmee-feh-ree]

material materiale (m) [mah-teh-ryah-leh]

matter (business) faccenda, questione (f) [fah-chehn-dah, kweh-styoh-neh]

maybe forse [fohr-seh]

me mi, me [mee, meh]

meadow prato [prah-toh]

meal pasto [pah-stoh]

mean (v) significare [see-nyee-fee-kah-reh]

meaning significato [see-nyee-fee-kah-toh]

meanwhile frattanto [frah-ttahn-toh]

measure (v) misurare [mee-soo-rah-reh]

measurement misura [mee-soo-rah]

meat carne (f) [kahr-neh]

Mediterranean Mediterraneo [meh-dee-teh-rrah-neh-oh]

meet (v) incontrare [een-kohn-trah-reh]

merchandise merce (f) [mehr-cheh]

middle mezzo [meh-zoh]; medio (adj) [meh-dyoh]; in the middle in mezzo [een meh-zoh]

midnight mezzanotte [meh-zah-noh-tteh]; at midnight a mezzanotte [ah meh-zah-noh-tteh]

minute minuto [mee-noo-toh]

misfortune sfortuna, disgrazia [sfohr-too-nah, dee-zgrah-tzyah]

miss (v) mancare [mahn-kah-reh]

Miss signorina [see-nyoh-ree-nah]

mistake sbaglio, errore (m) [zbah-lyoh, eh-rroh-reh]; by mistake erronea-mente, per sbaglio [eh-rroh-neh-ah-mehn-teh, pehr zbah-lyoh]; make a mistake (v) sbagliarsi [zbah-lyahr-see]

mistaken sbagliato [sbah-lyah-toh]

misunderstanding malinteso [mah-leen-teh-soh]

mixed misto [mee-stoh]

moderate moderato [moh-deh-rah-toh]

modern moderno [moh-dehr-noh]

mole molo [moh-loh]

moment momento, istante (m) [moh-mehn-toh, ee-stahn-teh]

money denaro [deh-nah-roh]

month mese (m) [meh-seh]

monthly mensile [mehn-see-leh]

mood umore (m) [oo-moh-reh]

moon luna [loo-nah]

more più [pyoo]; more than più che, più di [pyoo keh pyoo dee]; more or less più o meno [pyoo oh meh-noh]

morning mattino, mattina [ma-ttee-noh, mah-ttee-nah]; **in the morning** di mattina [dee mah-ttee-nah]
mosquito zanzara [zahn-zah-rah]
mother madre *(f)* [mah-dreh]
motive motivo [moh-tee-voh]
mountain monte *(m)* [mohn-teh]
move *(v)* cambiare casa, muovere [kahm-byah-reh kah-sah, mwoh-veh-reh]
moved commosso [koh-mmoh-ssoh]
movement movimento [moh-vee-mehn-toh]
Mrs. signora [see-nyoh-rah]
mud fango [fahn-ghoh]
music musica [moo-see-kah]

N

nail chiodo [kyoh-doh]
name nome *(m)* [noh-meh]
narrow stretto [streh-ttoh]
nation nazione *(f)* [nah-tzyoh-neh]
native of nativo di [nah-tee-voh dee]
natural naturale [nah-too-rah-leh]; **naturally** naturalmente [nah-too-rahl-mehn-teh]
nature natura [nah-too-rah]
near vicino a [vee-chee-noh ah]
necessary necessario [neh-cheh-ssah-ryoh]
necessity necessità [neh-cheh-ssee-tah]
necklace collana [koh-llah-nah]
need *(v)* aver bisogno di [ah-veh-reh bee-soh-nyoh dee]
needle ago [ah-goh]
negative negativo [neh-ghah-tee-voh]
neglect *(v)* trascurare [trah-skoo-rah-reh]
negligent negligente [neh-ghlee-jehn-teh]
neighbor vicino/vicina [vee-chee-noh/vee-chee-nah]
neighborhood quartiere [kwahr-tyeh-reh]
neither ... nor neppure, né...né [neh-ppoo-reh, neh ... neh]
nephew nipote *(m)* [nee-poh-teh]
nervous nervoso [nehr-voh-soh]
net rete *(f)* [reh-teh]
never mai [mah-ee]
nevertheless ciò nonostante, tuttavia [choh noh-noh-stahn-teh, too-ttah-vee-ah]
new nuovo, recente [nwoh-voh, reh-chehn-teh]
newborn neonato [neh-oh-nah-toh]
newness novità [noh-vee-tah]
news *(pl)* notizie [noh-tee-tzyeh]
news agent giornalaio [johr-nah-lah-yoh]

newspaper giornale *(m)* [johr-nah-leh]
next prossimo [proh-sse-moh]
next to last penultimo/ penultima [peh-nool-tee-moh/peh-nool-tee-mah]
nice simpatico, gentile [seem-pah-tee-koh, jehn-tee-leh]
niece nipote *(f)* [nee-poh-teh]
night notte *(f)* [noh-tteh]; **tonight** stanotte [stah-noh-ttoh]
no one nessuno [neh-ssoo-noh]; **in no way** in nessun caso [een neh-ssoon kah-soh]
noise rumore *(m)* [roo-moh-reh]
noisy rumoroso [roo-moh-roh-soh]
noon mezzogiorno [meh-zoh-johr-noh]; **at noon** a mezzogiorno [ah meh-zoh-johr-noh]
normal normale [nohr-mah-leh]
normally normalmente, di solito [nohr-mahl-mehn-teh, dee soh-lee-toh]
north nord *(m)* [nohrd]; **al nord** [ahl nohrd]; **north of** a nord di [ah nohrd dee]
not non [nohn]; **not even** neppure [neh-ppoo-reh]; **isn't it true?** non è vero? [nohn eh veh-roh]; **not again** non ancora [nohn ahn-koh-rah]
note *(v)* notare [noh-tah-reh]; **make note (of something)** *(v)* tenere a mente qlco [toh neh-reh ah mehn-teh kwahl-koh-sah]
note nota [noh-tah]
notebook quaderno [kwah-dehr-noh]
nothing niente [nyeh-nteh]; **nothing else** nient'altro [nyehn-tahl-troh]
notice annuncio [ah-nnoon-choh]
nourishing nutriente, nutrimento [noo-tree-ehn-teh, noo-tree-mehn-toh]
now ora [oh-rah]
nowhere in nessun luogo [een neh-ssoon lwoh-ghoh]
nude nudo [noo-doh]
number numero [noo-meh-roh]
numerous numeroso [noo-meh-roh-soh]
nun monaca, suora [moh-nah-kah, swoh-rah]
nurse infermiera [een-fehr-myeh-rah]

O

obey *(v)* ubbidire [oo-bee-dee-reh]
object oggetto [oh-djeh-ttoh]
obligation obbligo [oh-blee-ghoh]
obliged, to be *(v)* essere obbligato [eh-sseh-reh oh-bloo ghah toh]

A/Z

observe (v) osservare [oh-ssehr-vah-reh]
obtain (v) ottenere [oh-tteh-neh-reh]
occasionally occasionalmente (adj) [oh-kkah-syoh-nahl-mehn-teh]
occupied occupato [oh-kkoo-pah-toh]
odor odore (m) [oh-doh-reh]
offend (v) offendere [oh-ffehn-deh-reh]
offense offesa [oh-ffeh-sah]
offer (v) offrire, porgere [oh-ffree-reh, pohr-jeh-reh]
office ufficio [oo-ffee-choh]
officer ufficiale [oo-ffee-chah-leh]
official ufficiale [oo-ffee-chah-leh]
often spesso (adv) [speh-ssoh]
oil olio, olio combustibile [oh-lyoh, oh-lyoh kohm-boo-stee-bee-leh]
old (object) vecchio [veh-kkyoh]
on su, sopra [soo, soh-prah]; **on the Tiber** sul Tevere [sool teh-veh-reh]
one uno [oo-noh]
one fourth un quarto [oon kwhar-toh]
one third un terzo [oon tehr-tzoh]
only solo, soltanto, unico [soh-loh, sohl-tahn-toh, oo-nee-koh]
open (v) aprire [ah-pree-reh]
open aperto [ah-pehr-toh]
operate (v) operare [oh-peh-rah-reh]
opinion opinione (f) [oh-pee-nyoh-neh]; **in my opinion** secondo me [seh-kohn-doh meh]
opportunity occasione (f) [oh-kkah-syoh-neh]
opposite inverso, opposto [een-vehr-soh, oh-ppoh-stoh]; **in the opposite direction** nella direzione opposta [neh-llah dee-reh-tzyoh-neh oh-ppoh-stah]
or oppure [oh-ppoo-reh]
order (rel) ordine (m) [ohr-dee-neh]
ordinary ordinario [ohr-dee-nah-ryoh]
organize (v) organizzare, allestire [ohr-ghah-nee-zah-reh, ah-lleh-stee-reh]
other altro [ahl-troh]
otherwise altrimenti, se no, diversamente [ahl-tree-mehn-tee, seh noh, dee-vehr-sah-menh-teh]
out of stock esaurito [eh-sah-oo-ree-toh]
outdoors all'aperto [ah-llah-pehr-toh]
outline tratto [trah-ttoh]
outside fuori [fwoh-ree]; **from outside** dal di fuori [dahl dee fwoh-ree]
overseas oltremare (m) [ohl-treh-mah-reh]
oversee (v) sorvegliare [sohr-veh-lyah-reh]
own (v) possedere [poh-sseh-deh-reh]
owner proprietario [proh-pryeh-tah-ryoh]

P

pack (v) fare le valige, imballare, (baggage) fare le valigie [fah-reh leh vah-lee-jeh, eem-bah-llah-reh, fah-reh leh vah-lee-jeh]
package pacco [pah-kkoh]
packet pacchetto, pacco [pah-kkeh-tto, pah-kkoh]
packing imballaggio [eem-bah-llah-djoh]
pain dolore (m) [doh-loh-reh]
painful doloroso [doh-loh-roh-soh]
paint (v) dipingere [dee-peen-jeh-reh]
pair paio [pah-yoh]; **a pair of** un paio di, una coppia [oon pah-yoh dee, oo-nah koh-ppyah]
pale pallido [pah-llee-doh]
pamphlet manifesto, cartellone (m) [mah-nee-feh-stoh, kahr-teh-lloh-neh]
panorama panorama (m) [pah-noh-rah-mah]
parents genitori (pl) [jeh-nee-toh-ree]
park (v) parcheggiare [pahr-keh-djah-reh]
park parco, giardino pubblico [pahr-koh, jahr-dee-noh poo-blee-koh]
part parte (f) [pahr-teh]
particularly particolarmente [pahr-tee-koh-lahr-mehn-teh]
party comitiva, festa [koh-mee-tee-vah, feh-stah]
pass (time) (v) passare, passare (da qlcu/davanti a qlco) [pah-ssah-reh, pah-ssah-reh (dah kwahl-koo-noh/dah-vahn-tee ah kwahl-koh-sah)]
pass tessera [teh-sseh-rah]
passage passaggio [pah-ssah-djoh]; **passing (by)** (v) essere di passaggio [eh-sseh-reh dee pah-ssah-djoh]
passenger passeggero/a [pah-sseh-djeh-roh/-rah]
passport passaporto [pah-ssah-pohr-toh]
past passato [pah-ssah-toh]
path sentiero [sehn-tyeh-roh]
patience pazienza [pah-tzyehn-tzah]
patient paziente [pah-tzyehn-teh]
pavilion padiglione (m) [pah-dee-lyoh-neh]
pay (v) pagare [pah-ghah-reh]
pay attention (to) (v) fare attenzione (a), stare attento (a) [fah-reh ah-ttehn-tzyoh-neh, stah-reh ah-ttehn-toh]
pay in cash (v) pagare in contanti [pah-ghah-reh een kohn-tahn-tee]
payment pagamento [pah-ghah-mehn-toh]
peace pace (f) [pah-cheh]

pear pera [<u>peh</u>-rah]
pedestrian pedone *(m)* [peh-<u>doh</u>-neh]
people gente *(f)* [<u>jehn</u>-teh]
percent percento *(adj)* [pehr-<u>chehn</u>-toh];
  percentuale *(n)* [pehr-chehn-<u>twah</u>-leh]
perfect perfetto [pehr-<u>feh</u>-ttoh]
performance rappresentazione *(f)*,
  spettacolo [rah-ppreh-sehn-tah-<u>tzyoh</u>-
  neh, speh-<u>ttah</u>-koh-loh]
periphery periferia [peh-ree-feh-<u>ree</u>-ah]
permission permesso [pehr-<u>meh</u>-ssoh]
permit *(v)* permettere [pehr-<u>meh</u>-tteh-reh]
person persona [pehr-<u>soh</u>-nah]
personal personale *(m)* [pehr-soh-<u>nah</u>-
  leh]
personnel personale [pehr-soh-<u>nah</u>-leh]
perspire *(v)* sudare [soo-<u>dah</u>-reh]
persuade *(v)* persuadere [pehr-<u>swah</u>-
  deh-reh]
photo foto *(f)* [<u>foh</u>-toh]
photograph *(v)* fotografare [foh-toh-
  grah-<u>fah</u>-reh]
photograph foto(graphia) *(f)*,
  fotografia [foh-toh(grah-<u>fee</u>-ah), foh-toh-
  grah-<u>fee</u>-ah]
pick *(v)* cogliere [<u>koh</u>-lyeh-reh]
piece pezzo [<u>peh</u>-tzoh]; **a piece of
  bread** un pezzo di pane [oon <u>peh</u>-tzoh
  dee <u>pah</u>-neh]
pigeon piccione [pee-<u>choh</u>-neh]
pillow cuscino [koo-<u>shee</u>-noh]
pin spillo [<u>spee</u>-lloh]; **safety pin** spilla di
  sicurezza [<u>spee</u>-llah dee see-koo-<u>reh</u>-
  tzah]
pipe pipa, tubo [<u>pee</u>-pah, too-boh]
place luogo, località [<u>lwoh</u>-ghoh, loh-kah-
  lee-<u>tah</u>]
place (oneself) *(v)* mettersi [<u>meh</u>-ttehr-
  see]
plain pianura *(n)* [pyah-<u>noo</u>-rah]
plan pianta [<u>pyahn</u>-tah]
plant impianto [eem-<u>pyahn</u>-toh]
plate piatto [<u>pyah</u>-ttoh]
play *(v)* giocare [joh-<u>kah</u>-reh]; *(piano)*
  suonare [swoh-<u>nah</u>-re]
pleasant piacevole [pyah-<u>cheh</u>-voh-leh]
please prego; per favore [<u>preh</u>-ghoh,
  pehr fah-<u>voh</u>-reh]
pleasure piacere *(m)* [pyah-<u>cheh</u>-reh]
pledge pegno [<u>peh</u>-nyoh]
pliers tenaglie *(pl)* [teh-<u>nah</u>-lye]
pocket tasca [<u>tah</u>-skah]
point punto [<u>poon</u>-toh]
poison veleno [veh-<u>leh</u>-noh]
poisonous velenoso [veh-leh-<u>noh</u>-soh]
pole palo [pah-loh]

politics politica [poh-<u>lee-tee</u>-kah]
poor povero [<u>poh</u>-veh-roh]
porter facchino [fah-<u>kkee</u>-noh]
positive positivo [poh-see-<u>tee</u>-voh]
possession possesso [poh-<u>sseh</u>-ssoh]
possibility possibilità [poh-ssee-bee-lee-
  <u>tah</u>]
possible possibile [poh-<u>ssee-bee</u>-leh]
postcard cartolina postale [kahr-toh-<u>lee</u>-
  nah poh-<u>stah</u>-leh]
powerful potente [poh-<u>tehn</u>-teh]
practical pratico [<u>prah</u>-tee-koh]
practice *(v)* esercitare, praticare [eh-
  sehr-chee-<u>tah</u>-reh, prah-tee-<u>kah</u>-reh]
praise *(v)* lodare [loh-<u>dah</u>-reh]
pray *(v)* pregare [preh-<u>ghah</u>-reh]
prayer preghiera [preh-<u>ghye</u>-rah]
precaution precauzione *(f)* [preh-kah-
  oo-<u>tzyoh</u>-neh]
precision precisione *(f)* [preh-chee-<u>syoh</u>-
  neh]
prefer *(v)* preferire [preh-feh-<u>ree</u>-reh]
pregnant incinta, gravida [een-<u>cheen</u>-
  tah, <u>grah</u>-vee-dah]
prepare *(v)* preparare [preh-pah-<u>rah</u>-reh]
prescribe *(v)* prescrivere [preh-<u>skree</u>-
  veh-reh]
present *(v)* presentare [preh-sehn-<u>tah</u>-
  reh]
present *(time)* presente [preh-<u>sehn</u>-teh]
preserve *(v)* conservare [kohn-sehr-<u>vah</u>-
  reh]
press *(v)* *(button)* premere [<u>preh</u>-meh-
  reh]
price prezzo [<u>preh</u>-tzoh]; **admission
  price** prezzo del biglietto d'ingresso
  [<u>preh</u>-tzoh dehl bee-<u>lyeh</u>-ttoh deen-<u>greh</u>-
  sso]
priest prete *(m)* [<u>preh</u>-teh]
principal principal *(adj)* [preen-chee-
  <u>pah</u>-leh]
principally principalmente [preen-chee-
  pahl-<u>mehn</u>-teh]
private privato [pree-<u>vah</u>-toh]
prize premio [<u>preh</u>-myoh]
probability probabilità [proh-bah-bee-
  lee-<u>tah</u>]
procession processione *(f)* [proh-cheh-
  <u>ssyoh</u>-neh]
produce *(v)* produrre [proh-<u>doo</u>-rreh]
product prodotto [proh-<u>doh</u>-ttoh]
profession professione *(f)* [proh-feh-
  <u>ssyoh</u>-neh]
program programma *(m)* [proh-<u>grah</u>-
  mmah]
progress progresso [proh-<u>greh</u>-ssoh]

prohibit *(v)* proibire [proh-ee-<u>bee</u>-reh]
project progetto [proh-<u>jeh</u>-ttoh]
promise *(v)* prom**e**ttere [proh-<u>meh</u>-tteh-re]
promise promessa [proh-<u>meh</u>-ssah]
promote *(v)* prom**u**overe [proh-<u>mwoh</u>-veh-reh]
pronounce *(v)* pronunciare [proh-noon-<u>chah</u>-reh]
pronunciation pron**u**ncia [proh-<u>noon</u>-chah]
property tenuta, propriet**à** terriera [teh-<u>noo</u>-tah, proh-pryeh-<u>tah</u> teh-<u>rryeh</u>-rah]
proposal proposta [proh-<u>poh</u>-stah]
propose *(v)* proporre [pro-<u>poh</u>-rreh]
protect *(v)* prot**e**ggere [proh-teh-<u>djeh</u>-reh]
protection protezione *(f)* [proh-teh-<u>tzyoh</u>-neh]
protest *(v)* protestare [proh-<u>teh</u>-stah-reh]
provide *(v)* provvedere [proh-veh-<u>deh</u>-reh]
provisions provvista [proh-<u>vvee</u>-stah]
public authority autorit**à** p**u**bblica [ah-oo-toh-ree-<u>tah</u> poo-blee-kah]
public p**u**bblico *(adj)* [<u>poo</u>-blee-koh]
pull *(v)* tirare [tee-<u>rah</u>-reh]
punctual puntuale [poon-<u>twah</u>-leh]
punctually puntualmente [poon-twahl-<u>mehn</u>-teh]
punishment pena [<u>peh</u>-nah]
purchase c**o**mpera [<u>kohm</u>-peh-rah]
purchaser compratore *(m)* [kohm-prah-<u>toh</u>-reh]; **customer** cli**e**nte *(m)* [klee-<u>ehn</u>-teh]
purpose scopo [<u>skoh</u>-poh]
purse borsa [<u>bohr</u>-sah]
push *(v)* sp**i**ngere [speen-<u>jeh</u>-reh]
push spinta [<u>speen</u>-tah]
put (on) *(v)* m**e**ttere [<u>meh</u>-tteh-reh]
put down *(v)* deporre [deh-<u>poh</u>-rreh]
put on makeup *(v)* truccarsi [troo-<u>kkahr</u>-see]

Q

quality qualit**à** [kwah-lee-<u>tah</u>]
quantity quantit**à** [kwahn-tee-<u>tah</u>]
quarrel *(v)* bisticciarsi [bee-stee-<u>chahr</u>-see]
question domanda [doh-<u>mahn</u>-dah]
quick rapido, veloce, svelto *(adj)* [<u>rah</u>-pee-doh, veh-<u>loh</u>-cheh, <u>zvel</u>-toh]; presto, rapidamente, velocemente, in fretta *(adv)* [<u>preh</u>-stoh, rah-pee-dah-<u>mehn</u>-teh, veh-loh-cheh-<u>mehn</u>-teh, een <u>freh</u>-ttah]

quickly rapidamente [rah-pee-dah-<u>mehn</u>-teh]
quiet tranquillo [trahn-<u>kwee</u>-lloh]

R

radio r**a**dio *(f)* [<u>rah</u>-dyoh]
rain *(v)* pi**o**vere [<u>pyoh</u>-veh-reh]
raise *(v)* *(price)* aumentare, alzare [ah-oo-mehn-<u>tah</u>-reh, ahl-<u>tzah</u>-reh]
ramp passerella, pontile *(m)* [pah-sseh-<u>reh</u>-lla, pohn-<u>tee</u>-leh]
rare raro *(adj)* [<u>rah</u>-roh]
rarely raramente [rah-rah-<u>mehn</u>-teh]
rather piuttosto [pyoo-<u>ttoh</u>-stoh]
ray raggio [<u>rah</u>-djoh]
reach *(v)* *(a place)* raggiungere [rah-djoon-<u>jeh</u>-reh]
read *(v)* l**e**ggere [<u>leh</u>-djeh-reh]
ready pronto [<u>prohn</u>-toh]
real vero, aut**e**ntico [<u>veh</u>-roh, ahoo-<u>tehn</u>-tee-koh]
reality realt**à** [reh-ahl-<u>tah</u>]
realize *(v)* accorgersi (di) [ah-<u>kkohr</u>-jehr-see]
reason ragione *(f)* [rah-<u>joh</u>-neh]
reasonable ragion**e**vole [rah-joh-<u>neh</u>-voh-leh]
receipt ricevuta [ree-cheh-<u>voo</u>-tah]
receive *(v)* ric**e**vere [ree-<u>cheh</u>-veh-reh]
reception ricevimento, accettazione *(f)* [ree-cheh-vee-<u>mehn</u>-toh, ah-cheh-ttah-<u>tzyoh</u>-neh]
recognize *(v)* ricon**o**scere [ree-koh-noh-<u>sheh</u>-reh]
recollection ricordo [ree-<u>kohr</u>-doh]
recommend *(v)* raccomandare [rah-kkoh-mahn-<u>dah</u>-reh]
recommendation raccomandazione *(f)* [rah-kkoh-mahn-dah-<u>tzyoh</u>-neh]
reconcile *(v)* conciliare [kohn-chee-<u>lyah</u>-reh]
record disco [<u>dee</u>-skoh]
record player giradischi *(m)* [jee-rah-<u>dee</u>-skee]
rectify *(v)* rettificare/corr**e**gere qlco [reh-ttee-fee-<u>kah</u>-reh/koh-<u>rreh</u>-djeh-reh kwahl-<u>koo</u>-noh]
reduction riduzione *(f)* [ree-doo-<u>tzyoh</u>-neh]
refer (to) *(v)* riferirsi a [ree-feh-<u>reer</u>-see]
refreshments rinfreschi [reen-<u>freh</u>-skee]
refuse *(v)* rifiutare [ree-fyoo-<u>tah</u>-reh]
region regione *(f)* [reh-<u>joh</u>-neh]

regret *(v)* essere spiacente [eh-sseh-reh spyah-chehn-teh]

regret dispiacere *(m)* [dee-spyah-cheh-reh]

regular regolare [reh-ghoh-lah-reh]

regulations regolamenti [reh-ghoh-lah-mehn-tee]

reimburse *(v)* rimborsare [reem-bohr-sah-reh]

related imparentato [eem-pah-rehn-tah-toh]

remain *(v)* rimanere, restare [ree-mah-neh-reh, reh-stah-reh]

remaining rimanente [ree-mah-nehn-teh]

remember *(v)* ricordarsi [ree-kohr-dahr-see]

remind someone of something *(v)* ricordare a qlcu qlco [ree-kohr-dah-reh]

renew *(v)* rinnovare [ree-nnoh-vah-reh]

rent *(v)* affittare [ah-ffee-ttah-reh]

rent affitto [ah-ffee-ttoh]

repair *(v)* riparare [ree-pah-rah-reh]

repair riparazione *(f)* [ree-pah-rah-tzyoh-neh]; **auto repair shop** officina [oh-ffee-chee-nah]

repeat *(v)* ripetere [ree-peh-teh-reh]

report pagella, rapporto [pah-jeh-llah, rah-ppohr-toh]

request richiesta [ree-kyeh-stah]

reserve *(v)* prenotare, riservare [preh-noh-tah-reh, ree-sehr-vah-reh]

residence domicilio, residenza [doh-mee-chee-loe-oh, reh-see-dehn-tzah]

resolve *(v)* risolvere [ree-sohl-veh-reh]

respect riguardo [ree-gwahr-doo]; **without respect, thoughtless** senza riguardo, sconsiderato [sehn-tzah ree-gwahr-doh, skohn-see-deh-rah-toh]

responsible responsabile [reh-spohn-sah-bee-leh]

rest *(v)* riposarsi [ree-poh-sahr-see]

rest riposo [ree-poh-soh]

restaurant ristorante *(m)*, trattoria [ree-stoh-rahn-teh, trah-ttoh-ree-ah]

result risultato [ree-sool-tah-toh]

return *(v)* ritornare [ree-torh-nah-reh]

return ritorno [ree-tohr-noh]; **return trip** viaggio di ritorno [vyah-djoh dee ree-tohr-noh]

reward *(v)* ricompensare [ree-kohm-pehn-sah-reh]

reward ricompensa [ree-kohm-pehn-sah]

ribbon nastro [nah-stroh]

rich ricco [ree-kkoh]

riches ricchezza [ree-kkeh-tzah]

ridiculous ridicolo [ree-dee-koh-loh]

right destro, destra, giusto *(just, fair)* [deh-stroh, deh-strah, joo-stoh]; **to the right** a destra [ah deh-strah]; **right, to be** aver ragione [ah-veh-reh rah-joh-neh]

ring *(v)* suonare [swoh-nah-reh]

ring anello [ah-neh-lloh]

ripe maturo [mah-too-roh]

risk rischio [ree-skyoh]

river fiume *(m)* [fyoo-meh]

roast *(v)* arrostire [ah-rroh-stee-reh]

roast(ed) arrosto [ah-rroh-stoh]

rock roccia [roh-chah]

room sala [sah-lah]

rooster gallo [ghah-lloh]

rope corda [kohr-dah]

rough *(sea)* mosso [moh-ssoh]

round rotondo [roh-tohn-doh]

rude sgarbato [sghahr-bah-toh]

ruin *(v)* rovinare [roh-vee-nah-reh]

run *(v)* correre [koh-rreh-reh]

S

sad triste [tree-steh]

sale vendita [vehn-dee-dah]; **on sale** in vendita [een vehn-dee-tah]

same stesso [steh-ssoh]; **the same** lo stesso [loh steh-ssoh]

satiated *(full)* sazio, pieno [sah-tzyoh, pyeh-noh]

satisfied contento, soddisfatto [kohn-tehn-toh, soh-ddee-sfah-ttoh]

save *(v)* risparmiare [ree-spahr-myah-reh]

say *(v)* dire [dee-reh]

scarf foulard [foo lahr]

scary spaventoso [spah-vehn-toh-soh]

school scuola [skwoh-lah]

scissors forbici *(pl)* [fohr-bee-chee]

scold *(v)* sgridare [sgree-dah-reh]

scorpion scorpione *(m)* [skohr-pyoh-neh]

screw dado [dah-doh]

sea mare *(m)* [mah-reh]

sea urchin riccio (di mare) [ree-choh dee mah-reh]

seagull gabbiano [ghah-byah-noh]

season stagione *(f)* [stah-joh-neh]

seat sede *(f)* [seh-deh]

secluded appartato [ah-ppahr-tah-toh]

second secondo [seh-kohn-doh]

second-hand usato [oo-sah-toh]

secondly secondo, in secondo luogo [seh-kohn-doh, een seh-kohn-doh lwoh-ghoh]

secret segreto [seh-<u>greh</u>-toh]
secretly di nascosto [dee nah-<u>skoh</u>-stoh]
security sicurezza, cauzione *(f)* [see-koo-<u>reh</u>-tzah, kah-oo-<u>tzyoh</u>-neh]; *(guarantee)* garanzia [ghah-rahn-<u>tzee</u>-ah]
see *(v)* vedere [veh-<u>deh</u>-reh]
see again *(v)* rivedere [ree-veh-<u>deh</u>-reh]
seem *(v)* sembrare [sehm-<u>brah</u>-reh]
seize *(v)* afferrare [ah-ffeh-<u>rrah</u>-reh]
send *(v)* inviare, mandare, spedire [een-vee-<u>ah</u>-reh, mahn-<u>dah</u>-reh, speh-<u>dee</u>-reh]
send back *(v)* rimandare [ree-mahn-<u>dah</u>-reh]
send for *(v)* mandare a prendere [mahn-<u>dah</u>-reh ah <u>prehn</u>-deh-reh]
sensitive sensibile [sehn-<u>see</u>-bee-leh]
sentence frase *(f)* [<u>frah</u>-seh]
separate *(v)* separare [seh-pah-<u>rah</u>-reh], dividere [dee-<u>vee</u>-deh-reh]
separated separato [seh-pah-<u>rah</u>-toh]
serene sereno [seh-<u>reh</u>-noh]
serious serio [<u>seh</u>-ryoh]
sermon predica [<u>preh</u>-dee-kah]
serve *(v)* servire [sehr-<u>vee</u>-reh]
service servizio [sehr-<u>vee</u>-tzyoh]
set out *(v)* avviarsi [ah-vvee-<u>ahr</u>-see]; mettersi in moto [<u>meh</u>-ttehr-see een <u>moh</u>-toh]
settle a matter *(v)* sbrigare un affare [sbree-<u>gah</u>-reh oo-nah-<u>ffah</u>-reh]
sex sesso [<u>seh</u>-ssoh]
shade ombra [<u>ohm</u>-brah]
shape *(v)* formare [fohr-<u>mah</u>-reh]
sharp aguzzo, a punta [ah-<u>goo</u>-tzoh, ah <u>poon</u>-tah]
shave *(v)* radere/radersi, fare la barba [<u>rah</u>-deh-reh/<u>rah</u>-dehr-see, <u>fah</u>-reh lah <u>bahr</u>-bah]
sheep pecora [<u>peh</u>-koh-rah]
sheet *(paper)* foglio [<u>foh</u>-lyoh]
shine *(v)* brillare [bree-<u>llah</u>-reh]
shoe scarpa [<u>skahr</u>-pah]
shoot *(v)* sparare [spah-<u>rah</u>-reh]
shop window vetrina [veh-<u>tree</u>-nah]
shopping spese *(pl)* [<u>speh</u>-seh]
short basso [<u>bah</u>-ssoh]; *(length)* corto [<u>kohr</u>-toh]; *(duration)* breve [<u>breh</u>-veh]; **briefly** a breve termine/scadenza [ah <u>breh</u>-veh skah-<u>dehn</u>-tzah]; **shortly** tra breve [trah <u>breh</u>-veh]
show *(v)* mostrare, indicare [moh-<u>strah</u>-reh, en-dee-<u>kah</u>-reh]
show spettacolo [speh-<u>ttah</u>-<u>koh</u>-loh]
sick malato [mah-<u>lah</u>-toh]; **become sick** *(v)* ammalarsi [ah-mmah-<u>lahr</u>-see]
side lato [<u>lah</u>-toh]

sidewalk marciapiede [mahr-chah-<u>pyeh</u>-deh]
sign *(v)* firmare [feer-<u>mah</u>-reh]
sign insegna, targa, segnale *(m)* [een-<u>seh</u>-nyah, <u>tahr</u>-ghah, seh-<u>nyah</u>-leh]
signature firma [<u>feer</u>-mah]
silence silenzio [see-<u>lehn</u>-tzyoh]
silent silenzioso [see-lehn-<u>tzyoh</u>-soh]
similar simile [<u>see</u>-mee-leh]
simple semplice [<u>sehm</u>-plee-cheh]
since da [dah]; **since when?** da quando? [dah <u>kwahn</u>-doh]
sing *(v)* cantare [kahn-<u>tah</u>-reh]
single singolo [<u>seen</u>-goh-loh]
sister sorella [soh-<u>reh</u>-llah]
sit down *(v)* sedersi [seh-<u>dehr</u>-see]
situated, to be *(v)* trovarsi [troh-<u>vahr</u>-see]
situation condizione *(f)*, situazione *(f)* [kohn-dee-<u>tzyoh</u>-neh, see-twah-<u>tzyoh</u>-neh]
sky cielo [<u>cheh</u>-loh]
skyscraper grattacielo [grah-ttah-<u>cheh</u>-loh]
sleep *(v)* dormire [dohr-<u>mee</u>-reh]
sleep sonno [<u>soh</u>-nnoh]
sleeping car vagone letto [vah-<u>ghoh</u>-neh <u>leh</u>-ttoh]
sleeping pill sonnifero [soh-<u>nnee</u>-feh-roh]
slender snello [<u>sneh</u>-lloh]
slice fetta [<u>feh</u>-ttah]
slide *(photo)* diapositiva [dyah-poh-see-<u>tee</u>-vah]
slope pendio [pehn-<u>dee</u>-oh]
slow lento [<u>lehn</u>-toh]
slowly lentamente, piano [lehn-tah-<u>mehn</u>-teh, <u>pyah</u>-noh]
small piccolo [<u>pee</u>-kkoh-loh]
smoke *(v)* fumare [foo-<u>mah</u>-reh]
smoke fumo [<u>foo</u>-moh]
smooth liscio [<u>lee</u>-shoh]
smuggle *(v)* fare contrabbando [<u>fah</u>-reh kohn-trah-<u>bahn</u>-doh]
snack spuntino [spoon-<u>tee</u>-noh]
snake serpente *(m)* [sehr-<u>pehn</u>-teh]
sneeze *(v)* starnutire [stahr-noo-<u>tee</u>-reh]
snore *(v)* russare [roo-<u>ssah</u>-reh]
snow *(v)* nevicare [neh-vee-<u>kah</u>-reh]
so then dunque, allora [<u>doon</u>-kweh, ah-<u>lloh</u>-rah]
softly piano [<u>pyah</u>-noh]; **speak softly** *(v)* parlare a bassa voce [pahr-<u>lah</u>-reh ah <u>bah</u>-ssah <u>voh</u>-cheh]
soil suolo [<u>swoh</u>-loh]
solemn solenne [soh-<u>leh</u>-nneh]

some alcuni, alcune, poco, qualche [ahl-koo-nee, ahl-koo-neh, poh-koh, kwahl-keh]; **some, a little** un po' [oon poh]; **some of** un po' di [oon poh dee]; **in some way** in qualche modo [een kwahl-keh moh-doh]

someone qualcuno [kwahl-koo-noh]

something qualcosa [kwahl-koh-sah]

somewhere altrove [ahl-troh-veh]

son figlio [fee-lyoh]

song canzone (f) [kahn-tzoh-neh]

soon presto [preh-stoh]; **as soon as possible** al più presto possibile [ahl pyoo preh-stoh poh-ssee-bee-leh]

sound suono [swoh-noh]

south sud (m) [sood]

southern del sud, meridionale [dehl sood, meh-ree-dyoh-nah-leh]; **south of** a sud di [ah sood dee]

space spazio [spah-tzyoh]

spark scintilla [sheen-tee-llah]

sparkle (v) luccicare [loo-chee-kah-reh]

sparkling brillante [bree-llahn-teh]

special speciale [speh-chah-leh]

spectator spettatore (m) [speh-ttah-toh-reh]

speed velocità [veh-loh-chee-tah]

spell (out) (v) sillabare [see-llah-bah-roh]

spend (v) spendere [spehn-deh-reh]

spicy piccante [pee-kkahn-teh]

spoiled guasto, corrotto [gwah-stoh, koh-rroh-ttoh]

sport sport (m) [spohrt]

sports field campo sportivo [kahm-poh spohr-tee-voh]

spot macchia [mah-kkyah]; **spot/stain remover** smacchiatore (m) [smah-kkyah-toh-reh]

spring (water) sorgente (f), fonte (f) [sohr-jehn-teh, fohn-teh]

square piazza [pyah-tzah]

stabilize (v) stabilire [stah-bee-lee-reh]

stair(case) scala [skah-lah]

stamp francobollo [frah-koh-boh-lloh]

stand (v) stare (in piedi) [stah-reh (een pyeh-dee)]

star stella [steh-llah]

start again (v) rimettersi [ree-meh-ttehr-see]

state (government) stato (m) [stah-toh]

stay (v) rimanere [ree-mah-neh-reh]

stay for the night (v) pernottare [pehr-noh-ttah-reh]

steal (v) rubare [roo-bah-reh]

steep ripido [ree-pee-doh]

stick bastone (m) [bah-stoh-neh]

sting (v) pungere [poon-jeh-reh]

stink (v) puzzare [poo-tzah-reh]

stone pietra [pyeh-trah]

stony sassoso, pietroso [sah-ssoh-soh, pyeh-troh-soh]

stop (v) fermare, fermarsi, smettere [fehr-mah-reh, fehr-mahr-see, smeh-tteh-reh]

stop fermata [fehr-mah-tah]

stop! alt! [ahlt]

store negozio [neh-ghoh-tzyoh]

storm tempesta, temporale (m) [tehm-peh-stah, tehm-poh-rah-leh]

stove stufa [stoo-fah]

straight diritto [dee-ree-ttoh]

stranger straniero/straniera [strah-nyeh-roh/strah-nyeh-rah]

street via, strada [vee-ah, strah-dah]

strength forza [fohr-tzah]

strike (v) colpire, battere [kohl-pee-reh, bah-tteh-reh]

string spago [spah-ghoh]

strive (v) sforzarsi [sfohr-tzahr-see]

stroll passeggiata, giro [pah-sseh-djah-tah, jee-roh]

strong forte [fohr-teh]

study (v) studiare [stoo-dyah-reh]

stupid stupido, scemo [stoo-pee-doh, sheh-moh]

substitute (v) sostituire [soh-stee-too-ee-reh]

suburb sobborgo [soh-bohr-ghoh]

success successo [soo-cheh-ssoh]

such tale [tah-leh]

sudden improvviso [eem-proh-vvee-soh]

suitcase valigia [vah-lee-jah]

summit cima, punta, apice (m) [chee-mah, poon-tah, ah-pee-cheh]

sun sole (m) [soh-leh]

sunglasses occhiali da sole (pl) [oh-kkyah-lee dah soh-leh]

sunny soleggiato, assolato [soh-leh-djah-toh, ah-ssoh-lah-toh]

sunrise sorgere del sole (m) [sohr-jeh-roh dehl soh-leh]

sunset tramonto (del sole) [trah-mohn-toh (dehl soh-leh)]

superfluous superfluo [soo-pehr-flwoh]

supermarket supermercato [soo-pehr-mehr-kah-toh]

supply (v) fornire [fohr-nee-reh]

supply with (v) rifornire di [ree-fohr-nee-reh dee]

suppose (v) supporre [soo-ppoh-reh]

supposition (f) [soo-ppoh-see-tzyoh-neh]

sure sicuro [see-koo-roh]

surprise sorpreso [sohr-<u>preh</u>-soh]
suspicious sospetto [soh-<u>speh</u>-ttoh]
sweet dolce [<u>dohl</u>-cheh]
swim (v) nuotare [nwoh-<u>tah</u>-reh]
swimming pool piscina [pee-<u>shee</u>-nah]
swindle (v) imbrogliare [eem-broh-<u>lyah</u>-reh]
swindler imbroglione (m) [eem-broh-<u>lyoh</u>-neh]
swollen gonfio [<u>ghohn</u>-fyoh]

T

table tavolo, tavola [<u>tah</u>-voh-loh, <u>tah</u>-voh-lah]
take (v) prendere, andare a prendere [<u>prehn</u>-deh-reh, ahn-<u>dah</u>-reh ah <u>prehn</u>-deh-reh]; **take/bring** (v) portare, portare con sé [pohr-<u>tah</u>-reh, pohr-<u>tah</u>-reh kohn seh]
take away (v) portar via, togliere [pohr-<u>tah</u>-reh vee-ah, toh-<u>lyeh</u>-reh]
take leave (v) congedarsi, accomiatarsi, prendere congedo [kohn-djeh-<u>dahr</u>-see, ah-kkoh-myah-<u>tahr</u>-see, <u>prehn</u>-deh-reh kohn-<u>jeh</u>-doh]
take part (in) (v) prendere parte (a) [<u>prehn</u>-deh-reh <u>pahr</u>-teh (ah)]
take place (v) aver luogo [ah-<u>veh</u>-reh <u>lwoh</u>-ghoh]
tall alto [<u>ahl</u>-toh]
tanned abbronzato [ah-brohn-<u>zah</u>-toh]
taste (v) assaggiare, gustare [ah-ssah-<u>djah</u>-reh, ghoo-<u>stah</u>-reh]
taste gusto, sapore (m) [<u>ghoo</u>-stoh, sah-<u>poh</u>-reh]
taxes tasse (pl) [<u>tah</u>-sseh]
taxi tassì (m) [tah-<u>ssee</u>]
teach (v) insegnare [een-seh-<u>nyah</u>-reh]
team (sport) squadra [<u>skwah</u>-drah]
tear (v) strappare [strah-<u>ppah</u>-reh]
telephone (v) telefonare [teh-leh-foh-<u>nah</u>-reh]
telescope cannochiale (m) [kah-nnoh-<u>kyah</u>-leh]
tell (v) raccontare [rah-kkohn-<u>tah</u>-reh]
temporary provvisorio [proh-vvee-<u>soh</u>-ryoh]
tender tenero [<u>teh</u>-neh-roh]
tent tenda [<u>tehn</u>-dah]
terrible terribile [teh-<u>rree</u>-bee-leh]
thank (v) ringraziare [reen-grah-<u>tzyah</u>-reh]
thank you grazie [<u>grah</u>-tzyeh]

that quello, quella [<u>kweh</u>-lloh, <u>kweh</u>-llah]
that, who che [keh]
then dopo, poi [<u>doh</u>-poh, <u>poh</u>-ee]
there là, lì [lah, lee]
there is c'è [cheh]; **there are** ci sono [chee <u>soh</u>-noh]
therefore perciò [pehr-<u>choh</u>]
these questi/queste [<u>kweh</u>-stee/<u>kweh</u>-steh]
thick fitto, spesso [<u>fee</u>-ttoh, <u>speh</u>-ssoh]
thin magro [<u>mah</u>-groh]
thing cosa [<u>koh</u>-sah]
think (v) pensare, credere [pehn-<u>sah</u>-reh, <u>kreh</u>-deh-reh]
think of (v) pensare a [pehn-<u>sah</u>-reh ah]
think of (someone) (v) pensare a [pehn-<u>sah</u>-reh ah]
third terzo, terza [<u>tehr</u>-tzoh/<u>tehr</u>-tzah]
thirdly terzo, in terzo luogo [tehr-tzoh, een <u>tehr</u>-tzoh <u>lwoh</u>-ghoh]
thirst (v) sete (f) [<u>seh</u>-teh]; **to be thirsty** (v) avere sete [ah-<u>veh</u>-reh <u>se</u>-teh]
thirsty assetato [ah-sseh-<u>tah</u>-toh]
this questo/questa [<u>kweh</u>-stoh/<u>kweh</u>-stah]
those quelli/quelle [<u>kweh</u>-llee/<u>kweh</u>-lleh]
thought pensiero [pehn-<u>syeh</u>-roh]
thread filo [<u>fee</u>-loh]
throw (v) gettare [jeh-<u>ttah</u>-reh]
throw lancio, tiro [<u>lahn</u>-choh, <u>tee</u>-roh]
thus così [koh-<u>see</u>]
ticket biglietto [bee-<u>lyeh</u>-ttoh]
tie up (v) legare [leh-<u>ghah</u>-reh]
time tempo [<u>tehm</u>-poh]; **a period of time** un periodo di tempo [oon peh-ree-<u>oh</u>-doh dee <u>tehm</u>-poh]; **from time to time** di tanto in tanto [dee <u>tahn</u>-toh een <u>tahn</u>-toh]; **at the time/now** al momento, attualmente [ahl moh-<u>mehn</u>-toh, ah-ttwahl-<u>mehn</u>-teh]
time (occurrence) volta [<u>vohl</u>-tah]; **once** una volta [<u>oo</u>-nah <u>vohl</u>-tah]; **twice, two times** due volte [<u>doo</u>-eh <u>vohl</u>-teh]; **every time** ogni volta [<u>oh</u>-nyee <u>vohl</u>-tah]
tired stanco [<u>stahn</u>-koh]
tiring faticoso [fah-tee-<u>koh</u>-soh]
to a [ah]
tobacco tabacco [tah-<u>bah</u>-kkoh]
today oggi [<u>oh</u>-djee]
together comune (adj) [koh-<u>moo</u>-neh]; insieme (adv) [een-<u>syeh</u>-meh]
toilet toilette (f), gabinetto [<u>twah</u>-leht, ghah-bee-<u>neh</u>-ttoh]; **toilet paper** carta igienica [<u>kahr</u>-tah ee-<u>jeh</u>-nee-kah]
tone tono [<u>toh</u>-noh]

tonight stasera, stanotte [stah-<u>seh</u>-rah, stah-<u>noh</u>-tteh]
too troppo [<u>troh</u>-ppoh]
too much troppo [<u>troh</u>-ppoh]
touch (v) toccare [toh-k<u>kah</u>-reh]
tour giro [<u>jee</u>-roh]
tourist turista (m/f) [too-<u>ree</u>-stah]
toy giocattolo [joh-<u>kah</u>-ttoh-loh]
trace traccia [<u>trah</u>-chah]
traffic traffico [<u>trah</u>-ffee-koh]
training formazione (f), istruzione (f), educazione (f) [fohr-mah-<u>tzyoh</u>-neh, ee-stroo-<u>tzyoh</u>-neh, eh-doo-kah-<u>tzyoh</u>-neh]
translate (v) tradurre [trah-<u>doo</u>-rreh]
transport (v) trasportare [trah-spohr-<u>tah</u>-reh]
travel (v) viaggiare [vee-ah-<u>djah</u>-reh]
travel agency agenzia di viaggi [ah-jehn-<u>tsee</u>-ah dee <u>vyah</u>-djee]
travel bureau/agency ente (m) per il turismo [<u>ehn</u>-teh pehr eel too-<u>ree</u>-smoh]
traveler viaggiatore (m) [vee-ah-djah-<u>toh</u>-reh]
treasure tesoro [teh-<u>soh</u>-roh]
treat (v) trattare, curare [trah-<u>ttah</u>-reh, koo-<u>rah</u>-reh]
treatment trattamento, cura [trah-ttah-<u>mehn</u>-toh, <u>koo</u>-rah]
tree albero [<u>ahl</u>-beh-roh]
trip viaggio [<u>vyah</u>-djoh]
true vero [<u>veh</u>-roh]
trust fiducia [fee-<u>doo</u>-chah]
trust someone (v) fidarsi di qlcu [fee-<u>dahr</u>-see dee kwahl-<u>koo</u>-noh]
trusting fiducioso [fee-doo-<u>choh</u>-soh]
trustworthy fidato [fee-<u>dah</u>-toh]
truth verità [veh-ree-<u>tah</u>]
try (v) tentare, provare [tehn-<u>tah</u>-reh, proh-<u>vah</u>-reh]
try prova [<u>proh</u>-vah]
tube tubo [<u>too</u>-boh]
turn (v) girare, voltare [jee-<u>rah</u>-reh, vohl-<u>tah</u>-reh]; **turn right/left** (v) [jee-<u>rah</u>-reh ah <u>deh</u>-strah/see-<u>nee</u>-strah]
turn off (v) (light) chiudere [<u>kyoo</u>-deh-reh]
turn on (v) (light) accendere [ah-<u>chehn</u>-deh-reh]
type specie (f) [<u>speh</u>-cheh]
typical tipico, caratteristico [<u>tee</u>-pee-koh, kah-rah-<u>tteh</u>-<u>ree</u>-stee-koh]

U

ugly brutto [<u>broo</u>-ttoh]
umbrella ombrello [ohm-<u>breh</u>-lloh]
unaware senza conoscenza [<u>sehn</u>-tzah koh-noh-<u>shehn</u>-tzah]
uncertain incerto [een-<u>chehr</u>-toh]
uncertainty incerto, dubbio [cen-<u>chehr</u>-toh, <u>doo</u>-byoh]
uncle zio [<u>tzee</u>-oh]
uncomfortable scomodo [<u>skoh</u>-moh-doh]
unconscious svenuto [zveh-<u>noo</u>-toh]
undecided indeciso [een-deh-<u>chee</u>-soh]
under sotto [<u>soh</u>-ttoh]
underpass sottopassaggio [soh-ttoh-pah-<u>ssah</u>-djoh]
understand (v) capire [kah-<u>pee</u>-reh]
undress (v) svestirsi, spogliarsi [sveh-<u>steer</u>-see, spoh-<u>lyahr</u>-see]
unemployed disoccupato [dee-soh-kkoo-<u>pah</u>-toh]
unexpected inaspettato [ee-nah-speh-<u>ttah</u>-toh]
unfavorable sfavorevole [sfah-voh-<u>reh</u>-voh-leh]
unfortunately sfortunatamente, per disgrazia, purtroppo [sfohr-too-nah-tah-<u>mehn</u>-teh, pehr dee-<u>zgrah</u>-tzyah, poor-<u>troh</u>-ppoh]
ungrateful ingrato [een-<u>grah</u>-toh]
unhappy infelice, sfortunato, scontento [een-feh-<u>lee</u>-cheh, sfohr-too-<u>nah</u>-toh, skohn-<u>tehn</u>-toh]
unimportant poco importante [<u>poh</u>-koh eem-pohr-<u>tahn</u>-teh]
unknown sconosciuto [skoh noh-<u>shoo</u>-toh]
unload (v) scaricare [skah-ree-<u>kah</u>-reh]
unnecessary non necessario [nohn neh-cheh-<u>ssah</u>-ryoh]
unpack (v) disfare (la valigia) [dee-<u>sfah</u>-reh (lah vah-<u>lee</u>-jah)]
unpleasant spiacevole [spyah-<u>cheh</u>-voh-leh]
unsuitable inadatto [ee-nah-<u>dah</u>-ttoh]
until fino a [<u>fee</u>-noh ah]; **until now** fino-ra [fee-<u>noh</u>-rah]
unusual insolito [een-<u>soh</u>-lee-toh]
unwelcoming poco accogliente [<u>poh</u>-koh ah-kkoh-<u>lyehn</u>-teh]
unwell indisposto [een-dee-<u>spoh</u>-stoh]
unwilling malvolentieri [mahl-voh-<u>lehn</u>-tyeh-ree]
up there lassù [lah-<u>ssoo</u>]

urgent urgente [oor-<u>jehn</u>-teh]

use *(v)* servirsi, prendere, usare [sehr-<u>veer</u>-see, <u>prehn</u>-deh-reh, oo-<u>sah</u>-reh]

use uso, applicazione *(f)* [<u>oo</u>-soh, ah-pplee-kah-<u>tzyoh</u>-neh]

used to, to get *(v)* abituarsi a [ah-bee-too-<u>ahr</u>-see]

useful comodo, utile [<u>koh</u>-moh-doh, <u>oo</u>-tee-leh]

useless inutile [ee-<u>noo</u>-tee-leh]

usual solito, consueto, abituale [<u>soh</u>-lee-toh, kohn-<u>sweh</u>-toh, ah-bee-too-<u>ah</u>-leh]

V

vacation vacanza, ferie *(pl)* [vah-<u>kahn</u>-tza, <u>feh</u>-ryeh]

valid valido [<u>vah</u>-lee-do]

validity validità [vah-lee-dee-<u>tah</u>]

valuable objects oggetti *(pl)* di valore [oh-<u>djeh</u>-ttee dee vah-<u>loh</u>-reh]

value valore *(m)* [vah-<u>loh</u>-reh]; **be valuable** *(v)* avere un grande valore [ah-<u>veh</u>-re oon grahn-deh vah-<u>loh</u>-reh]

varied diverso [dee-<u>vehr</u>-soh]

vase vaso [<u>vah</u>-soh]

vending machine distributore *(m)* automatico [dee-stree-boo-<u>toh</u>-reh ah-oo-toh-mah-<u>tee</u>-koh]

very molto [<u>mohl</u>-toh]

view vista, panorama *(m)* [<u>vee</u>-stah, pah-noh-<u>rah</u>-mah]

villa villa [<u>vee</u>-llah]

village villaggio [vee-<u>llah</u>-djoh]

vineyard vigneto, vigna [vee-<u>nyeh</u>-toh, <u>vee</u>-nyah]

visible visibile [vee-<u>see</u>-bee-leh]

visit visita [<u>vee</u>-see-tah]

visit someone *(v)* far visita a qlcu [fahr <u>vee</u>-see-tah ah kwahl-<u>koo</u>-noh]

visit (something) *(v)* visitare [vee-see-<u>tah</u>-reh]

voice voce *(f)* [<u>voh</u>-cheh]

volume volume *(m)* [voh-<u>loo</u>-meh]

vote *(v)* votare [voh-<u>tah</u>-reh]

W

wait *(v)* aspettare [aı-speh-ttah-reh]

wait (for) *(v)* aspettare [ah-speh-<u>ttah</u>-reh]

wake *(v)* svegliare, alzare [sveh-<u>lyah</u>-reh, ahl-<u>tzah</u>-reh]

wake up *(v)* svegliarsi [sveh-<u>lyahr</u>-see]

walk *(v)* passeggiare [pah-sseh-<u>djah</u>-reh]

walk passeggiata [pah-sseh-<u>djah</u>-tah]; **take a walk/stroll** *(v)* fare una passeggiata [<u>fah</u>-reh <u>oo</u>-nah pah-sseh-<u>djah</u>-tah]

wall parete *(f)* [pah-<u>reh</u>-teh]

wallet portafoglio [pohr-tah-<u>foh</u>-lyoh]

want *(v)* volere [voh-<u>leh</u>-reh]

war guerra [<u>gweh</u>-rrah]

warm calore *(m)* [kah-<u>loh</u>-reh]

warm up *(v)* riscaldare [ree-skahl-<u>dah</u>-reh]

warn *(v)* avvertire (di) [ah-vvehr-<u>tee</u>-reh (dee)]

wash *(v)* lavare [lah-<u>vah</u>-reh]

wasp vespa [<u>veh</u>-spah]

watch *(v)* guardare [gwahr-<u>dah</u>-reh]

watch orologio da polso [oh-roh-<u>loh</u>-joh dah <u>pohl</u>-soh]; **wall clock** orologio da parete [oh-roh-<u>loh</u>-joh dah pah-<u>reh</u>-teh]

watchman guardiano [gwahr-<u>dyah</u>-noh]

water acqua [<u>ah</u>-kwah]

watt *(el)* watt *(m)* [vahtt]

way via [<u>vee</u>-ah]

we noi [<u>noh</u>-ee]; *(dir/ind obj)* ci [chee]; **to us** a noi [ah <u>noh</u>-ee]

weak debole [<u>deh</u>-boh-leh]

weakness debolezza [deh-boh-<u>leh</u>-tzah]

weather tempo [<u>tehm</u>-poh]

wedding nozze *(pl)* [<u>noh</u>-tzeh]

week settimana [seh-tte-<u>mah</u>-nah]; **in a week** fra una settimana [frah <u>oo</u>-nah seh-ttee-<u>mah</u>-nah]; **during the week** durante la settimana [doo-<u>rahn</u>-teh lah seh-ttee-<u>mah</u>-nah]

weekly settimanale *(adj)* [seh-ttee-mah-<u>nah</u>-leh]; ogni settimana *(adv)* [<u>oh</u>-nyee seh-ttee-<u>mah</u>-nah]

weigh *(v)* pesare [peh-<u>sah</u>-reh]

weight peso [<u>peh</u>-soh]

welcome *(v)* accogliere [ah-<u>kkoh</u>-lyeh-reh]

welcome accoglienza, benvenuto [ah-kkoh-<u>lyehn</u>-tzah, behn-veh-<u>noo</u>-toh]

welcoming accogliente [ah-kkoh-<u>lyehn</u>-teh]; **comfortable** confortevole [kohn-fohr-<u>teh</u>-<u>voh</u>-leh]

well bene *(m)* [<u>beh</u>-neh]; **be well** *(v)* trovarsi bene [troh-<u>vahr</u>-see <u>beh</u>-neh]

well-known noto [<u>noh</u>-toh]; **to be well-known** *(v)* essere noto [eh-<u>sseh</u>-reh <u>noh</u>-toh]

well-off benestante [beh-neh-<u>stahn</u>-teh]

West Occidente *(m)* [oh-chee-<u>dehn</u>-teh]

western occidentale [oh-chee-dehn-<u>tah</u>-leh]

wet bagnato, inzuppato [bah-<u>nyah</u>-toh, een-zoo-<u>ppah</u>-toh]

what cosa, che cosa [koh-sah keh koh-sah]
when quando [kwahn-doh]
while durante *(prep)*; mentre *(conj)* [doo-rahn-teh, mehn-treh]
whoever qualsiasi *(adj)* [kwahl-see-ah-see]; chiunque *(pron)* [kee-oon-kweh]
why perché [pehr-keh]
wicked malvagio, cattivo, brutto [mahl-vah-joh, kah-ttee-voh, broo-ttoh]
wide largo, ampio [lahr-ghoh, uhm-pyuh]
wife moglie *(f)* [moh-lyeh]
wild selvaggio, feroce [sehl-vah-djoh, feh-roh-cheh]
willingly volentieri [voh-lehn-tyeh-ree]; **unwilling(ly)** di mala voglia [dee mah-lah voh-lyah]
win *(v)* vincere [veen-cheh-reh]
win vincita, guadagno [veen-chee-tah, gwah-dah-nyoh]
windy ventoso [vehn-toh-soh]
wish *(v)* desiderare [deh-see-deh-rah-reh]
wish augurio [ah-oo-goo-ryoh]
with con [kohn]
withdraw *(v)* ritirarsi [ree-tee-rahr-see]
without senza [sehn-tzah]
witness testimone *(m)* [teh-stee-moh-neh]
woman donna [doh-nnah]
wonderful meraviglioso [meh-rah-vee-lyoh-soh]
wood legno [leh-nyoh]
word parola [pah-roh-lah]

work *(v)* *(machine)* funzionare, lavorare [foon-tzyoh-nah-reh, lah-voh-rah-reh]
work lavoro [lah-voh-roh]
workdays nei giorni feriali [neh-ee johr-nee feh-ryah-lee]
world mondo [mohn-doh]
worm verme *(m)* [vehr-meh]
worried irrequieto, agitato, preoccupato [ee-rreh-kwych-toh, ah-jee-tah-toh, preh-oh-kkoo-pah-toh]
worry (about) *(v)* inquietarsi (di), preoccuparsi (di) [een-kwyeh-tahr-see (dee), preh-oh-kkoo-pahr-see (dee)]
worthless senza valore [sehn-tzah vah-loh-reh]
wrap up *(v)* avvolgere [ah-vvohl-jeh-reh]
write *(v)* scrivere [skree-veh-reh]
wrong *(injustice)* ingiustizia [een-joo-stee-tzyah]
wrong, to be *(v)* aver torto [ah-vehr tohr-toh]

Y

year anno [ah-nnoh]
yield *(v)* dare la precedenza [dah-re lah preh-cheh-dehn-tzah]
young giovane [joh-vah-neh]
your (il) tuo [(oel) too-oh]
youth gioventù *(f)* [joh-vehn-too]; **young people** i giovani [ee joh-vah-nee]
youth hostel ostello per la gioventù

ITALIAN–ENGLISH DICTIONARY

A

a [ah] to; **vicino a** [vee-<u>cheh</u>-noh ah] near

a Bologna [ah boh-<u>loh</u>-nyah] in, to Bologna

abbandonare [ah-bahn-doh-<u>nah</u>-reh] to abandon

abbassare [ah-bah-<u>ssah</u>-reh] *(price)* to lower

abbastanza [ah-bah-<u>stahn</u>-tzah] enough

abbigliamento [ah-bee-lyah-<u>mehn</u>-toh] clothing

abbondante [ah-bohn-<u>dahn</u>-teh] abundant

abbracciare [ah-bra-<u>chah</u>-reh] to embrace

abbreviazione [ah-breh-vyah-<u>tzyoh</u>-neh] *(f)* abbreviation

abbronzato [ah-brohn-<u>zah</u>-toh] tanned

abile [<u>ah</u>-bee-leh] able

abitante [ah-bee-<u>tahn</u>-teh] *(m/f)* inhabitant

abitare [ah-bee-<u>tah</u>-reh] to live

abituale [ah-bee-too-<u>ah</u>-leh] usual

abituarsi a [ah-bee-too-<u>ahr</u>-see] to get used to

abitudine [ah-bee-<u>too</u>-dee-neh] *(f)* custom, habit

abusare [ah-boo-<u>sah</u>-reh] to abuse

abuso [ah-<u>boo</u>-soh] abuse

accadere [ah-kkah-<u>deh</u>-reh] to happen

accelerare [ah-cheh-lleh-<u>rah</u>-reh] to accelerate

accendere [ah-<u>chehn</u>-deh-reh] to light, to turn on *(light)*

accendino [ah-chehn-<u>dee</u>-noh] cigarette lighter

accento [ah-<u>chehn</u>-toh] accent

accesso [ah-<u>cheh</u>-ssoh] access

accettare [ah-cheh-<u>ttah</u>-reh] to accept, to receive

accettazione [ah-cheh-ttah-<u>tzyoh</u>-neh] *(f)* reception (desk)

accogliente [ah-kkoh <u>lyehn</u>-teh] welcoming; **poco accogliente** [<u>poh</u>-koh ah-kkoh-<u>lyehn</u>-teh] unwelcoming

accoglienza [ah-kkoh-<u>lyehn</u>-tzah] welcome

accogliere [ah-<u>kkoh</u>-lyeh-reh] to welcome

accomiatarsi [ah-kkoh-myah-<u>tahr</u>-see] to say good-bye

accompagnamento [ah-kkohm-pah-nyah-<u>mehn</u>-toh] accompaniment

accompagnare [ah-kkohm-pah-<u>nyah</u>-reh] to accompany

acconsentire [ah-kkohn-sehn-<u>tee</u>-reh] to agree

accordare [ah-kkohr-<u>dah</u>-reh] *(music)* to tune

accordarsi [ah-kkohr-<u>dahr</u>-see] to agree

accordarsi su [ah-kkohr-<u>dahr</u>-see soo] to agree on

accordo [ah-<u>kkohr</u>-doh] agreement; **essere d'accordo** [<u>eh</u>-seeh-reh dah-<u>kkohr</u>-doh] to agree

accorgersi (di) [ah-<u>kkohr</u>-jehr-see (dee)] to realize

accuratezza [ah-kkoo-rah-<u>teh</u>-tzah] care

accurato [ah-kkoo-<u>rah</u>-toh] careful

acerbo [ah-<u>chehr</u>-boh] unripe

acido [<u>ah</u>-chee-doh] sour, acidic

acqua [<u>ah</u>-kwah] water

acuto [ah-<u>koo</u>-toh] sharp

adatto [ah-<u>dah</u>-ttoh] suitable

addizionare [ah-ddee-tzyoh-<u>nah</u>-reh] to add up

addormentarsi [ah-ddohr-mehn-<u>tahr</u>-see] to fall asleep

aderire [ah-deh-<u>ree</u>-reh] to agree (to something)

adoperare [ah-doh-peh-<u>rah</u>-reh] to use

Adriatico [ah-dree-<u>ah</u>-tee-koh] Adriatic Sea

adulto/adulta [ah-<u>dool</u>-toh/ah-<u>dool</u>-tah] adult

aerare [ah-eh-<u>rah</u>-re] to aerate

affamato [ah-ffah-<u>mah</u>-toh] hungry, starving

affare [ah-<u>ffah</u>-reh] *(m)* business

affermare [ah-ffehr-<u>mah</u>-reh] to affirm

afferrare [ah-ffeh-<u>rrah</u>-reh] to seize, to get hold of

affettuoso [ah-ffeh-<u>ttwoh</u>-soh] loving, affectionate

affittare [ah-ffee-<u>ttah</u>-reh] to rent, to lease

affitto [ah-<u>ffee</u>-ttoh] rent

affollato [ah-ffoh-<u>llah</u>-toh] crowded

affrettarsi [ah-ffreh-<u>ttahr</u>-see] to hurry

agenzia [ah-jehn-<u>tzee</u>-ah] agency; **agenzia di viaggi** [ah-jehn-<u>tzee</u>-ah dee <u>vyah</u>-djee] travel agency

aggiungere [ah-<u>djoon</u>-jeh-reh] to add

aggredire [ah-gghre-<u>dee</u>-reh] to attack

agitato [ah-jee-<u>tah</u>-toh] worried; *(sea)* rough

ago [<u>ah</u>-ghoh] needle

aguzzo [ah-<u>ghoo</u>-tzoh] sharp

aiutare qlcu [ah yoo-<u>tah</u>-reh kwahl-<u>koo</u>-noh] to help someone

aiuto [ah-<u>yoo</u>-toh] help; **essere d'aiuto a qlcu** [<u>eh</u>-sseh-reh dah-<u>yoo</u>-toh ah kwahl-<u>koo</u>-noh] to be of help to someone

albero [<u>ahl</u>-beh-roh] tree

alcool [<u>ahl</u>-kohl] *(m)* alcohol

alcuni/alcune [ahl-<u>koo</u>-nee/ahl-<u>koo</u>-neh] *(with pl noun)* some, a few

alghe [<u>ahl</u>-gheh] *(pl)* algae

alimentari [ah-lee-mehn-<u>tah</u>-ree] *(m/pl)* groceries

alimentazione [ah-lee-mehn-tah-<u>tzyoh</u>-neh] *(f)* food, diet

alimento [ah-lee-<u>mehn</u>-toh] food

alleanza [ah-lleh-<u>ahn</u>-tzah] alliance

allegato [ah-lleh-<u>ghah</u>-toh] enclosure

allegro [ah-<u>lleh</u>-ghroh] merry; **un po' allegro** [oon poh ah-<u>lleh</u>-ghroh] tipsy

allestire [ah-lleh-<u>stee</u>-reh] to prepare

alloggio [ah-<u>lloh</u>-djoh] lodging

allora [ah-<u>lloh</u>-rah] then, so

allungare [ah-lleh-<u>ghah</u>-reh] to lengthen

almeno [ahl-<u>meh</u>-noh] at least

alt! [ahlt] stop!

altezza [ahl-<u>teh</u>-tzah] height

alto [<u>ahl</u>-toh] *(stature)* tall; high

altoparlante [ahl-toh-pahr-<u>lahn</u>-teh] *(m)* loudspeaker

altrettanto [ahl-treh-<u>ttahn</u>-toh] likewise, the same

altrimenti [ahl-tree-<u>mehn</u>-tee] otherwise

altro/altra [<u>ahl</u>-troh/<u>ahl</u>-trah] other; **un altro** [oon ahl-troh] another; **l'altro giorno** [lahl-troh johr-noh] the other day

altrove [ahl-<u>troh</u>-veh] somewhere else

alzare [ahl-<u>tzah</u>-reh] to lift up; *(price)* to raise

alzarsi [ahl-<u>tzahr</u>-see] to get up

amabile [ah-<u>mah</u>-boo-leh] amiable

amabilità [ah-mah-bee-lee-<u>tah</u>] amiability

amare [ah-<u>mah</u>-reh] to love

amaro [ah-<u>mah</u>-roh] bitter

ambasciata [ahm-bah-<u>shah</u>-tah] embassy

ambiente [ahm-<u>byehn</u>-teh] *(m)* environment

amichevole [ah-mee-<u>keh</u>-<u>voh</u>-leh] friendly

amicizia [ah-mee-<u>chee</u>-tzyah] friendship; **essere in amicizia** [<u>eh</u>-sseh-reh een ah-mee-<u>chee</u>-tzyah] to be friends

amico/amica [ah-<u>mee</u>-koh/ah-<u>mee</u>-kah] friend

ammalarsi [ah-mmah-<u>lahr</u>-see] to get sick

ammenda [ah-<u>mmehn</u>-dah] fine (ticket)

amministrazione [ah-mmee-nee-strah-<u>tzyoh</u>-ne] *(f)* management, administration

ammirare [ah-mmee-<u>rah</u>-reh] to admire

ammobiliare [ah-mmoh-bee-<u>lyah</u>-reh] to furnish

amore [ah-<u>moh</u>-reh] *(m)* love

ampio [<u>ahm</u>-pyoh] wide

anche [<u>ahn</u>-keh] also

ancora [ahn-<u>koh</u>-rah] again, yet; **ancora una volta** [ahn-<u>koh</u>-rah oo-nah <u>vohl</u>-tah] once again

andare [ahn-<u>dah</u>-reh] to go; **andar via** [ahn-<u>dah</u>-reh <u>vee</u>-ah] to go away; **andare a** [ahn-<u>dah</u>-reh ah] to go to; **andare a bordo** [ahn-<u>dah</u>-reh ah <u>bohr</u>-doh] to get on board; **andare a letto** [ahn-<u>dah</u>-reh ah <u>leh</u>-ttoh] to go to bed; **andare diritto** [ahn-<u>dah</u>-reh ah dee-<u>ree</u>-ttoh] to go straight ahead; **andare su** [ahn-<u>dah</u>-reh soo] to go up; **andare a prendere** [ahn-<u>dah</u>-reh ah <u>prehn</u>-deh-reh] to go get

anello [ah-<u>noh</u>-lloh] ring

angolo [<u>ahn</u>-ghoh-loh] corner

animale [ah-nee-<u>mah</u>-loh] *(m)* animal

anno [<u>ah</u>-nnoh] year

annuale [ah-<u>nnwah</u>-leh] yearly

annunciare [ah-nnon-<u>chah</u>-reh] announce

annuncio [ah-<u>nnoon</u>-choh] announcement, notice

anticipo [ahn-<u>tee</u>-chee-poh] advance; **essere in anticipo** [<u>eh</u>-sseh-reh een ahn-<u>tee</u>-chee-poh] to be early

antico [ahn-<u>tee</u>-koh] old

anticoncezionale [ahn-tee-kohn-cheh-tzyoh-<u>nah</u>-leh] *(m)* contraceptive

antipasto [ahn-tee-<u>pah</u>-stoh] hors-d'oeuvre, appetizer

anzi [<u>ahn</u>-tzee] in fact, indeed

anzitutto [ahn-tzee-<u>too</u>-ttoh] first of all

ape [<u>ah</u>-peh] *(f)* bee

aperto [ah-<u>pehr</u>-toh] open; **all'aperto** [ahl-lah-<u>pehr</u>-toh] outside

apice [<u>ah</u>-pee-cheh] *(m)* top, summit

apparecchio [ah-ppah-<u>reh</u>-kkyoh] appliance, set

apparentemente [ah-ppah-rehn-teh-<u>mehn</u>-teh] apparently

A/Z

apparenza [ah-ppah-<u>rehn</u>-tzah] appearance

apparire [ah-ppah-<u>ree</u>-reh] to appear

appartamento [ah-ppahr-tah-<u>mehn</u>-toh] apartment; **appartamento ammobiliato** [ah-ppahr-tah-<u>mehn</u>-toh ah-mmoh-bee-<u>lyah</u>-toh] furnished apartment

appartato [ah-ppahr-<u>tah</u>-toh] remote

appartenere [ah-ppahr-teh-<u>neh</u>-reh] to belong

appena [ah-<u>ppeh</u>-nah] hardly

appendere [ah-<u>ppehn</u>-deh-reh] to hang (up)

appetito [ah-ppeh-<u>tee</u>-toh] appetite

applauso [ah-<u>pplah</u>-oo-soh] applause

applicare [ah-pplee-<u>kah</u>-reh] to apply

applicazione [ah-pplee-kah-<u>tzyoh</u>-neh] (f) application

appoggio [ah-<u>ppoh</u>-djoh] support, backing

apposta [ah-<u>ppoh</u>-stah] deliberately, on purpose

appuntamento [ah-ppoon-tah-<u>mehn</u>-toh] appointment

aprire [ah-<u>pree</u>-reh] to open

apriscatole [ah-pree-<u>skah</u>-toh-leh] (m) can opener

argomento [ahr-ghoh-<u>mehn</u>-toh] subject, topic

aria [<u>ah</u>-ryah] air

aringa [ah-<u>reen</u>-gah] herring

arrabbiarsi [ah-rrah-<u>byahr</u>-see] to get angry; **arrabbiarsi per** [ah-rrah-<u>byahr</u>-see pehr] to get angry about

arrabbiato [ah-rrah-<u>byah</u>-toh] angry, mad

arrestare [ah-rreh-<u>stah</u>-reh] to stop

arrivare [ah-rree-<u>vah</u>-reh] to arrive

arrostire [ah-rroh-<u>stee</u>-reh] to roast

arrosto [ah-<u>rroh</u>-stoh] roast(ed)

articolo [ahr-<u>tee</u>-koh-loh] article

ascensore [ah-shehn-<u>soh</u>-reh] (m) elevator

asciugare [ah-shoo-<u>ghah</u>-reh] to dry

asciutto [ah-<u>shoo</u>-ttoh] dry

ascoltare (qlcu) [ah-skohl-<u>tah</u>-reh kwahl-<u>koo</u>-noh] to listen to someone

asino [<u>ah</u>-see-noh] donkey, ass

aspettare [ah-speh-<u>ttah</u>-reh] to wait (for)

aspro [<u>ah</u>-sproh] sour, tart

assaggiare [ah-ssah-<u>djah</u>-reh] to taste

assente [ah-<u>ssehn</u>-teh] absent

assetato [ah-sseh-<u>tah</u>-toh] thirsty

assicurare [ah-ssee-koo-<u>rah</u>-reh] to assure, to insure

assicurazione [ah-ssee-koo-rah-<u>tzyoh</u>-neh] (f) insurance

associazione [ah-ssoh-chah-<u>tzyoh</u>-neh] (f) association

assolato [ah-ssoh-<u>lah</u>-toh] sunny

assolutamente [ah-ssoh-loo-tah-<u>mehn</u>-teh] absolutely

assomigliare [ah-ssoh-mee-<u>lyah</u>-reh] to be like

assumere [ah-<u>ssoo</u>-meh-reh] to hire

attaccare [ah-ttah-<u>kkah</u>-reh] to attack

attenersi [ah-tteh-<u>nehr</u>-see] to keep, to stick to something

attento [ah-<u>ttehn</u>-toh] careful; attentive

attenzione! [ah-ttehn-<u>tzyoh</u>-neh] careful, **fare attenzione (a)** [<u>fah</u>-reh ah-ttehn-<u>tzyoh</u>-neh (ah)] to pay attention to

attestato [ah-tteh-<u>stah</u>-toh] certificate

attività [ah-ttee-vee-<u>tah</u>] activity

attraversare [ah-ttrah-vehr-<u>sah</u>-reh] to go across

attraverso [ah-ttrah-<u>vehr</u>-soh] across

attualmente [ah-ttwal-<u>mehn</u>-teh] presently

augurio [ah-oo-<u>ghoo</u>-ryoh] wish

aumentare [ah-oo-mehn-<u>tah</u>-reh] (price) to increase, to raise

autentico [ah-oo-<u>tehn</u>-tee-koh] real, authentic

autista [ah-oo-<u>tee</u>-stah] (m) driver

auto [<u>ah</u>-oo-toh] (f) car

autoambulanza [ah-oo-tohm-boo-<u>lahn</u>-tzah] ambulance

automatico [ah-oo-toh-<u>mah</u>-tee-koh] automatic

autorità pubblica [ah-oo-toh-ree-<u>tah</u> poo-blee-kah] public authority

autorizzato [ah-oo-toh-ree-<u>zah</u>-toh] authorized

avanti [ah-<u>vahn</u>-tee] ahead; come in!

avanzare [ah-vahn-<u>tzah</u>-reh] to advance

avere [ah-<u>veh</u>-reh] to have; **aver bisogno di** [ah-<u>veh</u>-reh bee-<u>soh</u>-nyoh dee] to need; **aver fretta** [ah-<u>veh</u>-reh <u>freh</u>-ttah] to be in a hurry; **aver ragione/torto** [ah-<u>veh</u>-reh rah-<u>joh</u>-neh/<u>tohr</u>-toh] to be right/wrong; **aver l'aspetto** [ah-<u>veh</u>-reh lah-<u>speh</u>-ttoh] to resemble

avvenimento [ah-vveh-nee-<u>mehn</u>-toh] event; incident

avvertire (di) [ah-vvehr-<u>tee</u>-reh (dee)] to warn (about)

avviarsi [ah-vvee-<u>ahr</u>-see] to set out

avvicinarsi [ah-vvee-chee-<u>nahr</u>-see] to get near

azione [ah-<u>tsyoh</u>-neh] (f) action

A/Z

B

baciare [bah-<u>chah</u>-reh] to kiss
bacio [<u>bah</u>-choh] kiss
bagnato [bah-<u>nyah</u>-toh] wet
bagno [<u>bah</u>-nyoh] bath; **fare il bagno** [<u>fah</u>-reh eel <u>bah</u>-nyoh] to take a bath
baita [<u>bah</u>-ee-tah] *(mountain)* hut
ballo [<u>bah</u>-lloh] dance, ball
bambino [bahm-<u>bee</u>-noh] child
bambola [<u>bahm</u>-boh-lah] doll
banca [<u>bahn</u>-kah] bank
banconota [bahn-koh-<u>noh</u>-tah] banknote
banda (musicale) [<u>bahn</u>-dah (moo-see-<u>kah</u>-leh)] *(music)* band
barattolo [bah-<u>rah</u>-ttoh-loh] jar, can
barca [<u>bahr</u>-kah] boat
barzelletta [bahr-zeh-<u>lleh</u>-ttah] joke
basso [<u>bah</u>-ssoh] low; *(stature)* short; **a bassa voce** [ah <u>bah</u>-ssah <u>voh</u>-cheh] in a low voice
bastare [bah-<u>stah</u>-reh] to be enough
bastone [bah-<u>stoh</u>-neh] *(m)* stick, cane
battere [<u>bah</u>-tteh-reh] to beat, to strike (hour)
batteria [bah-tteh-<u>ree</u>-ah] battery
bellezza [beh-<u>lleh</u>-tzah] beauty
bello/bella [<u>beh</u>-lloh/<u>beh</u>-llah] nice, beautiful, handsome
benché [behn-<u>keh</u>] although
bene [<u>beh</u>-neh] *(adv)* well
benessere [beh-<u>neh</u>-sseh-reh] *(m)* well-being
benestante [beh-neh-<u>stahn</u>-teh] well-off
benevolo [beh-<u>neh</u>-voh-loh] benevolent
benvenuto [behn-veh-<u>noo</u>-toh] welcome
benzina [behn-<u>zee</u>-nah] gas
bere [<u>beh</u>-reh] to drink
biancheria (per il letto) [byahn-keh-<u>ree</u>-ah (pehr eel <u>leh</u>-ttoh)] bed linens;
biancheria intima [byan-keh-<u>ree</u>-ah een-tee-mah] underwear, lingerie
bicchiere [bee-<u>kkyeh</u>-reh] *(m)* drinking glass
bidone delle immondizie [bee-<u>doh</u>-neh <u>deh</u>-lleh ee-mmohn-<u>dee</u>-tzyeh] *(m)* garbage can
biglietto (d'ingresso) [bee-<u>lyeh</u>-ttoh (<u>deen</u>-ghreh-ssoh)] admission ticket
bilancia [bee-<u>lahn</u>-chah] scale
binocolo [bee-<u>noh</u>-koh-loh] binoculars
bisticciarsi [bee-stee-<u>chahr</u>-see] to quarrel
bollire [boh-<u>llee</u>-reh] to boil *(water)*
borsa [<u>bohr</u>-sah] purse, bag
bottiglia [boh-<u>ttee</u>-lyah] bottle

bottone [boh-<u>ttoh</u>-neh] *(m)* button
brace [<u>brah</u>-cheh] *(f)* embers
bravo [<u>brah</u>-voh] good
breve [<u>breh</u>-veh] short; **a breve termine/scadenza** [ah <u>breh</u>-veh <u>tehr</u>-mee-neh/skah-<u>dehn</u>-tzah] short-term
brillante [bree-<u>llahn</u>-teh] sparkling, brilliant *(color)*
brillare [bree-<u>llah</u>-reh] to shine
brillo [bree-<u>lloh</u>] tipsy
bruciare [broo-<u>chah</u>-reh] to burn
brutto [<u>broo</u>-ttoh] ugly; *(weather)* nasty
bucato [boo-<u>kah</u>-toh] washing, laundry
buco [<u>boo</u>-koh] hole
bugia [boo-<u>jee</u>-ah] lie
buono [<u>bwoh</u>-noh] *(adj)* good; **buono** coupon; **buona fortuna!** [<u>bwoh</u>-nah fohr-<u>too</u>-nah] good luck!
bussare [boo-<u>ssah</u>-reh] to knock
bussola [<u>boo</u>-ssoh-lah] compass

C

c'è [cheh] there is
cabina [kah-<u>bee</u>-nah] booth
cadere [kah-deh-reh] to fall
caduta [kah-<u>doo</u>-tah] fall, drop *(in temperature)*
caffè [kah-<u>tteh</u>] *(m)* coffee, café
calcolare [kahl-koh-<u>lah</u>-reh] to calculate
caldo [<u>kahl</u>-doh] warm, hot
calligrafia [kah-llee-grah-<u>fee</u>-ah] handwriting
calore [kah-<u>loh</u>-reh] *(m)* heat, warmth
calzolaio [kahl-tzoh-lah-yoh] shoemaker
cambiamento [kahm-byah-<u>mehn</u>-toh] change
cambiare [kahm-<u>byah</u>-reh] to change; **cambiare casa** [kahm-byah-reh kah-sah] to move
cambiarsi [kahm-<u>byahr</u>-see] to change into
cambio [<u>kahm</u>-byoh] exchange *(money)*, gearshift
camera [<u>kah</u>-meh-rah] room; **camera da letto** [<u>kah</u>-meh-rah dah <u>leh</u>-ttoh] bedroom
camminare [kah-mmee-<u>nah</u>-reh] to walk
campanello [kahm-pah-<u>neh</u>-lloh] bell
campione [kahm-<u>pyoh</u>-neh] *(m)* sample
campo [<u>kahm</u>-poh] field; **campo sportivo** [<u>kahm</u>-poh spohr-<u>tee</u>-voh] sports field
canale [kah-nah-leh] *(m)* canal

cancello [kahn-<u>cheh</u>-lloh] gate
candela [kahn-<u>deh</u>-lah] candle
cane [<u>kah</u>-neh] *(m)* dog
canneto [kah-<u>nneh</u>-toh] *(pl)* **canne** [kah-nneh] field of cane
cannochiale [kah-nnoh-<u>kyah</u>-leh] *(m)* telescope
cantare [kahn-<u>tah</u>-reh] to sing
canto [<u>kahn</u>-toh] singing
canzone [kahn-<u>tzoh</u>-neh] *(f)* song
capace [kah-<u>pah</u>-cheh] able
capanna [kah-<u>pah</u>-nnah] hut
capire [kah-<u>pee</u>-reh] to understand
capitale [kah-pee-<u>tah</u>-leh] *(f)* capital
capo [<u>kah</u>-poh] head, leader
cappella [kah-<u>ppeh</u>-llah] chapel
caratteristico [kah-rah-tteh-<u>ree-stee</u>-koh] *(adj)* characteristic
carbone [kahr-<u>boh</u>-neh] *(m)* coal
caricare [kah-ree-<u>kah</u>-reh] to load *(camera)*
carne [<u>kahr</u>-neh] *(f)* meat
caro [<u>kah</u>-roh] dear, expensive **non caro** [nohn <u>kah</u>-roh] inexpensive
carta [<u>kahr</u>-tah] paper; **carta d'identità** [<u>kahr</u>-tah dee-dehn-<u>tee</u>-tah] identification card; **carta geografica** [<u>kahr</u>-tah jeh-oh-<u>ghrah</u>-fee-kah] land map; **carta igienica** [<u>kahr</u>-tah ee-<u>jeh</u>-nee-kah] toilet paper
cartella [kahr-<u>teh</u>-llah] school bag
cartellone [kahr-teh-<u>lloh</u>-neh] *(m)* placard, poster
cartolina [kahr-toh-<u>lee</u>-nah] card; **cartolina postale** [kahr-toh-<u>lee</u>-nah poh-<u>stah</u>-leh] postcard
casa [<u>kah</u>-sah] house; **casa di campagna** [<u>kah</u>-sah dee kahm-<u>pah</u>-nyah] country house
caso [<u>kah</u>-soh] chance; **caso (fortuito)** [<u>kah</u>-soh (fohr-<u>too</u>-ee-toh)] luck; **nel caso** [nehl <u>kah</u>-soh] in case; **per caso** [pehr <u>kah</u>-soh] by chance
casomai [<u>kah</u>-soh <u>mah</u>-ee] if, in case
cassa [<u>kah</u>-ssah] case, cash register
castello [kah-<u>steh</u>-lloh] castle
catena [kah-<u>teh</u>-nah] chain
cattivo [kah-<u>ttee</u>-voh] bad, wicked
causa [<u>kah</u>-oo-sah] cause; **a causa di** [ah <u>kah</u>-oo-sah dee] because of
causare [kah-oo-<u>sah</u>-reh] to cause
cauto [<u>kah</u>-oo-toh] caution
cauzione [kah-oo-<u>tzyoh</u>-neh] *(f)* security, bail
cedere [<u>cheh</u>-deh-reh] to give

cedibile [cheh-<u>dee</u>-bee-leh] transferable
celare [cheh-<u>lah</u>-reh] to hide
celibe [<u>cheh</u>-lee-beh] bachelor
cento [<u>chehn</u>-toh] hundred; **cento volte** [<u>chehn</u>-toh <u>vohl</u>-teh] a hundred times
centrale [chehn-<u>trah</u>-leh] central
centro [<u>chehn</u>-troh] center, downtown
ceramica [cheh-<u>rah</u>-mee-kah] ceramics; **ceramiche** [cheh-<u>rah</u>-mee-keh] *(pl)* pottery
cercare [chehr-<u>kah</u>-reh] to look for
certamente [chehr-tah-<u>mehn</u>-teh] *(adv)* certainly
certificare [chehr-tee-fee-<u>kah</u>-reh] to certify
certificato [chehr-tee-fee-<u>kah</u>-toh] certificate
certo [<u>chehr</u>-toh] certain
cespuglio [cheh-<u>spoo</u>-lyoh] bushy
cesto [<u>cheh</u>-stoh] basket
che [keh] that, who; **che peccato!** [keh peh-<u>kkah</u>-toh] what a shame! **che cosa?** [keh <u>koh</u>-sah] what?
chiamare [kyah-<u>mah</u>-reh] to name, to call
chiamarsi [kyah-<u>mahr</u>-see] to be called, named
chiaro [<u>kyah</u>-roh] clear, bright, light *(color)*
chiasso [<u>kyah</u>-ssoh] din, racket
chiavistello [kyah-vee-<u>steh</u>-lloh] latch, bolt
chiedere [<u>kyeh</u>-deh-reh] to ask; **chiedere qlco a qlcu** [<u>kyeh</u>-deh-reh kwahl-<u>koh</u>-sah ah kwahl-<u>koo</u>-noh] to ask someone something; **chiedere un'informazione** [<u>kyeh</u>-deh-reh oo-neen-fohr-mah-<u>tsyoh</u>-neh] to get information; **chiedo scusa!** [<u>kyeh</u>-doh <u>skoo</u>-zah] I beg your pardon!
chiodo [<u>kyoh</u>-doh] nail
chitarra [kee-<u>tah</u>-rrah] guitar
chiudere [<u>kyoo</u>-deh-reh] to close; **chiudere a chiave** [<u>kyoo</u>-deh-re ah <u>kyah</u>-veh] to lock
chiunque [kee-<u>oon</u>-kweh] *(pron)* whoever
chiuso [<u>kyoo</u>-soh] closed
chiusura [kyoo-<u>soo</u>-rah] closing
ci [chee] *(pron)* (to) us, ourselves; *(adv)* there
ci sono [chee <u>soh</u>-noh] there are
ciao [<u>chah</u>-oh] hi, bye *(inf)*
ciascuno [chah-<u>skoo</u>-noh] *(pron)* everyone, each (one)
cibo [<u>chee</u>-boh] food

cieco [cheh-koh] blind
cielo [cheh-loh] sky
ciò nonostante [choh noh-noh-stahn-teh] in spite of
cima [chee-mah] top, summit
cinghia [cheen-ghyah] belt, strap
circa [cheer-kah] around, about
circolare [cheer-koh-lah-reh] to circulate
circostanze [cheer-koh-stahn-tzeh] *(pl)* circumstances
città [chee-ttah] city
classe [klah-sseh] *(f)* class
cliente [klee-ehn-teh] *(m)* customer
clima [klee-mah] *(m)* climate
cogliere [koh-lyeh-reh] to pick, gather
cognata [koh-nyah-tah] sister-in-law
cognato [koh-nyah-toh] brother-in-law
cognome [koh-nyoh-meh] *(m)* family name
collana [koh-llah-nah] necklace
collega [koh-lleh-ghah] *(m/f)* colleague
collera [koh-lleh-rah] anger; **in collera** [een koh-lleh-rah] angry
collezione [koh-lleh-tzyoh-neh] *(f)* collection
collina [koh-llee-nah] hill
collisione [koh-llee-syoh-neh] *(f)* collision
colorato [koh-loh-rah-toh] dyed
colore [koh-loh-reh] *(m)* color
colpa [kohl-pah] guilt
colpire [kohl-pee-reh] to hit, to blow
colpo [kohl-poh] blow, strike
come [koh-meh] how; **come d'abitudine** [koh-meh dah-bee-too-dee-neh] as usual; **come se** [koh-meh seh] as if
cominciare [koh-meen-chah-reh] to begin
comitiva [koh-mee-tee-vah] (tourist) party
commestibile [koh-mmeh-stee-bee-leh] edible
commissione [koh-mmee-ssyoh-neh] *(f)* errand
commosso [koh-mmoh-ssoh] moved, touched
comodità [koh-moh-dee-tah] comfort
comodo [koh-moh-doh] useful, comfortable
compaesano/compaesana [kohm-pah-eh-sah-noh/kohm-pah-eh-sah-nah] fellow countryman/-woman
compagnia [kohm-pah-nyee-ah] company
comparare [kohm-pah-rah-reh] to compare
compassione [kohm-pah-ssyoh-neh] *(f)* compassion, pity

compenso [kohm-pehn-soh] payment
compera [kohm-peh-rah] purchase
competente [kohm-peh-tehn-teh] competent
compilare (un modulo) [kohm-pee-lah-reh (oon moh-doo-loh)] to fill out a form
compleanno [kohm-pleh-ah-nnoh] birthday
completamente [kohm-pleh-tah-mehn-teh] *(adv)* completely
completo [kohm-pleh-toh] *(adj)* full; **essere al completo** [eh-sseh-reh ahl kohm-pleh-toh] to be full (no vacancy)
comportamento [kohm-pohr-tah-mehn-toh] behavior
comprare [kohm-prah-reh] to buy
compratore [kohm-prah-toh-reh] *(m)* purchaser
comprendere [kohm-prehn-deh-reh] to understand
compreso [kohm-preh-soh] included
comune [koh-moo-neh] *(adj)* common
comunicare [koh-moo-nee-kah-reh] to communicate; *(tel)* to connect
comunicazione [koh-moo-nee-kah-tzyoh-neh] *(f)* communication; *(tel)* connection
con [kohn] with
concedere [kohn-cheh-deh-reh] to grant
conciliare [kohn-chee-lyah-reh] to reconcile, to settle
concorso [kohn-kohr-soh] competition
condizione [kohn-dee-tzyoh-neh] *(f)* condition
condoglianze [kohn-doh-lyahn-tzeh] *(pl)* condolences
conducente [kohn-doo-chehn-teh] *(m)* driver
condurre [kohn-doo-rreh] to drive
conduttore [kohn-doo-ttoh-reh] *(m)* (train) conductor
conduttura [kohn-doo-ttoo-rah] *(gas, water)* main
confermare [kohn-fehr-mah-reh] to confirm
confezionare [kohn-feh-tzyoh-nah-reh] to wrap up
confine [kohn-fee-neh] *(m)* border
confortevole [kohn-fohr-teh-voh-leh] comforting, comfortable
confrontare [kohn-frohn-tah-reh] to compare
confronto [kohn-frohn-toh] comparison
congedarsi [kohn-djeh-dahr-see] to take leave

A/Z

congratularsi [kohn-ghrah-too-<u>lahr</u>-see] to congratulate

coniugi [<u>koh</u>-<u>nyoo</u>-jee] *(pl)* husband and wife

conoscente [koh-noh-<u>shen</u>-teh] *(m/f)* acquaintance

conoscenza [koh-noh-<u>shehn</u>-tzah] knowledge, acquaintance; **fare la conoscenza di qlcu** [<u>fah</u>-reh lah koh-noh-<u>shehn</u>-tzah dee kwahl-<u>koo</u>-noh] to meet someone; **senza conoscenza** [<u>sehn</u>-tzah coh-noh-<u>shehn</u>-tzah] without knowledge

conoscere [koh-<u>noh</u>-sheh-reh] to know; **conoscere qlcu** [koh-<u>noh</u>-sheh-reh kwahl-<u>koo</u>-noh] to know someone

consegnare [kohn-seh-<u>nyah</u>-reh] to deliver

conservare [kohn-sehr-<u>vah</u>-reh] to preserve, to keep

considerare [kohn-see-deh-<u>rah</u>-reh] to consider

considerevole [kohn-see-deh-<u>reh</u>-voh-leh] considerable

consigliare [kohn-see-<u>lyah</u>-reh] to advise

consiglio [kohn-<u>see</u>-lyoh] advice

consolato [kohn-soh-<u>lah</u>-toh] consulate

consueto [kohn-<u>sweh</u>-toh] usual, habitual

consultare [kohn-sool-<u>tah</u>-reh] to consult

consumare [kohn-soo-<u>mah</u>-reh] to consume

consumo [kohn-<u>soo</u>-moh] consumption, waste

contadino [kohn-tah-<u>dee</u>-noh] farmer, peasant

contare [kohn-<u>tah</u>-reh] to count

contatto [kohn-<u>tah</u>-ttoh] contact

contemporaneo [kohn-tehm-poh-<u>rah</u>-neh-oh] simultaneously

contenere [kohn-teh-<u>neh</u>-reh] to contain

contento [kohn-<u>tehn</u>-toh] happy, satisfied

contenuto [kohn-teh-<u>noo</u>-toh] contents

continuare [kohn-tee-<u>nwah</u>-reh] to continue

conto [<u>kohn</u>-toh] account, bill

contrario [kohn-<u>trah</u>-ryoh] contrary; **al contrario** [ahl kohn-<u>trah</u>-ryoh] on the contrary; **essere contrario a** [<u>eh</u>-sseh-reh kohn-<u>trah</u>-ryoh ah] to be opposed to

contrassegnare [kohn-trah-sseh-<u>nyah</u>-reh] to mark

contrattare [kohn-trah-<u>ttah</u>-reh] to negotiate

contrattempo [kohn-trah-<u>ttehm</u>-poh] mishap, incident

contratto [kohn-<u>trah</u>-ttoh] contract

contro [<u>kohn</u>-troh] against

controllare [kohn-troh-<u>llah</u>-reh] to check, to verify

conversare [kohn-vehr-<u>sah</u>-reh] to converse, to talk

conversazione [kohn-vehr-sah-<u>tzyoh</u>-neh] *(f)* conversation

conversione [kohn-vehr-<u>syoh</u>-neh] *(f)* conversion

coperta [koh-<u>pehr</u>-tah] blanket, bedspread

coperto [koh-<u>pehr</u>-toh] overcast

copia [<u>koh</u>-pyah] copy

coppia [<u>koh</u>-ppyah] couple, pair

coprire [koh-<u>pree</u>-reh] to cover

corda [<u>kohr</u>-dah] cord, rope

cordialità [kohr-dyah-lee-<u>tah</u>] cordiality

cordialmente [kohr-dyahl-<u>mehn</u>-teh] cordially

coro [<u>koh</u>-roh] choir *(church)*

corpo [<u>kohr</u>-poh] body

corpulento [kohr-poo-<u>lehn</u>-toh] corpulent

corredo [koh-<u>rreh</u>-doh] equipment

correggere [koh-<u>rreh</u>-djeh-reh] to correct

corrente [koh-<u>rrehn</u>-teh] *(f)* current, stream *(adj)* current; **(el) corrente elettrica** [koh-<u>rrehn</u>-teh eh-<u>leh</u>-tree-kah] *(f)* current; **corrente d'aria** [koh-<u>rrehn</u>-teh <u>dah</u>-ryah] *(f)* draft

correre [koh-<u>rrehn</u>-teh] to run

corretto [koh-<u>rreh</u>-ttoh] correct

corridoio [koh-rree-<u>doh</u>-yoh] passage, corridor

corrispondenza [koh-rree-spohn-<u>dehn</u>-tzah] correspondence

corrotto [koh-<u>rroh</u>-ttoh] corrupt

corso [<u>kohr</u>-soh] course; **corso di cambio** [<u>kohr</u>-soh dee <u>kahm</u>-byoh] exchange rate

cortese [kohr-<u>teh</u>-zeh] courteous

cortesia [kohr-teh-<u>zee</u>-ah] courtesy

cortile [kohr-<u>tee</u>-leh] *(m)* courtyard

corto [<u>kohr</u>-toh] short

cosa [<u>koh</u>-sah] thing; **per che cosa** [pehr keh <u>koh</u>-sah] for what?; **cosa è successo?** [<u>koh</u>-sah eh soo-<u>cheh</u>-ssoh] what happened?

cosciente [koh-<u>shehn</u>-teh] aware

coscienzioso [koh-shehn-<u>tzyoh</u>-soh] conscientious

così [koh-<u>see</u>] like this, so, thus; **così ... come** [koh-<u>see</u> ... <u>koh</u>-meh] so ... that

costa [<u>koh</u>-stah] cost

costare [koh-<u>stah</u>-reh] to cost

costituzione [koh-stee-too-<u>tzyoh</u>-neh] (*f*) constitution

costoso [koh-<u>stoh</u>-soh] expensive

costringere [koh-<u>streen</u>-jeh-reh] to compel

costruire [koh-stroo-<u>ee</u>-reh] to build

costume [koh-<u>stoo</u>-meh] (*m*) custom; **costume regionale** [koh-<u>stoo</u>-meh reh-joh-<u>nah</u>-leh] regional custom

cotto [<u>koh</u>-ttoh] cooked

creativo [kreh-ah-<u>tee</u>-voh] creative

credere [<u>kreh</u>-deh-reh] to believe

credito [<u>kreh</u>-dee-toh] credit

crescere [<u>kreh</u>-sheh-reh] to grow

criticare [kree-tee-<u>kah</u>-reh] to criticize

cucina [koo-<u>chee</u>-nah] kitchen, cooking

cucinare [koo-chee-<u>nah</u>-reh] to cook

cugino/cugina [koo-<u>jee</u>-noh/koo-<u>jee</u>-nah] cousin

culmine [<u>kool</u>-mee-neh] (*m*) summit, top

cuoio [<u>kwoh</u>-yoh] leather

cuore [<u>kwoh</u>-reh] (*m*) heart

cura [<u>koo</u>-rah] treatment

curare [koo-<u>rah</u>-reh] to take care of, to cure

curioso [koo-<u>ryoh</u>-soh] curious

curva [<u>koor</u>-vah] curve, bend

cuscino [koo-<u>shee</u>-noh] pillow

custodire [koo-stoh-<u>dee</u>-reh] to look after

D

da [dah] from, since; **da qualche parte** [dah <u>kwahl</u>-keh <u>pahr</u>-teh] from somewhere; **da quando** [dah <u>kwahn</u>-doh] since; **da quando?** since when?; **una lettera da Roma** [<u>oo</u>-nah <u>leh</u>-tteh-rah dah <u>roh</u>-mah] a letter from Rome

dabbasso [dah-<u>bah</u>-ssoh] downstairs

dado [<u>dah</u>-doh] screw, nut

danneggiare [dah-nneh-<u>djah</u>-reh] to damage

danno [<u>dah</u>-nnoh] damage

dannoso [dah-<u>nnoh</u>-soh] harmful

danza [<u>dahn</u>-tzah] dance

dappertutto [dah-ppehr-<u>too</u>-ttoh] everywhere

dare [<u>dah</u>-reh] to give; **dare aria** [<u>dah</u> rch <u>ah</u>-ryah] to air; **dare delle indicazioni** [<u>dah</u>-reh een-deh-kah-<u>tzyoh</u>-nee] to give directions; **darsi appuntamento** [<u>dahr</u>-see ah-ppoon-tah-<u>mehn</u>-toh] to make an appointment; **darsi per**

vinto [<u>dahr</u>-see pehr <u>veen</u>-toh] to give up

data [<u>dah</u>-tah] date

davanti [dah-<u>vahn</u>-tee] front; **davanti a** [dah-<u>vahn</u>-tee ah] in front of

debito [<u>deh</u>-bee-toh] debt

debole [<u>deh</u>-boh-leh] weak

debolezza [deh-boh-<u>leh</u>-tzah] weakness

decidere [deh-<u>chee</u>-deh-reh] to decide

decidersi [deh-<u>choo</u> dohr see] to make up one's mind

decisione [deh-chee-<u>syoh</u>-neh] (*f*) decision

definitivamente [deh-fee-nee-tee-vah-<u>mehn</u>-teh] (*adv*) once and for all

definitivo [deh-fee-nee-<u>tee</u>-voh] (*adj*) final

delega [<u>deh</u>-leh-ghah] delegation

delicato [deh-lee-<u>kah</u>-toh] delicate, fine

deluso [deh-<u>loo</u>-soh] disappointed

denaro [deh-<u>nah</u>-roh] money

dentro [<u>dehn</u>-troh] in, inside

denuncia [deh-<u>noon</u>-chah] indictment

denunciare [deh-noon-<u>chah</u>-reh] to declare, to report

deporre [deh-<u>poh</u>-rreh] to put

depositare [deh-poh-see-<u>tah</u>-reh] to deposit

derivare [deh-ree-<u>vah</u>-reh] to derive, to come from

descrivere [deh-<u>skree</u>-veh-reh] to describe

descrizione [deh-skree-<u>tzyoh</u>-neh] (*f*) description; **descrizione dettagliata** [deh-skree-<u>tzyoh</u>-neh deh-ttah-<u>lyah</u>-tah] detailed description

desiderare [doh-see-deh-<u>rah</u>-reh] to wish, to want

desiderio [deh-see-<u>deh</u>-ryoh] wish, desire

destra [<u>deh</u>-strah] right hand, right; **a destra** [ah <u>deh</u>-strah] to the right

dettagliatamente [deh-ttah-lyah-tah-<u>mehn</u>-teh] in detail

dettaglio [deh-<u>ttah</u>-lyoh] detail

di [dee] from; (*material, origin*) of; **è di Roma** [eh dee <u>roh</u>-mah] he/she is from Rome; **un vestito di seta** [oon veh-<u>stee</u>-toh dee <u>seh</u>-tah] a silk dress/suit

diagnosi [dee-ah-<u>nyoh</u>-see] (*f*) diagnosis

diapositiva [dyah-poh-see-<u>tee</u>-vah] (*photo*) slide

dibattito [dee-<u>bah</u>-ttee-toh] debate, discussion

dichiarare [dee-kyah-<u>rah</u>-reh] to declare

A/Z

dietro [dyeh-troh] behind
difendere [deh-fehn-deh-reh] to defend
difetto [dee-feh-ttoh] defect
difettoso [dee-feh-ttoh-soh] defective
differenza [dee-ffeh-rehn-tzah] difference
difficile [dee-ffee-chee-leh] difficult
difficoltà [dee-fee-kohl-tah] difficulty
diffidare di qlco/qlcu [dee-ffee-dah-reh dee kwahl-koo-noh] to distrust something/someone
dilazione [dee-lah-tzyoh-neh] (f) delay
diligente [dee-lee-jehn-teh] diligent
dimagrire [dee-mah-ghree-reh] to lose weight
dimenticare [dee-mehn-tee-kah-reh] to forget
diminuire [dee-mee-noo-ee-reh] to reduce
Dio [dee-oh] God
dipingere [dee-peen-jeh-reh] to paint
dire [dee-reh] to say
direttamente [dee-reh-ttah-mehn-teh] (adv) directly
diretto [dee-reh-ttoh] (adj) direct
direttore [dee-reh-ttoh-reh] (m), **direttrice** [dee-reh-ttree-cheh] (f) director
direzione [dee-reh-tzyoh-neh] (f) direction, management, administration; **nella direzione opposta** [neh-llah dee-reh-tzyoh-neh oh-ppoh-stah] in the opposite direction
diritto [dee-ree-ttoh] straight
discendere [dee-shehn-deh-reh] to go down
disco [dee-skoh] record
discorrere [dee-skoh-rreh-reh] to discuss
discoteca [dee-skoh-teh-kah] discotheque
disdire [dee-sdee-reh] to retract
disegnare [dee-seh-nyah-reh] to draw
disfare (la valigia) [dee-sfah-reh (la vah-lee-jah)] to unpack
disgrazia [dee-sghrah-tzyah] misfortune; **per disgrazia** [pehr dee-sghrah-tzyah] unfortunately
disoccupato [dee-soh-kkoo-pah-toh] unemployed
disordine [dee-sohr-dee-neh] (m) disorder, confusion
disperato [dee-speh-rah-toh] despairing
dispiacere [dee-spyah-cheh-reh] (m) regret, sorrow
disputa [dee-spoo-tah] dispute
distanza [dee-stahn-tzah] distance
distinguere [dee-steen-gweh-reh] to distinguish; **distinguersi da** [dee-steen-gwehr-see dah] to distinguish oneself from

distinto [dee-steen-toh] distinctive
distribuire [dee-stree-boo-ee-reh] to distribute
distributore automatico [dee-stree-boo-toh-reh ah-oo-toh-mah-tee-koh] (m) vending machine
distribuzione [dee-stree-boo-tzyoh-neh] (f) distribution
distruggere [dee-stroo-djeh-reh] to destroy
disturbare [dee-stoor-bah-reh] to disturb
disturbo [dee-stoor-boh] trouble
ditta [dee-ttah] firm, business
diventare [dee-vehn-tah-reh] to become
diversamente [dee-vehr-sah-mehn-teh] (adv) otherwise
diverso [dee-vehr-soh] (adj) different
divertente [dee-vehr-tehn-teh] entertaining, amusing
divertimento [dee-vehr-tee-mehn-toh] amusement, entertainment
divertirsi [dee-vehr-teer-see] to enjoy oneself
dividere [dee-vee-deh-reh] to divide; **dividere con qlcu** [dee-vee-deh-reh kohn kwahl-koo-noh] to share with someone
divieto [dee-vyeh-toh] prohibition; **divieto di fumare** [dee-vyeh-toh dee foo-mah-reh] no smoking
documento [doh-koo-mehn-toh] document
dogana [doh-ghah-nah] customs; **diritti doganali** [dee-ree-ttee doh-ghah-nah-lee] duty tax; **doganiere** [doh-ghah-nyeh-reh] customs officer
dolce [dohl-cheh] sweet, gentle
dolore [doh-loh-reh] (m) pain
doloroso [doh-loh-roh-soh] painful
domanda [doh-mahn-dah] question
domicilio [doh-mee-chee-lyoh] residence
donna [doh-nnah] woman
dopo [doh-poh] (prep) after
doppiamente [doh-ppyah-mehn-teh] (adv) doubly
doppio [doh-ppyoh] (adj) double
dormire [dohr-mee-reh] to sleep
dottore [doh-ttoh-reh] (m) doctor
dovere [doh-veh-reh] (m) to have to, must
dubbio [doo-byoh] doubt; **senza dubbio** [sehn-tzah doo-byoh] without a doubt
dubbioso [doo-byoh-soh] doubtful
dubitare di qlcu [doo-bee-tah-reh] to doubt someone
due [doo-eh] two; **due volte** [doo-eh vohl-teh] twice, two times; **tutti e due** [too-ttee eh doo-eh] both

dunque [doon-kweh] also
durante [doo-rahn-teh] *(prep)* during
durare [doo-rah-reh] to last
durata [doo-rah-tah] duration, length
durezza [doo-reh-tzah] hardness
duro [doo-roh] hard

E

e [eh] and; **e così via** [eh koh-see vee-ah] and so on
eccellente [eh-cheh-llehn-teh] excellent
eccessivo [eh-cheh-ssee-voh] excessive
eccetera [eh-cheh-teh-rah] etcetera
eccetto [eh-cheh-ttoh] except, but
eccezione [eh-cheh-tzyoh-neh] *(f)* exception
economico [eh-koh-noh-mee-koh] economical, cheap
edicola (dei giornali) [eh-dee-koh-lah (deh-ee johr-nah-lee)] kiosk, newspaper stand
edificio [eh-dee-fee-choh] building
educazione [eh-doo-kah-tsyoh-neh] *(f)* upbringing
effetto [eh-ffeh-ttoh] effect
efficace [eh-ffee-kah-cheh] effective
elenco [eh-lehn-koh] phone book
elettrico [eh-leh-ttree-koh] electric
emancipato [oh-mahn-chee-pah-toh] emancipated
ente per il turismo [ehn-teh pehr eel too-ree-smoh] *(m)* tourist organization
entrare [ehn-trah-reh] to enter
entrata [ehn-trah-tah] entrata
entro [ehn-troh] *(time)* within, in
entusiasta (di) [ehn-too-syah-stah (dee)] enthusiastic (about)
equipaggio [eh-kwee-pah-djoh] crew
equivalente [eh-kwee-vah-lehn-teh] *(m/adj)* equivalent
erroneamente [eh-rroh-neh-ah-mehn-teh] by mistake
errore [eh-rroh-reh] *(m)* mistake
esagerato [eh-sah-jeh-rah-toh] exaggerated
esame [eh-zah-moh] *(m)* exam(ination)
esaminare [eh-zah-mee-nah-reh] to examine
esaurito [eh-sah-oo-ree-toh] sold out, out of stock
escluso [eh-skloo-zoh] excepted, excluded
eseguire [eh-seh-gwee-reh] to carry out
esempio [eh-sehm-pyoh] example; **per esempio** [pehr eh-sehm pyoh] for example

esente da dazio [eh-sehn-teh dah dah-tzyoh] tax-free
esercitare [eh-sehr-chee-tah-reh] to exercise, to carry on
esercizio [eh-sehr-chee-tzyoh] exercise
esigere [eh-see-jeh-reh] to require
esitare [eh-see-tah-reh] to hesitate
esperienza [eh-speh-ryehn-tzah] experience
esperto [eh-spehr-toh] *(adj)* expert
esportare [eh-spohr-tah-reh] to export
espressamente [eh-spreh-ssah-mehn-teh] expressly
espressione [eh-spreh-ssyoh-neh] *(f)* expression
essere [eh-sseh-reh] to be; **essere capace di** [eh-sseh-reh kah-pah-cheh dee] to be capable of; **essere contrario** [eh-sseh-reh kohn-trah-ryoh] to be against; **essere costituito da** [eh-sseh-reh koh-stee-too-ee-toh dah] to consist of; **essere deciso** [eh-sseh-reh deh-chee-soh] to be decided; **essere favorevole** [eh-sseh-reh fah-voh-reh-voh-leh] to be favorable; **essere obbligato** [eh-sseh-reh oh-blee-ghah-toh] to be obliged; **essere presente** [eh-sseh-reh preh-sehn-teh] to be present; **essere pubblicato** [eh-sseh-roh poo-blee-kah-toh] to be published; **essere spiacente** [eh-sseh-reh spyah-chehn-teh] to be sorry
est [ehst] *(m)* east
estendersi [eh-stehn-dehr-see] to stretch
esteriore [eh-steh-ryoh-reh] outside
esterno [eh-stehr-noh] exterior
estero [eh-steh-roh] foreign; **all'estero** [ah-lleh-steh-roh] abroad
estintore [eh-steen-toh-reh] *(m)* fire extinguisher
età [eh-tah] age
Europa [eh-oo-roh-pah] Europe
europeo [eh-oo-roh-peh-oh] European
europeo/europea [eh-oo-roh-peh-oh/eh-oo-roh-peh-ah] European (person)
eventualmente [eh-vehn-twahl-mehn-teh] *(adv)* eventually
evitare [eh-vee-tah-reh] to avoid

F

fabbrica [fah-bree-kah] factory
faccenda [fah-chehn-dah] business
facchino [fah-kkee-noh] porter
facile [fah-chee-leh] easy
falso [fahl-soh] false

fame [<u>fah</u>-meh] *(f)* hunger; **avere fame** [ah-<u>veh</u>-reh <u>fah</u>-meh] to be hungry
famiglia [fah-<u>mee</u>-lyah] family
famoso [fah-<u>moh</u>-soh] famous
fango [<u>fahn</u>-ghoh] mud
fare [<u>fah</u>-reh] to do, to make; **far benzina** [fahr behn-<u>zee</u>-nah] to fill up the tank; **fare colazione** [<u>fah</u>-reh koh-lah-<u>tzyoh</u>-neh] *(f)* to have breakfast; **fare contrabbando** [<u>fah</u>-reh kohn-trah-<u>bahn</u>-doh] to smuggle; **fare escursioni** [<u>fah</u>-reh eh-skoor-<u>syoh</u>-nee] to take an excursion; **far fare** [fahr fah-reh] to have (something) done; **far lezione** [fahr leh-<u>tzyoh</u>-neh] to have a lesson/class; **far male** [fahr <u>mah</u>-leh] to hurt; **far visita a qlcu** [fahr <u>vee</u>-see-tah ah kwahl-<u>koo</u>-noh] to visit someone; **fare gli auguri** [<u>fah</u>-reh lyee ah-oo-<u>goo</u>-ree] to give best wishes; **fare la barba** [<u>fah</u>-reh lah <u>bahr</u>-bah] to shave; **fare la conoscenza di qlcu** [<u>fah</u>-reh lah koh-noh-<u>shehn</u>-tzah dee kwahl-<u>koo</u>-noh] to meet; **fare la coda** [<u>fah</u>-re lah <u>koh</u>-dah] to line up; **fare la spesa** [<u>fah</u>-reh lah <u>spe</u>-sah] to do the shopping; **fare le valigie** [<u>fah</u>-reh leh vah-<u>lee</u>-jeh] to pack; **fare una passeggiata** [<u>fah</u>-reh <u>oo</u>-nah pah-sseh-<u>djah</u>-tah] to take a walk
faro [<u>fah</u>-roh] headlight
fasciatura [fah-shah-<u>too</u>-rah] bandage
faticoso [fah-tee-<u>koh</u>-soh] tiring
fatto [<u>fah</u>-ttoh] fact, deed; **fatto a mano** [<u>fah</u>-ttoh ah <u>mah</u>-oh] handmade
fattoria [fah-tto-<u>ree</u>-ah] farm
favore [fah-<u>voh</u>-reh] *(m)* favor; **a favore (di)** [ah fah-<u>voh</u>-reh (dee)] in favor of; **per favore** [pehr fah-<u>voh</u>-reh] please
favorevole [fah-voh-<u>reh</u>-voh-leh] favorable
fazzoletto [fah-tzoh-<u>leh</u>-ttoh] handkerchief
fede [<u>feh</u>-deh] *(f)* faith
fedele [feh-<u>deh</u>-leh] faithful
felice [feh-<u>lee</u>-cheh] happy
felicità [feh-lee-chee-<u>tah</u>] happiness
femminile [feh-mmee-<u>nee</u>-leh] feminine
ferie [<u>feh</u>-ryeh] *(pl)* holidays, vacation; **andare in ferie** [ahn-<u>dah</u>-reh een <u>feh</u>-ryeh] to go on vacation
ferito/ferita [feh-<u>ree</u>-toh/feh-<u>ree</u>-tah] wounded
fermare [fehr-<u>mah</u>-reh] *(mech)* to stop
fermarsi [fehr-<u>mahr</u>-see] to stop
fermata (d'autobus) [fehr-<u>mah</u>-tah (<u>dah</u>-oo-toh-boos)] bus stop

fermo [<u>fehr</u>-moh] firm
feroce [feh-<u>roh</u>-cheh] ferocious
ferro [<u>feh</u>-rroh] iron; **ferro da stiro** [<u>feh</u>-rroh dah <u>stee</u>-roh] iron *(appliance)*
festa [<u>feh</u>-stah] party
fetta [<u>feh</u>-ttah] slice
fiamma [<u>fyah</u>-mmah] flame
fiammifero [fyah-<u>mmee</u>-feh-roh] match
fidanzarsi con [fee-dahn-<u>tzahr</u>-see kohn] to be engaged to
fidanzata [fee-dahn-<u>tzah</u>-tah] fiancée
fidanzato [fee-dahn-<u>tzah</u>-toh] fiancé
fidarsi di [fee-<u>dahr</u>-see dee] to trust; **non fidarsi di qlco/qlcu** [nohn fee-<u>dahr</u>-see dee kwahl-<u>koh</u>-sah/kwahl-<u>koo</u>-noh] to mistrust something/someone
fidato [fee-<u>dah</u>-toh] trustworthy
fiducia [fee-<u>doo</u>-chah] trust
fiducioso [fee-doo-<u>choh</u>-soh] trusting
fiera [<u>fyeh</u>-rah] fair
figlia [<u>fee</u>-lyah] daughter
figlio [<u>fee</u>-lyoh] son
fila [<u>fee</u>-lah] line; **fare la coda** [<u>fah</u>-reh la <u>koh</u>-dah] to line up
filiale [fee-<u>lyah</u>-leh] *(f)* branch (office)
film [feelm] *(m)* film
filo [<u>fee</u>-loh] thread, wire
filtro [<u>feel</u>-troh] filter
finale [fee-<u>nah</u>-leh] *(m)* last, final
finalmente [fee-nahl-<u>mehn</u>-teh] finally
fine [<u>fee</u>-neh] *(f)* end; **alla fine** [<u>ah</u>-llah <u>fee</u>-neh] in the end, at last
finire [fee-<u>nee</u>-reh] to finish, to end
finito [fee-<u>nee</u>-toh] finished
fino a [<u>fee</u>-noh ah] until
finora [fee-<u>noh</u>-rah] till now
fiore [<u>fyoh</u>-reh] *(m)* flower
fiorire [fyoh-<u>ree</u>-reh] to bloom
firma [<u>feer</u>-mah] signature
firmare [feer-<u>mah</u>-reh] to sign
fisso [<u>fee</u>-ssoh] fixed *(price)*
fitto [<u>fee</u>-ttoh] rent
fiume [<u>fyoo</u>-meh] *(m)* river
flash [flehsh] *(m)* *(photo)* flash
flirt [flehrt] *(m)* flirt
fodera [<u>foh</u>-deh-rah] lining
foglia [<u>foh</u>-lyah] leaf
foglio [<u>foh</u>-lyoh] sheet of paper
folla [<u>foh</u>-llah] crowd
fontana [fohn-<u>tah</u>-nah] fountain
fonte [<u>fohn</u>-teh] *(f)* spring *(water)*
foraggio [foh-<u>rah</u>-djoh] fodder
forbici [<u>fohr</u>-bee-chee] *(pl)* scissors
forestiero/forestiera [foh-reh-<u>styeh</u>-roh/foh-reh-<u>styeh</u>-rah] foreigner

forfait [fohr-<u>feh</u>] *(m)* lump sum

forma [<u>fohr</u>-mah] form, shape; **in forma** [een <u>fohr</u>-mah] fit

formare [fohr-<u>mah</u>-reh] to form; **formare il numero** [fohr-<u>mah</u>-reh eel <u>noo</u>-meh-roh] *(tel)* to dial the number

formato [fohr-<u>mah</u>-toh] format, size

formazione [fohr-mah-tzyoh-neh] *(f)* training

formulario [fohr-moo-lah-ryoh] formulary

fornello a spirito [fohr-<u>neh</u>-lloh ah <u>spee</u>-ree-toh] kerosene stove

fornire [fohr-<u>nee</u>-reh] to supply

forse [<u>fohr</u>-seh] perhaps, maybe

forte [<u>fohr</u>-teh] strong

fortuna [fohr-<u>too</u>-nah] luck

fortunato [fohr-too-<u>nah</u>-toh] lucky

forza [<u>fohr</u>-tzah] strength

forzare [fohr-<u>tzah</u>-reh] to force

foto [<u>foh</u>-toh] *(f)* photo, snapshot

fotografare [foh-toh-ghrah-<u>fah</u>-reh] to photograph

fotografia [foh-toh-ghrah-<u>fee</u>-ah] photograph

foulard [foo-<u>lahr</u>] scarf

fra [frah] between, among; **fra l'altro** [frah <u>lahl</u>-troh] among other things; **fra una settimana** [frah oo-nah seh-ttee-<u>mah</u>-nah] (with)in a week

fragile [<u>frah</u>-jee-leh] weak, fragile

fraintendere [frah-een-<u>tehn</u>-deh-reh] to misunderstand

francobollo [frah-koh-<u>boh</u>-lloh] stamp

frase [<u>frah</u>-seh] *(f)* sentence

fratello [frah-<u>teh</u>-lloh] brother

frattanto [frah-<u>ttahn</u>-toh] meanwhile

freddo [<u>freh</u>-ddoh] cold; **aver freddo** [ah-<u>vehr</u> <u>freh</u>-ddoh] to be cold *(person)*

fresco [<u>freh</u>-skoh] fresh, cool

fretta [<u>freh</u>-ttah] haste; **in fretta** [een <u>freh</u>-ttah] *(adv)* in a hurry

frettoloso [freh-ttoh-<u>loh</u>-soh] hasty, hurried

friggere [<u>free</u>-djeh-reh] to fry

frode [<u>froh</u>-deh] *(f)* fraud

fronte [<u>frohn</u>-teh] *(f)* forehead; **di fronte a** [dee frohn-teh ah] opposite

frontiera [frohn-<u>tyeh</u>-rah] border

fulmine [<u>fool</u>-mee-neh] *(m)* lightning

fumare [foo-<u>mah</u>-roh] to smoke

fumo [<u>foo</u>-moh] smoke

funzionare [foon-tzyoh-<u>nah</u>-reh] to work, to function

fuochi d'artificio [<u>fwoh</u>-kee dahr-tee-<u>fee</u>-choh] *(pl)* fireworks

fuoco [<u>fwoh</u>-koh] fire

fuori (di) [<u>fwoh</u>-ree (dee)] outside; **dal di fuori** [dahl dee <u>fwoh</u>-ree] from outside; **fuori stagione** [<u>fwoh</u>-ree stah-<u>joh</u>-neh] off season; **fuori moda** [<u>fwoh</u>-ree <u>moh</u>-dah] unfashionable, passé

furbo [<u>foor</u>-boh] cunning

futuro [foo-<u>too</u>-roh] futuro

G

gabbiano [ghah-<u>byah</u>-noh] seagull

gabinetto [ghah-bee-<u>neh</u>-ttoh] toilet, closet

galleria [ghah-lleh-<u>ree</u>-ah] gallery, tunnel

gallo [<u>ghah</u>-lloh] rooster

gancio [<u>ghahn</u>-choh] hook; **gancio (dell'attaccapanni)** [<u>ghahn</u>-choh deh-llah-ttah-kkah-<u>pah</u>-nnee] clothes hanger

garage [ghah-<u>rahj</u>] *(m)* garage

garanzia [ghah-rahn-<u>tzee</u>-ah] guarantee

gatta/gatto [<u>ghah</u>-ttoh/<u>ghah</u>-ttah] cat

gelato [jeh-<u>lah</u>-toh] ice cream

generale [jeh-neh-<u>rah</u>-leh] general; **in generale** [een jeh-neh-<u>rah</u>-leh] usually

generalità [jeh-neh-rah-lee-<u>tah</u>] *(pl)* generality

genitori [jeh-nee-<u>toh</u>-ree] *(pl)* parents

gente [<u>jehn</u>-toh] *(f)* people

gentile [john-<u>tee</u>-leh] kind

gentilezza [jehn-tee-<u>leh</u>-tzah] kindness

gesso [<u>jeh</u>-ssoh] chalk

gettare [jeh-<u>ttah</u>-reh] to throw

getto d'acqua [<u>jeh</u>-ttoh dah-kwah] waterfall

ghiaccio [<u>ghyah</u>-choh] ice

già [jah] already

giardino [jahr-<u>dee</u>-noh] garden; **giardino pubblico** [jahr-<u>dee</u>-noh poo-blee-koh] public garden, park

giù [joo] down; **in giù** [een joo] downwards

giocare [joh-<u>kah</u>-reh] to play *(sport, game)*

giocattolo [joh-<u>kah</u>-ttoh-loh] toy

gioia [<u>joh</u>-yah] joy

giornalaio [johr-nah-<u>lah</u>-yoh] news vendor/agent

giornale [johr-<u>nah</u>-leh] *(m)* newspaper

giorno [<u>johr</u>-noh] day; **di giorno** [dee <u>johr</u>-noh] by day; **giorno festivo** [<u>johr</u>-noh feh-<u>stee</u>-voh] holiday; **nei giorni feriali** [<u>neh</u>-ee <u>johr</u>-nee feh-<u>ryah</u>-lee] (on) workdays

giovane [<u>joh</u>-vah-neh] young; **i giovani** [ee <u>joh</u>-vah-nee] *(pl)* young people

A/Z

gioventù [joh-vehn-<u>too</u>] *(f)* youth
giradischi [jee-rah-<u>dee</u>-skee] *(m)* record player
girare [jee-<u>rah</u>-reh] to tour
giro [<u>jee</u>-roh] stroll, tour
gita [<u>jee</u>-tah] trip, excursion
giudicare [joo-dee-<u>kah</u>-reh] to judge
giudizio [joo-<u>dee</u>-tzyoh] judgment
giusto [<u>joo</u>-stoh] just, fair
(gli) avanzi [lyee ah-<u>vahn</u>-tzee] leftovers
goccia [<u>ghoh</u>-chah] drop
gocciolare [ghoh-choh-<u>lah</u>-reh] to drip
godere [ghoh-<u>deh</u>-reh] to enjoy
godimento [ghoh-dee-<u>mehn</u>-toh] enjoyment
golfo [<u>ghohl</u>-foh] gulf
gomma da masticare [ghoh-<u>mmah</u> dah mah-stee-<u>kah</u>-reh] chewing gum
gonfiare [ghohn-<u>fyah</u>-reh] to pump up
gonfio [<u>ghohn</u>-fyoh] inflated
governo [ghoh-<u>vehr</u>-noh] government
grado [<u>ghrah</u>-doh] degree, rank
grande [<u>ghrahn</u>-deh] big, great, large
grandezza [ghrahn-<u>deh</u>-tzah] greatness, bigness
grandioso [ghran-<u>dyoh</u>-soh] grandiose
grasso [<u>ghrah</u>-ssoh] *(person)* fat
gratis [<u>ghra</u>-tees] free
grato [<u>ghrah</u>-toh] grateful
grattacielo [ghrah-ttah-<u>cheh</u>-loh] skyscraper
gratuito [ghrah-<u>too-ee</u>-toh] free
grave [<u>ghrah</u>-veh] heavy, serious
gravida [<u>ghrah</u>-vee-dah] pregnant
grazie [<u>ghrah</u>-tzyeh] thank you; **grazie a Dio!** [<u>ghrah</u>-tzyeh ah <u>dee</u>-oh] Thank God!
grazioso [ghrah-<u>tzyoh</u>-soh] pretty, graceful
gridare [ghree-<u>dah</u>-reh] to shout
grosso [<u>ghroh</u>-ssoh] big, large
grossolano [ghroh-ssoh-<u>lah</u>-noh] coarse
gruppo [<u>ghroo</u>-ppoh] group
guadagnare [gwah-dah-<u>nyah</u>-reh] to earn
guadagno [gwah-<u>dah</u>-nyoh] gain, earnings
guardare [gwahr-<u>dah</u>-reh] to look (at)
guardiano [gwahr-<u>dyah</u>-noh] keeper
guasto [<u>gwah</u>-stoh] waste
guerra [<u>gweh</u>-rrah] war
guida [<u>gwee</u>-dah] *(f)* guide; **guida** *(f)* tourist guidebook
guidare [gwee-<u>dah</u>-reh] to guide, to drive
gusto [<u>ghoo</u>-stoh] taste

H

hobby [<u>oh</u>-bee] *(m)* hobby
hotel [oh-<u>tehl</u>] *(m)* hotel

I

idea [ee-<u>deh</u>-ah] idea; **non ne ho idea!** [nohn neh oh ee-<u>deh</u>-ah] I have no idea!
illuminato [ee-lloo-mee-<u>nah</u>-toh] lit up
illustrazione [ee-lloo-mee-nah-<u>tzyoh</u>-neh] *(f)* illustration
imballaggio [eem-bah-<u>llah</u>-djoh] wrapping
imballare [eem-bah-<u>llah</u>-reh] to wrap
imboccatura [eem-boh-kkah-<u>too</u>-rah] entrance
imbrogliare [eem-broh-<u>lyah</u>-reh] to swindle, to cheat
imbroglione [eem-<u>broh</u>-lyoh-neh] *(m)* swindler
imbucare [eem-boo-<u>kah</u>-reh] to post
immediatamente [ee-mmeh-dyah-tah-<u>mehn</u>-teh] *(adv)* immediately
immediato [ee-mmeh-<u>dyah</u>-toh] *(adj)* immediate
immondizia [ee-mmohn-<u>dee</u>-tzyah] trash
impacco [eem-<u>pah</u>-kkoh] *(med)* compress
imparare [eem-pah-<u>rah</u>-reh] to learn
imparentato [eem-pah-<u>rehn</u>-tah-toh] related
impedire [eem-peh-<u>dee</u>-reh] to hinder, to prevent
impianto [eem-<u>pyahn</u>-toh] plant, installation
impiegare [eem-pyeh-<u>ghah</u>-reh] *(time)* to spend, to use
impiego [eem-<u>pyeh</u>-ghoh] employment, job
importante [eem-pohr-<u>tahn</u>-teh] important; **poco importante** [<u>poh</u>-koh eem-pohr-<u>tahn</u>-teh] unimportant
importanza [eem-pohr-<u>tahn</u>-tzah] importance
importazione [eem-pohr-tah-<u>tzyoh</u>-neh] *(f)* importation, import
importo [eem-<u>pohr</u>-toh] amount; **importo forfettario** [eem-<u>pohr</u>-toh fohr-feh-<u>ttah</u>-ryoh] lump sum
impossibile [eem-poh-<u>ssee</u>-bee-leh] impossible
imprecare [eem-pre-<u>kah</u>-reh] to curse
impreciso [eem-preh-<u>chee</u>-soh] imprecise
impresa [eem-<u>preh</u>-sah] enterprise
impressione [eem-preh-<u>ssyoh</u>-neh] *(f)* impression
improbabile [eem-proh-<u>bah</u>-bee-leh] improbable
improvviso [eem-proh-<u>vvee</u>-soh] sudden; **all'improvviso** [ah-lleem-proh-<u>vvee</u>-soh] suddenly
imprudente [eem-proo-<u>dehn</u>-teh] unwise

impugnatura [eem-poo-nyah-<u>too</u>-rah] handle

in [een] in; **in Francia** [een <u>frahn</u>-chah] in France; **in italiano** [een ee-tah-<u>lyah</u>-noh] in Italian; **in viaggio** [een vyah-djoh] on a trip, traveling

inadatto [ee-nah-<u>dah</u>-ttoh] unsuitable

inalterabile [ee-nahl-teh-<u>rah</u>-bee-leh] unchangeable

inaspettato [ee-nah-speh-<u>ttah</u>-toh] unexpected

incantato [een-kahn-<u>tah</u>-toh] enchanted

incantevole [een-kahn-<u>teh</u>-voh-leh] charming

incapace [een-kah-<u>pah</u>-cheh] incapable

incendio [een-<u>chehn</u>-dyoh] fire

incerto [een-<u>chehr</u>-toh] uncertain

incidente [een-chee-<u>dehn</u>-teh] (*m*) accident; **avere un incidente** [ah-<u>veh</u>-reh oon een-chee-<u>dehn</u>-teh] to have an accident

incidere [een-<u>chee</u>-deh-reh] to engrave, to cut

incinta [een-<u>cheen</u>-tah] pregnant

includere [een-<u>kloo</u>-deh-reh] to include

incompiuto [een-kohm-<u>pyoo</u>-toh] unfinished

incompleto [een-kohm-<u>pleh</u>-toh] incomplete

incontrare [een-kohn-<u>trah</u>-reh] to meet

inconveniente [een-kohn-veh-<u>nyehn</u>-teh] (*m*) inconvenient

incredibile [een-kreh-<u>dee</u>-bee-leh] incredible

incrocio [een-<u>kroh</u>-choh] (*street*) crossing, crossroad

indecente [een-deh-<u>chen</u>-teh] indecent

indeciso [en-deh-<u>chee</u>-soh] undecided

indennizzo [een-deh-<u>nnee</u>-zoh] indemnity

indesiderato [een-deh-see-deh-<u>rah</u>-toh] undesired

indeterminato [een-deh-tehr-mee-<u>nah</u>-toh] indeterminate

indicare [een-dee-<u>kah</u>-reh] to indicate, to show, to point

indicazione [een-dee-kah-<u>tzyoh</u>-neh] (*f*) information, direction

indietro [een-<u>dyeh</u>-troh] behind; **all'indietro** [ah-llen-<u>dyeh</u>-troh] backwards

indigeno [een-dee-<u>jeh</u>-noh] native

indirizzare [een-dee-ree-<u>tzah</u>-reh] to address

indirizzo [een-dee-<u>ree</u>-tzoh] address

indispensabile [een-dee-spehn-<u>sah</u>-bee-leh] essential

indisposto [een-dee-<u>spoh</u>-stoh] indisposed, unwell

indizio [een-<u>dee</u>-tzyoh] indication, sign

indovinare [een-doh-vee-<u>nah</u>-reh] to guess

inesperto [ee-neh-<u>spehr</u>-toh] inexperienced

inevitabile [ee-neh-vee-<u>tah</u>-bee-leh] inevitable

infastidire [een-fah-stee-<u>dee</u>-reh] to annoy

infatti [een-<u>fah</u>-ttee] in fact

infelice [een-feh-<u>lee</u>-cheh] unhappy

inferiore [een-feh-<u>ryoh</u>-reh] inferior, lower

infermiera [een-fehr-<u>myeh</u>-rah] nurse

infiammabile [een-fyah-<u>mmah</u>-bee-leh] inflammable

informare [een-fohr-<u>mah</u>-reh] to inform; **informare qlcu di qlco** [een-fohr-<u>mah</u>-reh kwahl-<u>koo</u>-noh dee kwahl-<u>koh</u>-sah] to inform/acquaint someone

informarsi [een-fohr-<u>mahr</u>-see] to inquire

informazione [een-fohr-mah-<u>tzyoh</u>-neh] (*f*) information

infortunio [een-fohr-<u>too</u>-nyoh] accident, mishap; **avere un infortunio** [ah-<u>veh</u>-reh oo-neen-fohr-<u>too</u>-nyoh] to have an accident

inturiato [een-foo-<u>ryah</u>-toh] furious

ingannare [een-ghah-<u>nnah</u>-reh] to deceive, to fool

inganno [een-<u>ghah</u>-nnoh] deceit

ingiustizia [een-joo-<u>stee</u>-tzyah] injustice, unfairness

ingiusto [een-<u>joo</u>-stoh] unfair

inglese [een-<u>ghleh</u>-seh] English

ingrassare [een-ghrah-<u>ssah</u>-reh] to fatten, to grease

ingrato [een-<u>ghrah</u>-toh] ungrateful

ingresso [een-<u>ghreh</u>-ssoh] entrance; **ingresso principale** [een-<u>ghreh</u>-ssoh preen-chee-<u>pah</u>-leh] main entrance

iniziare [ee-nee-<u>tzyah</u>-reh] to start

inizio [ee-<u>nee</u>-tzyoh] beginning

innocente [ee-nnoh-<u>chehn</u>-teh] innocent

inoltre [ee-<u>nohl</u>-treh] besides, moreover

inquietarsi [een-kwee-eh-<u>tahr</u>-see] to worry

insegna [een-<u>seh</u>-nyah] sign

insegnare [een-seh-<u>nyah</u>-reh] to teach

insetto [een-<u>seh</u>-ttoh] insect

insicuro [een-see-<u>koo</u>-roh] insecure

insieme [een-<u>syeh</u>-meh] (*adv*) together

insistere su [een-<u>see</u>-steh-reh soo] to insist on

insolito [een-<u>soh</u>-lee-toh] unusual

insopportabile [een-soh-ppohr-<u>tah</u>-bee-leh] intolerable

instabile [een-<u>stah</u>-bee-leh] unstable
insufficiente [een-soo-ffee-<u>chehn</u>-teh] insufficient
intasato [een-tah-<u>sah</u>-toh] clogged
intelligente [een-teh-llee-<u>jehn</u>-teh] intelligent
intelligenza [een-teh-llee-<u>jehn</u>-tzah] intelligence
intendere [een-<u>tehn</u>-deh-reh] to intend
intendersi [een-<u>tehn</u>-dehr-see] to come to an agreement
intenzione [een-tehn-<u>tzyoh</u>-neh] (f) intention; **avere l'intenzione di** [ah-<u>veh</u>-reh leen-tehn-<u>tzyoh</u>-neh dee] to have the intention to
interamente [een-teh-rah-<u>mehn</u>-teh] (adv) completely
interessante [een-teh-reh-<u>ssahn</u>-teh] interesting
interessarsi (di) [een-teh-reh-<u>ssahr</u>-see (dee)] to be interested in
interesse [een-teh-<u>reh</u>-sseh] (m) interest
internazionale [een-tehr-nah-<u>tzyoh</u>-nah-leh] international
interno [een-<u>tehr</u>-noh] internal, interior
interrompere [een-teh-<u>rrohm</u>-peh-reh] to interrupt
interruttore [een-teh-rroo-<u>ttoh</u>-reh] (m) switch
interruzione [een-teh-rroo-<u>tzyoh</u>-neh] (f) interruption
intimidire [een-tee-mee-<u>dee</u>-reh] to intimidate
intorno a [een-<u>tohr</u>-noh] around, about
inutile [ee-<u>noo</u>-tee-leh] useless, unnecessary
invano [een-<u>vah</u>-noh] in vain
invece di [een-<u>veh</u>-cheh dee] instead of
inventare [een-<u>vehn</u>-tah-reh] to invent
inverso [een-<u>vehr</u>-soh] opposite, contrary
inviare [een-vee-<u>ah</u>-reh] to send, to forward
invitare [een-vee-<u>tah</u>-reh] to invite
invito [een-<u>vee</u>-toh] invitation
involtare [een-vohl-<u>tah</u>-reh] to wrap (up)
involucro [een-<u>voh</u>-loo-kroh] covering
inzuppato [een-zoo-<u>ppah</u>-toh] soaked
io [ee-oh] I
irregolare [ee-rreh-ghoh-<u>lah</u>-reh] irregular
irrequieto [ee-rreh-<u>kwyeh</u>-toh] restless
iscriversi [ee-<u>skree</u>-<u>vehr</u>-see] to enroll
isola [ee-<u>soh</u>-lah] island
istante [ee-<u>stahn</u>-teh] (m) instant, moment
istruzione [ee-stroo-<u>tzyoh</u>-neh] (f) instruction

Italia [ee-<u>tah</u>-lyah] Italy
italiano [ee-tah-<u>lyah</u>-noh] Italian; **in italiano** [een ee-tah-<u>lyah</u>-noh] in Italian
italiano/italiana [ee-tah-<u>lyah</u>-noh/ee-tah-<u>lyah</u>-nah] (adj) Italian
itinerario [ee-tee-neh-<u>rah</u>-ryoh] itinerary

L

là [lah] there; **al di là** [ahl dee lah] on the other side
laggiù [lah-djoo] down there, below, over there
lago [lah-<u>ghoh</u>] lake
lamentarsi (di) [lah-mehn-<u>tahr</u>-see (dee)] to complain about
lampada [<u>lahm</u>-pah-dah] lamp
lampadina [lahm-pah-<u>dee</u>-nah] light bulb
lampeggiare [lahm-peh-<u>djah</u>-reh] (auto) to blink (lights)
lancio [<u>lahn</u>-choh] throw
largo [<u>lahr</u>-ghoh] broad, wide
lasciare [lah-<u>shah</u>-reh] to leave; **lasciar detto** [lah-shahr deh-ttoh] to leave word
lassù [lah-<u>ssoo</u>] up there
lato [<u>lah</u>-toh] side
lavanderia a secco [lah-vahn-deh-<u>ree</u>-ah ah <u>seh</u>-kkoh] drycleaner's
lavare [lah-<u>vah</u>-reh] to wash
lavorare [lah-voh-<u>rah</u>-reh] to work
lavoro [lah-<u>voh</u>-roh] work
leale [leh-<u>ah</u>-leh] loyal, fair
legare [leh-<u>ghah</u>-reh] to tie (up)
leggere [<u>leh</u>-djeh-reh] to read
leggero [leh-<u>djeh</u>-roh] light (weight)
legna [<u>leh</u>-nyah] firewood
legno [<u>leh</u>-nyoh] wood
Lei [<u>leh</u>-ee] (pol) you; **lei** [<u>leh</u>-ee] she, her
lentamente [lehn-tah-<u>mehn</u>-teh] slowly
lento [<u>lehn</u>-toh] (adj) slow
lettera [<u>leh</u>-tteh-rah] letter
letto [<u>leh</u>-ttoh] bed
lezione [leh-<u>tzyoh</u>-neh] (f) lesson
lì [lee] there
libero [<u>lee</u>-beh-roh] free
libro [<u>lee</u>-broh] book
lieto (di) [<u>lyeh</u>-toh (dee)] happy to
lieve [<u>lyeh</u>-veh] light, slight
linea [<u>lee</u>-neh-ah] line; **linea aerea** [<u>lee</u>-neh-ah ah-<u>eh</u>-reh-ah] airline; **linea ferroviaria** [<u>lee</u>-neh-ah feh-rroh-<u>vyah</u>-ryah] railroad
lingua [<u>leen</u>-gwah] tongue
liquido [<u>lee</u>-kwee-doh] liquid
liscio [<u>lee</u>-shoh] smooth

lista [lee-stah] list
lite [lee-teh] (f) quarrel
litigare [lee-tee-ghah-reh] to quarrel
locale [loh-kah-leh] (m) local
località [loh-kah-lee-tah] locality; **località marittima** [loh-kah-lee-tah mah-ree-ttee-mah] seaside location
lodare [loh-dah-reh] to praise
logico [loh-jee-koh] logical
lontananza [lohn-tah-nahn-tzah] distance
lontano [lohn-tah-noh] distant, remote
loro [loh-roh] (pl) them, they, (pol) you
luccicare [loo-chee-kah-reh] to shine, to sparkle
luce [loo-cheh] (f) light
lui [loo-ee] him, he
luna [loo-nah] moon
lunghezza [loon-gheh-tzah] length
lungo [loon-ghoh] long
luogo [lwoh-ghoh] place; **luogo di nascita** [lwoh-ghoh dee nah-shee-tah] birthplace; **aver luogo** [ah-veh-reh lwoh-ghoh] to take place; **in quel luogo** [een kwehl lwoh-ghoh] in this place
lusso [loo-ssoh] luxury
lussuoso [loo-sswoh-soh] luxurious

M

ma [mah] but
macchia [mah-kkyah] spot
macchina [mah-kkee-nah] car
macchina fotografica [mah-kkee-nah foh-toh-ghrah-fee-kah] camera
madre [mah-dreh] (f) mother
magari [mah-ghah-ree] if only
magazzino [mah-ghah-zee-noh] store; **grandi magazzini** [ghrahn-dee mah-ghah-zee-nee] department stores
magnifico [mah-nyee-fee-koh] magnificent
magro [mah-ghroh] thin
mai [mah-ee] never
malato [mah-lah-toh] sick
male [mah-leh] (adv) badly; **mi sento male** [mee sehn-toh mah-leh] I don't feel well
malgrado [mahl-ghrah-doh] in spite of
malinteso [mah-leen-teh-soh] misunderstanding
malsano [mahl-sah-noh] unhealthy
malvagio [mahl-vah-joh] wicked
malvolentieri [mahl-voh-lehn-tyeh-ree] unwillingly

mancanza [mahn-kahn-tzah] lack
mancare [mahn-kah-reh] to miss, to lack
mandare [mahn-dah-reh] to send; **mandar via** [mahn-dahr vee-ah] to send away, to dismiss; **mandare a prendere** [mahn-dah-reh ah prehn-deh-reh] to send for
mangiare [mahn-jah-reh] to eat
mangime [mahn-jee-meh] (m) fodder
maniera [mah-nyeh-rah] manner, fashion
manifestazione [mah-nee-feh-stah-tzyoh-neh] (f) display, event, performance
manifesto [mah-nee-feh-stoh] pamphlet
mano [mah-noh] (f) hand
marca [mahr-kah] brand
marcia [mahr-chah] (auto) gear
marcio [mahr-choh] rotten
mare [mah-reh] (m) sea
marito [mah-ree-toh] husband
marrone [mah-rroh-neh] brown
martello [mahr-teh-lloh] hammer
maschile [mah-skee-leh] masculine
massimo [mah-ssee-moh] maximum; **al massimo** [ahl mah-ssee-moh] at the most
materiale [mah-teh-ryah-leh] (m) material
matrimonio [mah-tree-moh-nyoh] marriage
mattina [mah-ttee-nah] morning; **di mattina** [dee mah-ttee-nah], **al mattino** [ahl mah-ttee-nh] in the morning
maturo [mah-too-roh] ripe
mazzo [mah-tzoh] bunch
me [meh] me; **a me** [ah meh] to me
mediatore [meh-dyah-toh-rch] (m) broker, agent
medicina [meh-dee-chee-nah] medicine
medio [meh-dyoh] (adj) middle; **in media** [een meh-dyah] (adv) on the average
Mediterraneo [meh-dee-teh-rrah-neh-oh] Mediterranean
medusa [moh doo-sah] jelly fish
meglio [meh-lyoh] better; **meglio che/di** [meh-lyoh keh/dee] better than
menù [meh-noo] (m) menu
meno [meh-noh] minus, less; **di meno** [dee meh-noh] less, fewer; **il meno** [eel meh-noh] the least; **per lo meno** [pehr loh meh-noh] at least
mensile [mehn-see-leh] monthly
mentre [mehn-treh] (conj) while
meravigliarsi di [meh-rah-vee-lyahr-see] to be amazed

A/Z

meraviglioso [meh-rah-vee-lyoh-soh] wonderful

mercato [mehr-kah-toh] market; **a buon mercato** [ah bwohn mehr-kah-toh] cheap

merce [mehr-cheh] *(f)* merchandise

meridionale [meh-ree-dyoh-nah-leh] southern

meritare [meh-ree-tah-reh] to deserve

merito [meh-ree-toh] merit

merletto [mehr-leh-ttoh] lace

mese [meh-seh] *(m)* month

messa [meh-ssah] *(rel)* mass

meta [meh-tah] goal

metà [meh-tah] half

mettere [meh-tteh-reh] to put, to put on; **mettere in comunicazione** [meh-tteh-reh een koh-moo-nee-kah-tzyoh-neh] *(tel)* to connect

mettersi [meh-ttehr-see] to place oneself; **mettersi in cammino** [meh-ttehr-see een kah-mmee-noh] to go walking; **mettersi in moto** [meh-ttehr-see een moh-toh] to start the car

mezzanotte [meh-zah-noh-tteh] midnight; **a mezzanotte** [ah meh-zah-noh-tteh] at midnight

mezzo [meh-zoh] half, middle

mezzogiorno [meh-zoh-johr-noh] midday, noon; **a mezzogiorno** [ah meh-zoh-johr-noh] at noon

mi [mee] me, to me

migliorare [mee-lyoh-rah-reh] to improve

migliore [mee-lyoh-reh] *(m/f)* best

minuto [mee-noo-toh] minute

mio [mee-oh] my; **da parte mia** [dah pahr-teh mee-ah] on my part

misto [mee-stoh] mixed

misura [mee-soo-rah] *(shoe)* measurement

misurare [mee-soo-rah-reh] to measure

mite [mee-teh] mild

mobile [moh-bee-leh] *(m) (piece)* furniture

moda [moh-dah] fashion

modello [moh-deh-lloh] model

moderato [moh-deh-rah-toh] moderate

moderno [moh-dehr-noh] modern

modificare [moh-dee-fee-kah-reh] to modify

modo [moh-doh] way; *(pl)* manners

modulo [moh-doo-loh] form

moglie [moh-lyeh] *(f)* wife

molla [moh-llah] spring

molo [moh-loh] dock

molto [mohl-toh] much, very; *(pl)* many;

molto lieto/a [mohl-toh lyeh-toh/ah] very happy; **mucchio di** [moo-kkyoh dee] a lot

momento [moh-mehn-toh] moment; **al momento** [ahl moh-mehn-toh] at the moment

monaca [moh-nah-kah] nun

mondo [mohn-doh] world

moneta [moh-neh-tah] coin

monte [mohn-teh] *(m)* mountain

morbido [mohr-bee-doh] soft, delicate

mordere [mohr-deh-reh] to bite

morire [moh-ree-reh] to die

morte [mohr-teh] *(f)* death

morto [mohr-toh] dead

mosca [moh-skah] fly

mosso [moh-ssoh] *(sea)* rough

mostra [moh-strah] show, exhibit

mostrare [moh-strah-reh] to show

motivo [moh-tee-voh] reason; **per questo motivo** [pehr kweh-stoh moh-tee-voh] for this reason

movimento [moh-vee-mehn-toh] movement

mucca [moo-kkah] cow

multa [mool-tah] fine

multicolore [mool-tee-koh-loh-reh] multicolored

muovere [mwoh-veh-reh] to move

musica [moo-see-kah] music

N

nascita [nah-shee-tah] birth

nascondere [nah-skohn-deh-reh] to hide; **di nascosto** [dee nah-skoh-stoh] *(adv)* secretly

nastro [nah-stroh] ribbon

nativo di [nah-tee-voh dee] native of, from

nato [nah-toh] born

natura [nah-too-rah] nature

naturale [nah-too-rah-leh] *(adj)* natural

naturalmente [nah-too-rahl-mehn-teh] *(adv)* naturally

nazione [nah-tzyoh-neh] *(f)* nation

né … né [neh.....neh] neither ... nor

nebbioso [neh-byoh-soh] foggy

necessario [neh-cheh-ssah-ryoh] necessary; **non necessario** [nohn neh-cheh-ssah-ryoh] unnecessary

necessità [neh-cheh-ssee-tah] necessity

negare [neh-gah-reh] to deny

negativo [neh-ghah-tee-voh] negative

negligente [neh-ghlee-jehn-teh] negligent

negozio [neh-<u>ghoh</u>-tzyoh] store
neonato [neh-oh-<u>nah</u>-toh] newborn
neppure [neh-<u>ppoo</u>-reh] neither, nor
nervoso [nehr-<u>voh</u>-soh] nervous
nessuno [neh-<u>ssoo</u>-noh] no one; **in nessun caso** [een neh-<u>ssoon</u> kah-soh] in no way; **in nessun luogo** [een neh-<u>ssoon</u> lwoh ghoh] nowhere
nevicare [neh-vee-<u>kah</u>-reh] to snow
niente [<u>nyehn</u>-teh] nothing; **nient'altro che** [nyehn-<u>tahl</u>-troh keh] nothing but; **nient'altro** [nyehn-<u>tahl</u>-troh] nothing else; **per niente** [pehr <u>nyehn</u>-teh] for nothing
nipote [nee-<u>poh</u>-teh] *(m/f)* nephew, niece
nodo [<u>noh</u>-doh] knot
noi [<u>noh</u>-ee] we, us; **a noi** [ah <u>noh</u>-ee] to us
noioso [noh-<u>yoh</u>-soh] annoying
nolo [<u>noh</u>-loh] freight
nome [<u>noh</u>-meh] *(m)* name
non [nohn] not; **non ancora** [nohn ahn-<u>koh</u>-rah] not yet; **non è vero?** [nohn eh <u>veh</u>-roh] isn't it true? right?
nonna [<u>noh</u>-nnah] grandmother
nonno [<u>noh</u>-nnoh] grandfather
nord [nohrd] *(m)* north; **a nord (di)** [ah nohrd (dee)] north of
normale [nohr-<u>mah</u>-leh] normal
normalmente [nohr-mahl-mehn-teh] normally
nota [<u>noh</u>-teh] note
notare [noh-tah-reh] to note
notizia [noh-<u>tee</u>-tzyah] (piece of) news; *(pl)* news
noto [<u>noh</u>-toh] well-known; **essere noto** [<u>eh</u>-sseh-reh <u>noh</u>-toh] to be well-known
notte [<u>noh</u>-tteh] *(f)* night; **di notte** [dee <u>noh</u>-tteh] at night
novità [noh-vee-<u>tah</u>] newness, novelty
nozione [noh-<u>tzyoh</u>-neh] *(f)* notion, idea
nozze [<u>noh</u>-tzeh] *(f pl)* wedding; **viaggio di nozze** [vyah-<u>djoh</u> dee <u>noh</u>-tzeh] honeymoon
nubile [<u>noo</u>-bee-leh] unmarried woman
nudo [<u>noo</u>-doh] nude
numerare [noo-meh-<u>rah</u>-reh] to number
numero [<u>noo</u>-meh-roh] number, figure
numeroso [noo-meh-<u>roh</u>-soh] numerous
nuocere [<u>nwoh</u>-cheh-reh] to harm
nuotare [nwoh-<u>tah</u>-reh] to swim
nuovo [<u>nwoh</u>-voh] new; **di nuovo** [dee <u>nwoh</u>-voh] again

nutriente [noo-tree-<u>ehn</u>-teh] nourishing
nutrimento [noo-tree-<u>mehn</u>-toh] nourishment

O

o… o [oh… oh] either… or
obbligo [<u>oh</u>-bloo-ghoh] obligation, duty
obiettivo [oh-byeh-<u>ttee</u>-voh] *(photo)* lens
occasionalmente [oh-kah-syoh-nahl-<u>mehn</u>-teh] *(adv)* occasionally
occasione [oh-kkah-<u>syoh</u>-neh] *(f)* opportunity
occhiali [oh-<u>kkyah</u>-lee] *(pl)* eyeglasses; **occhiali da sole** [oh-<u>kkyah</u>-lee dah soh-leh] sunglasses
occhio [<u>oh</u>-kkyoh] eye; **gli occhi** *(pl)* eyes
occidentale [oh-chee-dehn-<u>tah</u>-leh] western
Occidente [oh-chee-<u>dehn</u>-teh] *(m)* West
occupare un posto [oh-kkoo-<u>pah</u>-reh oon poh-stoh] to have a job
occuparsi di [oh-kkoo-<u>pahr</u>-see dee] to occupy oneself with
occupato [oh-kkoo-<u>pah</u>-toh] taken; *(tel)* engaged
oceano [oh-cheh-ah-noh] ocean
odore [oh-<u>doh</u>-roh] *(m)* smell, scent
offendere [oh-<u>ffehn</u>-deh-reh] to offend
offesa [oh-<u>ffeh</u>-sah] offense
officina [oh-ffe-<u>chee</u>-nah] (work)shop
offrire [oh-<u>ffree</u>-reh] to offer
oggetto [oh-<u>djeh</u>-ttoh] object; **oggetti di valore** [oh-<u>djeh</u>-ttee dee vah-<u>loh</u>-reh] valuable objects
oggi [<u>oh</u>-djee] today
ogni [<u>oh</u>-nyee] *(adj)* every; **in ogni caso** [een oh-nyee <u>kah</u>-soh] in every case; **ogni volta** [oh-nyee <u>vohl</u>-tah] everytime; **ogni due ore** [<u>oh</u>-nyee <u>doo</u>-eh <u>oh</u>-reh] every two hours; **ogni settimana** [<u>oh</u>-nyee seh-ttee-<u>mah</u>-nah] every week, weekly
ognuno [oh-<u>nyoo</u>-noh] *(pron)* everybody, everyone
olio [oh-lyoh] oil; **olio combustibile** [oh-lyoh kohm-boo-<u>stee</u>-bee-leh] fuel oil
oltremare [ohl-treh-<u>mah</u>-reh] *(m)* overseas
ombra [<u>ohm</u>-brah] shade
ombrello [ohm-<u>breh</u>-lloh] umbrella
ombrellone [ohm-breh-<u>lloh</u>-neh] *(m)* beach umbrella

onomastico [oh-noh-<u>mah</u>-stee-koh] saint's day, name day

onorario [oh-noh-<u>rah</u>-ryoh] honorarium, fee

onore [oh-<u>noh</u>-reh] *(m)* honor

operare [oh-peh-<u>rah</u>-reh] to operate

opinione [oh-pee-<u>nyoh</u>-neh] *(f)* opinion

opportuno [oh-ppohr-<u>too</u>-noh] opportune

opposto [oh-<u>ppoh</u>-stoh] opposite, contrary

oppure [oh-<u>ppoo</u>-reh] or

ora [<u>oh</u>-rah] hour, now; **un quarto d'ora** [oon <u>kwahr</u>-toh <u>doh</u>-rah] a quarter of an hour; **una mezz'ora** [<u>oo</u>-nah meh-<u>zoh</u>-rah] a half hour

orario d'apertura (al pubblico) [oh-<u>rah</u>-ryoh dah-pehr-too-rah (ahl <u>poo</u>-blee-koh)] (opening) hours

ordinario [ohr-dee-<u>nah</u>-ryoh] ordinary

ordinato [ohr-dee-<u>nah</u>-toh] orderly

ordine [<u>ohr</u>-dee-neh] *(m)* order, religious order

organizzare [ohr-ghah-nee-<u>zah</u>-reh] to organize

orlo [<u>ohr</u>-loh] edge

orologio [oh-roh-<u>loh</u>-joh] clock; **orologio da parete** [oh-roh-<u>loh</u>-joh dah pah-<u>reh</u>-teh] wall clock; **orologio da polso** [oh-roh-<u>loh</u>-joh dah <u>pohl</u>-soh] wristwatch

osare [oh-<u>sah</u>-reh] to dare

oscuro [oh-<u>skoo</u>-roh] dark

ospitalità [oh-spee-tah-lee-<u>tah</u>] hospitality

ospite [<u>oh</u>-spee-teh] *(m)* guest; *(m/f)* host, hostess

osservare [oh-ssehr-<u>vah</u>-reh] to observe, to watch, to notice

oste [<u>oh</u>-steh] *(m)* host, innkeeper

ostello per la gioventù [oh-<u>steh</u>-lloh pehr lah yohn-vehn-<u>too</u>] youth hostel

ottenere [oh-tteh-<u>neh</u>-reh] to obtain

otturato [oh-ttoo-<u>rah</u>-toh] plugged; filled (tooth)

P

pacchetto [pah-<u>kkeh</u>-ttoh] small package, packet

pacco [<u>pah</u>-kkoh] parcel

pace [<u>pah</u>-cheh] *(f)* peace

padiglione [pah-dee-<u>lyoh</u>-neh] *(m)* pavilion

padre [<u>pah</u>-dreh] *(m)* father

padrone [pah-<u>droh</u>-neh] *(m)* boss; **padrone/padrona di casa** [pah-<u>droh</u>-neh dee <u>kah</u>-sah] man/woman of the house

paese [pah-<u>eh</u>-seh] *(m)* country

pagamento [pah-ghah-<u>mehn</u>-toh] payment

pagare [pah-<u>ghah</u>-reh] to pay; **pagare in contanti** [pah-<u>ghah</u>-reh een kohn-<u>tahn</u>-tee] to pay in cash

pagella [pah-<u>jeh</u>-llah] report

pagina [<u>pah</u>-jee-nah] page

paio [<u>pah</u>-yoh] pair; **un paio di** [oon <u>pah</u>-yoh dee] a pair of

palla [<u>pah</u>-llah] (small) ball

pallido [<u>pah</u>-llee-doh] pale

pallone [pah-<u>lloh</u>-neh] *(m)* (large) ball

palo [<u>pah</u>-loh] pole, post

palude [pah-<u>loo</u>-deh] *(f)* marsh

panchina [pahn-<u>kee</u>-nah] bench

panno [<u>pah</u>-nnoh] cloth

panorama [pah-noh-<u>rah</u>-mah] *(m)* view, panorama

paragone [pah-rah-<u>ghoh</u>-neh] *(m)* comparison

parcheggiare [pahr-keh-<u>djah</u>-reh] to park

parco [<u>pahr</u>-koh] park

parete [pah-<u>reh</u>-teh] *(f)* wall

parlare [pahr-<u>lah</u>-reh] to speak; **parlar forte** [pahr-<u>lahr</u> <u>fohr</u>-teh] to speak loudly

parola [pahr-<u>roh</u>-lah] word

parte [<u>pahr</u>-teh] *(f)* part; **a parte** [ah <u>pahr</u>-teh] apart from; **dall'altra parte** [dah-<u>llahl</u>-trah <u>pahr</u>-teh] from someplace else

partenza [pahr-<u>tehn</u>-tzah] departure

particolare [pahr-tee-koh-<u>lah</u>-reh] *(m)* particular

particolarmente [pahr-tee-koh-lahr-<u>mehn</u>-teh] particularly

partire [pahr-<u>tee</u>-reh] to leave *(da* from); *(per* for)

party [<u>pahr</u>-tee] party

passaggio [pah-<u>ssah</u>-djoh] passage; **essere di passaggio** [<u>eh</u>-sseh-reh dee pah-<u>ssah</u>-djoh] to be passing by

passaporto [pah-ssah-<u>pohr</u>-toh] passport

passare [pah-<u>ssah</u>-reh] to pass; *(time)* to elapse, to go by; **passare davanti a qlcu/a qlco** [pah-<u>ssah</u>-reh dah-<u>vahn</u>-tee ah kwahl-<u>koo</u>-noh] to go past someone, something

passato [pah-<u>ssah</u>-toh] *(temporal)* past, last

passeggero [pah-sseh-<u>djeh</u>-roh] passenger

passeggiare [pah-sseh-<u>djah</u>-reh] to walk, to stroll

passeggiata [pah-sseh-<u>djah</u>-tah] walk, stroll

passerella [pah-sseh-<u>reh</u>-llah] ramp, gangway

passo [pah-ssoh] passage, pass

pasto [pah-stoh] meal

patria [pah-tryah] country, native land

patto [pah-ttoh] agreement, pact

paura [pah-oo-rah] fear; **aver paura di** [ah-vehr pah-oo-rah dee] to be afraid

pavimento [pah-vee-mehn-toh] floor

paziente [pah-tzyehn-teh] patient

pazienza [pah-tzyehn-tzah] patience

pazzo [pah-tzoh] mad, crazy

peccato (che)! [peh-kkah-toh (keh)] what a shame! **è un peccato** [eh oon peh-kkah-toh] it's a pity, shame

pecora [peh-koh-rah] sheep

pedone [peh-droh-neh] (m) pedestrian

peggio [peh-djoh] worse

pegno [peh-nyoh] pledge

pelle [peh-lleh] (f) skin, hide

pelliccia [peh-llee-chah] fur

pellicola [peh-llee-koh-lah] film

pelo [peh-loh] hair, fur

pena [peh-nah] punishment

pendio [pehn-dee-oh] slope

penna [peh-nnah] feather

pensare [pehn-sah-reh] to think; **pensare a** [pehn-sah-reh ah] to think of (something)

pensiero [pehn-syeh-roh] thought

pentola [pehn-toh-lah] cooking pot

penultimo/penultima [peh-nool-tee-moh/peh-nool-tee-mah] next-to-the-last

per [pehr] through, for, in; **per iscritto** [pehr ee-skree-ttoh] written; **per me** [pehr meh] for me

pera [peh-rah] pear

percento [pehr-chehn-toh] percent

percentuale [pehr-chehn-twah-leh] (f) percentage

perché [pehr-keh] why, because

perciò [pehr-choh] so, therefore

perdere [pehr-deh-reh] to lose

perdita [pehr-dee-tah] loss

perdonare [pehr-doh-nah-reh] to pardon

perfetto [pehr-feh-ttoh] perfect

pericolo [peh-ree-koh-loh] danger

pericoloso [peh-ree-koh-loh-soh] dangerous

periferia [peh-ree-feh-ree-ah] outskirts

periodo [poh-ree-oh-doh] period; **un periodo di tempo** [oon peh-ree-oh-doh dee tehm-poh] a period of time

però [peh-roh] however

permesso [pehr-meh-ssoh] permission; **permesso di transito** [pehr-meh-ssoh dee trahn-see-toh] travel permit

permettere [pehr-meh-tteh-reh] to permit

pernottare [pehr-noh-ttah-reh] to spend the night

persona [pehr-soh-nah] person

personale [pehr-soh-nah-leh] (m) personnel

persuadere [pehr-swah-deh-reh] to persuade

pesante [peh-sahn-teh] heavy

pesare [peh-sah-reh] to weigh

pescare [peh-skah-reh] to fish; **pescare con l'amo (la lenza)** [peh-skah-reh kohn lah-moh (lah lehn-tzah)] to angle

pesce [peh-sheh] (m) fish

pescivendolo [peh-shee-vehn-doh-loh] fishmonger

peso [peh-soh] weight

pessimo [peh-ssee-moh] very bad

pezzo [peh-tzoh] piece; **un pezzo di pane** [oon peh-tzoh dee pah-neh] a piece of bread

piacere [pyah-cheh-reh] to please; (m) pleasure; **per piacere** [pehr pyah-cheh-reh] please

piacevole [pyah-cheh-voh-leh] pleasant, agreeable

piangere [pyahn-jeh-reh] to cry

piano [pyah-noh] (adj) flat; (adv) slowly; (m) story, floor

pianoterra [pyah-noh-teh-rrah] ground floor

pianta [pyahn-tah] map; **pianta della città** [pyahn-tah deh-llah chee-ttah] city map

pianterreno [pyahn-teh-rreh-noh] ground floor

pianura [pyah-noo-rah] plain

piatto [pyah-ttoh] (adj) flat; (m) plate, dish, course

piazza [pyah-tzah] square

piccante [pee-kkahn-teh] spicy

piccolo [pee-kkoh-loh] little, small

piegare [pyeh-ghah-reh] to fold up, to bend

pieno [pyeh-noh] full

pietanza [pye-tahn-tzah] main course

pietra [pyeh-trah] stone

pietroso [pyeh-troh-soh] stony

pigione [pee-joh-neh] (f) pigeon

pigro [pee-ghroh] lazy

più [pee-oo] more; **in più** [een pee-oo] moreover; **più che/più di** [pee-oo keh/pee-oo dee] more than; **più o meno** [pee-oo oh meh-noh] more or less

pila [pee-lah] (small) battery

piovere [pyoh-veh-reh] to rain

pipa [pee-pa] pipe

piscina [pee-<u>shee</u>-nah] swimming pool
piuttosto [pyoo-<u>ttoh</u>-stoh] *(adv)* rather
pizzicare [pee-tzee-<u>kah</u>-reh] to pinch
pizzo [<u>pee</u>-tzoh] bribe
plastica [<u>plah</u>-stee-kah] plastic art
plastico [<u>plah</u>-stee-koh] plastic
poco [<u>poh</u>-koh] little, not much; **un po'** [oon poh] some, a little; **un po' di** [oon poh dee] some of
poi [<u>poh</u>-ee] then, later
poiché [poh-ee-<u>keh</u>] as, since
politica [poh-<u>lee</u>-tee-kah] politics
polvere [<u>pohl</u>-veh-reh] *(f)* dust
pomeriggio [poh-meh-<u>ree</u>-djoh] afternoon; **di pomeriggio** [dee poh-meh-<u>ree</u>-djoh] in the afternoon
pompiere [pohm-<u>pyeh</u>-reh] *(m)* firefighter
pontile [pohn-<u>tee</u>-leh] *(m)* wharf, pier
popolo [<u>poh</u>-poh-loh] people, nation
porgere [<u>pohr</u>-jeh-reh] to offer
porta [<u>pohr</u>-tah] door; **porta d'ingresso** [<u>pohr</u>-tah deen-<u>greh</u>-ssoh] entrance
portafoglio [pohr-tah-<u>foh</u>-lyoh] wallet
portamonete [pohr-tah-moh-<u>neh</u>-teh] *(m)* purse
portare [pohr-<u>tah</u>-reh] to bring, to carry, to wear; **portar via** [pohr-<u>tahr vee</u>-ah] to take away; **portare con sé** [pohr-<u>tah</u>-reh kohn seh] to take
portata [pohr-<u>tah</u>-tah] *(meal)* course
portone [pohr-<u>toh</u>-neh] *(m)* door
positivo [poh-see-<u>tee</u>-voh] positive, real
posizione [poh-see-<u>tzyoh</u>-neh] *(f)* position
possedere [poh-sseh-<u>deh</u>-reh] to possess, to have
possesso [poh-<u>sseh</u>-ssoh] possession
possibile [poh-<u>ssee</u>-bee-leh] possible
possibilità [poh-ssee-bee-lee-<u>tah</u>] possibility
posta [<u>poh</u>-stah] post office, mail; **alla posta** [<u>ah</u>-llah <u>poh</u>-stah] at the post office
posto [<u>poh</u>-stoh] place; **del posto** [dehl <u>poh</u>-stoh] local
potabile [poh-<u>tah</u>-bee-leh] drinkable
potente [poh-<u>tehn</u>-teh] powerful
potere [poh-<u>teh</u>-reh] to be able to, can; *(m)* power
povero [<u>poh</u>-vch roh] poor
pranzo [<u>prahn</u>-tzoh] lunch
praticare [prah-tee-<u>kah</u>-reh] to practice
pratico [<u>prah</u>-tee-koh] practical; **poco pratico** [<u>poh</u>-koh <u>prah</u>-tee-koh] impractical
prato [<u>prah</u>-toh] meadow, lawn

precauzione [preh-kah-oo-<u>tzyoh</u>-neh] *(f)* precaution
precedenza [preh-cheh-<u>dehn</u>-tsah] right of way; **dare la precedenza** [<u>dah</u>-reh lah preh-cheh-<u>dehn</u>-tsah] to yield
precisione [preh-chee-<u>syoh</u>-neh] *(f)* precision
preciso [preh-<u>chee</u>-soh] precise
predica [<u>preh</u>-dee-kah] sermon
preferire [preh-feh-<u>ree</u>-reh] to prefer
pregare [preh-<u>ghah</u>-reh] to pray
preghiera [preh-<u>ghyeh</u>-rah] prayer
pregio [<u>preh</u>-joh] esteem
prego [<u>preh</u>-ghoh] please
premere [<u>preh</u>-meh-reh] to press (a button)
premio [<u>preh</u>-myoh] prize, reward
prendere [<u>prehn</u>-deh-reh] to take; **prendere congedo** [<u>prehn</u>-deh-reh kohn-<u>jeh</u>-doh] to take leave; **prendere parte (a)** [<u>prehn</u>-deh-reh <u>pahr</u>-teh (ah)] to take part in; **prendere su** [<u>prehn</u>-deh-reh soo] to take up
prenotare [preh-noh-<u>tah</u>-reh] to reserve, to book
preoccuparsi di [preh-oh-koo-<u>pahr</u>-see] to worry
preoccupato [preh-oh-kkoo-<u>pah</u>-toh] worried
preoccupazione [preh-oh-koo-pah-<u>tzyoh</u>-neh] *(f)* worry
preparare [preh-pah-<u>rah</u>-reh] to prepare
prescrivere [preh-<u>skree</u>-veh-reh] to prescribe
presentare [preh-sehn-<u>tah</u>-reh] to present
presentazione [preh-sehn-tah-<u>tzyoh</u>-neh] *(f)* presentation
presente [preh-<u>sehn</u>-teh] present
preservativo [preh-sehr-vah-<u>tee</u>-voh] condom
prestare [preh-<u>stah</u>-reh] to lend
presto [<u>preh</u>-stoh] *(adv)* soon, early; **al più presto possibile** [ahl pee-oo <u>preh</u>-stoh poh-<u>ssee</u>-bee-leh] as soon as possible
prete [<u>preh</u>-teh] *(m)* priest
pretesa [preh-<u>teh</u>-sah] claim
pretesto [preh-<u>teh</u>-stoh] excuse
prezzo [<u>preh</u>-tzoh] price; **prezzo del biglietto d'ingresso** [<u>preh</u>-tzoh dehl bee-<u>lyeh</u>-tto deen-<u>ghreh</u>-ssoh] admission price
prima [<u>pree</u>-mah] before, first; **di prima qualità** [dee <u>pree</u>-mah kwah-lee-<u>tah</u>] best, top quality; **prima di** [<u>pree</u>-mah dee] before

primo/prima [pree-moh/pree-mah] first;
  in primo luogo [een pree-moh lwoh-
  ghoh] in the first place
principale [preen-chee-pah-leh] (adj)
  main, principal
principalmente [preen-chee-pahl-mehn-
  teh] mainly
privato [pree-vah-toh] private
probabile [proh-bah-bee-leh] probable
probabilità [proh-bah-bee-lee-tah] probability
probabilmente [proh-bah-beel-mehn-teh]
  probably
problema [proh-bleh-mah] (m) problem
processione [proh-cheh-ssyoh-neh] (f)
  procession
procurare [proh-koo-rah-reh] to get
prodotto [proh-doh ttoh] product, produce; **prodotto alimentare** [proh-doh-
  ttoh ah-lee-mehn-tah-reh] food
produrre [proh-doo-rreh] to produce
professione [proh-feh-ssyoh-neh] (f) profession
profilattico [proh-fee-lah-ttee-koh] condom
profondo [proh-fohn-doh] deep
progetto [proh-jeh-ttoh] plan, project
programma [proh-ghrah-mmah] (m) program
progresso [proh-ghreh ssoh] progress
proibire [proh-ee-bee roh] to prohibit
prolungare [proh-loon-ghah-reh] to pro-
  long, to extend
promessa [proh-meh-ssa] promise
promettere [proh-meh-tteh-reh] to
  promise
promuovere [proh-mwoh-veh-reh] to promote
pronto [prohn-toh] ready; (tel) hello;
  pronto soccorso [prohn-toh soh-kkohr-
  soh] first aid
pronuncia [proh-noon-chah] pronuncia
  tion
pronunciare [proh-noon-chah-reh] to pronounce
proporre [proh-poh-rreh] to propose, to
  suggest
proposta [proh-poh-stah] proposal
proprietario [proh-peh-tah-ryoh] owner,
  landlord
proprietà [pro-pryeh-tah] property, **proprietà terriera** [proh-pryeh-tah teh-
  rryeh-rah] real estate
proprio [proh-pryoh] (adv) just, exactly;
  proprio in questo minuto [proh-pryoh
  een kweh-stoh mee-noo-toh] at this very
  minute; **proprio ora** [proh-pryoh oh-
  rah] right now

prospetto [proh-speh-ttoh] view,
  prospectus
prossimo [proh-ssee-moh] near(by)
proteggere [proh-teh-djeh-reh] to protect
protestare [proh-teh-stah-reh] to protest
protezione [proh-teh-tzyoh-neh] (f) protection
prova [proh-vah] proof, test
provare [proh vah-reh] to prove
provenire (da) [proh-veh-nee rch(dah)] to
  come (from)
provvedere [proh-vveh-deh-reh] to provide
provvisoriamente [proh-vvee-soh-ryah-
  mehn-teh] (adv) temporarily
provvisorio [proh-vvee-soh-ryoh] temporary
provviste [proh-vvee-steh] (f/pl) provisions
prudente [proo-dehn-teh] careful
prudere [proo-deh-reh] to itch
pubblico [poo-blee-koh] (n/adj) public
pulire [poo-lee-reh] to clean, to wash
pulito [poo-lee-toh] clean
pungere [poon-jeh-reh] to prick, to sting
punta [poon-tah] point, tip, end; **punta
  del dito** [poon-tah deh dee-toh] fingertip
punto [poon-toh] point; **punto culmi-
  nante** [poon-toh kool-mee-nahn-teh] cli-
  max
puntuale [poon-twah-leh] (adj) punctual
puntualmente [poon-twahl-mehn-teh]
  (adv) punctually
pure [poo-reh] also, even
purtroppo [poor-troh-ppo] unfortunately
puzzare [poo-tzah-reh] to stink

Q

quaderno [kwah-dehr-noh] notebook
quadrangolare [kwah-drahn-ghoh-lah-reh]
  quadrangular
quadrato [kwah-drah-toh] square
quadro [kwah-droh] picture, painting
qualche [kwah-keh] some; **in qualche
  modo** [een kwahl-keh moh-doh] in
  some way; **in qualche posto** [een
  kwahl-keh poh-stoh] somewhere
qualcosa [kwahl-koh-sah] something
qualcuno [kwahl-koo-noh] someone
quale [kwah-leh] ... ? which ... ?; what
  ...?
qualità [kwah-lee-tah] quality
qualsiasi [kwahl-see-ah-see] (adj) any
quando [kwahn-doh] when
quantità [kwahn-tee-tah] quantity

A/Z

quartiere [kwahr-<u>tyeh</u>-reh] *(m)* neighborhood, district
quarto [<u>kwahr</u>-toh] fourth, quarter
quasi [<u>kwah</u>-see] almost, nearly
quello/quella [<u>kweh</u>-lloh/<u>kweh</u>-lla] that
questione [kweh-<u>styoh</u>-neh] *(f)* matter, issue
questo/questa [<u>kweh</u>-stoh/<u>kweh</u>-stah] this
qui [kwee] here

R

rabbia [<u>rah</u>-byah] anger
raccogliere [rah-kkoh-<u>lyeh</u>-reh] to pick, to gather
raccolta [rah-<u>kkohl</u>-tah] harvest, collection
raccomandare [rah-kkoh-mahn-<u>dah</u>-reh] to recommend
raccomandazione [rah-kkoh-mahn-dah-<u>tzyoh</u>-neh] *(f)* recommendation
raccontare [rah-kkohn-<u>tah</u>-reh] to tell; **raccontare bugie** [rah-kkohn-tah-<u>reh</u> boo-<u>jee</u>-eh] to tell lies
radersi [<u>rah</u>-dehr-see] to shave
radio [<u>rah</u>-dyoh] *(f)* radio
ragazza [rah-<u>ghah</u>-tzah] girl
ragazzo [rah-<u>ghah</u>-tzoh] boy
raggio [<u>rah</u>-djoh] ray, beam
raggiungere [rah-<u>djoon</u>-jeh-reh] to reach, to arrive (at a place)
ragione [rah-<u>joh</u>-neh] *(f)* reason; **aver ragione** [<u>ah</u>-vehr rah-<u>joh</u>-neh] to be right
ragionevole [rah-joh-<u>neh</u>-voh-leh] reasonable
rallegrarsi di [rah-lleh-<u>ghrahr</u>-see] to be glad about something
rammendare [rah-mmehn-<u>dah</u>-reh] to darn
rapidamente [rah-pee-dah-<u>mehn</u>-teh] *(adv)* quickly, swiftly
rapido [<u>rah</u>-pee-doh] *(adj)* quick, fast
rapporto [rah-<u>ppohr</u>-toh] report
rappresentazione [rah-ppreh-sehn-tah-<u>tzyoh</u>-neh] *(f)* performance
raramente [rah-rah-<u>mehn</u>-teh] *(adv)* rarely
raro [<u>rah</u>-roh] *(adj)* rare
reale [reh-<u>ah</u>-leh] real
realizzare [reh-ah-lee-<u>zah</u>-reh] to carry out, to achieve
realtà [reh-ahl-<u>tah</u>] reality
recente [reh-<u>chehn</u>-teh] recent, new
recipiente [reh-chee-<u>pyehn</u>-teh] *(m)* container

reclamare [reh-klah-<u>mah</u>-reh] to claim
reclame [reh-<u>klah</u>-meh] *(f)* advertisement
reclamo [reh-<u>klah</u>-moh] complaint
regalare [reh-ghah-<u>lah</u>-reh] to present (something to someone)
regalo [reh-<u>ghah</u>-loh] gift
regione [reh-<u>joh</u>-neh] *(f)* region
registrare [reh-jee-<u>strah</u>-reh] to register
regolamento [reh-ghoh-lah-<u>mehn</u>-toh] *(pl)* regulations
regolare [reh-ghah-<u>lah</u>-reh] to regulate, to adjust; *(adj)* regular
relazione [reh-lah-<u>tzyoh</u>-neh] *(f)* relation
rendere [<u>rehn</u>-deh-reh] to give back; **render noto** [<u>rehn</u>-deh-reh <u>noh</u>-toh] to make known; **render possibile** [<u>rehn</u>-dehr poh-<u>ssee</u>-bee-leh] to make possible
replicare [reh-plee-<u>kah</u>-reh] to reply
residenza [reh-see-<u>dehn</u>-tzah] residence
respingere [reh-<u>speen</u>-jeh-reh] to reject
respirazione [reh-spee-rah-<u>tzyoh</u>-neh] *(f)* breathing
respiro [reh-<u>spee</u>-roh] breath
responsabile [reh-spohn-<u>sah</u>-bee-leh] responsible
restare [reh-<u>stah</u>-reh] to stay
restituire [reh-stee-too-<u>ee</u>-reh] to give back
resto [<u>reh</u>-stoh] remainder, rest; **del resto** [dehl <u>reh</u>-stoh] moreover
rete [reh-teh] *(f)* net
retribuzione [reh-tree-boo-<u>tzyoh</u>-neh] *(f)* payment
rettificare [reh-ttee-fee-<u>kah</u>-reh] to rectify, to correct
riavere [reh-ah-<u>veh</u>-reh] to get back
ricchezza [ree-<u>kkeh</u>-tsah] wealth, riches
riccio (di mare) [ree-<u>choh</u> (dee <u>mah</u>-reh)] sea urchin
ricco [ree-<u>choh</u>] rich, wealthy
ricevere [ree-<u>cheh</u>-veh-reh] to receive
ricevimento [ree-cheh-vee-<u>mehn</u>-toh] receiving, reception
ricevuta [ree-cheh-<u>voo</u>-tah] receipt
richiesta [ree-<u>kyeh</u>-stah] request
ricompensa [ree-kohm-<u>pehn</u>-sah] reward
ricompensare [ree-kohm-pehn-<u>sah</u>-reh] to reward
riconoscere [ree-koh-<u>noh</u>-sheh-reh] to recognize
ricordare a qlcu/qlco [ree-kohr-<u>dah</u>-reh ah kwahl-<u>koo</u>-noh] to remind someone of something **ricordarsi** [ree-kohr-<u>dahr</u>-see] to remember
ricordo [ree-<u>kohr</u>-doh] recollection, souvenir
ridare [ree-<u>dah</u>-reh] to give again

ridere [ree-deh-reh] to laugh

ridicolo [ree-dee-koh-loh] ridiculous

riduzione [ree-doo-tzyoh-neh] *(f)* reduction

riempire [ree-ehm-pee-reh] to fill (up)

rientro [ree-ehn-troh] return, reentry

riferire [ree-feh-ree-reh] to report, to refer

riferirsi a [ree-feh-reer-see] to refer to (something)

rifiutare [ree-fyoo-tah reh] to refuse, to reject

rifiutarsi [ree-fyoo-tahr-see] to refuse

rifornire di [ree-fohr-nee-reh] to supply with

riguardo [ree-gwahr-doh] care; **senza riguardo** [sehn-tzah ree-gwahr-doh] regardless

rilevare [ree-leh-vah-reh] to notice

rimandare [ree-mahn-dah-reh] to send back

rimanente [ree-mah-nohn-teh] remaining

rimanere [ree-mah-neh-reh] to stay, to remain

rimborsare [reem-bohr-sah-reh] to reimburse

rimettere [ree-meh-tteh-reh] to put back

rimettersi [ree-meh-ttehr-see] to start again

rinfreschi [reen-freh-skee] refreshments

ringraziare [reen-ghrah-tzyah-reh] to thank

rinnovare [ree-nnoh-vah-reh] to renew

rinunciare [ree-noon-chah-reh] to give up

riparare [ree-pah-rah-reh] to repair

riparazione [ree-pah-rah-tsyoh-neh] *(f)* repair

ripetere [ree-peh-teh-reh] to repeat

ripido [ree-pee-doh] steep

riportare [ree-pohr-tah-reh] to bring back

riposarsi [ree-poh-sahr-see] to rest

riposo [ree-poh-soh] rest

risarcimento [ree-sahr-chee-mehn-toh] compensation

risarcimento dei danni [ree-sahr-chee-mehn-toh deh dah-nnee] compensation for damages

risarcire [ree-sahr-chee-reh] to compensate

riscaldare [ree-skahl-dah-reh] to warm up

rischio [ree-skyoh] risk

riservare [ree-sehr-vah-reh] to keep, to reserve

risoluzione [ree-soh-loo-tzyoh-neh] *(f)* resolution

risolvere [ree-sohl-veh-reh] to resolve

risparmiare [ree-spahr-myah-reh] to save

risplendere [ree-splehn-deh-reh] to shine

rispondere [ree-spohn-deh-reh] to respond

risposta [ree-spoh-stah] response

ristabilimento [ree-stah-bee-lee-mehn-toh] restoration

ristorante [ree-stoh-rahn teh] *(m)* restaurant

risultato [ree-sool-tah-toh] result

ritardare [ree-tahr-dah-reh] to delay

ritenere [ree-teh-neh-reh] to think, to consider

ritirarsi [ree-tee-rahr-see] to withdraw

ritornare [ree-tohr-nah-reh] to return, to go/come back

ritorno [re-tohr-noh] return; **ritorno in patria** [ree-tohr-noh een pah-tryah] return to one's country

rivedere [ree-veh-deh-reh] to see again

rivista [ree-vee-stah] magazine

rivolgersi (a) qlcu [ree-vohl-jehr-see] to address someone

roccia [roh-chah] rock

rompere [rohm-peh-reh] to break

rotondo [roh-tohn-doh] round, plump

rotto [roh-ttoh] broken

rovinare [roh-vee-nah-roh] to ruin

rubare [roo-hah-reh] to steal

rubinetto [roo-bee-neh-ttoh] faucet

rumore [roo-moh-reh] *(m)* noise

rumoroso [roo-moh-roh-soh] loud

russare [roo-ssah-reh] to snore

S

sacchetto [sah-kkeh-ttoh] small bag

sacco [sah-kkoh] sack, bag

sala [sah-lah] room

saldo [sahl-doh] sale

salire [sah-lee-reh] to get on, in (a vehicle), to go up; **salire in macchina** [sah-loo reh een mah-kkee-nah] to get in the car; **in salita** [sah-lee-tah] ascent

saltare [sahl-tah-reh] to jump

salutare [sah-loo-tah-roh] to greet

salute [sah-loo-teh] *(f)* health

salvare [sahl-vah-reh] to save

sano [sah-noh] healthy

santo [sahn-toh] holy

sapere [sah-peh-reh] *(m)* to know (something); **sapere di** [sah-peh-reh dee] to know of/about

sapore [sah-poh-reh] *(m)* taste, flavor

A/Z

sassoso [sah-<u>ssoh</u>-soh] stony

satollo [sah-<u>toh</u>-lloh] satiated, overfed

sazio [<u>sah</u>-tsyoh] full, satiated

sbadigliare [zbah-dee-<u>lyah</u>-reh] to yawn

sbagliare [zbah-<u>lyah</u>-reh] to make a mistake

sbagliarsi [zbah-<u>lyahr</u>-see] to be wrong, to be mistaken

sbagliato [zbah-<u>lyah</u>-toh] wrong

sbaglio [<u>zbah</u>-lyoh] mistake; **per sbaglio** [pehr <u>zbah</u>-lyoh] by mistake

sboccare [zboh-<u>kkah</u>-reh] *(river, street)* to flow (into)

sbocco [<u>zboh</u>-kkoh] mouth (of a river), opening

sbrigare [zbree-<u>gah</u>-reh] to finish off, to settle; **sbrigare un affare** [zbree-<u>gah</u>-reh oon ah-<u>ffah</u>-reh] to settle a matter

scadenza [skah-<u>dehn</u>-tsah] term (maturity)

scala [<u>skah</u>-lah] staircase, stairs

scambiare [skahm-<u>byah</u>-reh] to exchange, to change, to switch

scambio [<u>skahm</u>-byoh] exchange

scampolo [<u>skahm</u>-poh-loh] remnant

scarafaggio [skah-rah-<u>fah</u>-djoh] cockroach

scaricare [skah-ree-<u>kah</u>-reh] to discharge

scarpa [<u>skahr</u>-pah] shoe

scarso [<u>skahr</u>-soh] scarce

scassinare [skah-ssee-<u>nah</u>-reh] to force open

scatola [<u>skah</u>-toh-lah] box, can; **scatola di fiammiferi** [<u>skah</u>-toh-lah dee fyah-<u>mmee</u>-feh-ree] matchbox; **scatola di conserva** [<u>skah</u>-toh-lah dee kohn-sehr-vah] can

scegliere [sheh-<u>lyeh</u>-reh] to choose

scelta [<u>shehl</u>-tah] choice

scemo [<u>sheh</u>-moh] stupid, idiot

scendere [<u>shehn</u>-deh-reh] to go down, to get off

scintilla [sheen-tee-llah] spark

scommessa [skoh-<u>mmeh</u>-ssah] bet

scommettere [skoh-<u>meh</u>-tteh-reh] to bet

scomodo [<u>skoh</u>-moh-doh] uncomfortable

sconosciuto [skoh-noh-<u>shoo</u>-toh] unknown, strange

sconsiderato [skohn-see-deh-<u>rah</u>-toh] inconsiderate

scontento [skohn-<u>tehn</u>-toh] displeased

sconto [<u>skohn</u>-toh] discount

scontro [<u>skohn</u>-troh] collision, crash

scopo [<u>skoh</u>-poh] aim, purpose

scoppiare [skoh-<u>ppyah</u>-reh] to explode

scoprire [skoh-<u>pree</u>-reh] to discover, to find

scorciatoia [skohr-chah-<u>toh</u>-yah] shortcut

scorpione [skohr-<u>pyoh</u>-neh] *(m)* scorpion

scortese [skohr-<u>teh</u>-seh] rude, impolite

scrivere [<u>skree</u>-veh-reh] to write

scultura [skool-<u>too</u>-rah] sculpture

scuola [<u>skwoh</u>-lah] school

scuro [<u>skoo</u>-roh] dark

scusa [<u>skoo</u>-zah] excuse

scusare [skoo-<u>zah</u>-reh] to excuse; **scusarsi** [skoo-<u>zahr</u>-see] to excuse oneself; **scusi tanto!** [<u>skoo</u>-zee tahn-toh] many excuses! so sorry!

sdoganare [zdoh-ghah-<u>nah</u>-reh] to clear through customs

sdraiarsi [zdrah-<u>yahr</u>-see] to lie down

se [seh] if; **se no** [seh noh] but

seccante [seh-<u>kkahn</u>-teh] annoying, tiresome

secco [<u>seh</u>-kkoh] dry

seconda [seh-<u>kohn</u>-dah] second

secondo [seh-<u>kohn</u>-doh] second *(in rank, order)*; **in secondo luogo** [een seh-<u>kohn</u>-doh <u>lwoh</u>-ghoh] secondly; **secondo me** [seh-<u>kohn</u>-doh meh] in my opinion

sede [<u>seh</u>-deh] *(f)* seat

seder(si) [seh-<u>dehr</u>-see] to sit down

sedia [<u>seh</u>-dyah] chair

segnalatore d'incendio [seh-nyah-lah-<u>toh</u>-reh deen-<u>chehn</u>-dyoh] *(m)* fire alarm

segnale [seh-nyah-<u>lah</u>-reh] *(m)* signal; *(tel)* ringing

segno [<u>seh</u>-nyoh] sign

segreto [seh-<u>ghreh</u>-toh] secret

seguace [seh-<u>gwah</u>-cheh] *(m/f)* follower, supporter

seguire [seh-<u>gwee</u>-reh] to follow

selvaggina [sehl-vah-<u>djee</u>-nah] wild game

selvaggio [sehl-<u>vah</u>-djoh] wild

sembrare [sehm-<u>brah</u>-reh] to seem, to appear

semplice [<u>sehm</u>-plee-cheh] simple

sempre [<u>sehm</u>-preh] always

sensibile [sehn-<u>see</u>-bee-leh] sensitive

senso [<u>sehn</u>-soh] sense, direction

sentiero [sehn-<u>tyeh</u>-roh] path

sentimento [sehn-tee-<u>mehn</u>-toh] feeling

sentire [sehn-<u>tee</u>-reh] to feel, to hear, to smell

senza [<u>sehn</u>-tsah] without; **senza impegno** [<u>sehn</u>-tsah eem-peh-<u>nyoh</u>] with no obligation

separare [seh-pah-<u>rah</u>-reh] to separate
separato [seh-pah-<u>rah</u>-toh] separated
sera [<u>seh</u>-rah] evening
sereno [seh-<u>reh</u>-noh] serene
serio [<u>seh</u>-ryoh] serious
serpente [sehr-<u>pehn</u>-teh] *(m)* snake
serratura [seh-rrah-<u>too</u>-rah] *(door)* lock
servire [sehr-<u>vee</u>-reh] to serve, to wait on (someone)
servirsi (di) [sehr-<u>veer</u>-see (dee)] to use, to make use of something
servizio [sehr-<u>vee</u>-tsyoh] service
sesso [<u>seh</u>-ssoh] sex
sete [<u>seh</u>-teh] *(f)* thirst
settimana [seh-ttee-<u>mah</u>-nah] week; **durante la settimana** [doo rahn-teh lah seh-ttee-<u>mah</u>-nah] during the week
settimanale [seh-ttee-mah-<u>nah</u>-leh] *(adj)* weekly
severo [seh-<u>veh</u>-roh] strict
sfacciato [sfah-<u>chah</u>-toh] impudent
sfavorevole [sfah-voh-<u>reh</u>-voh-leh] unfavorable
sfociare [sfoh-<u>chah</u>-reh] *(river)* to flow
sfortuna [sfohr-<u>too</u>-nah] misfortune bad luck
sfortunatamente [sfohr-too-nah-tah-<u>mehn</u>-teh] unfortunately
sfortunato [sfohr-too-<u>nah</u>-toh] unfortunate, unlucky
sforzarsi [sfohr-<u>tzahr</u>-see] to strive hard
sforzo [<u>sfohr</u>-tzoh] effort, strain
sgarbato [zgahr-<u>bah</u>-toh] rude
sgridare [sgree-<u>dah</u>-reh] to scold, to chide
sguardo [<u>sgwahr</u>-doh] glance
se [seh] if
sì [<u>see</u>] yes
sicurezza [see-koo-<u>reh</u>-tzah] certainty
sicuro [see-<u>koo</u>-roh] *(adj)* sure, certain
sigaretta [see-ghah-<u>reh</u>-ttah] cigarette
sigaretto [see-glah-reh-ttoh] cigarillo
sigaro [<u>see</u>-ghah-roh] cigar
significare [see-nyee-fee-<u>kah</u>-reh] to mean, to signify
significato [see-nyee-fee-<u>kah</u>-toh] meaning
signor [see-<u>nyohr</u>] *(before name)* Mr.
signora [see-<u>nyoh</u>-rah] Mrs., woman
signore [see-<u>nyoh</u>-reh] gentleman, Mr.
signorina [see-nyoh-<u>ree</u>-nah] Miss, young woman
silenzio [see-<u>lehn</u>-tzyoh] silence
silenzioso [see-lehn-<u>tzyoh</u>-soh] silent
sillabare [see-llah-<u>bah</u>-reh] to spell

simile [<u>see</u>-mee-leh] similar
simpatico [seem-<u>pah</u>-tee-koh] nice
singolo [<u>seen</u>-ghoh-loh] single
sinistro/sinistra [see-<u>nee</u>-stroh/see-<u>nee</u>-strah] left; **a sinistra** [ah see-<u>nee</u>-strah] to the left
situazione [see-twah-<u>tzyoh</u>-neh] *(f)* situation, position
smacchiatore [smah-kkyah-toh-re] *(m)* stain remover
smarrirsi [smah-<u>rreer</u>-see] to get lost
smettere [<u>smeh</u>-tteh-reh] to stop, to give up
snello [<u>sneh</u>-lloh] slender, slim
sobborgo [soh-<u>bohr</u>-ghoh] suburb
società [soh-cheh-<u>tah</u>] company
soddisfatto [soh-ddoo ofah-ttoh] satisfied
soffitto [soh-<u>ffee</u>-ttoh] ceiling
soggiorno [soh-<u>djohr</u>-noh] living room
sognare [soh-<u>nyah</u>-reh] to dream
sogno [<u>soh</u>-nyoh] dream
sole [<u>soh</u>-leh] *(m)* sun
soleggiato [soh-leh-<u>djah</u>-toh] sunny
solenne [soh-leh-nneh] solemn
solitario [soh-lee-<u>tah</u>-ryoh] lonely
solito [<u>soh</u>-lee-toh] usual; **di solito** [dee <u>soh</u>-lee-toh] usually
solo [<u>soh</u>-loh] alone, only
soltanto [sohl-<u>tahn</u>-toh] only
somma [<u>soh</u>-mmah] addition, sum, amount
sommare [soh-<u>nyah</u>-re] to add, to sum up
sonnifero [soh-<u>nnee</u>-feh-roh] sleeping pill
sonno [<u>soh</u>-nnoh] sleep
sopportare [soh-ppohr-<u>tah</u>-reh] to tolerate
sopra [<u>soh</u>-prah] on, upon, above
soprattutto [soh-prah-<u>ttoo</u>-ttoh] above all
sorella [soh-<u>reh</u>-llah] sister
sorgente [sohr-<u>jehn</u>-teh] *(f)* *(water)* spring
sorgere del sole [<u>sohr</u>-jeh-re dehl <u>soh</u>-loh] *(m)* sunrise
sorpassare [sohr-pah-<u>ssah</u>-reh] to pass, to overtake a car
sorpreso [sohr-<u>pah</u>-soh] surprised
sorso [<u>sohr</u>-soh] draft, sip
sorvegliare [sohr-veh-<u>lyah</u>-reh] to oversee
sospetto [soh-<u>speh</u>-ttoh] suspicious
sostituire [soh-stee-too-<u>ee</u>-reh] to replace
sottile [soh-<u>ttee</u>-leh] thin, fine
sotto [<u>soh</u>-ttoh] under

sottopassaggio [soh-ttoh-pah-ssah-djoh] underpass

spago [spah-ghoh] string

sparare [spah-rah-reh] to shoot

sparire [spah-ree-reh] to disappear

spaventare [spah-vehn-tah-reh] to frighten

spaventoso [spah-vehn-toh-soh] frightening, terrible

spazio [spah-tzyoh] space

spazzatura [spah-tzah-too-rah] garbage

spazzola [spah-tzoh-lah] brush

spazzolare [spah-tzoh-lah-reh] to brush

speciale [speh-chah-leh] special, of top quality

specie [speh-cheh] (f) kind

spedire [speh-dee-reh] to send

spegnere [speh-nyeh-reh] to extinguish; **spegnere la luce** [speh-nyeh-reh lah loo-cheh] to turn off the light

spendere [spehn-deh-reh] to spend

sperare [speh-rah-reh] to hope

spese [speh-seh] (pl) charges; **fare le spese** [fah-reh leh speh-seh] to do the shopping

spesso [speh-ssoh] (adj) thick; (adv) often

spettacolo [speh-ttah-koh-loh] performance, show

spettatore [speh-ttah-toh-reh] (m) spectator

spezzare [speh-tzah-reh] to break

spiacevole [spyah-cheh-voh-leh] unpleasant

spiaggia [spyah-djah] beach

spiccioli [spee-choh-lee] (pl) small change

spiegare [spyeh-ghah-reh] to explain

spillo [spee-lloh] pin; **spillo di sicurezza** [spee-lloh dee see-koo-reh-tzah] safety pin

spingere [speen-jeh-reh] to push, to shove

spinta [speen-tah] push, shove

spirito [spee-ree-toh] spirits, alcohol

splendido [splehn-dee-doh] wonderful

spogliarsi [spoh-lyahr-see] to undress

sponda [spohn-dah] (river) bank

sporcizia [spohr-chee-tzyah] dirt

sporco [spohr-koh] dirty

sport [spohrt] (m) sport

sportello [spohr-teh-lloh] counter

sposare [spoh-sah-reh] to marry; **sposato con** [spoh-sah-toh kohn] to get married to

spuntino [spoon-tee-noh] snack

squadra [skwah-drah] (sport) team

stabilimento balneare [stah-bee-lee-mehn-toh bahl-neh-ah-reh] seaside resort

stabilire [stah-bee-lee-reh] to stabilize

stagione [stah-joh-neh] (f) season; **alta stagione** [ahl-tah stah-joh-neh] peak season; **fuori stagione** [fwoh-ree stah-joh-neh] off-season

stanco [stahn-koh] tired

stanotte [stah-noh-tteh] tonight

stare (in piedi) [stah-reh (een pyeh-dee)] to stand; **stare attento** [stah-reh ah-ttehn-toh] (a) to pay attention to

starnutire [stahr-noo-tee-reh] to sneeze

stasera [stah-seh-rah] this evening, tonight

stato [stah-toh] state

statura [stah-too-rah] height

stella [steh-llah] star

stesso [steh-ssoh] same; **lo stesso** [loh steh-ssoh] the same

stimare [stee-mah-reh] estimate

stoffa [stoh-ffah] material, fabric

storia [stoh-ryah] history

straccio [strah-choh] rag, cloth

strada [strah-dah] street, way; **per la strada** [pehr lah strah-dah] in the street; **per strada** [pehr strah-dah] on the way

straniero/straniera [strah-nyeh-roh] stranger

strano [strah-noh] strange

straordinario [strah-ohr-dee-nah-ryoh] extraordinary

strappare [strah-ppah-reh] to tear

stretto [streh-ttoh] tight, narrow

studiare [stoo-dyah-reh] to study

stufa [stoo-fah] stove

stupido [stoo-pee-doh] stupid

su [soo] on, upon; **in su** [een soo] up; **sul Tevere** [sool teh-veh-reh] on the Tiber; **sulla strada** [soo-llah strah-dah] on/in the street

subito [soo-bee-toh] at once, immediately

succedere [soo-cheh-deh-reh] to follow, to happen

successo [soo-cheh-ssoh] success

sud [sood] (m) south; **a sud di** [ah sood dee] south of; **del sud** [dehl sood] southern

sudare [soo-dah-reh] to sweat

sufficiente [soo-ffee-chen-teh] enough

suggerimento [soo-djeh-ree-mehn-toh] suggestion

suolo [swoh-loh] soil

suonare [swoh-nah-reh] to ring, to sound

suono [swoh-noh] sound

suora [swoh-rah] sister, nun

superfluo [soo-<u>pehr</u>-flwoh] unnecessary
supermercato [soo-pehr-mehr-<u>kah</u>-toh] supermarket
supplementare [soo-ppleh-mehn-<u>tah</u>-reh] additional
supporre [soo-<u>ppoh</u>-rreh] to suppose
supposizione [soo-ppoh-see-<u>tzyoh</u>-neh] *(f)* guess, supposition
svantaggio [svahn-<u>tah</u>-djoh] disadvantage
sveglia [<u>sveh</u>-lyah] alarm clock
svegliare [sveh-<u>lyah</u>-reh] to wake
svegliarsi [sveh-<u>lyahr</u>-see] to wake up
sveglio [<u>sveh</u>-lyaoh] awake
svelto [<u>svehl</u>-toh] *(adj)* quick, slim
svendita [<u>svehn</u>-dee-tah] sale
svenuto [svee-<u>noo</u>-toh] unconscious
svestirsi [sveh-<u>steer</u>-see] to undress
sviluppare [svee-loo-<u>ppah</u>-reh] to develop
sviluppo [svee-<u>loo</u>-ppoh] development
svolgere [<u>svohl</u>-jeh-reh] to unwrap, to carry out *(an activity)*
svolgersi [<u>svohl</u>-jehr-see] to take place, to happen
svoltare [svohl-<u>tah</u>-reh] to turn; **svoltare a destra/sinistra** [svohl-<u>tah</u>-reh ah <u>deh</u>-strah/see-<u>nee</u>-strah] to turn right/left

T

tabacco [tah-bah-<u>kkoh</u>] tobacco
tacco [<u>tah</u>-kkoh] *(shoe)* heel
tacere [tah-<u>cheh</u>-reh] to quiet
tagliando [tah-<u>lyahn</u>-doh] coupon
tagliare [tah-<u>lyah</u>-reh] to cut
tale [<u>tah</u>-leh] such
tanto [<u>tahn</u>-toh] so, so much; **di tanto in tanto** [dee <u>tahn</u>-toh een tahn-toh] every now and then; **tanto... quanto** [<u>tahn</u>-toh... <u>kwahn</u>-toh] both... and
tardare [tahr-<u>dah</u>-reh] to be late
tardi [<u>tahr</u>-dee] late; **più tardi** [pyoo <u>tahr</u>-dee] later
targa [<u>tahr</u>-ghah] license plate
tasca [<u>tah</u>-skah] pocket
tasse [<u>tah</u>-sseh] *(pl)* taxes
tassì [tah-<u>ssee</u>] *(m)* taxi
tasse d'interesse [<u>tah</u>-ssee deen-teh-<u>reh</u>-sseh] interest (tax)
tavola [<u>tah</u>-voh-lah] table; **a tavola** [ah <u>tah</u>-voh-lah] at the table
tavolo [<u>tah</u>-voh-loh] table
tazza [<u>tah</u>-tsah] cup
te [the] you, to you
telefonare [teh-leh-foh-<u>nah</u>-reh] to telephone

temere [teh-<u>meh</u>-reh] to fear
tempesta [tehm-<u>peh</u>-stah] storm
tempo [<u>tehm</u>-poh] time, weather; **in tempo** [een tehm-poh] *(adv)* on time; **a tempo** [ah tehm-poh] *(adv)* at the right time; **un periodo di tempo** [oon peh-<u>ree</u>-oh-doh dee <u>tehm</u> poh] a period of time
temporale [tehm-poh <u>rah</u>-leh] *(m)* thunderstorm
temporaneo [tehm-poh-<u>rah</u>-neh-oh] temporary
tenaglie [teh-<u>nah</u>-lyeh] *(pl)* pliers
tenda [<u>tehn</u>-dah] tent
tenere [teh-<u>neh</u>-reh] to have, to hold; **tenere a mente qlco** [teh-<u>neh</u>-reh ah <u>mehn</u>-teh kwahl-<u>koh</u>-sah] to keep (something) in mind
tenero [<u>teh</u>-neh-roh] tender
tentare [tehn-<u>tah</u>-reh] to attempt
tentativo [tehn-tah-<u>tee</u>-voh] attempt
tenue [<u>teh</u>-nweh] thin, weak
tenuta [teh-<u>noo</u>-tah] estate
terminare [tehr-mee-<u>nah</u>-reh] to end
termine [<u>tehr</u>-mee-neh] *(m)* limit, boundary
terra [<u>teh</u>-rrah] earth, land
terracotta [teh-rrah-<u>koh</u>-ttah] terracotta
terreno [teh-<u>rreh</u>-noh] ground
terribile [teh-<u>rree</u>-bee-leh] terrible
territorio nazionale [teh-rree-<u>toh</u>-ryoh nah-tzyoh-<u>nah</u>-leh] national territory
terza [<u>tehr</u>-tzah] third
terzo [<u>tehr</u>-tzoh] third; **in terzo luogo** [een <u>tehr</u>-tzoh <u>lwoh</u>-ghoh] in the third place; **un terzo** [oon <u>tehr</u>-tzoh] one third
tesoro [teh-<u>soh</u>-roh] treasure
tessera [<u>teh</u>-sseh-rah] card, ticket, pass
tessuto [teh-<u>ssoo</u>-toh] cloth, fabric material
testimone [teh-stee-<u>moh</u>-neh] *(m)* witness
ti [tee] you, to you
timbro [<u>teem</u>-broh] stamp; **timbro postale** [<u>teem</u>-broh poh-<u>stah</u>-leh] postmark
tipico [<u>tee</u>-pee-koh] typical
tirare [tee-<u>rah</u>-reh] to pull
tiro [<u>tee</u>-roh] draft
toccare [toh-<u>kkah</u>-reh] to touch
togliere [<u>toh</u>-lyeh-reh] to take off
togliersi [<u>toh</u>-lyehr-see] *(clothes)* to take off
toletta/toiletta [toh-<u>leh</u>-ttah/to-ee-<u>leh</u>-ttah] *(f)* lavatory, toilet
tollerare [toh-lleh-<u>rah</u>-reh] to tolerate

A/Z

tonalità [toh-nah-lee-_tah_] tonality
tono [_toh_-noh] tone
torbido [_tohr_-be-doh] turbid, muddy
tornare indietro [tohr-_nah_-reh een-_dyeh_-troh] to turn back
tossire [toh-_ssee_-reh] to cough
tra [trah] between, among; **tra breve** [trah _breh_-veh] soon
traccia [_trah_-chah] track, trace
tradurre [trah-_doo_-rreh] to translate
traffico [_trah_-ffee-koh] traffic
tramonto (del sole) [trah-_mohn_-toh (dehl _soh_-leh)] sunset
tranne [_trah_-nneh] but, except
tranquillizzarsi [trahn-kwee-llee-_tzahr_-see] to calm down, to tranquilize
tranquillo [trahn-_kwee_-lloh] quiet, tranquil
transito [_trahn_-see-toh] transit
trascurare [trah-skoo-_rah_-reh] to neglect
trasmissione [trah-smee-_ssyoh_-neh] (f) (radio, television) broadcast
trasportare [trah-spohr-_tah_-reh] to transport, to carry
trattamento [trah-ttah-_mehn_-toh] cure, treatment
trattare [trah-_ttah_-reh] to treat, to deal (with)
trattativa [trah-ttah-_tee_-vah] negotiation
trattenersi [trah-tteh-_nehr_-see] to hold oneself back
tratto [_trah_-ttoh] outline, sketch
trattoria [trah-ttoh-_ree_-ah] restaurant
tribunale [tree-boo-_nah_-leh] (m) (law) court
triste [_tree_-steh] side
troppo [_troh_-ppoh] too much; (pl) too many
trovare [troh-_vah_-reh] to find; **trovarsi** [troh-_vahr_-see] to be situated; **trovarsi bene** [troh-_vahr_-see _beh_-neh] to feel well
truccarsi [troo-_kkahr_-see] to put on makeup
tu [too] you
tubo [_too_-boh] tube, pipe
tunnel [_too_-nnehl] (m) tunnel
turista [too-_ree_-stah] (m/f) tourist
tuttavia [too-ttah-_vee_-ah] but, yet, nevertheless
tutto [_too_-ttoh] (adj) all; (pl) every; **tutti i giorni** [_too_-ttee ee _johr_-nee] every day; **tutti e due** [_too_-ttee eh _doo_-eh] both; **tutto pieno** [_too_-ttoh _pyeh_-noh] all full

U

ubbidire [oo-bbee-_dee_-reh] to obey
ubriacarsi [oo-bryah-_kahr_-see] to get drunk
ubriaco [oo-_bryah_-koh] drunk
uccello [oo-_cheh_-lloh] bird
udire [oo-_dee_-reh] to hear
ufficiale [oo-ffee-_chah_-leh] official
ufficio [oo-_ffee_-choh] office, department; **ufficio doganale** [oo-_ffee_-choh doh-ghah-_nah_-leh] customs office; **ufficio informazioni** [oo-_ffee_-choh een-fohr-mah-_tyoh_-nee] information office; **ufficio oggetti smarriti** [oo-_ffee_-choh oh-_djeh_-ttee smah-_rree_-tee] lost and found department
uguale [oo-_gwah_-leh] equal
ultimo/ultima [_ool_-tee-moh/_ool_-tee-mah] last
umano [oo-_mah_-noh] human
umido [_oo_-mee-doh] humid
umore [oo-_moh_-reh] (m) mood
un/una/uno [oon/oonah/oonh] a, an; **una volta** [oo-nah _vohl_-tah] one time (occurrence)
uncino [oon-_chee_-noh] hook
unico [_oo_-nee-koh] only
uno [_oo_-noh] one; **l'un l'altro** [loon _lahl_-troh] both; **uno e mezzo** [_oo_-noh eh _meh_-zoh] one and a half
uomo [_woh_-moh] man
uovo [_woh_-voh] egg
urgente [oor-_jehn_-teh] urgent
usare [oo-_sah_-reh] to use
usato [oo-_sah_-toh] second-hand
uscire [oo-_shee_-reh] to go out, to check out (book)
uscita [oo-_shee_-tah] going out, exit
uso [_oo_-soh] use; **in uso** [een **OO-soh**] in use
utile [_oo_-tee-leh] useful

V

vacanza [vah-_kahn_-tzah] vacation
vagone [vah-_ghoh_-neh] (m) (train) car; **vagone letto** [vah-_ghoh_-neh _leh_-ttoh] sleeping car
validità [vah-lee-dee-_tah_] validity
valido [_vah_-lee-doh] valid; **essere valido** [_eh_-sseh-reh _vah_-lee-doh] to be valid; **non valido** [nohn _vah_-lee-doh] invalid

valigia [vah-<u>lee</u>-jah] suitcase

valore [vah-<u>loh</u>-reh] (m) worth, value; **avere un grande valore** [ah-<u>veh</u>-reh oon ghrahn vah-<u>loh</u>-reh] to be valuable; **senza valore** [<u>sehn</u>-tsa vah-<u>loh</u>-reh] worthless

valutare [vah-loo-<u>tah</u>-reh] to estimate

valvola (di sicurezza) [<u>vahl</u>-voh-lah dee see-koo-<u>reh</u>-tsah] safety valve

vantaggio [vahn-<u>tah</u>-djoh] advantage

vantaggioso [vahn-tah-<u>djoh</u>-soh] advantageous

variabile [vah-<u>ryah</u>-bee-leh] variable

varietà [vah-ryeh-<u>tah</u>] (m) variety show

vario [<u>vah</u>-ryoh] varied

vaso [<u>vah</u>-soh] vase

vecchio [<u>veh</u>-kkyoh] old

vedere [veh-<u>deh</u>-reh] to see

veleno [veh-<u>leh</u>-noh] poison

velenoso [veh-leh-<u>noh</u>-soh] poisonous

veloce [veh-<u>loh</u>-cheh] (adj) fast

velocemente [veh-loh-cheh-<u>mehn</u>-teh] (adv) quickly

velocità [veh-loh-<u>chee</u>-tah] speed

vendere [<u>vehn</u>-deh-reh] to sell

vendita [<u>vehn</u>-dee-tah] sale; **in vendita** [een <u>vehn</u>-dee-tah] for sale

venire [veh-<u>nee</u>-reh] to come; **venire a sapere** [veh-<u>nee</u>-reh ah sah-<u>peh</u>-reh] to get to know; **venire dentro** [veh-<u>nee</u>-reh <u>dehn</u>-troh] to come inside

ventoso [vehn-<u>toh</u>-soh] windy

veramente [veh-rah-<u>mehn</u>-teh] (adv) really

verificare [veh-ree-fee-<u>kah</u>-reh] to verify

verità [veh-ree-<u>tah</u>] truth

verme [<u>vehr</u>-meh] (m) worm

vero [<u>veh</u>-roh] true, real

verso [<u>vehr</u>-soh] toward, about; **verso l'alto** [<u>vehr</u>-soh <u>lahl</u>-toh] upward

vespa [<u>veh</u>-spah] wasp

vestirsi [veh-<u>steer</u>-see] to get dressed

vetrina [veh-<u>tree</u>-nah] shop window

vetro [<u>veh</u>-troh] glass, pane

vi [vee] (pron) to you

via [<u>vee</u>-ah] street, way

viaggiare [vyah-<u>djah</u>-reh] to travel

viaggiatore [vyah-djah-<u>toh</u>-reh] (m) traveler

viaggio [<u>vyah</u>-djoh] trip, voyage; **in viaggio** [een <u>vyah</u>-djoh] traveling; **viaggio di ritorno** [<u>vyah</u>-djoh dee ree-<u>tohr</u>-noh] return trip

vicinanza [vee-chee-<u>nahn</u>-tsah] neighborhood

vicino(a) [vee-<u>chee</u>-noh (ah)] near; **vicino/vicina** [vee-<u>chee</u>-noh/vee-<u>chee</u>-nah] neighbor

vietato [vyeh-<u>tah</u>-toh] forbidden; **vietato l'ingresso** [vyeh-<u>tah</u>-toh leen-<u>ghreh</u>-ssoh] no admittance

vigili del fuoco [<u>vee</u>-jee-lee dehl <u>fwoh</u>-koh] firefighter

vigna, vigneto [<u>vee</u>-nyah, vee <u>nyeh</u>-toh] vineyard

villa [<u>vee</u>-llah] villa

villaggio [vee-<u>llah</u>-djoh] village

villano [vee-<u>llah</u>-noh] rustic, common, rule

vincere [<u>veen</u>-cheh-reh] to win

vincita [<u>veen</u>-chee-tah] win

violentare [vyoh-lehn-<u>tah</u>-reh] to rape, to force

violento [vyoh-<u>lehn</u>-toh] violent

visibile [vee-<u>see</u>-bee-leh] visible

visita [<u>vee</u>-see-tah] visit

visitare [vee-see-<u>tah</u>-reh] to visit; (med) to examine

vista [<u>vee</u>-stah] view

vita [<u>vee</u>-tah] life

vitto [<u>vee</u>-ttoh] food

vivace [vee-<u>vah</u>-cheh] lively

vivente [vee-<u>vehn</u>-teh] living

vivere [<u>vee</u>-veh-reh] to live

voce [<u>voh</u>-cheh] (f) voice

voglia [<u>voh</u>-lyah] wish, desire; **di mala voglia** [dee <u>mah</u>-lah <u>voh</u>-lyah] not willingly

voi [<u>voh</u>-ee] you (pl); **a voi** [ah <u>voh</u>-ee] to you

volare [voh-<u>lah</u>-reh] to fly

volentieri [voh-lehn-<u>tyeh</u>-ree] gladly

volere [voh-<u>leh</u>-reh] to want; **voler bene a qlcu** [voh-<u>lehr</u> <u>beh</u>-neh ah kwahl-<u>koo</u>-noh] to love someone

volgare [vohl-<u>ghah</u>-reh] vulgar

volt [vohlt] volt

volta [<u>vohl</u>-tah] time; **per volta** [pehr <u>vohl</u>-tah] at a time; **un'altra volta** [oo-<u>nahl</u>-trah <u>vohl</u>-tah] another time; **una volta** [oo-nah <u>vohl</u>-tah] once

voltare [vohl-<u>tah</u>-reh] turn

volume [voh-<u>loo</u>-meh] (m) volume

vostro [<u>voh</u>-stroh] your

votare [voh-<u>tah</u>-reh] vote

votazione [voh-tah-<u>tzyoh</u>-neh] (f) voting

vuoto [<u>vwoh</u>-toh] empty

A/Z

W

watt [vahtt] *(m)* watt

Z

zaino [<u>zah</u>-ee-noh] knapsack
zanzara [zahn-<u>zah</u>-rah] mosquito
zia [<u>zee</u>-ah] aunt
zio [<u>zee</u>-oh] uncle